Sheffield Hallam University
Learning and IT Services
Adsetts Centre City Campus
Sheffield S1 1WS

D1331030

Property Valuation

SHEFFIELD HALLAM UNIVERSITY
LEARNING CENTRE
WITHDRAWN FROM STOCK

This book is dedicated to my father and to the memory of my mother

Property Valuation

in an economic context

Peter Wyatt

University of the West of England
Bristol

Blackwell
Publishing

© 2007 by Peter Wyatt

Blackwell Publishing editorial offices:
Blackwell Publishing Ltd, 9600 Garsington Road, Oxford OX4 2DQ, UK
  Tel: +44 (0)1865 776868
Blackwell Publishing Inc., 350 Main Street, Malden, MA 02148-5020, USA
  Tel: +1 781 388 8250
Blackwell Publishing Asia Pty Ltd, 550 Swanston Street, Carlton, Victoria 3053, Australia
  Tel: +61 (0)3 8359 1011

The right of the Author to be identified as the Author of this Work has been asserted in accordance with the Copyright, Designs and Patents Act 1988.

All rights reserved. No part of this publication may be reproduced, stored in a retrieval system, or transmitted, in any form or by any means, electronic, mechanical, photocopying, recording or otherwise, except as permitted by the UK Copyright, Designs and Patents Act 1988, without the prior permission of the publisher.

Designations used by companies to distinguish their products are often claimed as trademarks. All brand names and product names used in this book are trade names, service marks, trademarks or registered trademarks of their respective owners. The Publisher is not associated with any product or vendor mentioned in this book.

This publication is designed to provide accurate and authoritative information in regard to the subject matter covered. It is sold on the understanding that the Publisher is not engaged in rendering professional services. If professional advice or other expert assistance is required, the services of a computer professional should be sought.

First published 2007 by Blackwell Publishing Ltd

3   2009

ISBN: 978-1-4051-3045-5

Library of Congress Cataloging-in-Publication Data
Wyatt, Peter, 1968-
Property valuation in an economic context / Peter Wyatt
p.cm.
Includes bibliographical references and index.
ISBN-13:978-1-4051-3045-5 (pbk. :alk. paper)
1. Commercial real estate–Great Britain–Valuation.
2. Real estate investment–Great Britain. I. Title.

HD1393.58.G7W93 2007
333.33'8720941–dc22

2007018632

A catalogue record for this title is available from the British Library

Set in 10/12 pt Sabon
by Newgen Imaging Systems (P) Ltd, Chennai, India
Printed and bound in Singapore
by C.O.S. Printers Pte Ltd

The publisher's policy is to use permanent paper from mills that operate a sustainable forestry policy, and which has been manufactured from pulp processed using acid-free and elementary chlorine-free practices. Furthermore, the publisher ensures that the text paper and cover board used have met acceptable environmental accreditation standards.

For further information on Blackwell Publishing, visit our website:
www.blackwellpublishing.com/construction

Contents

Preface

There is no denying it, this was a difficult book to write; satisfying and ultimately very rewarding but difficult nevertheless. The difficulty stems from defining the roots of valuation: conventionally regarded as a professional discipline it is only in recent years that valuation has undergone serious academic scrutiny and an attempt made to place it in an academic setting. The outcome of this scrutiny is a move away from valuation being taught as a branch of surveying and a move towards it being regarded as applied economics in a business finance context. The challenge does not stop there though, academically valuation might be regarded as applied economics but practically it requires the practitioner to call upon other disciplines, particularly law (including the ownership and use rights of property), finance and land economics, geography (including the physical attributes of land and human activities that take place on it) and management. These are enormous subjects in their own right and therefore this book navigates around them by not getting into the detail of case law, statutes and organisational behaviour. Also, I have not ventured far into the world of investment asset appraisal and portfolio analysis. There are already several excellent text books covering these topics and the reader is referred to them in the relevant places.

This book focuses on the valuation of commercial and industrial property (collectively referred to as business property) across three interlinked market sectors; namely the markets for investment, development and occupation. Chapter 1 places the property market and its various sectors in an economic context. Chapters 2 and 3 identify the basic principles of valuation, introducing the process and a broad range of methods. Chapters 4, 5 and 6 are concerned with the application of valuation techniques to the development, occupation and investment sectors of the market for business property. These three market sectors are interrelated and their analysis forms the backbone of the text. But it should be remembered that there is no one-to-one match between market participants and the sector in which they might operate. Ball *et al.* (1998) define three types of market participants, namely, users, developers and investors, and three types of relationship to property, namely, tenants, developers and owners, but users may own or rent, investors may own, develop, and so on. This book considers valuation from the standpoint of market participants because they are responsible for commissioning valuations. Although the focus is market valuation rather than worth appraisal, Chapter 7 considers how property valuation fits into an appraisal context. The chapter does no more than introduce appraisal concepts and methods and provides a springboard to more comprehensive texts already published on this subject matter. In covering this ground, the book attempts to combine the academic and practical roots of valuation. The various disciplines mean that terminology is a problem and so all the key terms emboldened in the text are defined in the glossary at the back of the book.

The primary dictionary definition of the term *property* is used in this book, namely the ownership of landed or real estate. The term property is, however, used interchangeably to describe the physical entity itself and the ownership of a legal interest in a piece of landed or real estate. The word property is also used to describe property in a singular and plural sense. Many of the calculations in the book were performed using a spreadsheet but appear as rounded figures so there may be some differences.

Reference

Ball, M., Lizieri, C. and MacGregor, B. (1998) *The Economics of Commercial Property Markets,* Routledge, London,UK.

Acknowledgements

My sincere thanks go to Steve Galliford, Richard Mollart, Danny Myers and Gerry Pitman at UWE, Madeleine Metcalfe at Blackwell Publishers and to Marcus Phillis at Brantano (UK) Ltd. I would also like to thank my wife Jemma and two sons, Sam and Tom, for putting up with the 'absent parent' for significant periods during 2006.

Chapter 1
The Economics of Property Value

1.1 Introduction

The legal ownership of land and buildings, collectively referred to as **property** throughout this book, confers legal rights on the owner that enable it to be developed, occupied or leased. The physical occupation of property is essential for social and economic activities including shelter, manufacture, commerce, recreation and movement. Typically, physical property ownership is not desired in its own right, although prestigious or landmark buildings can generate what Baum and Crosby (1995) refer to as 'psychic income'. Rather, demand for property is a derived demand; occupiers require property as a factor of production to help deliver the social and economic activities that take place within its fabric and investors require property as an investment asset. This concept of derived demand has a direct bearing on its valuation, as we shall see later.

This book is all about valuing *individual* properties or premises (units of occupation) within properties that are used for business purposes – what will often be referred to throughout this book as commercial property. Yet it is interesting at this early stage to consider the total value of *all* commercial property in the country. The Office for National Statistics publishes annual estimates of the net worth of various categories of assets, including business property. Table 1.1 shows the estimates of net worth of commercial, industrial and other non-domestic property between 1997 and 2005. So at the end of 2005 the total net worth of commercial property was estimated to be approximately £626 billion. By way of comparison, the UK National Accounts estimate that households occupy £3355.8 billion worth of residential property (not including housing association properties), a figure more than five times the size. Nevertheless, a huge amount of money is tied up in commercial property in the UK. The Investment Property Forum (IPF) estimated that around 80% is occupied by the core commercial land uses – retail, office and industrial space (IPF, 2005) – and that approximately half of the stock is owner-occupied, chiefly by private companies but also by

Table 1.1 National balance sheet asset totals for commercial, industrial and other buildings.

Year	Net worth (£ billion at end year)
1997	492.8
1998	477.4
1999	509.3
2000	599.7
2001	562.7
2002	588.4
2003	591.9
2004	626.0
2005	625.9

Source: UK National Accounts: *The Blue Book* (2006).

public and quasi-public bodies. The remaining half is owned by investors. It is argued that the proportion of owner-occupied commercial stock is falling as freehold interests in property are sold, and the properties are leased back by business occupiers as a means of releasing money that is tied up in the value of these properties and as a way of focusing investment in the core business activity (IPF, 2005).

The value of commercial property as estimated by the IPF was calculated by capitalising the assessments of rental value that the government assigns to individual commercial premises every 5 years for tax purposes. It is individual valuations of each commercial property like these that interest us most in this book and that is why we start with a look at microeconomics. The interaction between the supply of and demand for property generates exchange prices, and valuation is concerned with the estimation of those prices. Value is thus an economic concept and valuers are primarily concerned with how the market and sectors of the market measure value. This chapter will begin by explaining the microeconomic concepts that are relevant to property markets and estimates of exchange price therein. It will introduce microeconomic terms and concepts associated with the supply and demand of land and buildings, the concept of rent as a payment for the use of land and buildings, and some land use theory. The second part of the chapter will consider macroeconomic concepts, including the commercial property market and its constituent sectors; namely development, occupation and investment. In the case of investment a brief look at other major asset classes is included. The chapter ends with a look at macroeconomic property market cycles.

1.2   Microeconomic concepts

Economics is conventionally divided into two types of analysis: microeconomics and macroeconomics. **Microeconomics** studies how individuals and firms allocate scarce resources, whereas **macroeconomics** analyses economy-wide phenomena, resulting from decision-making in *all* markets. One way to understand the distinction between these two approaches is to consider some generalised examples. Microeconomics is concerned with determining how prices, values and rents emerge and change, and how firms respond. It involves an examination of the effects of new taxes and government incentives, the characteristics of demand, determination of a firm's profit, and so on. In other words, it tries to understand the economic motives of market participants such as landowners, developers, occupiers and investors. This diverse set of participants is rather fragmented and at times adversarial – but microeconomic analysis works on the basis that we can generalise about the behaviour of these parties. A particular branch of economics known as *urban land economics* is concerned with the microeconomic implications of scarcity and the allocation of urban property rights. Ball *et al.* (1998) in the preface to their book state that: 'The microeconomics of commercial property, proved to be the most difficult [area] to draw together. There simply does not exist an adequate and complete general microeconomic theory of urban property markets.' This is true and an attempt to develop such a theory is not attempted here! Instead this section brings together and explains the key microeconomic concepts and theories that have a bearing on urban property markets and the important work of authors such as Harvey (1981), Fraser (1993) and Myers (2006) in relating classical economic concepts and theories to urban land and property markets is acknowledged.

1.2.1   Supply and demand, markets and equilibrium price determination

This book does not seek to present all facets of microeconomics; the focus is on price determination. The world's resources – land, labour and capital – are used to create economic goods to satisfy human desires and needs, and **economics** is concerned with the allocation of these finite (limited in supply) resources to humanity's infinite wants. This problem is formally referred to as **scarcity**. In an attempt to reconcile this problem, economists argue that people must make careful choices – choices about what is made, how it is made and for whom it is made; or in terms of property, choices about what land should be developed, how it should be used and whether it should be available for purchase or rent. Indeed, at its simplest level, economics is 'the science of choice'. Because resources are scarce their use involves an **opportunity cost** – resources allocated to one use cannot be used simultaneously elsewhere, so the opportunity cost of using resources in a particular way is the value of alternative uses forgone. In other words, in a world of scarcity, for every want that is satisfied, some other want, or wants, remain unsatisfied. Choosing one thing inevitably requires giving up something else; an opportunity has been missed or forgone. This fundamental economic concept helps explain how economic decisions are made; for example, how property developers might decide which projects to proceed with and how investors might select the range of assets to include in their portfolios. To avoid understanding opportunity cost in a purely mechanistic way – where one good is simply chosen instead of another – we need to clarify how decisions between competing alternatives are made. Following Lancaster's theory of 'consumer behaviour', goods are rarely bought to yield a one-dimensional type of utility to the purchaser; the purchase of each good or service usually fulfils a range of needs. In other words, any good or service provides a number of attributes; the price paid satisfies a cluster of requirements. As Lancaster (1966) explained 'The good, *per se*, does not give utility to the consumer; it possesses characteristics, and these characteristics give rise to utility. In general ... many characteristics will be shared by more than one good.' For example, a commercial building provides a range of services for the tenant; office space for employees, a certain image, a specific location relative to transport and supplies, an investment, and so on.

An assumption must be made at this early stage that consumers of resources seek to maximise their welfare. Our concern is with commercial property and therefore businesses are the resource consumers and welfare to them means profit. Businesses seek to maximise their profit. A budget constraint limits the choices that businesses can make when choosing between resources in a market – in effect, desire, measured by opportunity cost, is limited by a budget constraint. The existence of a budget constraint is a reflection of the distribution of resource-buying capacity throughout an economy. In some economies this distribution might be state-controlled, in others it is itself left to competitive forces. In a market economy the allocation of scarce commercial property resources is facilitated by means of a **market**. In economic terms a market has particular characteristics; there are lots of decision-makers (firms in our case) and they behave competitively; any advantage some might have in terms of access to privileged information, for example, does not continue beyond the short-run. Each business will have particular preferences or requirements and a budget, and these will influence the price that can be offered for property and consequently the quantity obtained.

Let us simplify the commercial property market for a moment to one where landowners supply properties and businesses demand or 'consume' them. Suppliers interact with consumers in a market-place where property interests are exchanged, usually indirectly by means of money. The short-run[1] demand schedule illustrated in Figure 1.1 represents consumer behaviour and is a downward-sloping curve to show that possible buyers and renters of property demand a greater quantity at low prices than at high prices (assuming population, income, future prices, consumer preferences, etc. all remain constant). The short-run supply curve maps out the quantity of property interests available for sale or lease at various prices (assuming factors of production remain constant).[2] The higher the price that can be obtained the greater the quantity of property that will be supplied. Equilibrium price P^* is where demand for property equals supply at quantity Q^*. Price varies directly with supply and indirectly with demand.

The result of an efficiently functioning commercial property market in the long-run should be economic efficiency, achieved when resources have been

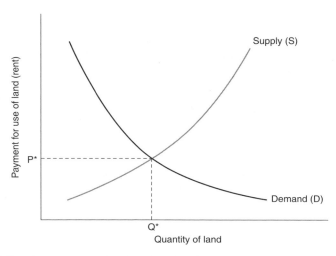

Figure 1.1   Short-run supply of and demand for property.

allocated in their optimum way – profit has been maximised and property resources could not be reallocated without making at least one consumer or business worse off – a concept known as Pareto optimality.

But what do businesses demand commercial property for? Property is demanded, and therefore leased or purchased, not for its own sake but as a means to an end; typically, as far as commercial property is concerned, for the production capabilities it offers, the services it supports or the profit it might generate. Demand of this type is known as **derived demand**. This is an important concept as it explains some of the complexity associated with valuation, especially as commercial property offers different utility opportunities for developers, occupiers and investors. This utility value is usually measured in monetary terms and might take the form of a rental value in the case of a tenant or a capital value in the case of an investor, developer or owner-occupier. So commercial property, particularly in its raw or undeveloped state, is a resource that is combined with other resources to produce those goods and services that businesses desire. Economists tend to refer to these resources as **factors of production** to emphasise that various factors need to be combined to produce any goods or services. The factors of production are usually classified into three groups, namely, land, capital and labour – and sometimes entrepreneurs are specifically identified as a fourth category. To construct buildings or infrastructure, for example, labour is required to develop a plot of land, and plant and equipment, which may be hired or bought, is required to facilitate the process. These manufactured resources are called capital, or more precisely **physical capital**. Each factor of production receives a specific kind of payment. Landlords, who provide the use of land over time, receive rent. Owners of physical capital, who often rely on credit, pay, directly or indirectly, in the form of interest. Workers receive wages and the entrepreneur gains profit. It is interesting that the Marxists challenge the logic of this model, as they understand land to be a gift of nature – a non-produced resource – that exists regardless of payment. From a pure Marxist perspective, therefore, land has no value and all property is regarded as theft! Indeed it is too easy to forget that the state or some collective arrangement could own and allocate land.

The Appraisal Institute (2001) summarises the situation: a property or, more correctly, a legal interest in a property cannot have economic value unless it has *utility* and is *scarce*. Its value will be determined by these factors together with *opportunity cost* and *budget constraint*. The way these four factors interact to create value is reflected in the basic economic principle of supply and demand, and valuation is the process of formalising this principle as a means of estimating the equilibrium price at which supply and demand takes place under 'normal' market conditions. Property, then, is required to produce goods and services and enters the economy in many ways. Capitalist market economies have developed systems of private property ownership and occupation and the trading of property rights between owners and occupiers as a means of competitive allocation. Economists try to understand the nature of payments that correspond with the trading of these property rights, and this is, from an economic perspective at least, the essence of valuation.

1.2.2   The property market and price determination

This Section introduces three interrelated economic concepts concerning the use of land for commercial activity. These are the following:

- The payment in the form of rent that is made for the use of land as a whole. Rent is a composite sum comprising two economic concepts known as **economic rent** and **transfer earnings**.
- Different rents for different land uses; competitive bidding between different users of land means that each site is allocated to its profit-maximising use.
- Land can vary in its intensity of use.

1.2.2.1   Rent for land as a whole

Commercial property has certain economic characteristics that distinguish it from other factors of production. It actually has two components: the land itself and (usually) improvements that have been made to the land in the form of buildings and other manmade additions. This has several implications, not least the existence of a separate market in land for development, which we will discuss in more detail in Chapter 6. Each unit of property is unique; it is a heterogeneous product if only because each land parcel on which a building is sited occupies a separate geographical position. This means that it will vary in quality – for urban land this is largely due to accessibility differences but will also differ in terms of physical attributes and institutional restrictions and will also be susceptible to external influences. Property tends to be available for purchase in large, indivisible and expensive units or lots so financing plays a significant role in market activity. Also, because property is durable, there is a big market for second-hand (existing or already developed) property and a much smaller market for development land on which to build new property. We also know that about half of the total stock of commercial property is owned by investors who receive rent paid by occupiers in return for the use of property. The other half own the property that they occupy outright but we can assume that the price or value of each property asset is the capitalised value of rent that would be paid if the property was owned as an investment. What this means is that we can focus our economic analysis of price determination in the property market on rental values and assume that capital values bear a relation to these, which we will describe in detail in Chapter 2.

Early classical economists regarded rent as a payment to a **landlord** by a **tenant** for the use of land in its 'unimproved' state (land with no buildings on it) typically for farming. The classical economist Ricardo (1817) set out a basic theory of agricultural land rent. The theory implied that land rent was entirely demand-determined because the supply of land as a whole was fixed and had a single use (to grow corn). The most fertile or productive land is used first and less productive land is used as the demand for the agricultural product increases. Rent on most productive land is based on its advantage over the least productive and competition between farmers ensures the value of the 'difference in productivity of land' is paid as rent (Alonso, 1964). Rent is therefore dependent on the demand (and hence the price paid) for the output from the land – a derived demand.

Now consider price determination in the market for new urban development land. Applying marginal productivity theory, land is a factor of production and a profit-maximising business in a competitive factor and product market will buy land up to a point at which additional revenue from using another unit of land is exactly offset by its additional cost. The additional revenue attributable to any factor is called the marginal revenue product (MRP) and it is calculated by multiplying the marginal revenue[3] (MR) obtained from selling another unit of output by the marginal product[4] (MP) of the factor. If other factors of production are fixed, as more and more land is used, its MP decreases due to the onset of **diminishing returns**. So if MR is constant and MP declines, the MRP of land will decline as additional units of land are used *ceteris paribus*. The declining MRP can represent a firm's demand schedule for the land factor as shown in Figure 1.1.[5] If the price of land falls relative to other factors of production, demand will increase; that is why the demand curve in Figure 1.1 is downward-sloping. If the productivity of land or the price of the commodity produced good/service increased then demand for all quantities of land and hence the rent offered would rise (the demand curve would shift upwards and to the right from D to D_1, as illustrated in Figure 1.2. On the supply side the situation is a little more unusual. In a market for a conventional factor or product, the supply curve would be upward-sloping as illustrated in Figure 1.1, but the supply of all land is completely (perfectly) inelastic and cannot be increased in response to higher demand – the only response is higher price. Price therefore is solely demand-determined.

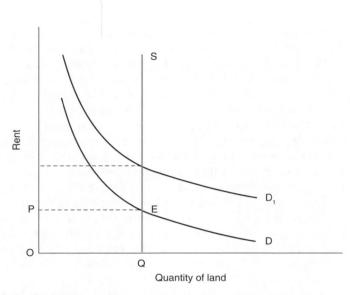

Figure 1.2   Elastic demand and inelastic supply of land for a single use under Ricardian rent theory.

Whatever the level of demand, supply remains fixed; the opportunity cost of using land is therefore zero and all earnings from land and, the corollary, all rent paid for its use (represented in Figure 1.2 by the area OPEQ) are an excess over opportunity cost – they represent economic rent – that part of earnings from a factor of production that results from it having some element of fixed or inelastic supply and there is competition to secure it (Harvey and Jowsey, 2004).

Ricardian rent theory applies to land as a whole since the ultimate supply of all land is fixed, that is why the supply curve is perfectly inelastic (vertical) and all rent is economic rent. But demand for urban development land (as for all commercial property) is a derived demand and, because each unit of land is spatially heterogeneous, different businesses will demand land in different locations for different uses. Consequently, they will be able to pay a price for land that depends on the revenue they think they can generate and the costs they will incur in the process. As Harvey (1981) puts it, users compete for land, being able to offer the difference between the revenue they think they can generate from using the land less other costs of production (including **normal profit**). So we can adapt the above theory to take into account different businesses wishing to use land in various locations in different ways.

1.2.2.2 Land use rents

The supply of land for a particular use will not be fixed (perfectly inelastic) unless, of course, it can only be used in one way. This is because, in response to an increase in demand, additional supply could be bid from and surrendered by other uses if the proposed change of use has a value in excess of its existing use value. The payment to the landowner for the use of land is still made in the form of rent but, since land can be used for alternative uses, supply is no longer perfectly inelastic and has an opportunity cost. Land rent, rather than comprising economic rent only as in Ricardian rent theory, can now be considered to consist of two elements: transfer earnings (a minimum sum or opportunity cost to retain land in its current use, which must be at least equal to the amount that could be obtained from the most profitable alternative use) and economic rent (a payment in excess of transfer earnings that reflects the scarcity value of the land). Generally urban land rents contain high transfer earning because of the overall usefulness of land and the possible returns from transferring it between uses (Button, 1976).

Diagrammatically, the supply curve is no longer vertical; instead it is upward-sloping. Figure 1.3 illustrates the demand for and supply of land for a particular use, warehousing perhaps. Q_1 represents the amount of land that would be supplied to the market if the rent was P_1 but, under our assumption of competition between users of land, interaction of supply and demand will lead to a supply of Q^* of land for this particular use, all of which will be demanded and for which the market equilibrium rent will be P^*. Because supply is not perfectly elastic, some of this rent is transfer earnings and the rest is economic rent. If the rent falls below the transfer earnings then the landowner will transfer from this land use or at least decide to supply less of it. Taking all the properties together their economic rent is shown by the shaded area. Property Q^* is the marginal property and is only just supplied at price P^* and all of the rent is transfer earnings. Assuming a homogeneous supply, the interaction of supply and demand leads to an equilibrium market rent for this type of land use and competition between uses ensures that this rent goes to the optimum use (Harvey, 1981).

The amount of price shift in response to a change in supply will depend on the elasticity of supply – the more inelastic the greater the change in price.

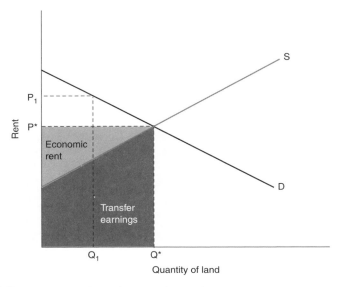

Figure 1.3 Elastic supply and elastic demand.

Using this neoclassical land use rent theory it is possible to look at the inter-action between supply and demand more closely in order to understand the nature of the rent payments for different land uses. Figure 1.4 shows that the rent for retail land use is almost entirely economic rent in the central area. Commercial floor-space that is restricted in supply such as shops in Oxford Street in London or offices in the City of London command a high com-mercial rent that is almost entirely made up of economic rent because of the scarcity of this type of space in these locations.

The more elastic supply of land for industrial use on the edge of an urban area means that the lower commercial rent for industrial land use is largely transfer earnings, see Figure 1.5. The proportion of transfer earnings and

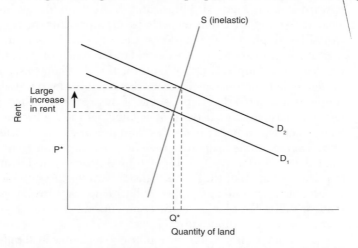

Figure 1.4   Rents for retail land in the central area under conditions of inelastic land supply.

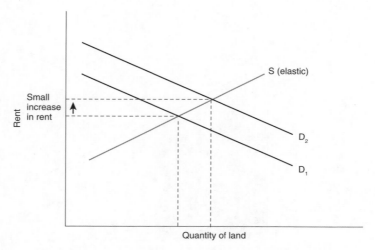

Figure 1.5   Industrial land rents on the edge of an urban area under conditions of elastic land supply.

economic rent depends on the elasticity of supply of land: the more inelastic the supply, the higher the economic rent while the more elastic the supply, the higher the transfer earnings element. Because urban land is fairly fixed in supply (inelastic) and is increasingly so near the centre, economic rent is also high for particular sites and forms an increasing proportion of total land rent as the centre of an urban area nears. So any increase in demand (or reduction in supply) for central sites is reflected in substantial rises in commercial rent, but on the outskirts an increase in demand (or decrease in supply) for land for a specific purpose only produces a small change in economic rent (and thus land rent as a whole) because land is less scarce.

A demand-side Ricardian rent theory would seem to be more applicable in circumstances where supply is very inelastic, in the centre of an urban area where land is scarce or where land use planning controls severely restrict the supply of land for a particular use (Evans, 2004). Neoclassical land use rent theory would be more appropriate where the supply of land for a particular use is relatively elastic, perhaps on the edge of an urban area. The theory assumes strong competition between prospective occupiers, ensuring that the rent for the most desirable/prime profit maximising locations (either in terms of revenue-generating attributes such as access to the market or cost-reducing attributes such as access to labour) attracts the highest rents. Price rations scarce supply among competing uses and this ensures land is put to its most profitable use in each location (Harvey and Jowsey, 2004).

Before we move on let us consider the effect of time on the elasticity of supply of and demand for commercial land. Taking office land as an example and using conventional equilibrium analysis, in the short-run supply will be inelastic[6] (S in Figure 1.6) and demand represented by D will be elastic, producing an equilibrium rent, r^*. If demand for offices increases to D_1 (perhaps an economic upturn has meant that more employees have been recruited and therefore there is a demand for more space) rent will rise to r_1.

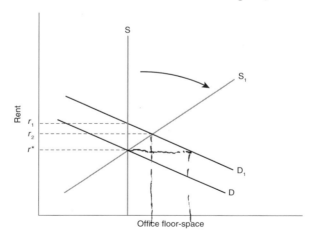

Figure 1.6 Equilibrium analysis of rent for office space (Adapted from Fraser 1993).

In the long-run, supply adjusts in response to this increase in demand because the increase in rent improves the profitability of property development activity. The assumption of inelasticity can therefore be relaxed and the supply of office land will increase to say S_1, settling rents back to r_2, assuming no further change in demand. It should be noted that this is a very simple model of a complex market that is seldom in a state of equilibrium (Fraser, 1993). In fact Ball *et al.* (1998) point out that, in practice, the short-run demand curve is unlikely to be very sensitive to rent levels and therefore tends to be inelastic. This is why rents tend to be sticky downwards because, faced with an inelastic demand curve, landlords would have to reduce rents significantly to have much impact on the quantity of space demanded. In the long-run the demand curve would become more elastic as businesses change production methods, space utilisation and location.

It is now time to turn our attention to the use of land *and* buildings (property) as a collective factor of production. The first thing to point out is the dominance of the existing stock of property over new stock. Because property is so durable it accumulates over time and new additions (say each year) add a tiny amount to the existing stock. Consequently new supply has negligible influence on price. Nowadays we think of rent as a payment for 'improved' land – typically land that has been developed in some way so that it now includes buildings too. Economists refer to this concept of rent as commercial rent. If the property is let to a tenant then the rent would include not only a payment for the use of the land but also some payment for the interest and capital in respect of the improvements that have been made to the land. But it is not easy to distinguish the rent attributable to buildings from that attributable to land. Land is, of course, permanent and although buildings do ultimately depreciate, usually due to a combination of deterioration and obsolescence factors which will be discussed in Chapter 6, they do last a long time. It can be assumed therefore that land and buildings are a fixed factor of production in any time frame except the very long-run, which the business occupier can combine with variable amounts of other factors (labour, capital and enterprise) to undertake business activity. We have also established that, in absolute terms, the physical supply of land as a whole is completely inelastic and the supply of land for *all* commercial uses is very inelastic. The supply of land and buildings (or property) for *specific* commercial uses is relatively inelastic in the short-run owing to the requirement for planning permission to change use and the time it takes to develop new property, but less so in the long-run as development activity reacts and changes in the intensity with which land is used are possible. Nevertheless, compared to the other factors of production, supply of property is the least flexible. So, because of the negligible influence on price of new supply, demand is the major determinant of rental value.

1.2.2.3   Land use intensity

It was stated above that the quantity of land that a user demands depends not only on its price and the price of the final product but also on its productivity.

The productivity of land can usually be increased in response to increased demand (or a price rise) by using it more intensively through the addition of capital. In economic terms we can add variable amounts of other factors of production (labour but, particularly, capital) to the fixed amount of land. As we are dealing with commercial property we are typically referring to the addition of variable amounts of building area or floor-space to a unit of land rather than, say, the addition of fertiliser to farmland. This idea was first expounded by the British economist Alfred Marshall who argued that as demand for a piece of land increases it will pay to provide more accommodation on the site (i.e. use it more intensively). By providing more accommodation on a given site, land area is being substituted by building area and the relative cost of land and building will determine how far this substitution will take place; if land is cheap it will not take much building before it will pay to acquire more land to provide more accommodation whereas, if land is expensive, a large amount of building may take place before building costs increase to a level where it pays to acquire more land to provide extra accommodation. It must be borne in mind though that the process of adding more and more capital to a fixed amount of land will be subject to the principle of diminishing returns. This concept is fundamental to urban land use so it is worth repeating it in Marshall's own words. Marshall (1920) stated that

> as in agriculture, there is a certain application of capital and labour to the acre which gives the highest return, and further applications after this give a less return, so it is in building. The amount of capital per acre which gives the maximum return varies in agriculture with the nature of the crops, with the state of the arts of production, and with the character of the markets to be supplied; and similarly in building, the capital per square foot which would give the maximum return, if the site had no scarcity value, varies with the purpose for which the building is wanted. But when the site has a scarcity value, it is worth while to go on applying capital beyond this maximum rather than pay the extra cost of land required for extending the site. In places where the value of land is high, each square foot is made to yield perhaps twice the accommodation, at more than twice the cost, than it would be made to give, if used for similar purposes where the value of land is low.

Marshall used the phrase '*the margin of building*' to describe that accommodation which it is only just worth obtaining from a given site and which would not be obtained if land were less scarce. This extra accommodation was likened to the top floor of a building which by erecting this floor instead of spreading the building over more ground yields a saving in the cost of land, which just compensates for the extra expense. The revenue that the accommodation on this top floor provides is only just enough to cover its costs without allowing anything for rent. In other words, the marginal revenue (MR) from this floor equals its marginal cost (MC).

So, for each unit of land, the land use rent theory must simultaneously allocate the optimum (profit maximising) use and intensity of that use. We have already examined allocation of land use, so now let us concentrate on the intensity of land use. Assume that the optimum land use of a particular site has already been determined. This means that land is a factor of production that has a fixed cost. What we want to know is the optimum amount of capital (which, it is assumed, means building floor-space) to add to the land. In other words, how intensively should the land be used or how much floor-space should be added to a particular piece of land to maximise profit? Assuming that perfect competition in the capital market keeps the cost per unit of capital the same regardless of the quantity required, as more capital (floor-space) is added to the fixed amount of land, the MRP of the land might initially increase because of economies of scale but the principle of diminishing returns means that eventually it will fall. This might be because the revenue that can be generated from upper floors is less than lower ones – think of how much higher rents for ground floor shops are compared to rents for office space above. Profit is maximised where the MRP of a unit of capital equals the (MC) of a unit of capital; in Figure 1.7 this is when OX units of capital are employed. If the business employs less than this amount the MR earned by an extra unit exceeds its MC and if more are employed the MC of each unit in excess of OX will be higher than its MR. OX is therefore the optimum amount of capital to combine with the land. The total revenue earned is represented by the area QYXO. Total cost (including profit) is area PYXO and surplus revenue is therefore QYP. If the current land use is the most profitable then land rent is QYP, that is, the surplus remaining after deducting costs of optimally employed factors of production from expected revenue (Fraser, 1993). The amount of land that a business user will demand depends on its price relative to other factors of production, the price of the good or service produced on or provided from the land and the productivity of the land. If the price obtained for goods and services produced from the land falls the MRP curve will drop from the solid line to the dashed line. Alternatively the production cost (the cost of each unit of capital) might fall, perhaps due to an improvement in construction technology or a fall in the cost of borrowing capital. This would shift the MC of capital line downwards. Either case will, *ceteris paribus*, affect the margin at which it is profitable to use the land, the commercial rent that can be charged and the intensity of use of the land. Similarly a more profitable use would have a higher MRP curve and could therefore afford to bid a higher rent. Competition between different land uses ensures that the land is allocated to its most profitable use and the land rent surplus QYP is maximised.

In terms of land use intensity, Figure 1.7 and the underlying land use rent theory shows that, in order to maximise revenue from a site, capital must be added to the point where MRP equals MC. As stated by Marshall (1920) this also has the effect of maximising the surplus revenue that is available to pay as rent: the highest bidder or rent payer is also the most intensive user of the land. So if land is cheap relative to other factors of production or if a particular use becomes more profitable, the business will demand more land, and if the land is expensive it will demand less and use it more intensively, by building higher, for example. This assumes that competition for land for various uses will ensure that the use of each site will be intensified up to a

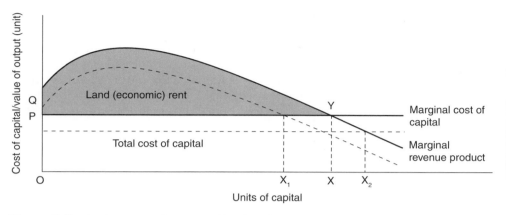

Figure 1.7 Optimum combination of land and capital (adapted from Fraser 1993).

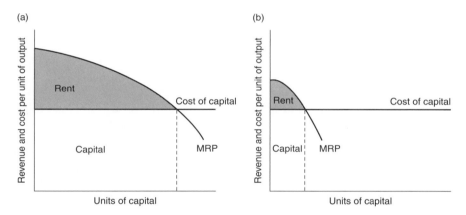

Figure 1.8 Demand and its effect on rent and intensity of land use: (a) intensive use of land and (b) extensive use of land (Harvey and Jowsey 2004).

point at which it is no longer profitable to add any more capital to the same site. In a market where supply is inelastic, as demand for business space in a locality increases, it becomes worthwhile to pay a higher and higher price for land in order to avoid the expense and inconvenience of forcing more accommodation from the same site. At the same time, the higher price of land means that it makes sense to economise its use. These forces of supply and demand cause capital to be applied to a piece of land – its use is intensified – and this continues up to the point where the production costs (excluding rent) are so high that it is more cost-effective to purchase additional land than use the existing site more intensively. So a factory owner in a central location may find that, on account of the high rent for the site, the revenue generated will not cover production costs and may decide to relocate and sell the site to an office user. Harvey and Jowsey (2004) illustrate this point by comparing two sites of the same size; (a) one in the city centre and (b) one in a suburb (Figure 1.8), which shows that it is the strength of demand (represented by the MRP curve) that determines land rent and intensity of land use. For reasons that will become clear in the next section, it is the city centre site from which a business user is able to extract more revenue per unit of output. From the landlord's perspective, where demand (reflected in the commercial rent obtainable) is high (high MRP curve) a more intensive use of land is profitable and rents are high.

This is a very simple model that will be developed a little further in Chapter 6 in the context of property development. Specifically it will be assumed that MC is not constant – as increasing amounts of capital are added to a fixed piece of land, it becomes progressively more expensive to do so, as is the case when building a high-rise office building or skyscraper. The MC curve therefore rises.

To summarise, the rent for land is regarded as a surplus and is determined largely by demand. Different users compete for each piece of land and com-petitive behaviour ensures that each piece is allocated to its most profitable use and its most profitable intensity of use. We have made a number of simplifying assumptions along the way and we shall come back to these at the end of the next section.

1.2.3   Location and land use

Our discussion so far has suggested that different users of land might be pre-pared to offer different rents for a piece of land because it offers the potential to earn different amounts of revenue depending on the use to which it is put. But what is this potential and why are different users able to offer or bid different rents to use it? Land offers certain attributes that some commercial users find more beneficial than others and we have to bring these into our discussion now. In developing our understanding of commercial rent we are not only concerned about supply and demand of land as a whole, of land for particular uses and the intensity with which those uses are employed on land but also where the land is. We need to understand this final part of the jigsaw because land, unlike other factors of production (labour and capital), is fixed in space so the location of each site influences the way in which it is used and its profit-making potential. In short, we need to know a little about the economics of space.

As well as formulating a theory of agricultural land rent on the basis of fer-tility, Ricardo also recognised that land near a market bears lower transport costs and so generates more revenue, with the surplus (over and above costs and normal profit) being paid as rent. Ricardo (1817) argued that '[I]f all land has the same properties, if it were unlimited in quantity, and uniform in quality, no charge could be made for its use, unless where it possessed pecu-liar advantages of situation.' So land that is close to the market or a supply of labour (a 'prime' site) will yield the same output as land that is further away (a 'secondary' site) but would incur lower labour and capital costs due to its accessibility advantages. In other words the distant land suffers greater diminishing returns. Assuming the exchange value or price of the output

Chapter 1

remains the same regardless of whether it was produced on prime or secondary land, the utility value of the prime site is greater and this value is transferred via competitive bidding from user to landlord in the form of rent.

In 1826 the German landowner Johann von Thünen applied Ricardian rent theory in a spatial context and demonstrated the relationship between the ability to pay agricultural rent for a piece of land and its distance from the market in which the farm produce is traded. The theory assumes that farmland exists in a boundless, featureless plain over which natural resources and climate are uniformly distributed, produce is traded at a central market that is connected to its catchment area by a uniformly distributed transport network. It was also assumed that although different agricultural goods can be produced, which differ in production costs and bulk so that cost of transportation varies, revenue from each product per unit area of land is the same; in other words, von Thünen's theory was a cost-based model that ignored intensity of land use and revenue differentials. Fixing all other costs, Figure 1.9 shows that, for a single land use, transport costs will increase as distance from the central market increases. Assuming competition between uses, any surplus profit over and above costs (which include normal profit to the farmer) is paid as rent to the landowner. As the theory assumes that the total revenue remains constant, the rent (surplus profit[7] in Figure 1.9) decreases as the distance to the market increases. Beyond distance Y this use is no longer profitable as costs exceed revenue.

Figure 1.10 introduces a second land use (A) for which fixed production costs are lower, OA, but the final product is more bulky than the original land use (B) and therefore incurs more steeply rising transport costs as distance to the market increases. Assuming revenue is the same from both

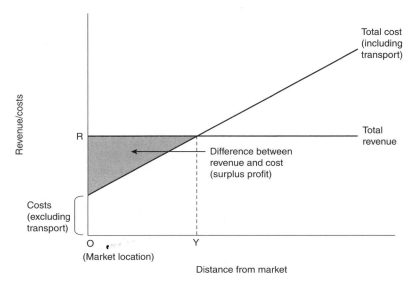

Figure 1.9 Von Thunen's single use revenue and cost model (Harvey and Jowsey 2004).

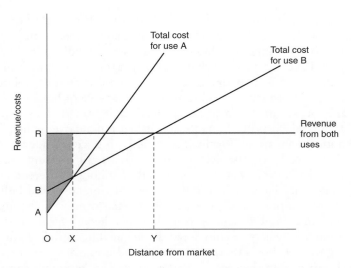

Figure 1.10   Von Thunen's two-use revenue and cost model (Harvey and Jowsey 2004).

products, close to the market land use A has the greatest surplus (revenue less costs) available to bid as rent (AR as opposed to BR). So land use A is able to outbid land use B but only up to distance X from the market, after which, because B's total production costs do not rise so steeply, it is able to outbid A.

As more land uses are added with different levels of fixed costs and different rates of rising transport costs, an agricultural land use rent theory is obtained by rotating Figure 1.10 through 180° and considering the rent-earning capacity (i.e. revenue less cost) of each land use on the y-axis. In Figure 1.11, which is adapted from Harvey and Jowsey (2004), the shaded areas (surplus profit) represent rent-earning capacity and the sizes of these are maintained for each land use. The revenue line is dropped as it is constant for all land uses. A rent curve MN is derived showing the rent for land at different distances from the market. Given a central market and a homogeneous agricultural plain, a series of concentric zones of land use is the result and the relationship between location, land use and rent should now be evident. Of course, reality confounds all of the simplifying assumptions made by von Thünen and we do not see concentric rings in the real world. Instead, natural features, the vagaries of the transport network and other irregularities, such as government trade policy, break up this simple pattern but the theory retains a robust logic that is hard to deny.

Building on Ricardo's observations and von Thünen's theory, Mill (1909) argued that in a country where land remains to be cultivated, the worst land in actual cultivation pays no rent and it is this marginal land that sets the standard for estimating the amount of rent yielded by all other land (beyond D in Figure 1.11). It does this by establishing a benchmark so that whatever revenue agricultural capital produces, beyond what is produced by the same

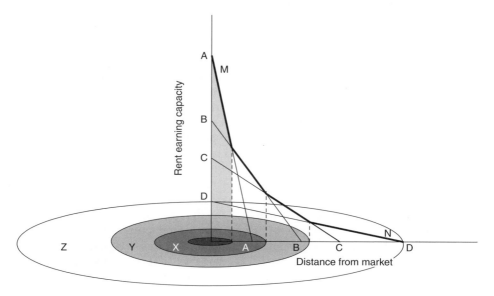

Figure 1.11   Land use bid–rent theory.

amount of capital on the worst soil, or under the most expensive mode of cultivation, that revenue will be paid as rent to the owner of the land on which it is employed. In other words

> Rent, in short, merely equalises the profits of different farming capitals, by enabling the landlord to appropriate all extra gains occasioned by superiority of natural advantages.   (Mill, 1909)

Like agricultural land uses, what urban land uses desire is accessibility, not just access to the market (where the customers are) but also access to factors of production (particularly labour but capital too) and to other complementary land uses.[8] The aim is to seek a location that minimises transport costs involved with marshalling factors of production but maximises access to the market and to complementary land uses. With a radial transport network around a central market and the other simplifying assumptions von Thünen's model can be applied to urban land uses. Consideration of the relationship between the location of urban land uses and rent began in earnest at the beginning of the twentieth century. Hurd (1903) applied the theory of economic competition among farmers for agricultural land to businesses in an urban area. In explaining the cause of different land values within an urban area, Hurd suggested that 'since value depends on economic rent, and rent on location and location on convenience, and convenience on nearness, we may eliminate the intermediate steps and say that value depends on nearness.' Theoretically, as Kivell (1993) points out, in a monocentric urban area the centre is where transport facilities maximise labour availability, customer flow and proximate linkages, and therefore attracts the highest capital and rental values. Haig (1926) suggested that 'rent appears as the charge which the owner of a relatively accessible site can impose because of the saving in transport costs which the use of the site makes possible.' His theory emphasised the correlation between rent and transport costs, the latter being the payment to overcome the 'friction of space'; the better the transport network, the less the friction. The theoretically perfect site for an activity is that which offers the desired degree of accessibility at the lowest costs of friction. Haig's hypothesis was therefore 'the layout of a metropolis ... tends to be determined by a principle which may be termed the minimising of the costs of friction' (Haig, 1926). Haig's hypothesis concentrated on the cost-side of profit maximisation but some land uses such as retail are able to derive a revenue-generating advantage from certain sites, particularly those most accessible to customers. Therefore, the revenue-generating potential of a site must be weighed against the costs of friction for these land uses. Marshall (1920) noted that demand for the highest value land comes from retail and wholesale traders rather than manufacturers because they can fit into smaller sites (i.e. develop land more intensively) in places where there are plenty of customers. Therefore 'In a free economy, the correct location of the individual enterprise lies where the net profit is greatest' (Losch, 1954).

In attempting to quantify spatial variation in rent and land use, Alonso (1964) adapted von Thünen's agricultural land use model to urban land use. Alonso suggested that activities can trade off falling revenue and higher costs (including transport) against lower site rents as distance from the centre increases. This can be illustrated by defining 'bid–rent' curves (similar in nature to indifference curves) that indicate the maximum rent that can be paid at different locations and still enable the business to earn normal profit, as shown in Figure 1.12. In other words, the lines join equilibrium locations where access and rent are traded off against each other. In a monocentric city market, the rent curve derived in Figure 1.11 can be superimposed. Businesses will endeavour to locate on the bid–rent curve nearest the origin; the equilibrium location is at X as this is the most profitable location at current rents.

Some urban land uses place greater emphasis on accessibility than others and these will have steeper bid–rent curves since a considerable drop in rent will be necessary to compensate for the falling revenue as distance from the central business district (CBD) increases. Rent gradients emerge, illustrated in Figure 1.13, for each land use where the steepest gradient prevails. Retailers outbid office occupiers because they are particularly dependent on a central location where the market is located, accessibility is maximised and transport costs are minimised. The availability of such sites is very limited and therefore supply is almost perfectly inelastic (consider the shops surrounding Oxford Circus in London as an example). Office occupiers, in turn, outbid industrial occupiers. Consequently rents generally decline as distance from the central area increases. Basically greater accessibility leads to higher demand, which, in turn, causes rents to rise and land use intensity to increase. This competitive bidding between perfectly informed landlords and occupiers within a simplified market allocates sites to their optimum use.

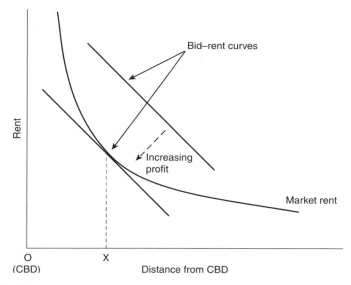

Figure 1.12   Bid–rent curves (Harvey and Jowsey 2004).

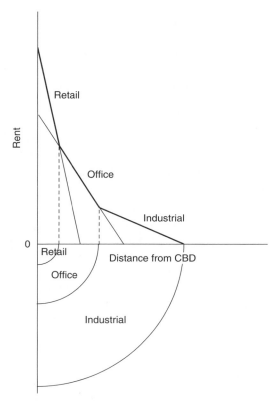

Figure 1.13   Alonso's bid–rent concept.

Alonso's theory rests on simplifying assumptions: a central market in an urban area and a perfect market for urban land, and agglomerating forces, spatial interdependence, special site characteristics and topographical irregularities are all ignored. If the main determinant of differences in urban rent in a city was accessibility and if transportation was possible in all directions and if the transport cost–distance functions were linear, then there would be a smooth land value gradient declining from the centre. In reality, the gradient falls steeply near the centre and levels off further out (Richardson, 1971). Other distortions result from trip destinations to places other than the centre such as out-of-town office, retail and leisure activities, and a non-uniform network of transport infrastructure. Despite the simplifying assumptions, this *bid–rent* theory is still regarded as an acceptable explanation of spatial variation in the demand for property. As Ball *et al.* (1998) argue, the rent or price paid for an owner-occupied property reflects its utility to the user. This utility is a function of land and building characteristics and location. Rents and capital values thus vary spatially and occupiers will choose a location based on an analysis of profit they can make at different locations. Competitive pricing should ensure that, in equilibrium, land is allocated to its most profitable use, but inertia and planning controls influence this. In reality, competitive bidding between users of land often results in mixed use on sites, retail outbidding on the ground floor and offices above (Harvey and Jowsey, 2004).

As Richardson (1971) notes, the central feature of the market is that land rent is an inverse function (typically a negative exponential function) of distance from the centre. This function is primarily a reflection of external and other agglomeration economies and transport costs.

> The significance of transport costs is obvious. People and activities are drawn into cities because of the need for mutual accessibility, especially between homes and workplaces. Even within cities, the distances between interrelated activities have to be minimised, and the existence of transport costs tends *ceteris paribus* to draw activities together. (Richardson, 1971)

The role of external economies and agglomeration economies is generally less obvious but probably more significant. Agglomeration economies include scale economies at the firm or industry level. External economies include access to a common labour market, benefits from personal contacts and access to market, and environmental factors.

The classical economic theories of urban rent and land use have been criticised primarily for their simplifying assumptions and the increasing influence of modern working practices and living habits on the way urban land use is organised. These criticisms are summarised below:

- The process of allocating a land use to a site is constrained by inertia (preventing a high proportion of urban land that is in suboptimal use from coming on to the market) and high mobility costs (preventing users from relocating) (Richardson, 1971).

- A change in the distribution or level of income or a change in the spatial pattern of consumer demand will cause a change in urban land values and the pattern of uses.
- A change in transport costs will have a greater effect on those uses that depend more heavily on transport.
- The theories have no regard for land use interdependence, sometimes referred to as complementarity between neighbouring land uses.
- Land use changes infrequently because of the long life of buildings, lease contracts, neighbourhood effects, expectations and uncertainty. Consequently, adjustments in supply and demand towards an equilibrium are slow.
- There is no uniform plane; geographical and economic factors, the rank and size of urban areas, proximity to other centres, history, favoured areas, cultural dispositions, existence of publicly owned land and ethnic mix all distort the perfect market assumption.
- The theories unrealistically assume a free market with no intervention and perfectly informed market players. In reality the major restriction on the competitive allocation of land uses to sites is land use planning control. This may restrict supply for some uses (leading to artificially higher rents) and over-supply other uses (leading to artificially lower rents). Diagrammatically, the result is suggested in Figure 1.14.
- Owners of property have monopoly power owing to heterogeneity of property.
- The theories ignore spill-over effects such as the filtering of land uses and property types and diseconomies such as traffic congestion.

The emergence of greater spatial flexibility as a result of increased car use, lower transport costs and better information and communications technology meant that, in the 1960s, the classical economic approach to explaining land use allocation, growth and pricing was challenged; see, for example, Meier (1962). Indeed, ubiquitous car ownership has led to the phenomenal growth of out-of-town leisure, retailing and office activity, causing rents to rise in outer areas, and developments in information and communication technology that facilitate home-working and internet shopping may have similarly dramatic impacts on land use patterns in the future. Yet, despite these shortcomings, the classical theories retain a logical appeal that is difficult to counter. As Lean and Goodall (1966) wrote

> An urban area consists of a great variety of interdependent activities and the choice of location of any activity is normally a rational decision made after an assessment of the relative advantages of various locations for the performance of the activity in question, given the general framework and knowledge prevailing.

In the long term each land use will tend to the location that offers the greatest relative advantage. This will be the profit maximisation location for businesses. The spatial differentiation of land use becomes more marked and complex as the degree of specialisation increases in significance and

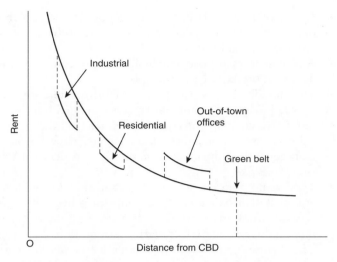

Figure 1.14   The effect of land use planning controls on bid–rent theory (Evans 2004).

complementarity linkages are more commonplace. The pattern of land use is a reflection of competition for sites between uses operating through the forces of supply and demand via the price mechanism.

The relationship between the location of urban land uses and the rents that they attract is a complex one. Land supply in the centre is limited and competition increases rents. At a certain size and level of transport provision, diseconomies of scale set in and lead to congestion. Other influences include planning, declining importance of manufacturing, rising administrative employment and more multiregional and multinational organisations. These influences, together with disadvantages of city centre locations such as congestion, parking, high rents and taxes, have led to decentralisation. But despite predictions that decentralisation would continue at an increasing rate, there has not been a wholesale abandonment of the city centre. The need for face-to-face contact with clients or complementary activities remains crucial to many businesses, and economies of concentration, agglomeration and complementarity can outweigh the problems associated with the city centre.

In summary, as Henneberry (1998) points out, the relationship between accessibility, property values and land use patterns preoccupied early theorists. Travel costs, it was suggested, were traded off against rents and population densities, from the central area to suburbs of a monocentric city. The centre has declined as the predominant location of employment and services in the modern city because accessibility is now heavily car-dependent and peripheral centres of activity have grown. In short, accessibility has become a more complicated phenomenon requiring more sophisticated treatment and it is important to study accessibility more rigorously in order to understand the locational advantages of individual properties rather than rely on traditional bid–rent theory that places the peak rent contour in the central area of a city. For example, if the relative transport costs of a site were reduced (either directly via a transport subsidy or indirectly via an increase in accessibility owing to public transport investment), it will result in increased demand, leading to a rise in rental values. If the changes in value are substantial enough they may trigger property investment and development, causing a change in or intensification of land use.

Key points

- Rent is regarded as a surplus amount paid to the landowner by the user after having deducted the unit costs of optimally employed factors of production involved in using land in its most profitable manner from the MRP generated.
- The pattern of urban land use is determined by supply and demand. Classical urban location theory states that on the supply side landowners will seek to maximise land value by allocating land to its optimum use, subject to planning regulation. On the demand side demand for urban land is a demand for space and occupiers or tenants of land pay occupation costs or bid rents that reflect a location's accessibility. This classical view of the relationship between land use and rent explains whether or not a site is brought into economic use, the intensity of that use and the rent that might be charged. The classical theories also posit that spatial variation in cost and revenue determines the optimum profit maximising location (Dunse *et al.*, 1998).
- An extreme view of the heterogeneity of land is that the supply of each unique parcel of land is perfectly inelastic but of course there will be many plots of land that are substitutable to a greater or lesser extent. When considering urban land, sites in the centre are less substitutable than those on the outskirts simply because there are less of them. Consequently the supply of these sites is more inelastic than others. But these sites are the ones in greatest demand because they are the most accessible to raw materials (labour and capital) and the market (consumers); so their rents are higher and they tend to be intensively developed. This inelastic supply means that economic rent is high in the central area and may even represent 100% of the total rent owing to the inability of supply to increase.

1.3   Macroeconomic concepts

In contrast to microeconomics, macroeconomics is concerned with the outcome of *all* decisions made in the economy as a whole. It takes account of purchases made by all consumers, total capital investments made by businesses, goods and services procured by central and local government and the level of exports demanded overseas. In short, macroeconomics deals with aggregates or totals analysing the overall level of prices, output and employment.

1.3.1   The commercial property market

The discussion in Section 1.2 on the theory of urban rent and land use leads us to the concept of a **market** that encompasses the exchange arrangements of owners and users of property. A market is an environment in which commodities (which may be goods or services and, in our case, legal interests in property) are traded between buyers and sellers through a price mechanism, usually without undue restriction, known as 'an open market' and can be local, regional, national or international. Buyers and sellers – market participants – interact and respond to supply–demand relationships and other price-setting factors as well as to their own constraints (such as budget and desired risk exposure), knowledge and understanding of the relative utility of the property for its intended purpose. The level of efficiency of a market is determined to some extent by the standardisation of the product and the degree of efficiency with which it functions. The stock market in a typical developed economy, for example, provides instant information worldwide about the prices and quantities of shares being bought and sold during the current trading period. By contrast, property markets are more informal, less structured and more diverse; in many ways each property market transaction can be regarded as unique. There are fewer, more heterogeneous transactions in the property market. Consequently it is more complex, buyers and sellers rarely come together and simply strike a bargain, as they usually need to appoint agents, with local knowledge, to act on their behalf and commission independent valuations to verify asking prices. As the Appraisal Institute (2001) points out: the property market has never been considered as strongly efficient because of decentralised trading, the heterogeneity and high cost of each unit of product, the high cost and lengthy transaction process that is common when buying and selling property (referred to as illiquidity), the relatively few buyers and sellers at a single point in time in one price range and location, paucity of market information at the individual property level and the opportunity to exercise monopoly power.

It is possible to gauge the level of market activity by monitoring the number of property transactions, shown in Figure 1.15. This is a very crude statistic as it does not separate residential from commercial transactions and does not classify them by property type or by location but it does provide a sense of market activity over time and gives some general idea of cyclical movements.

As a way of explaining how the commercial property market functions, we can define three interlinked sectors:

- The user, or occupier market, in which each property is either owned and occupied by the user or leased from a landlord who is holding the property as an investment.
- The investment market, where properties are regarded as financial assets. This sector proceeds on the basis that rational investors seek to maximise

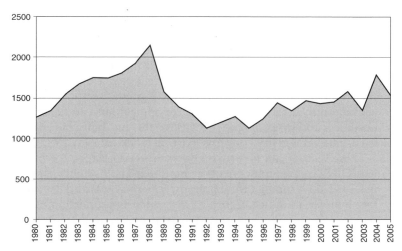

Figure 1.15 Number of property transactions in England and Wales (thousands) (Office for National Statistics).

returns on a range of assets and compare the risks of holding property against other investment opportunities. At the heart of investment theory and practice is a trade-off between risk and return with the aim of maximising return for a minimum acceptable level of risk. This market sector is driven by the opportunity cost of investment capital.

- The new property, or development market, where land is developed to create new stock or redeveloped to replace existing stock. For ease the developer can be regarded as a separate entity but in reality is a particular type of investor or is sometimes the occupier of the developed property. The developer is responsible for conceiving the scheme, acquiring the land, negotiating the finance and organising construction. Completed projects are subsequently let to occupiers and sold to investors or retained either as an investment or for own occupation.

This means that the same property or site can have different values depending on the market sector in which it is being traded. For occupiers, property represents a factor of production, the bid-price (rental value if let or capital value if purchased) that will depend on the specific use to which it is put; that is, its value to the business – this is what we have been discussing in the microeconomics section. Developers and investors, on the other hand, regard property as an investment opportunity and investment value will depend on its capacity to deliver a satisfactory return. But it should be remembered that the ability of a property to provide a satisfactory return to investors and developers is predicated on its value to users/occupiers, thus rental value is the key financial driver of commercial property market activity in all sectors. The three sectors are interdependent and values and market activity in each are influenced by signals from the others. Rental values are determined by the forces of supply and demand in the occupier sector and this demand is one that is derived from price signals in the market for the commodity that the property is being used to produce. In the investment sector capital values are determined by the expectations of occupier activity and its forecast effect on rental values. Both capital values in the investment sector and rental values in the occupier sector are theoretically affected by the supply of properties from the development sector, in which land values are determined by the supply of development land and demand for space by occupiers and investors but, because of the durability of property, the majority of market activity concerns existing stock (Fraser, 1993).

These sectors can be broken down into subsectors according to property use. Obvious examples are office buildings and business parks, retail properties such as shopping centres, shops, supermarkets and department stores; in fact high street outlets represent a significant proportion of the commercial sector. Less obvious are the industrial estates and traditional warehouses that formed an important part of the industrial age. Leisure outlets such as hotels, pubs and cinemas represent an increasing proportion of commercial property stock. Buyers and sellers of these various types of property are brought together in separate submarkets to determine exchange details. Furthermore, because property is physically immobile, each of these submarkets may operate differently depending on their location; office property in the West End of London is regarded as a separate market to similar space in the Mid-Town and City areas of Central London. More specific, specialised markets may also be identified on the basis of unit size, quality, investor and tenant characteristics, such as institutionally owned high-tech business parks let to 'blue-chip' tenants. The distinguishing characteristic of a market is the exchange of information about factors such as price, quality and quantity. In terms of property this can be interpreted as rental and capital values, location, physical (size, style, design, age, etc.) and legal (tenure, planning, etc.) attributes. The next three sections consider the principal commercial property market sectors described above in more detail.

1.3.2 Property occupation

From the occupier's perspective, property can either be rented or owned, the latter often debt financed, via a mortgage, for example. According to the IPF, in 2005 the total value of commercial property stock in the core commercial land uses of retail, office and industrial was £489 billion. The IPF also reports that, in the same year, approximately 52% of this stock was held as investment property and the remainder was owner-occupied. The IPF has researched information published by Companies House as a way of estimating the value of owner-occupied property. The results show that 755 companies hold property assets of more that £20 million each, according to figures reported on their balance sheets in 2003. Indeed 68 retail companies hold property assets valued at £38 billion in total (IPF, 2005). Table 1.2 shows estimates of net worth of commercial, industrial and other buildings categorised by use, and it can be seen that, out of a total net worth of all commercial

Table 1.2 National balance sheet totals for commercial, industrial and other buildings categorised by use for the year 2005.

Use	Sub-total (£ billion at end year)	Net worth (£ billion at end year)
Public non-financial corporations	26.5	
Private non-financial corporations	223.5	
Non-financial corporations		250.0
Financial corporations		131.1
Central government	76.2	
Local government	112.5	
General government		188.7
Households and non-profit institutions serving households		56.1

Source: UK National Accounts: *The Blue Book* (2006).

property assets at the end of 2005 of £625.9 billion, around a third (£215.6 billion) is in the public sector. As in 2003, a best estimate of total retail, office and industrial property held by the public sector is £20–25 billion, around £7 billion in central government and £15 billion in local authorities, with most of that stock in the office sector (IPF, 2005).

In the case of the owner-occupied property, annual occupation costs are often referred to as *imputed rent* but whether real or imputed, rent acts as a price signal to market participants and, through its rise and fall, clears the market by equating supply and demand (Ball *et al.*, 1998). For properties held as investments, the owner receives a return for the capital outlay (purchase price) in the form of rent from the occupier. Typically rental income from a property is fixed for 5 years at a time and thus offers a degree of price stability in the occupier market. This links to stability of investment income and hence capital values in the investment market (Fraser, 1993). Indeed, Fraser argues, prices of property investments tend to be more stable than other types of investment, especially in the short-term as investors often hold out for a price they expect rather than reduce their asking price when selling. So whereas the occupier is concerned with the property and its contribution to the business occurring on the premises, the investor is concerned with the rate of return on the investment. This ownership/occupation split will continue as long as occupiers in the commercial market prefer to rent rather than own property and occupiers show no sign of wishing to increase the amount of property that they own. Businesses may be reluctant to own property because it can tie up a considerable amount of capital and this money could be used in core business activities. Also property ownership requires management expertise to integrate the assets into core activities. This role is often contracted out to external agents who may not be familiar with corporate objectives and strategies of the company and this can result in under-occupied space and other inefficiencies. Alternative strategies have therefore been employed by companies and these have often been variations on the theme of a **sale and leaseback** arrangement where property owner-ship (and sometimes management) is transferred to an owner-investor and capital is released to the occupying business tenant (previously an owner-occupier) for investment in the business.

The requirements of commercial occupiers are constantly changing in terms of physical attributes such as size of accommodation, type of struc-ture and geographical location, and in terms of legal ownership. By way of example, whereas 20 years ago most commercial premises were let on 25 year leases, new leases granted in 2004 and 2005 averaged 11 years for retail property, just over 7 years for offices and just less than 7 years for industrial property (IPF, 2005). These changing property requirements result not only from shifts in economic activity but also from changes in the way many businesses operate; working practices, developments in informa-tion and communication technology, globalisation of resource and product markets have all had significant impacts. Increasingly big corporate organi-sations are trying to specify property that meets strict corporate criteria; some even want the building to be part of the branding. Hence bespoke owner-occupied commercial offices are slowly increasing in number; witness the change to the London skyline over the past 5 years or so. If the existing stock cannot supply the required assets then development must occur to meet the demand. These changing occupier requirements are considered in more detail in Chapter 4.

The UK Government publishes annual statistics on the number, size and value of occupied units of commercial and industrial property. These units are commonly referred to as 'business premises' but for property taxation purposes they are legally defined as **hereditaments** in England and Wales. Broadly speaking, these are either whole buildings or units of accommoda-tion exclusively occupied within a building. The data on which the statistics are based originate from the Valuation Office Agency (VOA). As an executive agency of Her Majesty's Revenue and Customs office, the role of the VOA is to estimate the rental value of all taxable hereditaments on a 5-year cycle as a basis on which to assess the amount of business rates that need to be paid by occupiers and owners of business premises. Much of the data relating to these assessments is in the public domain on a property-by-property basis and can be accessed by visiting the VOA website (www.voa.gov.uk). Since 2005 the VOA has published details of each hereditament that they have assessed for property tax purposes and an example of the type of information that is avail-able can be seen in Table 1.3.

Information like this is collected for all taxable hereditaments and Table 1.4 summarises these data by property type. The VOA uses the term 'bulk classes' to describe the main land uses of retail, office, factory and warehouse space; all other commercial land uses are termed 'non-bulk'. Incidentally, the 2005 rateable values are actually valuations as on 1 April 2003 – this gives the VOA time to value all business premises prior to publication of the entire data set. Retail premises account for the greatest proportion of bulk class hereditaments in England and Wales (39%), with offices making up around a quarter of hereditaments.

Table 1.3 Example of a tax assessment.

Address in Rating List:	1-6 ST GEORGES PLACE, BATH, BA1 3AA
Scheme Reference:	10219
Property Description:	SHOP AND PREMISES

Floor	Description	Area m²/units	£/m²	Value £
Ground	Retail zone A	154.20	125.00	19 275
Ground	Office	6.80	15.63	106
		161.00		19 381
Car parking: Spaces 6				1 200
Total value				**20 581**
Adopted rateable value				**20 500**

It can be seen that there are many shops but they are small in size where the opposite is true of factories. Factories accounted for 19% of bulk class hereditaments, but constituted 37% of floor-space in England and Wales (ODPM, 2006). The financial importance of the service sector (shops and offices) can be seen by looking at their rateable values; together they comprise approximately two-thirds of the total rateable value of taxable business premises. Warehouses have shown the greatest increase in average size from 656 m² in 1998 to 742 m² in 2005, reflecting an increase in demand for large storage and distribution premises as internet shopping and modern logistics take hold. Figure 1.16 shows how factory and warehouse land uses dominate other land uses in terms of sheer floor-space, especially in the north. The only region where it does not dominate is London.

Figure 1.17 illustrates the number of bulk class hereditaments in each region and shows London, the South East and the North West having the most premises, with Wales and the North East the fewest. Looking at the number of hereditaments and the rateable value of the main commercial land uses (Figure 1.18), the dominance of retail and office space is clear to see in all regions and particularly so in London.

In Figure 1.19 we can see the bid–rent theory at work; highest rents paid for retail space, followed by offices and then factories and warehousing.

Certain business premises are exempt from paying business rates altogether including churches, agricultural land and buildings, and fish farms. Another data set compiled by the Office for National Statistics encompasses a wider range of local business units, including agriculture, health and other public services. Table 1.5 shows the number of local units in value added tax (VAT) registered[9] enterprises on 18 March 2005. A local unit in this context means that an individual branch of a company is counted separately.

Many commercial property surveying firms also monitor and publish property information, usually on a quarterly, biannual or annual basis. The information is not as comprehensive as statistics compiled by the government

Table 1.4 Summary statistics for commercial and industrial hereditamentsa: England and Wales, 1 April 1998–2005.

	1998[b]	1999[b]	2000	2001	2002	2003	2004	2005
Hereditaments (number)								
Total	1711586	1716703	1716671	1723313	1732882	1742705	1749778	1745884
Retail premises	574796	571576	570611	567546	564933	562712	559651	548221
Offices	295451	297677	304939	309922	316508	322669	328642	324981
Commercial offices	241464	243343	248931	253778	260115	266022	271653	275527
'Other' offices	53987	54334	56008	56144	56393	56647	56989	49454
Factories[c]	265265	265550	263864	264716	264960	265218	264893	262156
Warehouses[c]	198650	198796	197351	198775	199933	201491	202807	200895
Other bulk premises	—	—	—	—	—	—	—	59194
Non-bulk	377424	383104	379906	382354	386548	390615	393785	350437
Floor-space (000 m^2)								
Total	573201	578552	594164	600522	607538	610174	609360	606259
Retail premises	101827	103053	106166	107459	108556	109704	110840	103095
Offices	82011	83131	93894	95517	97725	99765	101060	97875
Commercial offices	65181	66188	74205	75477	77581	79735	80943	80916
'Other' offices	16830	16944	19689	20039	20144	20029	20117	16959
Factories[c]	225964	224684	231936	230883	230791	228564	224398	220392
Warehouses[c]	130333	133039	138051	142402	146186	148598	151339	149007
Other bulk premises	—	—	—	—	—	—	—	20203
Non-bulk	33064	34644	24117	24260	24280	23544	21723	15687

Rateable value (£000)

Total	29 433 857	29 913 179	38 576 848	39 219 847	39 946 445	40 741 182	40 883 939	48 305 367
Retail premises	8 035 534	8 178 106	10 165 349	10 324 561	10 484 066	10 664 515	10 724 200	13 333 215
Offices	6 097 028	6 219 257	9 767 617	9 934 044	10 244 863	10 588 765	10 654 541	12 059 375
Commercial offices	5 206 163	5 320 918	8 455 426	8 592 038	8 906 229	9 246 956	9 310 565	10 660 780
'Other' offices	890 865	898 338	1 312 191	1 342 006	1 338 634	1 341 809	1 343 976	1 398 595
Factories[c]	4 956 210	4 914 172	5 670 247	5 681 850	5 679 637	5 660 379	5 587 704	6 226 390
Warehouses[c]	3 518 814	3 613 258	4 313 880	4 458 924	4 604 529	4 737 975	4 812 104	5 854 171
Other bulk premises	—	—	—	—	—	—	—	623 238
Non-bulk	6 826 271	6 988 388	8 659 756	8 820 469	8 933 350	9 089 548	9 105 390	10 208 977

Rateable value per m² (£)

Total[d]	40	41	51	51	52	53	53	64
Retail premises	79	79	96	96	97	97	97	129
Offices	74	75	104	104	105	106	105	123
Commercial offices	80	80	114	114	115	116	115	132
'Other' offices	53	53	67	67	66	67	67	82
Factories[c]	22	22	24	25	25	25	25	28
Warehouses[c]	27	27	31	31	31	32	32	39
Other bulk premises	—	—	—	—	—	—	—	31
Non-bulk[e]	17	17	18	18	18	19	19	43

[a]The broken lines show the years of revaluation (2000 and 2005). A revaluation affects rateable values and other information for hereditaments.
[b]Crown properties are not included in the statistics for 1998 and 1999.
[c]To prevent disclosure of information for individual properties at local authority district level, some bulk classes have been combined for some local authority districts. These combined totals are reflected in the statistics presented here.
[d]Based on rateable values of bulk and non-bulk hereditaments with floor-space.
[e]Non-bulk hereditaments with floor-space only.
Source: Office for National Statistics.

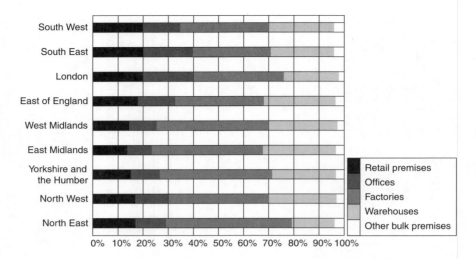

Figure 1.16 Floor-space of hereditaments by sector (bulk class) and region in 2005 (ODPM 2006).

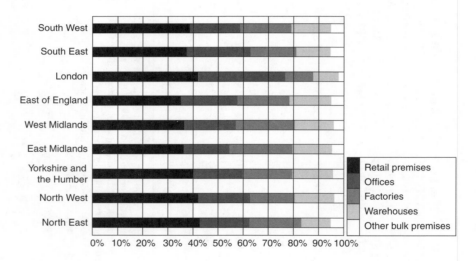

Figure 1.17 Number of hereditaments by sector and region in 2005 (ODPM 2006).

but it does tend to be more up to date. Typically the sort of information that is published includes supply, demand and resultant take-up figures and rents across the main urban areas. As an example, the information shown in Table 1.6 was published by CB Richard Ellis (CBRE) in relation to office property in Bristol in 2005.

There is no one definitive source, and firms often publish information relating to specific sectors of the markets such as big warehouse space or out-of-town retailing. Some of the larger surveying firms with offices in many countries publish international data. CBRE, for example, publishes an

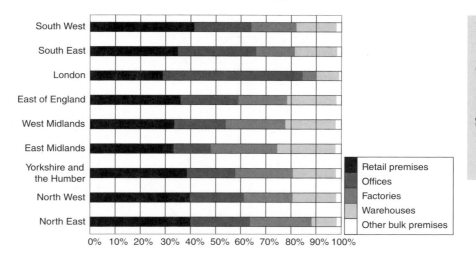

Figure 1.18   Rateable value of hereditaments by sector and region in 2005 (ODPM 2006).

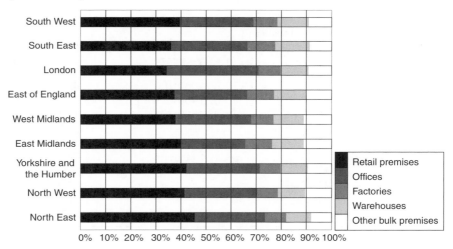

Figure 1.19   Rateable value of hereditaments by sector and region in 2005 (ODPM 2006).

index of global market rents and occupation costs for office space. It is interesting to note that the top ten most expensive locations to open an office in 2005 were (in descending order) London (West End), Tokyo (Inner), Tokyo (Outer), London (City), Paris, Moscow, Dublin, Hong Kong, Edinburgh and Manchester. Mumbai is now more expensive than Manhattan and China (Shanghai) does not appear until position 47.

Statistics offer a summary picture or overview of business activity and stock size across the country but they do not reveal detail at the property level and this is why property experts are required – to help interpret what is happening at the local level.

Table 1.5   Number of local units by broad industry group, 2005.

Activity	Number of local units in UK
Agriculture	138 850
Production	159 850
Construction	198 125
Motor trades	78 410
Wholesale	125 235
Retail	279 625
Hotels and catering	152 455
Transport	74 305
Post and telecom	22 490
Finance	35 180
Property and business services	533 010
Education	47 560
Health	37 215
Public Admin. and other services	185 620
TOTAL	**2 067 580**

Source: Office for National Statistics.

Table 1.6   Bristol Market Statistics 2005.

	City centre	Out-of-town
Take-up	654 000 ft^2	382 500 ft^2
5-year average	675 400 ft^2	334 745 ft^2
Availability	881 500 ft^2	200 000 ft^2
Prime rent (retail)		£185 per ft^2 (ITZA)
Prime rent (industrial)		£6.75 per ft^2
Prime rent (offices)	£24.50 per ft^2	£20.50 per ft^2
Investment transactions	£250 m	£30 m
Achievable prime yield (retail)		4.50%
Achievable prime yield (industrial)		6%
Achievable prime yield	5.2%	5.5%

Source: CBRE.

1.3.3   Property investment

Economists refer to **investment** as anything that adds to productive capacity. In other words, activities that make use of resources today in order to secure greater production in the future. For example, a business may put funds into new equipment or into building a new factory, either way it is making an investment to increase capacity in the future. In financial terms investment is the sacrifice of present capital for future gain, typically in the form of income and/or capital.

A key attraction of owning property is its suitability as an investment, particularly over the long term. It ranks alongside equities and bonds as a major component of any investment portfolio. Property is a tangible and durable asset so investment in property is typically viewed as a relatively long-term activity in comparison to equities and bonds (Sayce *et al.*, 2006). Investors rely on a combination of income and capital growth to generate required return and property benefits from real growth in rent and capital value; each operates in a separate submarket and is affected by different forces, so it is possible that rental growth may be strong one year because of high demand by tenants while capital growth may be limited because of sluggish demand from prospective investors. Commercial property delivers a relatively high return on income; in 2004 the income return on equities and gilts was 3.3% and 5.8%, respectively. For commercial property the comparable figure was 6.3%. Also property is regarded as a 'portfolio diversifier'. This means that levels of property risk can be hedged against non-correlated levels in other investment asset classes such as equities and bonds. An influence that causes a change in gilt yields may lead to an opposite change in property yields. For example, a rise in inflation can lead to higher gilt yields and therefore higher property yields (as the risk-free component of the latter is often based on the former). But the higher rate of inflation may also lead to a higher rental growth expectation and thus reduce property yields as property investment becomes more attractive and investors bid up prices. This reduction might cancel the increase and might explain why property yields are relatively stable when compared to yields from gilts and only follow significant trends (Fraser, 1993). Many of the larger, institutional portfolios contain a mix of investment types as a means of hedging against adverse market conditions in any single sector or location, and portfolio managers rebalance their assets from time to time as a response to market conditions. It is important to note that whereas all shares in a company are the same, property investments are heterogeneous and vary by size, location, use, age, construction and tenant (Sayce *et al.*, 2006).

Property can be invested in directly through ownership as an investor, developer or occupier. As with equities and bonds, property investments can be traded second-hand and indeed this market, rather than the market for new property, is where the vast majority investment trading activity takes place. It is also possible to invest in property indirectly by purchasing shares in property companies or companies that deal with property, property unit trusts and other securitised investment vehicles. There has been a large increase in demand for new unlisted investment vehicles such as pooled funds and limited partnerships fuelled by large net sales of property by owner-occupiers (IPF, 2005). The advantage of indirect property investment is that many of the problems associated with direct property investment such as illiquidity, high transaction costs and sale time disappear but the portfolio diversification benefits are reduced. On balance, indirect property investment is a good way of allowing small investors to pool their funds so that property can be acquired that could not be done so by these investors individually. Our concern in this book is with direct property investment but indirect property investment will be considered briefly in Chapter 7.

On the supply side property investments take the form of properties that are already in existence and occupied by one or more tenants paying rent. These 'standing investments' form the majority of assets in the property investment sector, but new ones come along all the time in the form of newly developed properties and transfers from owner occupation (these are often sale and leasebacks but other financial instruments are used too). As well as standing investments and new developments, property investments can be classified in terms of their risk/return profile. Offering the greatest potential return for the least risk are 'prime' property investments that have modern amenities, a flexible design and are typically found in excellent locations, and are occupied by blue-chip tenants. Moving up the risk scale, secondary property can be found in viable locations and typically comprise a structurally sound property construction with improvement potential and good tenants. Then tertiary properties are usually found in poor locations, may require significant structural work, may be occupied but struggle to attract tenants and require significant proactive management. Property investments can also be classified by their ownership characteristics. Freeholds offer a pure equity interest to the owner-occupier and an equity/bond mix to an investor because of the stepped income growth pattern obtained from properties let at rents that are reviewed every 5 years. Leasehold investments come in two main types. First, long leases on ground rents where the reversion is a long way off – like long-dated or undated gilts but without the same level of liquidity and with higher management and transaction costs, causing yields to be slightly higher. The second type of leasehold investment is shorter leases but these are not very popular. We will come back to these various property interests in Chapter 2.

On the demand side, property competes against other forms of investment, primarily bonds and equities. Perhaps as a consequence of the unique investment characteristics of commercial property (which we discuss in the next section), investment is dominated by a relatively small number of large financial institutions such as pension funds, insurance companies, investment and unit trusts. These organisations traditionally invested in property as a hedge against inflation but nowadays it is the relatively favourable return that provides the incentive. Pension funds (which have long-term inflation-linked liabilities) and life assurance companies (which have long-term fixed interest liabilities) seek to match their liability profiles with suitable investment assets (Sayce *et al.*, 2006). In addition to institutional investors, other investors include public and private property companies, investment and high street banks and building societies, private individuals and charitable organisations. Table 1.7 shows that the major investors in property are UK pension funds and insurance companies, accounting for £73 billion (29%) of the £254 billion core commercial total. But in recent years these traditional investors have been joined by overseas investors and private investors in the form of listed and unlisted property companies each with £36–37 billion portfolios (14% each of the total market).

Information on the nature of investors in direct property can also be obtained from the Investment Property Databank (IPD). IPD is an independent research company that provides investors, occupiers, advisors and

Table 1.7 The owners of the invested stock £billion, end-2003.

	Retail	Office	Industrial	Total	% of total
UK institutions	36	24	12	73	29
Overseas investors	7	29	1	37	15
UK unlisted property companies	21	15	1	37	15
UK listed property companies	20	14	1	36	14
Unitised and pooled funds	11	5	4	20	8
Limited partnerships	12	2	4	18	7
Traditional estates/charities	6	5	2	13	5
Other investors	8	1	3	12	5
UK private investors	2	5	1	8	3
Total invested property	**124**	**100**	**30**	**254**	**100**

Source: IPF, 2005.

Table 1.8 Composition of the IPD Databank, December 2005.

	All property	Retail	Office	Industrial	Other[a]
Capital value (£m)	147 334	74 131	44 564	23 582	5 069
No. of properties	11 010	4 220	2 957	3 129	704

[a]Includes residential, agricultural and other commercial property types.

researchers with property benchmarks and indices. The total value of properties included in the IPD at the end of December 2005 was £147 billion – equivalent to 45% of the total property assets of UK institutions and listed property companies, see Table 1.8. Table 1.9 shows the breakdown of direct property by investor type. The figures are quite different to those reported by the IPF in Table 1.7 but remember that IPD is a subset of all investment property in the UK and there are some differences in the way that the types of investor are classified.

Of the £235 billion of retail, office and industrial property that remains in the hands of owner-occupiers close to £100 billion is in industrial property, £80 billion in retail and £60 billion in offices. On average, the owner-occupied stock is far lower in terms of capital value than that held in the investment market, and this suggests that a very large element of the owner-occupied stock is below the quality currently considered desirable as an investment asset. But there are clearly large blocks of property still owned by large businesses or the public sector which, in terms of building quality and tenant quality, would meet the criteria set by investors (IPF, 2005).

The annual IPD UK Digest reports a great deal of statistical information about the prime direct property investment market. Perhaps a good place to start is to look at the level of net investment in the prime direct property market over the last couple of decades. This is shown in Figure 1.20 and categorises investment by sector. Level of net investment was pretty steady throughout the 1980s, tailed off during the recession of the early 1990s and

Table 1.9   IPD Databank by investor type, December 2004.

Investor type	Number of properties	Capital value (£m)	% Capital value	Average lot size (£m)	Number of funds	Average fund capital value (£m)
Insurance funds	4907	56823	47.1	11.6	77	738
Life funds	2294	40378	33.4	17.6	29	1392
Unit linked funds	1976	11672	9.7	5.9	39	299
Managed pension funds	637	4772	4.0	7.5	9	530
Segregated pension funds	2625	24317	20.1	9.3	74	329
Property companies	390	10151	8.4	26.0	7	1450
Property unit trusts	981	11949	9.9	12.2	28	427
Traditional estates	651	3373	2.8	5.2	11	307
Other types	1432	14147	11.7	9.9	46	308
Total	**10986**	**120760**	**100.0**	**11.0**	**243**	**497**

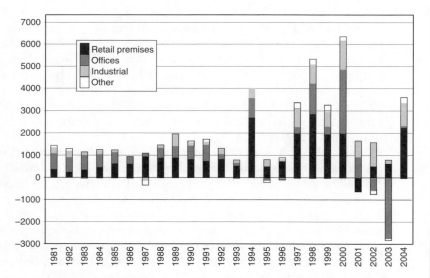

Figure 1.20   Net investment in direct property (£m) (IPD UK Digest 2005).

then picked up dramatically in 1994. Since that time net investment has displayed a great deal more volatility over the past decade.

If we now look more closely at the type of property that is being invested in and its general location, Table 1.10 summarises these statistics as at the end

Table 1.10   IPD UK Databank profile, December 2004.

Market segment	Total return (%)	Number of properties	Total CV (£ billion)	% Total CV
All retail	20.50	4359	64408	53.30
Standard shops	21.10	2639	15711	13.00
Central London	17.90	298	3717	3.10
Rest of London	23.70	296	1450	1.20
Southern England	22.60	650	2801	2.30
Rest of UK	21.80	1395	7743	6.40
Shopping centres	17.40	312	24442	20.20
In-town	18.20	296	18565	15.40
Out-of-town	14.60	16	5877	4.90
Retail warehouses	23.40	1048	21713	18.00
Retail parks	23.60	493	13400	11.10
Fashion parks	23.40	29	2776	2.30
Other retail warehouses	22.70	526	5537	4.60
Dept/variety stores	20.60	117	1350	1.10
Supermarkets	22.80	64	524	0.40
Other retail	19.90	178	668	0.60
All office	15.20	2947	33273	27.60
Standard offices	15.70	2576	27853	23.10
Central London	16.00	1032	15062	12.50
Rest of London	16.40	253	2675	2.20
Inner South East	14.30	455	3610	3.00
Outer South East	16.80	225	1285	1.10
Rest of UK	15.60	611	5220	4.30
Office parks	12.20	371	5420	4.50
London and the South East	12.20	223	4039	3.30
Rest of UK	12.20	148	1381	1.10
All industrial	16.90	2966	19298	16.00
Standard industrials	17.10	2636	15888	13.20
London	17.30	378	3369	2.80
Inner South East	15.20	349	2790	2.30

Source: IPD UK Digest 2005.

of 2004. Using capital value as the measure, the majority of investment is made in retail (53.3%) mainly in shopping centres (three quarters of which are out-of-town), retail warehouses (usually in the form of entire retail parks) and standard (high street) shops. Investment in offices accounts for 27.6% of investment by capital value and much of this is in the form of standard offices (as opposed to office parks) and is mainly situated in London. Of investment capital value, 16% was in industrial property. According to the IPF (2005) the value of total commercial property investment at £265 billion (£254 billion of which is in the core retail, office and industrial sectors) in 2003 compares with a total market capitalisation of the UK equities market of £1356 billion. On that basis a market-weighted portfolio would include 12% property on a gross asset value basis, but just below 10% when adjusted for debt financing of the investment stock.

As property must compete with other major investment types, primarily equities and bonds, it is important to understand the advantages and disadvantages of these alternatives. There are certain attributes that are desirable regardless of the type of investment: the level or amount of return on capital invested (this return may take the form of income or growth in capital value or a combination of the two); the security of capital and income (typically regarded as the risk inherent in an investment); accessibility of the invested funds (often referred to as the liquidity of an investment) and tax efficiency. Some investments will produce little or no income but will provide a return to the investor by way of capital growth, such as gold, works of art and precious gems. Other investments produce a high income but little or no capital growth. Inflation is a major factor affecting security of capital and income. High inflation quickly erodes capital and will also affect income if it is not regularly revised to ensure parity with real income levels. Investors generally prefer low-risk investments – they are risk-averse. The taxation or fiscal implications of any investment need to be considered, especially when comparing the returns across different investment assets as their tax status may differ significantly. Some investment returns are tax-free or at least received after tax has been paid at the basic rate, others are not tax-free and any income received will be subject to income tax. Normally there is a trade-off between liquidity and the rate of return (a current versus a 90 day building society account, for example). The importance placed on capital or income growth can also depend on tax position of the investor. Convenience refers to the amount of management that an investment asset requires; can an investor sit back and leave the investment to look after itself or will someone else look after it for them or does the investment require constant vigilance and attention from the investor? For example, building society accounts are very convenient and require virtually no attention; shares on the other hand require constant monitoring, while property investment returns can be enhanced through careful management. Because property competes as an investment asset against equity and fixed income investment assets, it is these to which we turn our attention now.

1.3.3.1   Fixed interest securities or 'bonds'

Government spending, which is not covered by tax revenue, produces a budget deficit that is financed by the sale of bonds. Private sector companies can also issue 'corporate' bonds to raise debt finance. Because government bond certificate used to be printed on gilt-edged paper they are referred to as 'gilt-edged' bonds or 'gilts' for short. In fact, the term 'gilt-edged' has become a metaphor for low risk and high quality. At the date of issue a new stock of bonds are sold at a 'par' value of £100 each. This is the nominal value representing how much the investor will receive at the specified maturity or redemption date. The bonds will also state the 'coupon' that is the fixed annual income return expressed as a percentage of the nominal value that they will pay throughout their term. The coupon on newly issued government bonds (gilts) is determined by the interest rate at the time of issue. Corporate bond interest rates depend on the creditworthiness of the issuer, length of loan term, economic climate as reflected by prevailing interest rate, inflation and output (Sayce *et al.*, 2006). The income is paid in arrears every 6 months. On redemption, the original nominal value of £100 per bond can be redeemed.

There is an enormous variety of bonds but they are grouped according to their period to redemption: short-dated bonds or 'shorts' will mature in up to 5 years' time, 'mediums' in 5–15 years, 'longs' over 15 years and finally there are a very small number of undated bonds that were issued by the government to finance World War I and which have no redemption date and therefore income is receivable in perpetuity. As time passes, longs become mediums and mediums become shorts but undated bonds will always remain so and will thus only ever provide an income return. There are also index-linked gilts where the interest paid and redemption (par) value are adjusted in line with the inflation rate as measured by the retail price index, thus providing a real return (Fraser, 1993).

Investors usually buy bonds 'second-hand' at a price higher or lower than the original £100 nominal value. If the second-hand market price is lower than £100 investors will obtain capital growth, if the price is higher than £100 the gilt will pay a higher rate of interest than the coupon rate and produce income rather than capital growth. For example, when the Treasury issued its 2021 stock of government bonds they had a stated coupon of 8%. At the date of issue, when the market price is the same as the nominal par value, the yield is the same as the coupon of 8%. If, subsequently, bonds become an increasingly popular form of investment this will tend to bid up the prices paid for these bonds, let us say to £160. Given that the coupon cannot change, this higher market price will reduce the current 'income yield' to 5%. This income yield of 5% is sometimes referred to as the 'running yield', since it provides a measure of income in relation to current bond prices (it is different from the coupon as it refers to the return an investor receives when buying the stock at the market price rather than the nominal value). The holder of the bond receives the coupon (interest) specified in the original bond but the yield relates to a new investment basis. When the loan is repaid at maturity the purchaser receives the par value plus any discount received or minus any premium paid at the time of acquisition. The 'gross redemption yield' comprises interest collected, plus any gain (or minus any loss) realised at maturity, and repayment. The important point to understand is that an increase in the market price of an undated bond (perhaps as a result of a drop in the rate of interest prevailing in the economy) will lead to a reduction in its yield and vice versa. The other important point to note is the rate of return on gilts provides a comparative reference for other investments because, in terms of security and liquidity, government bonds are regarded as risk-free.

1.3.3.2   Equities

An equity investment has none of the contractual certainty or specificity of a debt investment such as a bond (Appraisal Institute, 2001). Ordinary shares in companies can be purchased through a stock market or via a broker. Investors effectively own a share of the company's assets, that is, its equity, subject to prior claims of operating expenses and debt service, and will receive a regular income or dividend (based on company profits), usually twice a year. The 'dividend yield' is similar to the income or running yield on a bond and is calculated by dividing the dividend per share by the market price of the share. Unlike bonds income from equities is not known in advance as dividends are linked to profits which, in turn, are linked to company performance and economic activity. Also, there is no redemption date so shares must be sold on a secondary market to realise capital. Prices on the secondary market are determined by supply and demand and vary according to future cash-flow expectations and perception of risk (Ball *et al.*, 1998). Equity investments can yield a high rate of return but are more volatile and risky than debt investments such as bonds. Consequently market knowledge is needed if informed decisions are to be made and this incurs fees. Nevertheless, millions of pounds are traded in debt and equity markets daily, traders are sophisticated and well informed, investments are often professionally rated for risk and transaction prices are reported daily. Changes in yields of equities respond quickly to changes in supply and demand due to the efficiency of the equities market (Sayce *et al.*, 2006). Consequently data from these markets provide an objective basis for property market assumptions, particularly regarding expectations of debt capital performance (Appraisal Institute, 2001).

1.3.3.3   Property

Property may be regarded as an equity/bond hybrid investment. Property investments are like equities because they are capable of maintaining their value in real terms (keeping pace with inflation) and hopefully growing in real terms. This is achieved through growth in capital value and income. With regard to capital growth, as standing property investments trade on a second-hand market, capital values rise and fall depending on economic activity, just as they do for shares. But, unlike equities, the capital value of a property will not fall below its inherent land value regardless of the rent-earning capacity of the business currently in occupation. Regarding income growth, this is only receivable at rent reviews and lease renewals that usually take place every 5 years. Consequently property investments resemble a bond-type investment between rent reviews. Indeed, because rent reviews are almost always upward-only in the UK, if the market rent falls below the rent currently being paid by the tenant, the cash-flow has all the characteristics of a conventional fixed income bond where risk exposure depends almost entirely on the quality of the tenant. In contrast to bonds and equities, property represents a tangible investment asset that needs to be managed and maintained in order to secure a steady income stream. Despite this, property is considered to be an attractive investment for several reasons.

Return. There is potential for an inflation-proof or real return on income and capital. Unlike bonds, the income from property is uncertain and unlike shares income growth is not received annually. However, the rent received from an occupying tenant is usually prevented from being eroded by inflation through the use of rent reviews, which typically occur every 5 years. At the review the rent is adjusted (normally upwards) to the level of market rents at that time. Capital growth can depend on many factors: generally a shop located in the prime pitch of an urban area will attract the highest capital value in a town or city because of the demand to locate and trade from that particular position in the high street. However, there are many other considerations such as the quality of the tenant, precise lease terms, possible development potential and the way that financing for purchase of the property might be geared (see Chapter 7), which must be considered when attempting to explain or forecast capital growth and this is particularly difficult to do at a local level let alone at the level of the individual property. The major concern for an investor regarding income and capital return is whether they at least keep pace with inflation. As can be seen from Figure 1.21 total property return (income and capital return combined) has outperformed inflation over most of the last quarter of a century. Refer to Appendix 1A for an explanation of the way in which IPD calculate property returns. (See Appendix 1A at www.blackwellpublishing.com/wyatt)

Property and equities are inflation proof whereas bonds are inflation prone so even bonds produce a return which is uncertain (and therefore risky) in real terms (Baum and Crosby, 1995). Year-on-year returns for these three investment classes are shown in Figure 1.22.

Annualised returns, shown in Table 1.11, reveal property to have been a very strong performer in the first 5 years of this millennium. Over the long-term (25 years) equities were the strongest though.

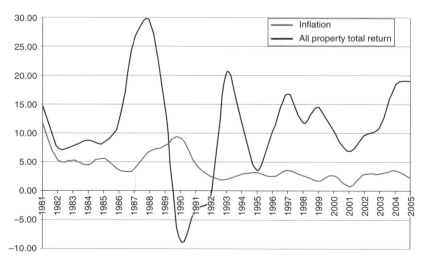

Figure 1.21 Inflation and all property total return % per annum (IPD).

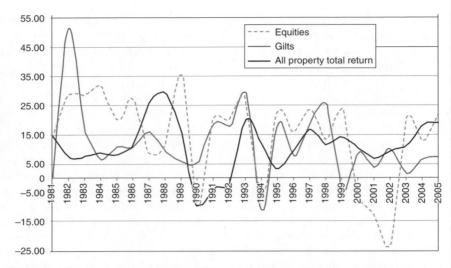

Figure 1.22 Returns from IPD Universe market standing investments, equities and medium-dated bonds (% per annum).

Table 1.11 Annualised returns from equities, gilts and property (%).

Year	Equities	Gilts (15–20) years	All property total return
1970–2004	13.80	10.80	12.20
1970–1980	14.20	10.20	16.30
1980–1990	18.80	12.80	11.60
1990–2000	13.70	12.10	9.90
2001–2005	2.20	6.00	12.80
1981–2005	13.90	10.90	10.90

Source: IPD.

Perhaps the most important performance measure is the annual total return and annualised returns on 'standing investments'. Standing investments are properties that existed at the start and end of the period over which the return is calculated, and therefore exclude new developments coming on-stream between measurement dates. Figure 1.23 illustrates the income and capital returns and clearly shows the prolonged recession of the early 1980s, the major boom and slump in the property market during the late 1980s and early 1990s, respectively and, more recently, the smaller boom and slump of the mid-1990s. The contribution of movements in capital values to movements in total return is clearly visible. Income return is much more stable.

Different types of commercial property display different investment characteristics. There are many types of shops and they are typically regarded as a secure investment because of the *goodwill* and capital invested by the tenant. Retail developments, such as a new shopping centre, can be more risky and so rent linked to turnover can provide a solution. There is also a wide

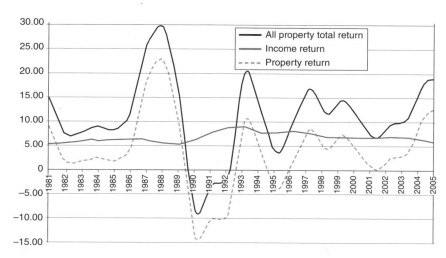

Figure 1.23   IPD Universe market standing investments (% per annum) (IPD UK Digest 2005).

range of office accommodation let on different lease terms. From an investor's perspective there are two main methods of leasing offices: the whole building may be let to a single tenant and this is usually regarded as the best option, alternatively the building can be split into suites that are let to separate tenants and the cost of maintenance of the building as a whole is recovered via a service charge to each tenant in addition to their rent. Historically, industrial property was not a popular form of investment owing to intense physical use, inflexibility of premises and the close relationship between risk/return profile and the declining manufacturing base since the 1970s. Attitudes have changed owing to the introduction of new types of premises that are typically of a modern, simple construction with a large, uninterrupted and well-lit floor-space, with ancillary offices, yard space and parking. 'High-tech' industrial units offer good communications, campus style accommodation, high specification space, proximity to skilled labour, and the flexibility to cope with changes in information, communication, production and distribution technologies. Nevertheless, investment in industrial property is subject to 'voids' because of economic conditions and changes in technology and manufacturing practice. Warehousing can be either purpose-built or conversions of existing properties but both are prone to voids as demand for warehousing varies significantly with economic activity. IPD measures total return by property sector and Figure 1.24 shows the investment performance of these three main property types over the past quarter of a century. Retail is the least volatile, industrial has performed surprisingly well and offices have shown the biggest downside owing, in part, to major problems in the London office market in early 1990s when there were lots of *over-rented property* investments. As with the whole property market, most of the shifts in total return can be explained by shifts in capital rather than income return. The boundaries between these very simplistic classifications

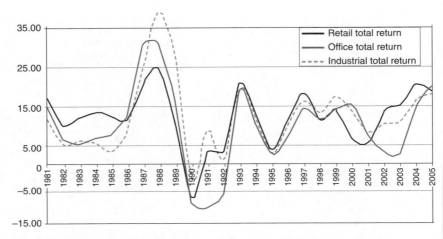

Figure 1.24   IPD universe market standing investment returns by sector (% per annum) (IPD UK Digest 2005).

Table 1.12   Returns annualised between 1999–2004 and 1994–2004 (%).

Last	5 years	10 years
Retail	12.3	12.1
Office	8.8	9.5
Industrial	12.1	12.0
Other	12.1	13.5
All	11.1	11.2

Source: IPD UK Digest 2005.

of retail, office and industrial investment property are changing; increasingly retail coexists with leisure activities and the distinction between office and industrial land use is sometimes rather blurred.

Most investors hold direct property investments for several years so it is important to monitor returns that have been annualised over periods that correspond to typical holding periods. Table 1.12 shows that offices have not been performing very well when compared with other sectors.

As well as providing performance measures and details of investment activity by main sector, market segment and region IPD also categorises these data by floor area and date of construction. The usefulness of these data will become apparent in later chapters so they will not be presented here.

Risk. Risk is the uncertainty surrounding expected investment return, both capital and income. Investors seek to minimise risk for an expected level of return from the investment, and property is regarded as a relatively secure or low-risk investment. Risk to capital refers to the possibility of losing some or all of the investment capital. For property investments, capital risk is

Table 1.13 Standard deviation of annual returns from the main investment classes (%).

Year	Equities	Gilts (15–20) years	Property
1981–2005	15.17	12.03	8.41
1996–2005	15.16	11.84	8.39
2001–2005	14.90	8.61	8.38

Source: IPD UK Digest 2005.

low because property is a tangible asset where proof of ownership is usually registered by law and its usefulness ensures a high opportunity cost (transfer earnings). Income risk is reduced by rent reviews helping to keep rent in line with inflation. Security of income is affected by factors such as the quality of the tenant and the nature of the lease terms, for example, how likely is the tenant to default on the rent and thus undermine the investment value or is there a break clause in the lease that may lead to a void or gap in rental income? Property income risk is similar to dividend risk in the case of equities although income from property investments is normally fixed for periods of 5 years rather than changing each year. But rent is a prior charge above dividend payments should a tenant go into receivership. Consider again the returns from equities, gilts and property, but this time focusing on the standard deviation of the annual returns between 1981 and 2005, between 1996 and 2005 and between 2001 and 2005, that is, over the last 25, 10 and 5 years. These are shown in Table 1.13. Using standard deviation as a measure of risk, we can see that the return on property is less volatile over all time periods according to this very basic statistic. Also, the return from direct property investment has been much greater per unit of risk than the other principal asset classes (IPF, 2005).

Other reasons. As well as providing a real return and offering a relatively secure investment opportunity, property can provide corporate identity, there may be tax advantages and it is a useful portfolio diversifier. This means that investing in property as part of a mixed portfolio of investments can help reduce the amount of risk that the portfolio as a whole is exposed to. Look at Figure 1.22 and see how total return from property investment moves in relation to the return on equities and gilts. Even within a property portfolio it is useful to hold a mix of property types because the returns may not always move in same way. Using the IPD UK Property Investors Digest for 2005, over the past 10 years the correlation between retail and office sectors is 0.3 and, more specifically, the correlation between standard shops in Central London and standard offices outside of London is 0.1 over the past 10 years. This illustrates the benefit of holding a mixed property portfolio. A final but important feature of property as an investment vehicle is the ability to borrow money to help purchase property investments. This allows investors to combine their equity with debt finance and thus invest in either bigger properties or in a larger number of properties than they would otherwise be able to do. This debt financing represents an advantage over the equity and bond investment markets.

However, property has a number of disadvantages too. First, it comes in large indivisible heterogeneous units that suffer from depreciation and obsolescence. Its lumpiness makes it difficult for smaller investors to acquire big, prime investments and almost impossible to acquire landmark developments such as shopping centres or prestigious office buildings. It also means that only the larger investors can afford to assemble balanced and sufficiently diversified portfolios (Sayce et al., 2006). Ways around this are to syndicate investment acquisitions or use debt finance. Second, property is an illiquid investment asset. This means transactions take time and money to complete. A sale of an investment property usually takes weeks or months rather than days – the norm in equity and bond markets – and in this respect property compares less favourably with other investments. The purchase of a property investment sometimes involves the acquisition of complex legal interests and negotiations between buyer and seller, and to agree on a price can take time and debt finance may have to be arranged. Transfer costs are usually higher for property investments than they are for other investment assets. Stamp Duty Land Tax[10] must be paid, surveyors are employed to survey the property and negotiate price and general lease terms, legal advisors are required to draft the lease and oversee the conveyance. Stamp duty, conveyancing/legal fees and agents fees on sale and purchase have been estimated to be in the region of 7% in every 5-year holding period and perhaps should be amortised over this period (Sayce et al., 2006). However, lot size and holding period are higher and longer respectively than for bonds and equities so the annual equivalent of costs is lower but probably still higher than for shares and bonds (Fraser, 1993). Third, there are high management costs covering rent collection, ensuring compliance with lease terms, negotiating rent reviews and lease renewals, revaluations, performance analysis, and so on (Fraser, 1993), and this means that net income might be significantly below gross income. But, on the plus side, proactive management, which might include refurbishment and renewal, can enhance income and capital value (Sayce et al., 2006). An investor will seek to minimise these costs and transfer liability wherever possible to the tenant. For example, a typical lease requires the tenant to be responsible for internal and external repairs and insurance of the premises.

Property is characterised by a decentralised and cyclical market with a paucity of market information in which a high degree of market knowledge is required. It is susceptible to external influences and government intervention in the form of planning, environmental controls, buildings regulations, rent control and security of tenure (Sayce et al., 2006). All aspects of property dealings, whether occupation, investment or development take time to respond to changes in economic activity and this leads to periods of over- and under-supply and hence greater volatility and risk (Ball et al., 1998). Consequently property is typically a long-term investment because a long holding period reduces the problems associated with illiquidity and the emphasis is on security of income and capital, especially in real terms.

1.3.4   Property development

In general terms, property development may be defined as a process by which buildings are constructed either for owner occupation or for retention or sale as an investment and in financial terms development becomes viable when the value of the completed scheme is at least equal to the development costs, which include the acquisition and preparation of the site, construction materials and labour costs, finance and a suitable profit element. In common with all other economic activity, the process of development requires the integration of land, capital, labour and enterprise and the process takes time; a site needs to be acquired, existing property demolished if necessary, planning permission has to be negotiated, construction activity has to be contracted, complex financial arrangements may need to be arranged, especially in the commercial sector where property is often developed as a speculative venture. Consequently it can take several years for a building or more complex scheme to progress from its development phase to completion, and there is inevitably a time lag before supply catches up with demand.

It is important to identify the optimum use that can be envisaged for a site and choices about design, planning, funding, construction, renting or selling need to be made. These are difficult decisions especially since, in most instances, commercial property development companies tend to be dominated by entrepreneurial talent and few other resources. In fact, apart from the really big institutional players in the market, developers of commercial property rarely own land in their own right. The success of any kind of development depends upon drawing together the other factors at the right time and at the best price. The importance, therefore, of the entrepreneur should not be overlooked. In a small development firm the manager-proprietor would be the entrepreneur; in a joint stock company the shareholders would take on that responsibility. In all market-driven organisations the entrepreneur organises the factors of production.

A characteristic of the development sector of the property market is the paucity of transaction information. Not only do development land transactions occur very infrequently (especially when compared with the volume of transactions that takes place in other financial markets or, indeed, the occupation and investment sectors of the property market) but also the market players – the buyers and sellers – are not inclined to share this information. Development success depends to a large extent on piecing together the various factors; the right site with relevant permission to develop, access to sufficient finance, labour and construction materials, a market for the completed development, and so on. Only if these ingredients lead to a successful development can a developer extract a profit as payment for the enterprise. The profit is a residual sum and is therefore very risky. As a way of reducing competition risk, secrecy surrounds the assembly of development sites, the securing of planning permission and finance.

One source of land value information is the Property Market Report published by the VOA (2006). This shows land values for the development of factories and warehouses in some of the main industrial areas in England, Scotland and Wales (excluding London). Figure 1.25 shows the data for January 2006.

Chapter 1

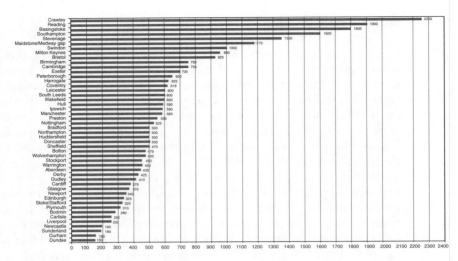

Figure 1.25 Capital value of industrial land (Valuation office agency).

Short-term finance is typically used to pay for the costs incurred throughout the development period and so money markets that deal in short-term loans are especially important to the property development sector. Development loans are usually short term with variable interest rates. If the rate increases, then construction becomes expensive and reduces the number of viable projects. Also the longer the development period the more uncertain developers are about future costs and the more risky it is to predict them. If the developer is looking to retain the scheme as an investment, an arrangement can be made with a lender on completion to repay the short-term finance that was taken out to fund the development. This long-term finance is typically obtained from the capital markets in the form of a **mortgage**. Traditional mortgage loans are for 20–30 years and the interest rate is lower than for short-term finance. If the developer sells the scheme on completion then long-term finance is not required.

In terms of development activity, new construction orders obtained by contractors over the past 10 years are shown in Figure 1.26. The figures are at 2000 prices and have been seasonally adjusted. The time series spans nearly half a century and a great deal of information about development activity over this period can be gleaned. The post-war redevelopment of public infrastructure that was funded by the government is evident from the steeply rising trend in public sector construction between 1955 and the end of the 1960s. After the energy crises in the 1970s, when development activity stagnated, a phenomenal boom in private sector construction can be seen. This boom was fuelled by the removal of regulatory restrictions on access to finance and privatisation of public utilities, infrastructure providers and other companies. After the slump of the late 1980s and early 1990s construction activity in all sectors has recovered well and remains buoyant. Infrastructure output was separately recorded from 1981 onwards.

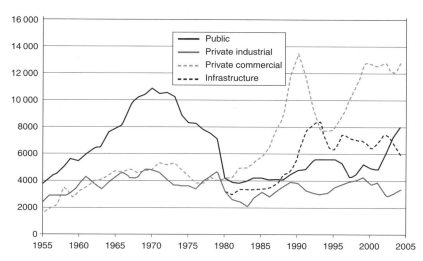

Figure 1.26   Non-housing construction output for Britain at constant, seasonally adjusted prices (DTI 2006).

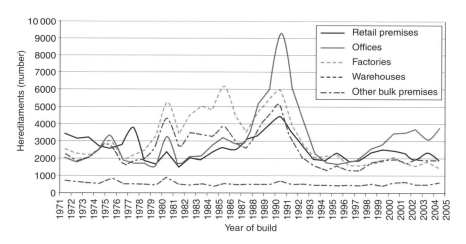

Figure 1.27   Year of build of bulk-class hereditaments in England and Wales, 1971–2004, from 1 April 2005 data (ODPM 2006).

Turning to the Commercial and Industrial Floor-space and Rateable Value Statistics that were introduced in Section 1.3.2, Figures 1.27 and 1.28 show the number of hereditaments and total floor-space built each year from 1971 to 2004 (ODPM, 2006). The year of build in this context can mean the year a building was finished and ready for beneficial occupation or it can be the year when a property underwent significant refurbishment or extension. As this is an age profile of the stock as on 1 April 2005, it is important to note that there will have been a substantial number of properties built in the earlier years that have subsequently been demolished. Consequently they are not included here. The number of hereditaments built each year followed an upward trend from 1971 until 1990. There was an increase from 1980 across all sectors and in the 4 years from 1986 the number of new hereditaments grew to over 25 000 in 1990. This is a reflection of both market cycles and increased VOA activity during the revaluation in 1990. The significant decline from 1990 to 1995 reflects the downturn in the property market at the start of this decade. The number of new hereditaments built each year between 1998 and 2004 was fairly constant at an average of 9500 hereditaments, only exceeding 10 000 in 2000. Figure 1.28 shows a fluctuating pattern of new floor-space for all of the sectors with distinct peaks and troughs occurring up to 1987, again probably a result of market cycles. This was followed by increased development activity during the period 1988–1991 with over 15 million m^2 of floor-space recorded as being built in 1990. The total amount of new floor-space then levelled off between 1998 and 2003 with around 7 million m^2 built each year. During this period of fairly constant floor-space levels, warehouses varied the most, although this might be expected as they tend to be considerably larger than retail premises and offices, and new additions will have a more pronounced effect on the statistic. At the sector level, new retail and office floor-space both grew gradually to a peak in 1990. Until 2004, new retail construction had been fairly constant with around 1.2–1.6 million m^2 being built each year. Offices suffered a decline in the number of builds with less than 800 000 m^2 built in 1995 but the amount has been growing steadily since then, with over 2 million m^2 of office floor-space built in 2002. There has been a steady decline in new factory floor-space that had its peak in 1980 unlike the other sectors that peaked in 1990. This trend has continued with the 2003 and 2004 figures of

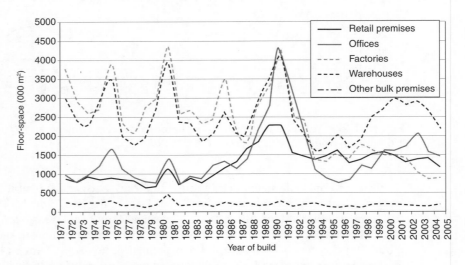

Figure 1.28 Year of build of bulk-class floor space in England and Wales, 1971–2004, from 1 April 2005 data (ODPM 2006).

around 900 000 m² being the lowest recorded over the period shown in the graph. The warehouse sector followed the early downward trend of factories, but since 1993 there has been a steady increase from 1.6 million m² in 1993 to nearly 3 million m² built in 2000 and 2002. There were 2.2 million m² of warehouse floor-space built in 2004.

1.3.5   Macroeconomic cycles

Decisions on the development and occupation of, and investment in, property require an assessment of the current and future macroeconomic conditions and an understanding of the related markets. For example, if interest rates rise sharply, consumer spending tends to decline and the demand for retail and manufacturing property reduces and in some instances may even become surplus to requirements. Figure 1.28 shows that, when the UK Government increased interest rates in the late 1980s, this precipitated a major downturn in investment returns from property. Property market activity responds to short- and long-term macroeconomic stimuli; the former are largely a function of availability of debt finance and the latter is a function of changes in employment, population, income and shifts in consumer preferences. Consequently, the property market does not operate in isolation; it is influenced by, but tends to lag, movements in the economy as a whole and in the financial markets in particular.

It is important therefore that valuers monitor key macroeconomic indicators and understand how their movements may influence the supply and demand of different types of property in different locations. Knowing this will facilitate more informed judgements about rental and capital values, rental growth, investment and occupier demand and development activity. Key macroeconomic indicators include gross domestic product, trade deficit, tax-to-GDP ratio, inflation, employment and unemployment figures, oil prices, house prices, household debt and debt as a percentage of income. A key money market indicator is the price of money that is expressed as an interest rate (i.e. the cost of borrowing money) influenced by supply and demand and set by the Bank of England. The interest rate is very important to the property market as most investment and development activity is a combination of debt and equity finance, typically a large amount of the former and a small amount of the latter. The cost and availability of equity and debt finance influence the quantity and quality of demand for and supply of property. The interest rate is also a component of yields and discount rates used in valuation, and so directly affects property values (Appraisal Institute, 2001). The UK economy has been characterised by a low interest rate since the early 1990s and the property market has benefited as rental yields have exceeded bond yields and the average cost of borrowing. It is also important to monitor government policy not just in relation to planning and development control but also legislation and other statutory controls regarding the environment, workplace, landlord and tenant relationship, licensing, and so on.

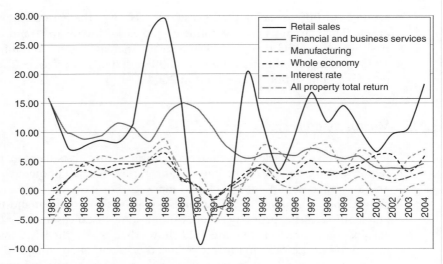

Figure 1.29   Macroeconomics indicators (IPD).

The property market, like the economy as a whole, is prone to cyclical fluctuations. Property cycles are identified by monitoring changes in key indicators of property market activity such as investment returns. What makes the property market interesting is the way in which the sectors of the market interact during these fluctuations – the varying leads and lags. Over the short term the supply of property is relatively inelastic, so disequilibrium can characterise the market in the short term when demand increases or decreases (Appraisal Institute, 2001). Fraser (1993) argues that supply and demand in the property market can be in disequilibrium for some time before market prices move to a 'market clearing' level. For there to be equilibrium in the overall property market, all submarkets must be in equilibrium simultaneously and this is not always rapidly achieved; markets are continually adjusting to new supply and demand conditions and therefore are unlikely to be in equilibrium at any one time. Because of longevity and fixed location of property, its high unit price and the terms of lease contracts, property markets take time to adjust (Ball *et al.*, 1998). By that time the market would have probably moved on so that market prices tend to lag changes in buying and selling pressure – a feature of an imperfect market. Consequently, the property market has been cyclical, displaying successive periods of expansion, decline, recession and recovery. Figure 1.30 illustrates how this cycle operates.

The position of property in its cycle is determined by supply and demand in the occupier market (measured by stock availability, rental value and rental growth) and supply and demand in the investor market (measured by yields and capital values). So, according to the Appraisal Institute (2001), trends in the property market as a whole can be observed by measuring vacancy rates, rental growth rates, yields and changes in supply but remembering that the property market is slow to react to new information. For example, the vacancy rate may begin to rise and rental growth to stagnate but new

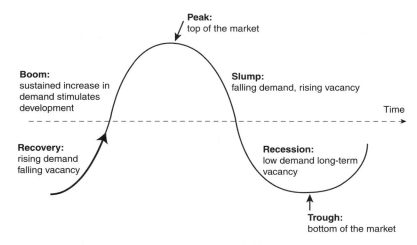

Figure 1.30 Property market cycle (Appraisal Institute 2001).

buildings will still be constructed in the short to medium term and landlords tend to be very reluctant to reduce rents unless they absolutely have to. The lag in construction activity can lead to over-supply and raise vacancy rates. This, in turn, causes a drop in rents and an increase in yields until demand increases to remove any surplus. However, development activity introduces only a small amount of new property each year in comparison to the size of the total stock and so tends not to significantly influence the property market as a whole. At the start of a market upturn supply lags the increase in demand, which causes the vacancy rate to drop and rents to rise and yields to fall. In the medium term, developers increase supply in response to rising demand. Building costs tend to follow general price levels over the long term but may vary in the short-term and may vary geographically. High building costs lead to increased demand for existing buildings and more refurbishment of existing buildings.

It is important for valuers to understand the position of the economy in its cycle because different types of valuation work might predominate at certain stages. For example, valuations in relation to foreclosures, bankruptcies and tax appeals might be more prevalent during a declining market or recession; valuations for lending purposes and in connection with investment and occupation market transactions would tend to dominate during a recovery or expansion phase; and at the peak of the market, valuers may lead with consulting on investments as investors may want to know when to buy and sell or redevelop their assets.

According to the Appraisal Institute (2001), although the general economic cycle influences the property cycle, it is typically not synchronised with it. As the economy expands competition for capital intensifies, the cost of commodities increases and this fuels inflation. If the Bank of England raises the cost of borrowing money by increasing the interest rate as a means of curbing inflationary pressure, the economy will slow down as demand for capital falls due to its increased price. Interest rates will eventually fall once more, the economy stabilises and the cycle is repeated. Although not synchronous, historically, the UK property market has shown a cyclical pattern that meets the qualitative definition conventionally applied to economic cycles, but cannot be described definitively by statistical techniques. The property cycle is the compounded result of cyclical influences from the wider economy, which are coupled with cyclical tendencies inherent to property markets. The critical linkage between property and economic cycles can, in the main, be captured in simple models that are intuitively plausible and statistically sound (RICS, 1999).

Key points

- Microeconomics involves the study of individual decision-making agents, whereas macroeconomics involves a broader study of aggregate activity. The concepts of scarcity, choice, opportunity cost and rent form the basis of property economics. A definition may describe it as a social science that studies how individuals choose to allocate scarce resources to satisfy the competing needs of society for various goods and services.
- The exchange of information between buyers and sellers about factors such as price, quality and quantity takes place in a market. Property is made up of a diverse range of market sectors and relative to all other markets, they have distinguishing characteristics: the market is decentralised and restricted to fewer transactions than consumer goods or services, the product is heterogeneous, physically immobile, durable and of finite supply.
- Commercial property exists to serve the needs of occupying businesses. It is a derived demand that can be classified by property type. A lot of this stock is not actually owned by business occupiers themselves but is owned by investors instead.
- Commercial property investments tend to be of interest to a wide range of institutional investors seeking real income and capital growth. There is a broad range of opportunities to choose from, each comprising a different set of attributes. Property, as an investment medium, exhibits some of the characteristics of equities and bonds. The risks and returns associated with property and other investment assets continually shift in absolute and relative terms as economic conditions change, driven by the level of the interest rate and the opportunity cost of capital invested elsewhere (Ball *et al.*, 1998).
- Developers play a key role in assembling sites and procuring the services of a professional team to bring forward property for investment and occupation.
- As in the general economic cycle, the property cycle consists of recurrent upswings and downswings that vary in length, scale and composition.

Notes

1. In economics the short-run is the decision-making time frame of a firm in which at least one factor of production remains fixed whilst in the long-run all factors of production may be varied and firms can respond to price changes.
2. Supply and demand schedules are referred to as curves but, for illustration purposes, these curves are normally depicted as straight lines because they are

simple representations of the general form of the schedule rather than an empirically based one.

3. In a competitive product market, price is constant so MR is also constant and equal to price.

4. MP of a factor is the addition to total product (output) obtained from using another unit of that factor.

5. Technically, the MRP schedule is equal to the demand schedule only if the firm uses a single factor but it can be proven that when more than one factor is used the demand schedule for each slopes downwards.

6. Even if supply was not fixed/perfectly inelastic in the short-run, the longevity of property means that new stock is a very small proportion of total stock and therefore stock availability/supply depends much more on the availability of existing stock, either via vacant premises or the ability of uses to change easily (Ball *et al.*, 1998).

7. The rent paid in respect of any particular use of the land is therefore a geared residual payment (unless there is monopoly ownership of land) but its volatility is reduced as the land can be transferred to the next most profitable and thus restrict drops in rent. Also, land rent is based on expectations of profitability rather than actual year-to-year profit revenue and this tends to reduce the volatility of land rent in the short term (Fraser, 1993).

8. Complementary land uses include things like comparison shopping and symbiotic business activities.

9. Companies that generate a turnover in excess of approximately £60 000 per annum must be registered for VAT purposes.

10. Stamp Duty Land Tax (SDLT) is a tax on the acquisition of a chargeable interest in property. The amount of tax is calculated as a percentage of the consideration for the property. For non-residential or mixed residential/non-residential property the rates are as follows: consideration (including a premium in lieu of rent) up to £150 000 the rate is 0%, £150 001–£250 000 it is 1%, £250 001–£500 000 it is 3% and £500 001 or more it is 4%. SDLT is also payable on the acquisition of leasehold interests with a net present value of more than £150 000 and the rate is 1%.

References

Alonso, W. (1964) *Location and Land Use: Toward a General Theory of Land Rent*, Harvard University Press, Cambridge, MA, USA.

Appraisal Institute (2001) *The Appraisal of Real Estate*, 12th edn, The Appraisal Institute, Chicago, IL, USA.

Ball, M., Lizieri, C. and MacGregor, B. (1998) *The Economics of Commercial Property Markets*, Routledge, London, UK.

Baum, A. and Crosby, N. (1995) *Property Investment Appraisal*, 2nd edn, Routledge, London, UK.

Button, K. (1976) *Urban Economics: Theory and Policy*, Macmillan, London, UK, September 1998.

CBRE (2005) Published at www.cbre.com

Dunse, N., Fraser, W., Jones, C. and Martin, D. (1998) The nature and structure of spatial industrial property markets, Cutting Edge Conference, RICS, Leicester, UK, September 1998.

Evans, A. (2004) *Economics, Real Estate and the Supply of Land*, Blackwell Publishing, Oxford, UK.

Fraser, W. (1993) *Principles of Property Investment and Pricing*, 2nd edn, Macmillan, Basingstoke, Hampshire, UK.

Haig, R. M. (1926) Toward an understanding of the metropolis, *Quarterly Economic Journal*, 40, May, 421–423.

Harvey, J. (1981) *The Economics of Real Property*, Macmillan, London, UK.

Harvey J. and Jowsey, E. (2004) *Urban Land Economics*, 6th edn, Palgrave Macmillan, Basingstoke, UK.

Henneberry, J. (1998) Transport investment and house prices, *Journal of Property Valuation and Investment*, 16, 2, 144–158.

Hurd, R. (1903) *Principles of City Land Values, The Record and Guide*, New York, NY, USA.

IPD (2005) Published at www.ipdindex.co.uk

IPF (2005) *Understanding Commercial Property Investment: A Guide for Financial Advisers*, 2005 edition, Investment Property Forum, London.

IVSC (2005) *International Valuation Standards*, 7th edn, International Valuation Standards Committee, London, UK.

Kivell, P. (1993) *Land and the City*, Routledge, London, UK.

Lancaster, K. (1966) A new approach to consumer theory, *Journal of Political Economy*, 74, 132.

Lean, W. and Goodall, B. (1966) *Aspects of Land Economics*, Estates Gazette Ltd, London, UK.

Losch, A. (1954) *The Economics of Location*, Yale University Press, New Haven, CT, USA.

Marshall, A. (1920) *Principles of Economics*, 8th edn, Macmillan, London, UK.

Meier, R. L. (1962) *A Communications Theory of Urban Growth*, MIT Press, Cambridge, MA, USA.

Mill, J. S. (1909) *Principles of Political Economy*, Augustus M Kelly, Fairfield, New Jersey, USA.

Myers, D. (2006) *Economics and Property*, 2nd edn, EG Books, London, UK.

ODPM (2006) Commercial and Industrial Floorspace and Rateable Value Statistics 2005 (2005 Revaluation), Office of the Deputy Prime Minister, London, UK.

RICS (1999) *The UK Property Cycle – a History from 1921 to 1997*, RICS and IPD, London, UK.

Ricardo, D. (1817) *On the Principles of Political Economy and Taxation*, John Murray, London, UK.

Richardson, H. (1971) *Urban Economics*, Penguin, Middlesex, UK.

Sayce, S., Smith, J., Cooper, R. and Venmore-Rowland, P. (2006) *Real Estate Appraisal: From Value to Worth*, Blackwell Publishers, Oxford, UK.

VOA (2006) Property Market Report, January 2006, Valuation Office Agency, www.voa.gov.uk/publications/property_market_report/pmr-jan-06/index.htm.

Chapter 2
Property Valuation Principles

2.1 Introduction

Chapter 1 explained how property values arise and it did this using economic principles and theories that have been developed and expounded over the past 200 years or so Building on the theories relating to the agricultural land market, the causes and spatial distribution of urban land and property uses and rents have been described. The first half of the chapter provided explanations for the causes of price differentials between land uses and over space. In doing so it homogenised the product to a large extent, only really differentiating between the main commercial land uses of retail, office and industrial space. In the second half of the chapter, macroeconomic influences were described that cause the property market to be dynamic, since it is subject to constantly changing market conditions and cyclical macroeconomic pressures. As a result the value of property varies over time, between different stakeholders – investors, users, developers and owner-occupiers – and across submarkets. In essence, Chapter 1 concentrated on property value, its nature and derivation. Chapter 2 focuses on property valuation and, in doing so, some of the simplifications made in Chapter 1 to make the economic theories work will be relaxed. This has to be done because the property market is complex and property values vary not just in response to microeconomic principles and macroeconomic influences but also because of a myriad of other factors. This chapter sets out to explain the nature, purpose and determinants of value and the process of its determination, namely, property valuation. The associated mathematics and related procedures that underpin the methods described in subsequent chapters are also introduced here.

2.2 What is valuation?

Chapter 1 explained that, under normal market conditions, the supply of and demand for property are in a constant state of flux but tend towards an equilibrium **exchange price**, being the outcome of the interaction of supply and demand. The more generic term **price** is used to describe the amount requested, offered or paid for a property whereas **cost** refers to the expense of producing it (constructing a building on a piece of land, for example). So, in a single conveyance or transaction of a property there might be an asking price advertised by the seller, a bid price offered by the potential buyer and finally, usually after some period of negotiation, an agreed exchange or sale price at which the property is conveyed or transacted.

The concept of **value** is more difficult to pin down. Adam Smith[1] first noted the ambiguity surrounding the word 'value', which can mean usefulness in one sense and purchasing power in another, referring to them as value-in-use and value-in-exchange, respectively (Mill, 1909). Given the definition of exchange price above, we are interested here in value-in-exchange and can say that it is an estimate of price, typically an estimate of the most likely price to be concluded at a specific point in time by buyers and sellers of a property that is assumed to be available for purchase. Consequently sale prices are by and large useful indicators of the value of properties. We will come back to value-in-use as a concept of worth in Chapter 7. As we saw in Chapter 1, scarcity and **utility** of property give rise to its value: scarcity of all land in terms of its limited supply relative to other factors of production and the unique spatial characteristics of each site, and utility of all property in terms of durability and the specific physical and legal attributes of each site. Individual properties will, of course, have different utility values to different people but in a market you would expect individuals to converge on an agreed exchange price.

Property **valuation** is the process of forming an opinion of value-in-exchange under certain assumptions. Supply and demand within the property market as a whole and in specific submarkets will be changing all the time and therefore a valuation is a snapshot estimate of exchange price at a particular point in time. Because people tend to buy and use commercial property for a variety of utility and investment reasons, most decisions are made after an assessment of their financial implications. Similarly, while a property is held as a business resource or as an investment asset, its financial contribution will be monitored. If a property no longer provides the return that an investor requires or if a property is no longer suited to a particular mode of occupation, then the financial impact of these effects will be estimated and a decision made. Part of the information set needed to make this decision will be a property valuation. Property valuations are financial estimates of the future net benefit of purchasing an interest in property, suitably discounted over time to reflect opportunity cost and risk. Consequently, the economic concepts of exchange price and opportunity cost are fundamental to property valuation theory.

A market valuation[2] is an economic concept that attempts to quantify the aspirations of buyers and sellers of a property in an 'open market' situation. It has a formal basis, which is defined in Section 2.2.3, and a methodology, which is firmly grounded in the analysis of market transactions. In Chapter 1 it was noted that property can be distinguished from many other commodities and, particularly as far as property investment is concerned, from bonds and equities, because relatively speaking it takes a long time to transact. Also property tends not to be as frequently traded as other types of investment asset and companies tend to hold on to property assets for long periods of time. Individual units of property are quite large and expensive – in Chapter 1, they were described as lumpy and illiquid. All of this, coupled with the perennial fact that each unit of property is unique, thus giving rise to separate submarkets for different types of property, means that there is a demand for professional **valuers** to help determine the market value of individual properties. Valuers are employed to analyse and make informed judgements about market value based on their analysis of market transaction information. Market value is an important concept because vast sums of debt and equity capital are committed annually to property investments and loans that are based on opinions of market value. Property taxation and legislation also refer to market values as we shall see in Chapter 4.

2.2.1 The need for valuations

Valuers are requested to provide advice about the capital and rental value of properties and the service is often closely associated with agency work where the client seeks advice on the appropriate asking price (in the case of a vendor) or the accuracy of an asking price (in the case of a prospective purchaser) and the terms of the transaction are negotiated. This close association allows valuers to have a strong link to current market activity and helps them spot the price signals. The term **appraisal** is often used in conjunction with valuation and refers to a wider consideration of issues that are expounded in Chapter 7.

Valuations are required for many purposes relating to the development and subsequent occupation and ownership of property. The purpose for which the valuation is required and the type of property that is to be valued will determine the nature of the valuation instruction, including the techniques employed and the basis on which value is to be estimated. Table 2.1 lists the chief reasons for commissioning a valuation of commercial property.

Developers need to know how much they should bid for a piece of development land or a building that is in need of redevelopment. Ever since the construction of the canals and railways during the Industrial Revolution, valuers have been employed to assess the amount of compensation that should be paid to landowners whose land has been compulsorily acquired to make way for these transport routes. In fact a professional body, the Institution of

Table 2.1 Reasons for valuing commercial property.

Development appraisal
Transfer of ownership
Monitoring of property investment performance
Reporting the value of property assets held by companies
Loan security
Tax matters; property tax, capital gains tax and inheritance tax
Insurance risk assessment

Surveyors (now known as the **Royal Institution of Chartered Surveyors or RICS**), was founded in 1868 to represent the collective interests of the valuation profession and regulate its activity. Land continues to be compulsorily acquired for many public sector and utility network projects including major transport infrastructure projects such as the Channel Tunnel, urban public transport networks and airport construction, for regeneration projects where sites in fragmented ownership need to be assembled, and for minor works such as the realignment of a road junction to improve sight lines. Compensation may also be paid to landowners where none of their land has been acquired but there has been a reduction in the value because of nearby public works, such as noise from a new road. Valuation for compulsory purchase and compensation is considered in Chapter 4.

A property owner who wishes to sell would need to advertise an asking price that will attract potential purchasers and the level is clearly dependent on market conditions. If the owner wishes to let the property, then advice will be sought regarding the level of rent that could be obtained, the lease terms that should be included and the type of tenant that can be expected. **Rent reviews** ensure that the rent paid by the tenant is periodically reviewed to market value and it is necessary (usually as a condition of the rent review clause in the lease) to employ a valuer to estimate the revised rent. If the property is already let and the tenant wishes to dispose of the lease then the lease must be assigned to a new tenant and a **premium** or reverse premium might be appropriate.

When an investor purchases a property and leases it to a tenant, the expectation is that it will generate sufficient income in the form of rent payments and capital appreciation to provide an adequate rate of return in comparison to other investment opportunities such as equities and bonds. After a period of time the investor may sell the property to another investor at a value that has risen over the holding period. Properties held as investments by financial institutions, developers, property companies and the like are valued on a regular basis as a means of monitoring investment performance. Indeed many property investors are legally required to revalue their property investment assets on a regular basis and annual, often monthly, valuations of properties in the portfolios of these investors are undertaken. Listed companies that own property carry out certain property-related transactions or they are companies primarily engaged in property activities and are subject to additional disclosure requirements, principally in relation to valuations. Many of these investment valuations are recorded in the IPD (see Chapter 1) and this enables investors to benchmark the performance of their property investment portfolios.

Historically companies reported the original cost of property assets in their balance sheets. This led to considerable under-valuation of company assets. Entrepreneurs could buy these businesses for a price that reflected their historic asset value and then release real value by disposing of valuable assets, including property, at current prices (a process known as 'asset stripping'). Companies may now elect to report the current value of their property assets in their annual accounts, and valuers are required to perform these valuations for corporate disclosure purposes. As businesses are acquired or merged, valuers are often asked to value the property assets of the companies concerned. The City Code on Takeovers and Mergers ensures equitable treatment of shareholders in relation to takeovers and substantial share acquisitions. Where a valuation of assets is given in connection with an offer it should be supported by the opinion of a named independent valuer. The London Stock Exchange Listing Rules set out the basis for company valuations of property assets – these follow the relevant accounting standard and we shall look at these in Chapter 4.

A lender who is offering a loan facility that is to be secured by property will invariably require a valuation of the property to ensure that it represents sufficient collateral. If a borrower defaults then the lender may wish to take possession of the property and sell it in order to realise its value and thus recover the debt. Recent debate in the valuation profession has focused on whether a loan security valuation should be to market value or whether some other basis that reflects the 'forced' sale of the property is more appropriate. A lender who is lending money for property development will clearly wish to be suitably reassured (with adequate allowance for the risk taken) as to the expected value of the completed development.

Valuations are also required for capital and revenue taxation purposes. Occupiers of commercial premises in England and Wales must pay a property tax, known as **business rates,** to the government. The tax liability is calculated by assessing the **rateable value** of the premises and multiplying this amount by a rate known as the Uniform Business Rate. The rateable value of a property is very similar to its annual rental value but with some simplifying assumptions. Valuers are employed by the Valuation Office Agency (an executive agency of the Government's HM Revenue and Customs Department) to assess the rateable value of every business property in the country. Valuers are also employed by occupiers who wish to ensure that the rateable value has been correctly assessed. Also, valuations are required for property on which Capital Gains Tax and Inheritance Tax are due.

Finally, most properties are insured against damage and destruction and valuers are required to estimate their replacement cost for insurance purposes. Strictly speaking this is less of an estimate of market value in the sense of an exchange price and more an assessment of the cost of a replacement building. Also, insurance companies must regularly revalue any property investment assets that they own in order to ensure that they are complying with statutory solvency requirements and to encourage them to maintain a prudent spread of investments in relation to their liabilities (RICS, 2003).

2.2.2 Types of property to be valued

Until this point the terminology surrounding the concept of property has been rather confusing and it is probably a good time to try and pin down some of the key terms that are used. A good place to start is the International Valuation Standards, IVS (IVSC, 2005), in which a parcel of **real estate** is defined as a physical entity comprising land and buildings. Incidentally, buildings on land are often referred to as improvements and therefore a piece of developed land might be called improved land. This term is not favoured in this book because 'improvements' is a rather generic term and in any case it is used later to refer to improvements that a tenant might carry out and which carry special meaning in law (see Chapter 4). The property market actually deals in property rights rather than the physical land and buildings themselves. So real estate is the physical entity whereas **real property** is a legal interest in real estate that entitles its owner to various rights, including the right to develop, lease, sell, donate, farm, mine, physically alter, subdivide or assemble into larger units. These real property rights are typically restricted and regulated by limitations imposed by national government such as taxation, compulsory acquisition, land use planning regulation or appropriation in cases of intestacy. Many statutes also affect the way in which property may be owned and occupied; under certain conditions tenants can obtain legal rights that protect their occupational interest and investment that they may have made to improve the premises and these will be discussed in Chapter 4. Other restrictions may be imposed by **deed** or **covenant,** which run with the land and may affect the use, development and transfer of ownership, or by **easement** (non-possessory and **incorporeal**) interests conveying use but not ownership of real estate, such as a right of way. The term real property is, then, used to describe ownership of real estate. From now on the prefix 'real' will be omitted and we will simply use the term 'property' to refer to the ownership of a legal interest in real estate.

But what about this term **legal interest**? Common law, as it relates to property, is derived from the system of feudal land tenure by which the monarch and his or her lords ruled the land. In the UK only the Crown can own land and historically lords merely 'held' their land under a system of **tenure.** The lords, in turn, granted lesser rights to hold property to others in return for loyalty, services or **rent.** The monarch or superior *land*lords could withdraw their patronage and reclaim their land at any time. This holding of land was categorised according to its duration and because of its derivation in the doctrine of legal estates it is more accurate to speak of someone holding an 'estate' (or bundle of rights) rather than owning physical land (Card *et al.*, 2003). The two most important estates are **freehold** and **leasehold.** A freeholder holds land in perpetuity from the Crown and is at liberty to use it for any purpose subject to statutory regulation and the legal protection afforded to third parties. The freeholder may be an occupier using the property for business purposes or the freeholder may be an investor (usually referred to as a **landlord** but sometimes as a **lessor**) deriving a rental income from a lease granted to an occupier. A leaseholder (usually referred to as a **tenant** but sometimes as a **lessee**) holds a property for a term of years, the duration of which is usually specified in or implied by the terms of the **lease** granted by the landlord.

There are two principal types of lease. Long *ground leases* are typically for a term of more than 100 years where the landlord grants a lease of, say, a vacant site to a tenant who in turn may construct a building on it and enjoy the economic benefits of doing so during the term of the ground lease. Historically these ground leases required a rent to be paid that typically remained the same during the entire term. As time passed, the real value of this rent diminished. Nowadays it is common to find rent reviews or some other arrangement inserted into ground leases that enable the landlord to participate in rental value growth. Shorter leases of say 5–25 years duration are granted in respect of existing land and buildings for occupation. Subject to the provisions of these *occupation leases* tenants can subdivide and sublet a property but only for durations of less than the length of any head-lease. During the lease the rent is usually reviewed upwards every 5 years and at the end of the lease term the business tenant may have a legal right to renew the lease. So a single unit of property may comprise more than one legal interest, each of which will have a market value providing it is capable of being freely exchanged (IVSC, 2005). Fraser (1993) notes that it is the longevity of property as a physical asset that enables its use to be separated from ownership and for a number of interests to exist in the same property at the same time. Figure 2.1 provides an example of the way in which legal interests in a single physical property might be structured but there is no limit to the number of leasehold interests that may be created in this way.

Leases can be for a fixed term or they can be periodic. Leases for a fixed term are the most common form of commercial tenancy. Periodic tenancies have no fixed duration and continue from period to period (weekly, monthly, quarterly or yearly) until determined at end of any period by a 'notice to quit' issued by either party. A recently introduced form of tenure known as **commonhold** is designed to replace the long lease and provide a form of collective ownership where property interests are interdependent (in a multilet office block, for example). Other important ownership and financial interests include trusts, where the interest of a beneficiary under a trust is an equitable interest as opposed to the legal interest of a trustee, and financial interests, which are created by a legal charge, if the property is used as collateral to secure finance (the owner's equity position is considered a separate financial interest). There are other, more minor, legal interests in land such as easements, covenants and licences that allow or restrict the use of land under specific conditions.

So far we have distinguished physical real estate from legal interests in real property and stated that the property market is concerned with exchanges of the latter. As valuation is concerned with the estimation of exchange price this

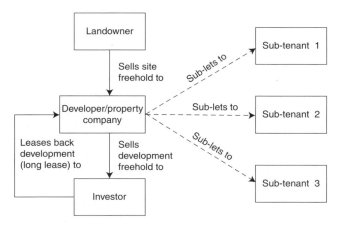

Figure 2.1 Legal estates in a property.

distinction between physical real estate and legal real property interests is critical – it is the real property interest that is valued rather than the real estate as a physical entity. For example, a lease might specify that the tenant has no right to sell or transfer the leasehold interest, making the interest unmarketable during the lease term and causing the exchange value to be zero. Instead, its value exists solely in terms of its use and occupancy rights, in other words it has a value-in-use but not a value-in-exchange. Similarly, onerous lease covenants, such as restrictions on the way that occupation of the property may be transferred, may adversely affect the market value of a leasehold interest (IVSC, 2005).

A property is usually valued as a distinct physical and legal entity designed for a specific use or range of uses, such as a factory, shop or office building, to which particular ownership rights apply. Having said this, the value of some properties is estimated by considering the profitability of the business that is operating therein and the property is a specialised asset of that business. As a result, property is often classified by legal interest (primarily freehold or leasehold) as well as by property type (retail, office, industrial, for example) and then more specifically by such descriptions as high-tech industrial, warehousing and factory space, by specific geographical locations such as South West, London West End or Central Leeds and by geographic abstractions such as in-town or out-of-town. These classifications are important to the analysis of market transactions because the values of similar types of properties in the same locality tend to correlate. The classifications are also important to valuation because methods vary depending on the type of property being valued. Table 2.2 illustrates the diversity of commercial property and attempts to classify them into recognisable submarkets. Overlaying this land use class classification will be the sort of geographical divisions mentioned above.

Ownership of a legal interest in an item other than real estate is known as personal property. Items of personal property can be tangible such as a chattel or intangible such as a licence. In a property context, tangible personal property includes items not permanently attached to real estate (IVSC, 2005) such as plant and machinery or fixtures and fittings. According to UK valuation guidance (RICS, 2003), plant and machinery that are usually valued with a property include service installations, utility equipment such as heating, hot water and air-conditioning that are not integral to any business process, and structures and fixtures such as chimneys, plant housings or railway track that are not an integral part of a process. Fixtures and fittings attached to a building by a tenant and used in conjunction with the business are removable upon lease expiry. International valuation guidance, in the form of International Valuation Standards or IVS for short, is slightly more generic in its approach to the valuation of personal property plant and equipment. According to the IVS Committee (IVSC), under 'Guidance Note 2 – Plant & Machinery', plant and equipment is a general class of tangible personal property that is typically moveable and depreciates more quickly than real property. Value can differ markedly depending on whether it is valued in combination with other assets in an operational unit or whether it is valued as an individual item for exchange and where it may be considered as either *in situ* or for removal. Personal property may need to be valued in conjunction with real property when valuing specialised trading property. **Specialised trading properties**

Table 2.2 Commercial property descriptions.

Standard property types

Offices	**Shops**	**Factories and warehouses**
Standard office	Kiosk	Factory
Business park	Standard unit	Works (e.g. quarry, pit, mine, tip)
	Post office, bank	Workshop
	Showroom	Light industrial business unit
	Supermarket/superstore	Warehouse
	Retail warehouse	Builders yard
	Retail park	Store
	(collection of retail warehouses)	Storage land
	Shopping centre	Storage depot
	(collection of standard units)	
	Department/variety store	
	Market stall	

Non-standard property types

Accommodation	**Licensed**	**Education**	**Leisure**	**Transport**
Camping park	Pubs and clubs	Day nursery	Golf course	Petrol station
Hotel	Market	School	Sports hall/	Car park
Self-catering	Restaurant	College	ground	Dock/wharf
unit	Café	University	Leisure centre	Marina/
Guest house	Food court	**Medical**	Cinema	mooring
Student	Betting shop	Surgery	Garden centre	Bus station
Miscellaneous	Casino	Health centre	Health club	Railway
Advertising	Bingo hall	Hospital	Theatre	Airport
right	Amusement	Nursing home	Amusement park	Vehicle
Utility works	arcade		Place of worship	dealership
Public service				
Library	Club-house	Sports centre	Swimming pool	Hostel
Museum/	Hall	Stadium	Cemetery/crema-	Home
gallery			torium	
Community	Playing field	Sports ground	Police/fire station	Toilets
centre				
Prison	Allotments	Sporting right	Law court	Park

(which will be discussed in detail in Chapter 3) are individual properties that usually change hands while remaining operational. The conveyance usually includes not only real property (land and buildings) but also personal property (plant, machinery, fixtures, fittings furniture, equipment) and a business component comprising the transferable elements of the business itself and intangible assets such as goodwill. As such, a specialised trading property is valued as an operational business entity or **going concern**. When valuing such property the valuer must decide whether personal property are to be valued as part of the transferable business or as separate assets and we will look at this decision process in more detail in Chapter 3. In addition to the case of specialised trading property, personal property must be distinguished from real property for other types of valuation including valuations for compulsory purchase and taxation. It may also be necessary to consider the impact of depreciation on personal property.

Finally, an important question arises when valuing a group of properties such as the estate of a business or the portfolio of an investor, that is, should the properties be valued individually or collectively? The market values may be different in each case. The RICS (2003) gives two examples of why this might be so: one is where physically adjacent land parcels are worth a certain amount individually but might be worth a great deal more when assembled as part of a development programme; another is where various properties are used in a functionally dependent way, such as an office with a car park down the road, a chain of retail outlets or a utility network. If the group of properties were to be sold at the same time this could 'flood' the market and the increase in supply might lead to a decrease in the prices obtained for each property. Conversely, an opportunity to purchase the group of properties might persuade a bidder to pay a premium and therefore increase the collective price paid. UK valuation guidance in the form of 'Guidance Note 3 – Valuations of Portfolios and Groups of Properties' (RICS, 2003) advises that the properties should be valued as though they were part of a group and in the way that they would most likely be offered for sale. If the purpose of the valuation is one that would ordinarily assume that a group of properties will remain in existing ownership and occupation (the valuation is for a set of company accounts, for example) then it is not appropriate to reduce the value owing to all properties flooding the market at the same time. But if the group of properties is being valued for, say, loan security, then the flooding effect should not be ignored. In such a case the assumption would normally be that the properties are marketed in an orderly way. Rees and Hayward (2000) add that purchasing a group of functionally or geographically related properties can mean reduced acquisition fees and a shorter transaction time on the part of the purchaser and this may lead to the payment of a 'lotting premium'. It may also allow the purchaser to obtain valuable personal property such as a brand name or design right. Whatever approach is adopted, all assumptions should be reported with the valuation and both group and individual valuations should be stated if they are different.

2.2.3   Bases of value

It is now time to think more carefully about the ambiguity that surrounds the term 'value'. It was mentioned above that a property can have a value-in-use or a value-in-exchange with estimates of the latter being the most commonly sought. To help clarify matters valuers talk about bases of value; a basis of valuation being a description, or definition, of a value of an interest in property within a given set of parameters (RICS, 2003). Before a valuation can be undertaken the valuer must identify a particular basis of value. **Market value**, being a basis that corresponds to the concept of value-in-exchange, is the most common but others exist.

The UK has adopted the international basis of market value, which is the estimated amount for which a property should exchange on the date of valuation between a willing buyer and a willing seller in an arm's length transaction after property marketing wherein the parties had each acted knowledgeably, prudently and without compulsion. [Practice Statement 3.2 – Market Value (RICS, 2003) and International Valuation Standard 1 – Market Value Basis of Valuation (IVSC, 2005)]

Notes on the conceptual framework for this definition can also be found from these sources. Because property valuations can be capital and rental, a definition of **market rent** is also published which is

the estimated amount for which a property, or space within a property, should lease on the date of valuation between a willing lessor and a willing lessee on appropriate lease terms, in an arm's-length transaction, after proper marketing wherein the parties had each acted knowledgeably, prudently and without compulsion. [Practice Statement 3.4 – Market Rent (RICS, 2003) and Guidance Note 2 – Valuation of Lease Interests, paragraph 3.1.9.1 (IVSC, 2005).]

'Appropriate lease terms' should be stated in the valuation and usually cover repair liability, lease duration, rent review pattern and incentives.

Market value will include 'hope value', which arises from expectations of changing circumstances surrounding the property such as development potential (even if there is no planning permission at the time of the valuation), and the possibility of **marriage value**, which arises from the merger of two or more physical properties or two or more legal interests within the same property. Assumptions may need to be added to the basis when estimating the market value of certain types of property; specialised trading properties were mentioned earlier and these are designed or adapted for specific uses and they often transfer as part of an operational business. Consequently the property tends not to be valued separately from the business as a whole and includes the value of personal property (as described above). Often a separate valuation of plant and machinery is required, particularly for industrial premises where such assets represent a significant component of the tangible assets of a company. Plant and machinery may be valued as a whole in its working place or for removal from the premises at the expense of the purchaser (RICS, 2003). If a property includes land that is mineral-bearing or is suitable for use as a waste management facility, an assumption may be necessary to reflect the potential for such uses in the valuation. An opinion of market value can also be expressed with 'special assumptions' attached. These special assumptions may include the anticipation of planning consent for development of the property; anticipation of a physical change (e.g. extension); anticipation of a new letting on given terms, or a known constraint that could prevent the property either being placed on, or adequately exposed to, the market. If such a valuation is provided, the special assumptions must be clearly stated together with a note of the effect on value.

Valuations for Capital Gains Tax, Inheritance Tax and Stamp Duty Land Tax purposes are based on statutory definitions of market value similar to the Red Book definition of market value. A definition for the basis of valuation for Capital Gains Tax can be found in Section 272 of the Taxation of Chargeable Gains Act 1992, for Inheritance Tax it is in Section 160 of the Inheritance Act 1984 and for Stamp Duty Land Tax it is in Section 118 of the Finance Act 2003. These current statutory definitions are similar to those used in earlier tax legislation and, over the years, case law has established that, in arriving at market value, the following assumptions must be made:

- the sale is hypothetical;
- the vendor and purchasers are hypothetical, prudent and willing parties to the transaction (unless the latter is considered a 'special purchaser');
- for the purposes of the hypothetical sale, the vendor would divide the property to be valued into whatever natural lots would achieve the best overall price, known as 'prudent lotting';
- all preliminary arrangements necessary for the sale to take place have been carried out prior to the valuation date;
- the property is offered for sale on the open market by whichever method of sale that will achieve the best price;
- adequate marketing has taken place before the sale;
- the valuation reflects the bid of any 'special purchaser' in the market (provided they are willing and able to purchase).

Further clarification on detailed aspects of the statutory definitions of market value, as established by case law can be found in sections three, four and five of 'UK Guidance Note 3.2 – Valuations for Capital Gains Tax (CGT), Inheritance Tax (IHT) and Stamp Duty Land Tax (SDLT)' of the RICS Appraisal and Valuation Standards (RICS, 2003).

There are other bases of value that are used in specific circumstances. These include **going concern value,** which is the value of the business as a whole and can only apply to a property that is a constituent part of a business (see Chapter 4), and **net realisable value,** which is an accounting concept used in relation to the value of fixed assets that include property.

Key points

- 'Property' is a term used to describe a legal real property interest in real estate. In economic terms a property can have a value-in-use and a value-in-exchange, the latter is an estimate of exchange price.
- A property valuation is the process of forming an opinion of value-in-exchange under certain assumptions and a market valuation requires those assumptions to establish an open market scenario.
- Valuations are required in connection with many activities, chiefly development appraisal, transfer of ownership, monitoring of property investment performance, reporting the value of property assets held by companies, loan security, tax matters and insurance risk assessment.
- The diversity of property makes valuation a difficult task, no two properties are ever the same, yet valuation relies on the comparison of properties to give an indication of value. To do this the valuer must be aware of, and be able to quantify, differences in type, location, legal interest, quality and the state of the market. These determinants of value are considered in more detail in Section 2.3.

2.3   Determinants of value

Chapter 1 set out the theoretical background to the concept of rent and its capitalised equivalent, capital value. The focus of that chapter was to consider the economic implications of changes in supply and demand and their effect on the rental value of land and buildings. To be able to place the concepts and the mechanisms described in Chapter 1 into a practical valuation context, it is necessary to identify those demand factors that underpin the rental bid for commercial property. Remembering that the demand for property is a derived demand and that property is a factor of production, the attributes that make a property attractive to an occupier are central to the understanding of the rental bid level and hence an estimate of value. This demand for occupation is fundamental to the supply decisions of developers with regard to new stock and is of paramount importance to investors as it provides the income return. This section considers those attributes considered desirable in a commercial property and therefore likely to influence its rental and capital value.

Influences on value can be classified as property-specific or market-related. Property-specific factors relate to the property itself and market-related factors to the market as a whole. Valuation methods have developed over the years to help the valuer quantify the effect of geographical, legal and physical influences on value. The wider market factors are less to do with the valuation itself and more to do with context and form part of the cognitive background that valuers bring to a valuation, including market knowledge and an awareness of the current legislative framework, environmental policy and economic activity. As Fraser (1993) argues, supply and demand, and hence prices and values, are affected by local, regional, national and international economic conditions and they can be influenced by political, legal and technological events that at first glance may seem remote and irrelevant.

2.3.1   Property-specific factors

Turning our attention to property-specific factors first, the principal physical qualities of the building are size, age, condition, external appearance (including aspect and visibility), internal specification and configuration. These qualities affect the performance of the building to varying degrees depending on the use to which it is put. For commercial properties the handling of materials, products and maintenance arrangements are important whereas the impact on the volume of business is important for retail property. Retail property value can be influenced by what would appear to be minor physical considerations such as aspect, lighting, internal configuration (including frontage length, depth, ground floor area, capacity for display, sale and storage space including upper floors and basement levels) and delivery facilities. Office occupiers often look for a prestigious address and good design features while occupiers of industrial property favour an uninterrupted ground floor area with good load-bearing capacity, generous eaves height, easy loading and access. Generous car parking, good ventilation and canteen facilities might also be desirable. These design features enhance the attractiveness of the property, its utility to an occupier and thus its value.

Running costs such as repairs and maintenance of common parts are important considerations and it is in the interest of the occupier to keep these to a minimum. Other financial considerations may be site development potential and adaptability of the premises in the face of changing production methods, technological advances or a rapidly expanding or contracting market. The ability to dispose of the property and the flexibility for possible changes of use are also value-significant considerations as they will enhance the marketability of the property should the current occupier wish to move. As well as flexibility for change of use, office-occupiers increasingly demand adaptable internal space so that it is capable of meeting their changing business requirements without having to move premises. Design considerations and corporate image are important to occupiers who may be using the premises as a headquarters or for a use that requires regular client contact. These characteristics help the property combat obsolescence – an issue to which we will return in Chapter 6.

Legal factors, although intangible and therefore sometimes overlooked, can have a significant impact on value. If the legal interest is a freehold then it is important to consider any easements or other statutory rights and obligations (such as restrictive covenants) over the land, the nature and extent of permitted use(s), potential for change of use and proposed development plans. If the freehold is held as an investment and let to an occupying tenant then the quality of that tenant is a primary concern, not only in terms of an ability to keep paying rent but also in complying with other lease terms such as repairs and maintenance. If the property is let to more than one tenant then the mix of tenants is important – an industrial estate with over-exposure to a particular trade (say car repair) will not enhance the value of the estate as a whole. Consequently, user restrictions are sometimes inserted into each lease contract to protect the landlord's balance of lettings. For example, if the landlord owns a large shopping mall then it would be wise to ensure that there is a wide variety of shops. To do this the landlord and each tenant must agree what limitations are to be placed on the trade that can occur in a particular shop unit. The landlord will wish to ensure that potential tenants are financially able to meet terms of lease and that they are of a sufficient standing so as not to harm the investment value of the shopping mall as a whole; references and guarantees are often taken up.

Special circumstances surrounding individual properties and owners also influence property value. Certain types of commercial property, garden centres or butchers are good examples, which can remain as family-run operations for years. Alternatively, a special bid by an adjacent landowner or a bidder with specific tax concerns may need to be considered. Valuers should also be aware of the potential liability on owners and occupiers for work to comply with the Disability Discrimination Act and other legislation, especially where the property is used for the provision of goods or services to the public such as shops, leisure property and certain types of office use.

When valuing a property for which a current certificate is required, valuers should make enquiries about the existence of a current certificate, any conditions it imposes and whether there have been any material alterations to the property or its use since the certificate was granted. Conditions which restrict the use of a property may impact on its value, as will any outstanding building works required to either maintain or obtain a certificate (to create or improve a means of escape, for example). The value of fully equipped trading entities could be significantly affected by the absence of a currently valid fire certificate. Valuers should also look out for high-voltage overhead transmission lines, disused mine workings and the use of building materials such as asbestos which are known to cause problems.

It is also important to consider how much rent is left after all expenditure has been accounted for. This **net rent** is usually calculated by deducting the cost of insurance, management and maintenance from the **gross rent**. Usually the precise amounts of expenditure are not known and percentage deductions from the gross rent are estimated instead (a 2.5% deduction to cover the cost of insurance, 10% for management costs, for example). Ideally investors want leases that oblige the tenant to be responsible for repairs and insurance. This (partly) explains why leasehold investments are less attractive; the additional repair and management responsibilities, the wasting nature of the asset and a lack of reversionary value (redevelopment potential perhaps) are not attractive characteristics to an investor. A primary concern of the landlord is the security of rent in real terms so the negotiation of a new rent at rent review or lease renewal is of great importance. If rent reviews were not inserted into the lease contract then the rent that the landlord receives would be eroded by inflation over the duration of the lease. Rent reviews ensure that the landlord receives an inflation-proof income. From an occupying tenant's perspective legal obligations contained in the lease can have a substantial impact on value. Of overriding concern is the amount of rent, length of the lease, repair and insurance liability and any other regular expenditure such as a **service charge**. But there are many other issues and lease provisions that the tenant must be mindful of; any restrictions on use and the ability to make changes to the premises, sub-letting or **assignment**, the nature and frequency of any rent reviews and options to renew or terminate the lease, known as **break options**, the nature of any incentives offered by the landlord (such as a rent-free period) or by the tenant (such as a premium) and the remedies for breach of lease terms. On the issue of assignment, this is where the tenant transfers the remaining term of the leasehold interest to another party. For leases granted before 1 January 1996, a legal concept known as 'privity of contract' meant that the contractual relationship between the original landlord and original tenant persisted throughout the entire duration of the lease even if the leasehold interest was assigned to another tenant. In effect, if any subsequent **assignee** breached a term of the lease, defaulted on rent payment, for example, the landlord would be able to seek damages from each **assignor** right back to the original tenant. This clearly provided the landlord with additional security of income but was regarded as rather harsh on previous tenants who had long since departed the property. After 1 January 1996 the Landlord and Tenant (Covenants) Act, 1995 came into effect and a tenant assigning a lease is generally released from any future liability under the lease. It is, however, permitted (and accepted market practice) for the landlord to require a guarantee from the outgoing tenant for the liabilities of the specific person to whom he assigns (IPF, 2005). Since the abolition of privity of contract, landlords have been more wary of allowing tenants to assign their leases to tenants of lesser financial standing as this will clearly have an impact on the value of their investments.

In Chapter 1, the influence of location on property value was considered at the scale of the urban area and it was argued that accessibility was the key determinant of the location for a business. In short the importance of accessibility is dependent upon the use to which the property is put and the various needs for accessibility result in a process of competitive bidding between different land uses and a property rent pattern emerges that is positively correlated with the pattern of accessibility. This usually means that the highest rents are paid in the centre of an urban area but there is an increasing number of exceptions to this simple assertion. Nevertheless, the theory is sound and empirical evidence supports it. But it is worth spending a few moments considering the accessibility advantages to specific land uses in a little more detail.

The prime location factor revolves around linkages to people and other uses measured in terms of accessibility to market(s) and factors of production (capital and labour). Accessibility refers to the ease with which contacts can be made considering the number, frequency and urgency of those contacts. If there is more reliance on access to customers there is more need to locate at the position of maximum accessibility to the market. The layout of transport routes and the cost of traversing them influence the pattern of accessibility. Retail property is highly dependent on market accessibility and it is a key objective to locate a shop where it has vehicular or pedestrian access to the greatest number of potential customers. Differences can be observed at the individual property level and are caused by the type of district, street, position in the street, and whether there are department stores, car parks or public transport nodes nearby. Certain types of office premises such as building societies, employment agencies and estate agents also require particularly accessible locations in order to attract customers. They try to locate at ground level in those locations where they are not outbid by retailers. Other more general office property, insurance companies and other financial institutions, for example, require access to a pool of labour and will locate in the centre of urban areas where commuter transport hubs are located. Within the urban area itself, headquarters and large branches of international firms regard accessibility and a prestigious address as very important, and professional institutions require similar attributes but often fail to outbid the first category and therefore locate near parks, squares or buildings of interest. Small professional firms and branch offices require access to a resident population and usually locate in a high street, suburb or near a public transport node. Local government and civil service offices used to be centrally located when land values were low but now tend to occupy cheaper sites on the edge of the central area.

Offices attached to industrial units locate where the industry's criteria are met. Compared with other land uses industrial relocation is uncommon owing to inertia and sunk costs; generally the more space extensive the industry, the less demand for central sites. Heavy industry requires access to raw material and heavy freight, while light industries are often located in, or on the periphery of, an urban area. If the firm's market is outside the urban area then intra-urban location is irrelevant with regard to sales but will differ on costs owing to land value variation, access to the labour market and the transport network. Other considerations include access to materials, parts and components, skilled labour, ancillary activities, owner's preferences, utilities and services. High-tech industrial units require a high quality 'green' environment with generous car parking, and close proximity to residential areas and amenities. Business and science parks require motorway access and proximity to a skilled labour force. Warehouses also need easy motorway access.

Other important location considerations are agglomeration economies and complementarity, collectively known as neighbourhood effects. These are the benefits that can accrue when properties of a similar nature cluster together. The amount of benefit depends on the need for contacts. Once sites in an area have been developed for a particular use, this will largely determine the best use for remaining sites because of advantages of concentration. Large multiple retailers and chain stores tend to cluster to provide comparison shopping and complementary shops cluster to offer a wider range of goods and services. As an example of retail agglomeration, big 'anchor' stores in shopping centres are usually able to capture a share of external economies through negotiated lower rents or incentive packages (Ball *et al.*, 1998). Offices cluster near shopping facilities and desirable residential neighbourhoods. Industry benefits from clustering the production sequence which in turn lowers costs because of external economies of scale. This explains the success of industrial estates. Smaller firms locate near the centre but larger firms have less dependency on agglomeration economies and complementarity because they are able to internalise their production processes. Incompatibility is the inverse of complementarity where properties locate apart to prevent higher costs or loss of revenue, for example, an obnoxious industry and food production. With regard to retail property 'dead frontage' such as a civic building or a church represent incompatible uses because of different opening hours and a lack of display frontage.

2.3.2   Market-related factors

Market-related factors are not specific to a particular property but relate to the property market as a whole or at least to a market sector. There are certain factors that affect the values of all properties regardless of type, although the extent to which they do so will vary depending on property type and location.

Market influences on property values include national output (as measured using the Gross Domestic Product metric), household disposable income, consumer spending levels and retail sales, employment rate, construction output, house building activity and net household formation, production costs (including wage levels), cost and availability of finance and inflation. Changes in the size and demographic profile of the population can affect demand for goods and services as well as the availability and cost of the workforce used to produce them. Economic factors that affect the value of retail property, in particular, centre on the propensity to attract custom, for example, purchasing power (credit restrictions), consumer behaviour (spending habits, changes in tastes or fashion) and population density. Whatever the property type, the valuer tries to ascertain market strengths and weaknesses, assess the likely supply of and demand for properties, comparable to the one being valued and determine the factors likely to impact on the value of properties in the market. Important local market characteristics include stock availability, rental growth rates, yields, rents, capital values, take-up rate, vacancy rate and the development pipeline. As a way of obtaining a mixture of macroeconomic information and market information, valuers are able to obtain summary statistics relating to the urban and regional location in which the property is located. The extent to which a valuer is concerned with national and regional economy depends on the size and type of property being valued; a large regional shopping centre or car assembly plant would require a great deal of market analysis at the national level whereas the valuation of a doctor's surgery or suburban shop would require analysis primarily at the local level. Perhaps the most important environmental factor for commercial property occupiers and owners as a whole is energy cost and this is going to become an increasingly important factor in the future.

Social factors will include tastes of consumers and clients and changes in those tastes. For example, a wholesale shift towards the purchase of organic produce, to working at home or internet-based retailing will clearly impact on various sectors of the property market including shops, warehousing, offices and transport logistics. Socioeconomic data is available from the FOCUS property information service (www.focusnet.co.uk)at county and town level and includes demographic, household and employment data, economic data and estimates of floor-space for the main commercial property market sectors (offices, shops and restaurants, and industrial and warehousing). Table 2.3 shows the sort of data that is available at the town/city level. It is possible to obtain market reports from property agents and data providers such as FOCUS and Property Market Analysis. These reports cover a broad spectrum of market intelligence summarised for the main market sectors defined in terms of land use (offices, shops, industrial space) and location (such as West End, Mid-Town and City of London). They are usually updated monthly, quarterly or half-yearly depending on the dynamic

Table 2.3 City/town level data available from FOCUS.

Infrastructure
  Details of road, rail and air communications
  Name and population size of nearest five centres by road distance, travel time
Demography
  Population and number of households in the town/city as at 1991 and 2001
  Population with five and ten kilometer radii as at 1994
  Gender and age structure of the resident population
Socio-economic; proportions of the population classified by
  CACI lifestyle groups, e.g. from wealthy executives and inner city adversity
  Census class groupings, for 2001 census these were
  AB. Higher and intermediate managerial/administrative/professional
  C1. Supervisory clerical junior managerial/administrative/professional
  C2. Skilled manual workers
  D. Semi-skilled and unskilled manual workers
  E. On state benefit unemployed lowest grade workers
  Car ownership
  Household tenure
Economy
  Employment profile (percentage of males and females in employed full-time
    and part-time, self-employed, unemployed, retired, studying, looking after
    the home, permanently disabled) and the proportions of the main sectors in
    which the working population is employed (manufacturing, primary indus-
    tries, construction, hotel and catering, transport and communication, bank-
    ing, finance and business services, other services, utilities, public admin and
    defence, retail)
  Name, activity and number of staff of the largest employers
Commercial property
  Prime rents for offices and shops
  Number of requirements for retail space, monthly
  Top 20 comparison goods multiple retailers and the percentage of the
    national top 20 retailers present in the town/city and the names of those not
    present
  The names of the top three shopping streets
  Annual spend on comparison and core convenience goods within the catch-
    ment area of the town/city
  Details of the main retail developments including the name, size, developer,
    date of opening, managing agent, landlord, details of anchor and other
    tenant(s)

of the market sector in question. For example, a market report on London office space might be updated each month whereas for Exeter retail once a year would suffice. The reports typically consist of some headlines and then report the availability (in terms of floor-space) of new, refurbished and second-hand business space and space under construction, the level of take-up (also measured in terms of floor-space), asking prices and quoted rents for new and second-hand space and the amount of vacant floor-space.

Finally, the property market is a market for a tangible product that has influences and implications beyond its straightforward economic use as a factor of production or as an investment asset. The aesthetic and architectural qualities of individual properties are there for all to see. Similarly the layout and design of property in its collective sense – across an urban area – imposes a skyline that influences not only how we feel about a place but also how we work, reside, interact with others and spend our leisure time. The 'invisible hand' of free trade is not always able to optimise these 'public' benefits and can sometimes impose unacceptable public or social costs on society. It is therefore the role of government to intervene. The main way that government intervention affects property values is through development control and land use regulation or planning, but other activities can also have a significant impact including compulsory purchase (see Chapter 4), legislation that may protect certain rights of occupiers (security of tenure, for example) and regulations that may affect revenue such as Sunday trading and gambling laws.

Key points

- Value influencing property characteristics can be property-specific or market-wide: the former refers to the spatial, physical and legal attributes of the property itself and the latter refers to the characteristics of the market as a whole or the market sector in which the property operates. Fundamentally, the market value of a property reflects its capacity to fulfil a function. If the property is a shop, for example, then its value will be determined by factors such as trading position, length of frontage, accessibility, planning restrictions and tenure. We shall see later how it is important to be able to quantify financially these value factors as part of the valuation process (comparison adjustment). This is not an easy task and provides substance to the argument that valuation is as much an art as it is a science.
- There are two levels of property value analysis: property-specific and market overview. The value of a property is largely determined by its competitive position in the market in which it operates. Therefore, both property-specific and market-wide factors must be considered to delineate the market by investigating property type features such as (single or multiple) occupancy, use, construction types, design, amenities, geographical extent, available substitutes and complementary land uses.
- The built environment cannot be treated like a clinical laboratory and in practice variations in valuations will occur. Rates of inflation will alter, market conditions will change the expected rates of return and unforeseen events will happen. The calculations performed in valuations assume *ceteris paribus*.

2.4   Valuation mathematics

We have now considered the economic concepts behind supply and demand decisions that give rise to exchange value and we have discussed the various

Chapter 2

attributes of properties that users require. If properties are to be exchanged, and they clearly are, then buyers and sellers are able to agree prices for the property or 'basket' of property attributes that they are acquiring. Individually these attributes are not easy to quantify; it is much easier to look at aggregate exchange prices than build them up from first principles – there is no point trying to make valuation harder than it already is! But sometimes it is necessary to resort to some of the underlying processes when comparison is not possible. Indeed, there have been many attempts to price the individual attributes that a particular type of property offers using multiple regression analysis (see Adair and McGreal, 1987 and Adair *et al.*, 1996, for examples). However, these studies focus on the explanation and the measurement of the importance of these attributes rather than the estimation of exchange price and nearly always concentrate on residential property values because the product is more homogeneous than commercial property. In a competitive market, suppliers and users of and investors in property must agree on exchange prices and valuation is all about estimating these. The best way of doing so, assuming you are not trying to measure and explain the relative contribution of the individual property attributes, is by comparison. But here is the paradox; the best evidence of the value of a property is the price recently achieved on the sale or letting of similar properties, yet each property is unique! This is, however, a simplification of reality and we can, in the main, group properties into relatively homogeneous market sectors defined by land use and location. Comparison only then becomes a problem in markets where the uniqueness of each property precludes attempts at meaningful comparison. In these cases it is sometimes necessary to look more closely at the financial decisions that underpin the prices agreed. As an example some specialised types of property are valued by quantifying the contribution of the property to business profit and we will look at these in Chapter 3. Chapter 3 will also describe how valuers interpret the market pricing signals and mechanisms as a way of helping them to estimate exchange prices. Before this, though, it is necessary to introduce the financial mathematics that underpins valuation methods. A word of caution first; it is not a good idea to hide the maths in valuation – it would be easy to relegate much of the upcoming material to an appendix and try to gloss over the detail. But to do so belittles the true nature of the valuation process. For many years valuers have tended to adopt fairly simple ratios between rental income and capital value and, in the presence of heterogeneity, make rudimentary adjustments to these ratios. This can be sufficient but increasingly it is not acceptable; a more fundamental understanding of the way in which the value factors, described in Section 2.3, influence value is required.

We know that property is usually demanded not as an end in itself but as a means to an end – as a factor of production or as an investment asset – it is a derived demand and the opportunity cost of capital invested in property must be measured against other factors of production for occupiers and other investment asset types for investors. Valuers rely on this feature of property demand when attempting to quantify financially the opportunity cost of owning or leasing property. Economists (and valuers) use financial mathematics when measuring the opportunity cost of capital spent on property and this is necessary because property usually requires large amounts of money to be invested over periods lasting several years, so the 'time value of money' must be factored into calculations. The time value of money is an expression used to refer to the fact that, although in nominal terms £1000 tucked under the mattress today will be £1000 in 10 years' time, in real terms it will actually be worthless because inflation will have partially eroded its value. Similarly, and more importantly as far as property investment is concerned, the further into the future an amount of money (rent, for example) is received the less it is worth in today's terms.

Occupation and ownership are separate for approximately half of the stock of commercial property in England, as we discovered in Chapter 1, and this feature provides a very good evidence base from which to derive financial measures of the opportunity cost of money invested in property and of the cost of occupying property; the prices and rents paid for investment (landlord) and occupation (tenant) interests, respectively. But in the absence of perfectly comparable evidence (sadly a luxury that only valuation text books can invent) valuation involves adjustment of comparable evidence using mathematical formulae that enable the time value of money to be expressed in financial terms. This process requires a finance mathematics framework within which to operate and this is provided by financial investment theory. This section begins by illustrating some of the frequently used formulae for calculating investment value that take into account the time value of money before describing simple ratios between the price paid and the financial return expected from a property acquisition. The focus is on acquisition as a standing investment but the theory is equally applicable to acquisitions for owner-occupation and development but the investor's required rate of return is replaced by measures like the 'weighted average cost of capital' (WACC) and developer's profit margin.

2.4.1   The time value of money

In order to be able to value property it is necessary to understand how future economic benefits, typically in the form of a cash-flow, can be expressed in terms of present value. As far as property is concerned, after an initial expenditure on acquisition, cash-flow revenue typically takes the form of rental income and would be a real rent to an investor and an imputed rent to an owner-occupier. Property-based cash-flow can take other forms though; capital profit from a completed development (capital payments such as premiums, for example), but let us keep things simple at this stage and just think about rental income. Mathematical formulae are used to measure the time value of regular income cash-flows such as rent. These formulae are founded on the premise that rational purchasers of property, whether for ownership, investment or development, would prefer to have money now rather than later because, in an inflationary economy, money has a time-value. In other words, its real value is eroded by the general rise in the cost of

Table 2.4 Variables.

Variable	Description
A	Amount originally invested as a lump sum or regular series of payments
S	Sinking fund payment
n	Number of years (or other period) over which the cash-flow is estimated
r	Rate of return or discount rate per annum (or per period)
y	Market yield
t	Tax rate

all goods and services (inflation) over time. This time-value is a function of property investment characteristics described in Chapter 1, namely loss of liquidity and costs associated with the management of the investment, inflation and risk. The principles of compounding and discounting measure the value of money over time and form the basis of the financial economics of cash-flows. By compounding it is possible to calculate the **future value** of any income or expenditure and by discounting it is possible to calculate the **present value** of any future income or expenditure.

Before the various formulae are described we need to introduce some mathematical notation so they can be presented in a succinct and consistent form. The basic notation that will be used is listed in Table 2.4 and it is also worth noting that the formulae assume that investment deposits are made at the start of each period and interest is payable at the end of each period (in arrears).

The **future value of £1 (FV £1)** is the amount to which £1 will accumulate at a given rate of return after n periods. For example, if £1 is invested at the beginning of year 1 at r rate of return, the capital accrued at the end of the year will be $1 + r$. If £1 is invested for 2 years the future value will be $(1 + r)(1 + r)$ or $(1 + r)^2$ and if it is to be invested for n periods:

$$FV£\,1 = (1+r)^n \qquad [2.1]$$

If A is the sum originally invested, rather than £1, the formula to calculate the amount accumulated becomes:

$$FV\,£A = A(1+r)^n \qquad [2.2]$$

For example, the roof of a factory will need replacing in 4 years' time as part of a rolling programme of maintenance. The current cost of the work is estimated to be £25 000. Building costs are forecasted to increase at an average annual rate of 3.5% pa over this period of time. The cost of the repair in 4 years' time will be

$$A(1+r)^n = £25\,000(1+0.035)^4 = £28\,688$$

If r accumulates at intervals m of less than 1 year:

$$FV\,£A = A\left(1+\frac{r}{m}\right)^{n \times m} \qquad [2.3]$$

The **present value of £1 (PV £1)** is the sum that needs to be invested at the present time in order to accumulate to £1 by the end of n periods at r rate of return. If an amount of money A is invested for n periods and earns an annual rate of return, r, so that at the end of period n the investor receives £1 (equal to the original amount plus the required return) we can solve for A using the FV £1 formula as follows:

$$A(1+r)^n = 1$$

So

$$A = \frac{1}{(1+r)^n} \qquad\qquad [2.4]$$

In this case, A is the PV £1 and the formula is the reciprocal of the FV £1. This reciprocal relationship is illustrated graphically in Figure 2.2 where £1 is assumed to compound at a rate of return of 10% per annum over periods ranging between 1 and 100 years, rising to a value of £13781 after 100 years using the FV £1 formula and then this figure is discounted at the same rate back down to £1 using the PV £1 formula.

If money can be invested in a secure bond investment and receive an annual return of 4% pa, how much capital should be invested now to meet the estimated future expenditure calculated in the roof repair example above?

$$A\left[\frac{1}{(1+r)^n}\right] = \frac{A}{(1+r)^n} = \frac{£28688}{(1+0.04)^4} = £24523$$

The FV £1 and the PV £1 are concerned with single deposit investments. Property investment typically provides a regular or multiple-period return and therefore the following formulae are concerned with regular flows of money. The **future value of £1 per annum (FV £1 pa)** is the amount to which a series of payments of £1 invested at the end of each period will accumu-

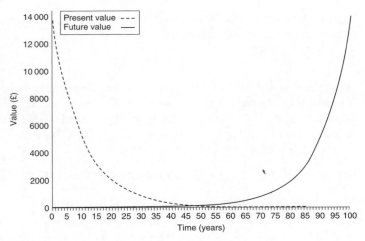

Figure 2.2 Future value of £1 and present value of £1.

Chapter 2

late at r rate of interest after n periods. It differs from the FV £1 because it is based on a number of deposits rather than a single deposit (remembering that the last payment accrues no interest because it is paid in arrears). The formula for the FV £1 pa is derived by adding the FV £1 for each successive year:

$$\text{FV£1 pa} = (1+r)^{n-1} + (1+r)^{n-2} + \cdots + (1+r)^2 + (1+r) + 1 \qquad [2.5]$$

This is an example of a geometric progression and we can use some of the recurring terms to simplify matters when we wish to calculate the sum of a geometric progression. This is achieved by looking at the general form of a geometric progression; $a, ar, ar^2, ar^3, ar^4, \ldots, ar^{n-1}$ where there are n terms, a is the first term and scale factor and r ($\neq 0$) is the common ratio. The sum of a geometric progression in its general form therefore looks like this:

$$\sum_{i=0}^{n} ar^i = a + ar + ar^2 + ar^3 + ar^4 + \cdots + ar^{n-1} \qquad [2.6]$$

If both sides of the above equation are multipied by r

$$r\sum_{i=0}^{n} ar^i = ar + ar^2 + ar^3 + ar^4 + ar^5 + \cdots + ar \qquad [2.7]$$

and Equation 2.6 is deducted from 2.7 we are left with the following since all the other terms cancel.

$$\sum_{i=0}^{n} ar^i - r\sum_{i=0}^{n} ar^i = a - ar^n \qquad [2.8]$$

Rearranging Equation 2.8 we get the following formula for the sum of a geometric progression:

$$\sum_{i=0}^{n} ar^i (1-r) = a(1-r^n)$$

$$\sum_{i=0}^{n} ar^i = \frac{a(r^n - 1)}{r - 1} \qquad [2.9]$$

This equation for calculating the sum of a geometric progression can now be used to construct a formula for the FV £1 pa by inserting 1 as the first term and $(1 + r)$ as the common ratio:

$$\text{FV £1 pa} = \frac{1(1+r)^n - 1}{(1+r) - 1} = \frac{(1+r)^n - 1}{r} \qquad [2.10]$$

So for any series of payments A the FV £1 pa for n periods is

$$\text{FV £1 pa} = A\left[\frac{(1+r)^n - 1}{r}\right] \qquad [2.11]$$

There are major repair works planned in 8 years' time for the entire industrial estate that you hold in your investment portfolio. Assuming that you can invest money at an average rate of return of 6.5% pa, how much will accrue if you invest £50 000 at the end of each year for the next 8 years?

$$A\left[\frac{(1+r)^n - 1}{r}\right] = £50\,000\left[\frac{(1+0.065)^8 - 1}{0.065}\right] = £50\,000 \times 10.0769 = £503\,845$$

A **sinking fund (SF)** is the amount which must be invested at the end of each period, accumulating at r rate of return, to provide £1 after n periods. The SF formula can be derived from the FV £1 pa formula. If A was invested at the end of each year at r rate of interest for n periods in order to accumulate to £1 at the end of the total number of periods, we can rearrange Equation 2.11 to solve for A. Substituting £1 as the amount to which the FV £1 pa must accrue:

$$1 = A\left[\frac{(1+r)^n - 1}{r}\right]$$

[2.12]

Then rearranging this equation to isolate A:

$$A = \left[\frac{r}{(1+r)^n - 1}\right]$$

[2.13]

A is the periodic amount that must be invested (the SF) to accumulate to £1. The formula is the reciprocal of the FV £1 pa formula:

$$SF£1 = \frac{r}{(1+r)^n - 1}$$

[2.14]

Rather than set aside a single capital amount now for the roof repair as we did in the PV £1 example above you decide to set aside equal annual instalments. What should these instalments be, assuming that the repair will still cost £28 688 in 4 years' time and you can invest money at a rate of return of 4% per annum?

$$A\left[\frac{r}{(1+r)^n - 1}\right] = £28\,688\left[\frac{0.04}{(1+0.04)^4 - 1}\right] = £28\,688 \times 0.2355 = £6756$$

In other words, £6756 should be invested at the start of each of the next 4 years to accrue £28 688 assuming an interest rate of 4% per annum paid annually in arrears. This can be checked using the FV of £1 pa formula to calculate the future value of £6756 invested in each of the next 4 years at 4% per annum. The answer should be £28 688. Sometimes you may see the term 'annual sinking fund' or ASF and this simply refers to a SF where the periodic investment deposits are made annually.

Despite the SF being a reciprocal of the FV £1 pa, graphically, the formulae do not plot symmetrical capital values as the FV £1 and PV £1 formulae do. Figure 2.3 shows the values produced when £1 is compounded at 10% per annum for between 1 and 100 years using the FV £1 pa formula.

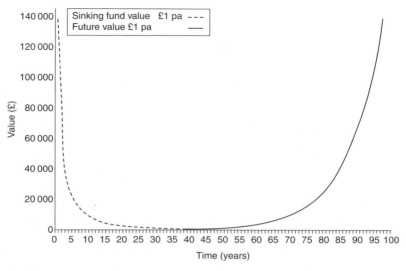

Figure 2.3 Future value of £1 per annum and sinking fund: 1–100 years.

The capital value of £137 796 produced after 100 years is then used to calculate SF amounts over the same time period and at the same rate of return.

The **present value of £1 per annum (PV £1 pa)** is the present value of the right to receive £1 at the end of each year for n years at r rate of return. It is the sum of the present values (PV £1s) over n years.

$$\text{PV £1 pa} = \frac{1}{(1+r)} + \frac{1}{(1+r)^2} + \frac{1}{(1+r)^3} + \cdots + \frac{1}{(1+r)^n} \qquad [2.15]$$

This is another geometric progression where the first term is $1/(1+r)$ and the common ratio is also, $1/(1+r)$ but, this time, because the common ratio is less than 1, we must reverse the equation for calculating the sum of a geometric progression. In other words it becomes

$$\sum_{i=0}^{n} ar^i = \frac{a(1-r^n)}{1-r} \qquad [2.16]$$

So substituting, we get

$$\text{PV £1 pa} = \frac{(1/(1+r))\left[1-(1/(1+r))^n\right]}{1-(1/(1+r))} = \frac{(1/(1+r))-(1/(1+r))^{n+1}}{1-(1/(1+r))}$$

$$\text{PV £1 pa} = \frac{(1/(1+r))-(1/(1+r)^{n+1})}{1-(1/(1+r))} \qquad [2.17]$$

If we multiply both sides of this equation by $(1 + r)$ it simplifies to

$$\text{PV £1 pa} = \frac{1-(1/(1+r)^n)}{r} \qquad [2.18]$$

For example, how much would you pay for the right to receive £50 000 per annum over the next 15 years assuming average investment returns of 8% per annum?

$$A\left[\frac{1-(1+r)^{-n}}{r}\right] = £50\,000\left[\frac{1-(1+0.08)^{-15}}{0.08}\right] = £50\,000 \times 8.5595 = £427\,975$$

The PV £1 pa formula is used to calculate the present capital value of regular cash-flows which, of course, include rent payments. If we replace the word 'calculate' with 'value' in the preceding sentence, the mathematical essence of valuation should now be apparent. The valuation of a finite (terminable) cash-flow involves capitalising the net income at a suitable discount rate r for the duration n that the income A is received. In other words, the PV £1 pa formula is used to convert a series of regular rent payments into a capital value. Conventionally, the PV £1 pa is referred to as the **years purchase (single rate)** by valuers, being the multiplier applied to the annual rent A to calculate the capital value of a property. It is called the 'years purchase', or YP for short, because the multiplier is the number of years that will pass before the income equals the capital value – like a payback period but taking the time value of money into account as well. So, in the example above, it will take approximately 8.56 years of receiving £50 000 pa to recoup the original outlay of £427 975 at the prevailing interest rate of 8% pa. In this respect, the YP is similar to the price:earnings ratio used to describe the quality of company shares on the stock market.

Now consider an investment that provides a constant annual income of £1 in arrears *in perpetuity*. If we assume a discount rate of 10% pa, as the time period n over which income received goes beyond about 50 or 60 years, the value of this investment levels out to a fraction under £10, as shown in Figure 2.4.

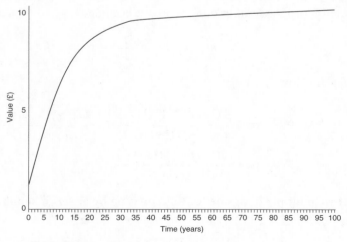

Figure 2.4   Present value of £1 pa: 1–100 years.

Mathematically, as n gets bigger the $1/(1 + r)^n$ term in Equation 2.18 gets smaller and the equation simplifies to

$$\text{PV £1 pa} = \frac{1}{r}$$

[2.19]

So, in terms of the mathematical accuracy typically required for the valuation of property investments, any stream of income receivable for 60 years or more may be regarded as receivable in perpetuity. This means that freehold and long leasehold property interests can be valued to an acceptable degree of accuracy by dividing the income by the rate of return, r. For example, a freehold shop investment is for sale and currently produces an annual rent of £80 000 pa. If investors generally require a 5% return on investments of this sort, what is the capital value of this investment?

$$\text{PV £80000 pa} = \frac{£80000}{0.05} = £1600000$$

When looking at property investment transactions that have recently taken place in the market it is possible to substitute r in Equation 2.19 to identify the market rate of return, known as the yield y (more of which later) given a price P (i.e. the PV £1 pa). Thus Equation 2.19 remains the same mathematically but the variables change:

$$P = \frac{1}{y}$$

[2.20]

And for any market rent MR other than £1 per annum

$$P = \frac{MR}{y}$$

[2.21]

By rearranging Equation 2.21 to isolate y

$$y = \frac{MR}{P}$$

[2.22]

It is then possible to use this formula to derive market yields from property investments that have recently transacted and, once this has been done, a suitable yield (known as an **all-risks yield**) can be estimated for the property being valued. For example, when valuing (calculating the present value PV) freehold properties where the annual rental income is assumed to be received in perpetuity, the market rent (MR) is divided by the yield y as in Equation 2.23, where V is the value. Do not worry too much about this at the moment; we will come back to it in Chapter 3.

$$V = \frac{MR}{y}$$

[2.23]

Finally, an **annuity £1 will purchase (Ann £1)** is the amount that will be paid back at the end of each period for n periods at r rate of return for £1 invested.

The return on an annuity is in the form of a constant income either for a fixed term or in perpetuity. For example, a life annuity is an annuity that is guaranteed for the rest of a person's life in return for a capital deposit and is calculated using 'life tables' (actuarial estimates of how long people are expected to live for). Mathematically the Ann £1 is the PV £1 pa viewed from the other end of the telescope. In other words, we are trying to find A given that the PV £1 pa is £1. So substituting £1 for the PV £1 pa and Ann £1 for A in Equation 2.18 as follows:

$$£1 = \text{Ann } £1 \left[\frac{1 - \left(1/(1+r)^n \right)}{r} \right]$$

We get

$$\text{Ann } £1 = \frac{r}{1 - \left(1/(1+r)^n \right)} \qquad [2.24]$$

The formula for the Ann £1 is the reciprocal of the PV £1 pa. As n gets bigger the denominator in Equation 2.24 gets smaller and the equation simplifies to

$$\text{Ann } £1 = r \qquad [2.25]$$

which is the inverse of $1/r$ that results when the PV £1 pa receivable in perpetuity is calculated.

Unlike a building society account or bond investment – where the capital invested remains, the capital invested in an annuity is not paid back. Instead the return from an annuity is partly a return *on* capital (at r) and partly a return *of* capital in the form of a sinking fund that must recoup the capital originally invested by the end of n periods. The formula for Ann £1 therefore comprises these two parts, r and SF:

$$\text{Ann } £1 = r + \text{SF} = r + \left[\frac{r}{(1+r)^n - 1} \right] \qquad [2.26]$$

Similarly;

$$\text{PV } £1 \text{ pa} = \frac{1}{r + \text{SF}} = \frac{1}{r + \left(r/(1+r)^n - 1 \right)} = \frac{1}{\text{Ann } £1} \qquad [2.27]$$

The reciprocal relationship between these versions of the Ann £1 and the PV £1 pa can again be proved as in Equation 2.24, by rearranging the PV £1 pa formula to calculate the fixed annuity income A that would be produced if £1 were invested at r for n years:

$$£1 = A \left[\frac{1}{r + \left(r/(1+r)^n \right) - 1} \right]$$

Therefore,

$$A = r + \left[\frac{r}{(1+r)^n - 1} \right] = r + \text{SF}$$

By now, assuming you are still awake, you may be thinking – hang on a minute; I spot two different formulae for calculating the PV £1 pa (Equations 2.18 and 2.27) and for calculating the Ann £1 (Equations 2.24 and 2.26). The reason for this concerns the way in which an investment provides a return *on* and a return *of* capital. To correctly calculate the present value of a cash-flow the PV £1 pa formula must include a sinking fund so that capital is recovered by the end of the investment period (the return of capital) while, at the same time, a return on capital is maintained at r. For example, what is the present value of an investment that offers an annual income of £10 000 over the next 4 years at a return of 5% pa? Using Equation (2.18)

$$\text{PV £10 000 pa} = \text{£10 000} \times \frac{1-\left(1/(1+0.05)^4\right)}{0.05} = \text{£10 000} \times 3.5460 = \text{£35 460}$$

And using Equation 2.27:

$$\text{PV £10 000 pa} = \text{£10 000} \times \frac{1}{0.05 + \left[0.05/(1+0.05)^4 - 1\right]} = \text{£35 460}$$

Table 2.5 shows the returns on and of capital broken down year-by-year.

The income provides for a return on capital at the accumulative rate (5% pa) and a return of capital at the remunerative rate (also at 5% pa). The sinking fund invests income at the remunerative rate to recover the original capital outlay of £35 460. Because the sinking fund is returning some of the capital at the end of each year the amount of capital outstanding reduces, caus-ing the return on capital to reduce too, leading to more of the fixed income being available for return of capital, and so on. Because the accumulative and remunerative rates are the same, the annuity and present value formulae are known as 'single rate' – the sinking fund is, in effect, a hypothetical one. The other versions of the Ann £1 and PV £1 pa formulae are known as 'dual rate' and are used when the remunerative rate r and the accumulative rate SF (or s for short) are different. So if we assume that the remunerative rate of return on a property with a capital value of £1 is r and the annual sinking fund to recoup the £1 at the end of a fixed term is s (the accumulative rate), the total income from the property will be $r + s$. We know from Equation 2.23 that

$$V = \frac{\text{MR}}{y}$$

Table 2.5 Breakdown of return on and return of capital invested.

Year	Capital outstanding	Income	Return on capital	Return of capital (sinking fund)
1	35 460	10 000	1 773	8 227
2	27 233	10 000	1 362	8 638
3	18 595	10 000	930	9 070
4	9 525	10 000	476	9 524
Total				35 460

and, rearranging, that

$$y = \frac{V}{MR}$$

Here $r + s$ is MR so

$$y = \frac{V}{r+s} = \frac{1}{r+s}$$

which is what we have in Equation 2.27.

Note that $1/(r + s)$ becomes $1/r$ when the period over which income is received is really long because the annual amount that needs to be invested in a sinking fund becomes negligible as n gets bigger, so s tends to 0 and the formula simplifies. We will come back to dual rate formulae in Chapter 3.

All of the formulae presented so far assume that the return on the investment is received annually in arrears. If income is received at the start of each period n instead of at the end this will, in effect, be at the end of year $n - 1$, so the PV £1 (received in advance) is

$$PV\ £1_{advance} = \frac{1}{(1+r)^{n-1}}$$

[2.28]

Regarding the PV £1 pa, if the income is receivable in advance (at the start of each period) £1 is received immediately so there is one less time period over which a payment is discounted. The series of present values that comprise the PV £1 pa with income received at the beginning of each period becomes

$$PV\ £1\ pa_{advance} = 1 + \frac{1}{(1+r)^1} + \frac{1}{(1+r)^2} + \frac{1}{(1+r)^3} + \cdots + \frac{1}{(1+r)^{n-1}}$$

And this simplifies to

$$PV\ £1\ pa_{advance} = \frac{1 - \left(1/(1+r)^{n-1}\right)}{r} + 1$$

[2.29]

Share dividends and coupons from bonds are usually received biannually in arrears but most leases on commercial property in the UK require the tenant to pay rent in quarterly instalments at the beginning of each quarter, usually on 'quarter days' at the end of December, March, June and September. Because the income is received sooner than if it was paid annually in arrears, these arrangements have a small but beneficial impact on the value of the investment. So, although rents are quoted as annual figures and used in valuations in this way, the actual return that an investor receives is enhanced by this payment method but not quite to the same extent as having all of the annual rent at the start of each year. To illustrate this, compare the present value of two investments that both yield a 6% annual return on an income of £10 000 for the next 5 years but one pays this income annually in advance and the other annually in arrears:

$$PV \; £10\,000 \, pa_{arrears} = £10\,000 \times \frac{1-\left(1/(1+0.06)^5\right)}{0.06} = £10\,000 \times 4.2124 = £42\,124$$

$$PV \; £10\,000 \, pa_{advance} = £10\,000 \times \frac{1-\left(1/(1+0.06)^{(5-1)}\right)}{0.06} + 1 = £10\,000 \times 4.4651 = £44\,651$$

Now assume that the income is from a property and therefore paid in four instalments of £2500 at the beginning of each quarter

$$PV \; £1\,pa_{quarterly \; advance} = \frac{1-\left(1/(1+r)^n\right)}{4\left[1-(1/(1+r)^{1/4})\right]} \qquad [2.30]$$

$$PV \; £10\,000 \, pa_{quarterly \; advance} = £10\,000 \times \frac{1-\left(1/(1+0.06)^5\right)}{4\left(1-(1/(1+0.06)^{1/4})\right)}$$

$$= £10\,000 \times 4.3692 = £43\,692$$

The yield from a completed investment transaction is usually reported as a simple annual income to capital value ratio, which assumes that the income is received annually in arrears. Given the above, we now know this to be slightly inaccurate and for property investments it is often desirable to adjust this yield so that it reflects the fact that income is received quarterly in advance. Assuming the property investment is a freehold or long leasehold interest and the income is receivable in perpetuity, the simple annually in arrears yield y_a that was derived in Equation 2.22 may be converted to a quarterly in advance yield y_q using the following formula:

$$y_q = \frac{1}{\left(1-(y_a/4)\right)^4} - 1 \qquad [2.31]$$

where y_q is quarterly in advance yield and y_a the annually in arrears yield. So, for example, if the £10 000 income in the example above was receivable in perpetuity rather than just 15 years and an investor paid £120 000 for the investment, the initial yield (y_a) is 8.3333%. But this assumes the income is paid annually in arrears. If the rent is paid quarterly in advance the yield (y_q) is 8.7861%.

Finally, let us consider the impact on valuation of income tax. When income is receivable in perpetuity income tax makes no difference to the valuation because income is perpetual and all return is on capital. Consider an investment where the net income is £10 000 per annum in perpetuity and the yield is 10%. Gross of tax valuation (present value of £10 000 in perpetuity) would be

$$£10\,000 \times \frac{1}{r} = £10\,000 \times \frac{1}{0.10} = £100\,000$$

For a net of income tax t at a rate of say 40%, the valuation would be

$$£10\,000(1-t) \times \frac{1}{r(1-t)} = £6000 \times \frac{1}{0.06} = £100\,000$$

If the income is terminable, for example, a leasehold property investment, then there is an impact on value. Consider profit rent of £10 000 receivable for 15 years on a 10% gross yield. Gross of tax the valuation (present value of £10 000 per annum for 15 years) would be:

$$\pounds 10\,000 \times \frac{1-(1+10)^{-15}}{0.10} = \pounds 10\,000 \times 7.6061 = \pounds 76\,061$$

But for a net of tax t, at 40% again, the valuation would be:

$$\pounds 10\,000(1-t) \times \frac{1-[1+r(1-t)]^{-15}}{r(1-t)} = \pounds 6\,000 \times \frac{1-[1+0.06]^{15}}{0.06} = \pounds 58\,273$$

Figure 2.5 illustrates this impact on capital value of paying tax on income received.

All of the formulae discussed in this section can, of course, be reproduced on a spreadsheet and Table 2.6 illustrates how they might be input. You may be pleased and somewhat relieved to know that valuation software is available commercially to help automate much of the mathematical calculations that we have explored so far. Your understanding of the underlying principles is essential, however, if you are going to be able to spot when such software presents you with erroneous output!

2.4.2 Yields and rates of return

It is easy to get confused by the many terms that are used in financial mathematics. As a simple rule of thumb, the term 'yield' is generally used to describe the return that an investment provides or yields; it is the ratio of annual income to value or price, whereas as the rate of 'return' refers to the desired return (on capital) that an investor would like. Using this terminology simple investment decision rules can be devised that compare the yield from an investment with the investor's required return; if the yield is below the required return then an investment looks bad.

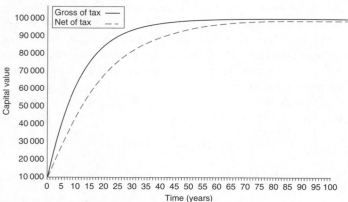

Figure 2.5 Gross and net of tax values.

Table 2.6 Valuation formulae in spreadsheet form.

Input variables	
Yield/rate of return (annually in arrears)	B4
Number of years	B6
Formulae	
FV £1	$= (1+B4)\wedge B6$
PV £1	$= 1/(1+B4)\wedge B6$
FV £1 pa	$= (1+B4)\wedge B6{-}1)/B4$
Annual sinking fund	$= B4/((1+B4)\wedge B6{-}1)$
Annuity £1 will purchase	$= B4/(1{-}(1/(1+B4)\wedge B6))$
PV £1 pa (YP) (single rate)	$= (1{-}(1/(1+B4)\wedge B6))/B4$
PV £1 pa (YP) in perpetuity	$= 1/B4$
True equivalent yield (quarterly in advance)	$= 1/(1{-}B4/4)\wedge 4{-}1$

Bond yields are regarded as fundamental benchmarks for the various financial markets and their movements set rate levels throughout money and capital markets. For example, the property development sector employs short- and medium-term finance, the cost of which significantly affects a project's economic feasibility (Appraisal Institute, 2001). Perhaps the most widely known rate of return is the one that the Bank of England Monetary Policy Committee reviews each month; the bank base rate or, as it is more generally known, the interest rate.

Having made this simple distinction between yields and rates of return we now need to complicate matters by explaining some of the other terms that are commonly used. As a way of imposing some sort of logic these terms will be described under the headings of 'yields' and 'rates of return' although, in real life it is not quite so straightforward.

2.4.2.1 Yields

The purchaser of a property investment is acquiring the right to receive income in the form of rent from an occupying tenant or tenants. The price is usually paid at the time of acquisition and, as stated above, the yield describes the ratio of annual income to price paid. For example, consider the freehold interest in a shop purchased for £375 000 and subsequently let at a rent of £30 000 pa. Given that this is a freehold interest we can assume that this income is receivable in perpetuity, thus, using Equation 2.22, the property produces a yield of 8%, that is, £30 000 ÷ £375 000 = 8%. The more precise term for this yield is the **income yield** as it measures the current income return. The income yield can be calculated at any time during the life of an investment. The **initial yield** is a particular type of income yield and is the net income received in the first year divided by purchase price, and is a common market measure of investment performance. The fact that initial yields from similar types of property investment are similar demonstrates that they typically sell for a certain multiplier of income. For example, if a shop is recently let at market rent of £100 000 pa and the investment was purchased for £1 667 000 the initial yield is £100 000 divided by £1 667 000, that is, 6%.

A good quality investment (a new building let to a large business perhaps) has a low yield as investors bid up the price in relation to income level. But supply of and demand for a particular investment (and hence the price paid) is affected by many other characteristics of the investment in addition to current income level. These were discussed in Section 1.3.4 and include expectations of income and capital growth and perceived risk which are, in turn, determined by the range of factors that we have already encountered in Section 2.3 of this chapter such as location, age, use, condition of the property, the financial standing of the tenant, and so on. Attention would also be paid to the returns obtainable from other investments and, of these, government bonds often form an important reference point. We consider how these factors might be expressed mathematically when we discuss how a rate of return might be derived below. As far as property investments are concerned the initial yield is usually lower than the rate of return that will actually be obtained over the life of the investment because the investor is paying a price that assumes the rent and capital value will appreciate over the holding period – the purchaser of a property investment would expect the rent paid by a tenant and the capital value of the property to increase over time. If income and capital value are expected to increase sufficiently, investors may be willing to accept an initial yield below what they could achieve from a risk-free, non-growth investment. If this should be the case, the difference between an initial yield of say 6% from a property investment and, say, 7% from a risk-free investment such as government bonds, is known as the **reverse yield gap** and is counter-intuitive to the notion that investors require a higher return for higher risk. The gap must be made good through growth.

In the absence of directly comparable exchange prices valuers use the initial yield as a unit of comparison for investment valuation. It is the rate at which rent (derived in the occupier market) is capitalised in the investor market (Ball *et al.*, 1998). Baum and Crosby (1995) argue that because the market for a particular type of investment usually generates comparable price and income information this leads to widespread use of initial yield as a market comparison metric. In doing so the term **all-risks yield (ARY)** is given to the unit of comparison used to value property investments. The ARY is usually derived by analysing the initial yields from recent comparable property investment transactions. When using the ARY to value a property, adjustments are made to initial yields in recent comparable transactions to reflect any differences between them and the property being valued, such as those described in the preceding paragraph. For example, the higher the expectation of future income and/or capital growth the more an investor is prepared to pay for the investment *ceteris paribus* and, as a consequence, the initial yield that an investor is prepared to accept will be lower. Yields tend to be comparable for similar property investments in similar locations because their income growth prospects and risk to capital and income will tend to be similar.

For property investments where the rent passing is below the market rent but is likely to revert to market rent in the future, the **reversionary yield** refers to the ratio between the reversionary market rent and the capital value. When valuing reversionary property investments, which we will look at in detail in Chapter 3, valuers tend to apply a slightly higher yield to the reversionary income stream to reflect perceived risk inherent in a future and slightly uncertain income. The **equivalent yield** is an overall yield that can be used to capitalise both the current and reversionary incomes. Its derivation is not easy and we will leave the detail until the next chapter; the best approach is by iteration on a spreadsheet. Nowadays reversions to a higher rent usually take place within a 5-year period owing to the frequency with which rent reviews occur and, unless the reversion is many years away or the term income is very low compared to the reversionary income, the equivalent yield will be very close to the ARY. It is important to note that the equivalent yield, as with the ARY, is a growth-implicit yield, and therefore any future growth in the income stream is implied by the choice of the yield.

Figure 2.6 shows IPD data on yield levels across market sectors between 1981 and 2005. Focusing on the equivalent yields for the main sectors, it can be seen that yields on industrial property investments are higher than on retail and office investments. What this shows is that investors pay a lower price for each unit of rent from industrial property than for shops and offices. They do this because they perceive industrial property to be more risky. It is also possible to see how the initial yield from all property is lower than the equivalent yield, revealing an expectation of reversionary growth.

Figure 2.7 reveals the economic impact of rising inflation and interest rates in the late 1980s on retail sales and, after a time-lag, how this impacted retail equivalent yields.

2.4.2.2   Rates of Return

The rate of return that is expected from a property investment is often referred to as the **target rate of return (TRR)** and also as the **discount rate** because it is the rate used in the PV £1 pa formula to discount future income to a present capital value. Rather confusingly, the TRR is also referred to as

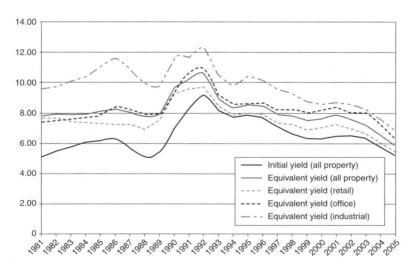

Figure 2.6   Yields from the main property market sectors (IPD UK Property Digest).

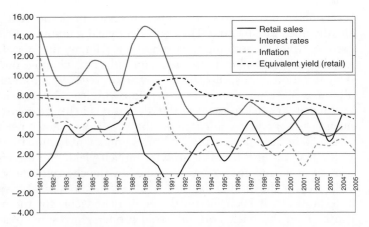

Figure 2.7 Movement in retail equivalent yields in response to economic shifts (IPD UK Property Digest).

an **equated yield**. The TRR depends on a range of factors and these, along with supply-side factors, determine the price that will be paid and the resultant initial yield that will be obtained. We have already listed some of these factors in Section 1.3.3 of Chapter 1 and in Section 2.3 of this Chapter but we need to consolidate them if we are going to handle them mathematically in a rate of return. Fisher (1930) argued that the total return expected from an investment may be made up of three economic variables. First, the prevailing market rate of interest, as this determines the cost of acquiring the capital to invest and sets a minimum level of return that could be obtained if we simply put the funds into a savings account – a measure of opportunity cost or loss of **liquidity**. Second, the anticipated rate of inflation; if inflation is expected to increase then the target rate should increase to compensate. Third, a premium could be added to cover risk. According to the Appraisal Institute (2001), risk is the chance of incurring a financial loss and the uncertainty of realising projected future benefits. Investors expect a reward for taking risk; the greater the perceived risk the greater the return necessary to attract investment. Risk may be categorised as market risk or as property risk. Market risk refers to events that might affect the return on all property investments such as shifts in supply and demand, unexpected inflation, availability and cost of equity and debt finance, liquidity problems and returns available from other types of investment. An additional premium might be added to reflect property-specific risks associated with the type of tenant (breaches of lease terms, for example), the sector (industrial more risky than retail, for example), the location and physical condition of the property and how this might have an impact on depreciation of capital and rental value and management costs. The amount added to the discount rate as a **risk premium** will vary for each investor and each investment, and each type of risk can influence separately or in combination, so things can get pretty complicated. It is important to keep sight of the fact that a *market* value is being estimated; so factors considered to be more investor-orientated than market-orientated should be considered in an appraisal context rather than a market valuation (see Chapter 7).

Obtaining rates to reflect these three components of total return allowed Fisher (1930) to construct an equation so that the target rate of return r required by an investor may be expressed as

$$r = (1+i)(1+d)(1+RP) - 1 \qquad [2.32]$$

where i is the prevailing interest rate, d is the rate of inflation and RP is the risk premium.

As noted in Chapter 1, government bonds are a risk-free investment (except for the risk of *un*expected inflation) but are inflation-prone so investors in bonds will expect a return that adequately compensates them in terms of opportunity cost of capital and expected inflation. The rate of return that investors expect from short- and medium-dated government bonds provides a useful combined measure of i and d. It is worth pointing out at this stage an inconsistency in the terminology: the return obtained from bonds includes income flow to its maturity (return *on* capital) and a return *of* capital; it is the **internal rate of return**, that is, the rate which discounts future cash-flows to their net present value and equates this figure to the market price of the bond. But this *rate of return* is referred to as the *gross redemption yield*, so the concept of a yield in the property market is different to that used in the bond markets (Sayce *et al.*, 2006). Regardless of the terminology, the gross redemption yield or internal rate of return on short- and medium-dated government bonds is used as a benchmark risk-free rate on which to build target rates of return for other types of investment. As far as property investments are concerned the current tendency is to base the risk-free rate on long-dated gilt yields because property is regarded as a long-term investment asset but, as lease lengths shorten, it may be more appropriate to consider using medium-term gilt yields. It is also important to remember that there are factors that affect the return on gilts in one way and property returns in another. For example, if long-dated gilts increase by 2% due to increased government borrowing, then the valuer might be justified in increasing property yields too but if it was because of an expectation of higher inflation then, as property is regarded as an inflation hedge and rents might be expected to increase, property yields might be expected to remain unchanged (Sayce *et al.*, 2006).

To recap, we can say that the minimum return on invested capital is usually referred to as the risk-free rate RFR and is indicated by the rate of return on government bonds (Appraisal Institute, 2001). Mathematically the RFR required from government bonds may be expressed as

$$RFR = (1+i)(1+d) - 1 \qquad [2.33]$$

So the RFR can now be inserted into Equation 2.32 as follows:

$$r = (1+RFR)(1+RP) - 1 \qquad [2.34]$$

And, as Baum and Crosby (1995) note, an approximation of this is given by

$$r = RFR + RP \qquad [2.35]$$

Often an investor's choice of target rate of return will be affected by the actual returns that have been achieved within the sector or as revealed in indices such as the Investment Property Databank (IPD) index. The important point to remember is that if the target rate is set too high good investments will be rejected, if it is set too low uneconomic investments will be accepted.

2.4.2.3   Yields and rates of return

Gordon (1958) argued that the initial yield y from an investment can be related to the target rate of return r in terms of the growth in net income that is anticipated:

$$y = r - g \qquad [2.36]$$

So, combining Fisher and Gordon

$$y = \text{RFR} + \text{RP} - g \qquad [2.37]$$

Ball *et al*. (1998) extend this model to include an annual rate of property depreciation

$$y = \text{RFR} + \text{RP} - g + d \qquad [2.38]$$

where g is the expected average annual income growth in perpetuity and d is the expected average annual depreciation rate in perpetuity.

So y can be determined using valuation rules to adjust market-derived initial yields to an ARY as described in the 'yields' section or by applying financial economic principles to derive a TRR based bond rates plus a risk premium less growth. Although the construction of a target rate can be helpful in understanding these components it should not be considered as a replacement means of developing a market discount rate for use in valuation. Analysis of yields obtained from comparable investments is the best way to estimate a market discount rate for a particular property investment. But, as we shall see in Chapter 6, deriving a target rate of return from financial economic principles as an aid to valuation has many merits in certain situations.

Key points

- Commercial property ownership and occupation are often separate interests and the capital amount paid for a property is therefore a function of its income-producing potential.
- Even when occupiers buy property for their own occupation they must consider the opportunity cost of the capital and the financial return the asset may produce. With such properties, valuation is the estimation of the future financial benefits derived from the ownership expressed in terms of their present value.
- The valuer needs to be able to estimate future net benefits and discount them at a suitable rate to calculate present value.
- The mathematical content of valuation is often very simple; difficulties arise when attempting to quantify and adjust for differences between properties.
- The terminology surrounding yields and rates of return is confusing. Table 2.7 attempts to clarify the situation.

Table 2.7 Yields and return measures in the main investment markets.

	Income return	Total return
Bonds	Income yield	Gross redemption yield (for a undated bond this is mathematically the same as the income yield)
Equities	Dividend yield	Holding period return
Property	Initial yield	Target rate of return or equated yield

Source: Ball *et al.* (1998).

2.5   Valuation process

After that foray into the world of financial mathematics that underpins valuation methods, it is perhaps timely to take a deep breath and consider, in the final section of this chapter, the bigger picture – the valuation process as a whole. This will establish the context for the valuation methods that are considered in the next chapter. Fundamentally valuation methods and techniques are broadly similar throughout the world. The IVSC formulates and publishes IVS, reveals differences in the drafting and application of national standards and seeks to harmonise them. The reason for doing this is to facilitate cross-border property transactions and promote transparency of property markets (IVSC, 2005).

In the UK, valuation procedures are regulated to a large extent by the Royal Institution of Chartered Surveyors (RICS). The RICS ensures accountability, establishes education and training requirements, sets standards and imposes disciplinary procedures on its members. As far as valuation is concerned, the key set of standards are contained within the RICS Appraisal and Valuation Standards manual (RICS, 2003), commonly referred to as the 'Red Book'. The Standards regulate valuation process rather than the methods employed and it does this by promoting the use of consistent definitions, bases of valuation and reporting standards. The Standards also provide a framework for certain statutory valuations and regulate procedural protocols agreed with client bodies such as the Council of Mortgage Lenders and the British Bankers Association. Most valuations undertaken in the UK are subject to Red Book regulations, which stipulate that they must be prepared or supervised by an appropriately qualified valuer with sufficient market knowledge, skills and competence to undertake the valuation, and that valuers act with independence, integrity and objectivity. Also the valuer

> must have sufficient current local, national and international (as appropriate) knowledge of the particular market and skills and understanding necessary to undertake the valuation competently.   (RICS, 2003)

Valuations that are not subject to Red Book regulations include those provided as part of advice during the course of litigation or as an expert witness before a court, tribunal or committee; those provided during arbitrations and similar disputes with surveyors acting as arbitrators, independent experts or mediators; those provided during negotiations; internal valuations by internal valuers solely for use by their organisation and those provided during certain agency work.

Procedural tasks associated with a typical valuation are listed in Table 2.8 and include; confirming the valuation instruction, agreeing terms of engagement (assumptions under which the valuation is conducted), inspecting the property, gathering and analysing comparable evidence, performing the valuation itself and producing the report. Each of these tasks is considered in more detail below.

Table 2.8   Procedural tasks associated with a typical valuation.

Preliminary questions:
  Determine purpose of valuation
  Ensure valuer is suitably qualified and there is no conflict of interest that cannot be
    managed
  Determine whether the valuation is exempt from standards, whether there are any
  UK Practice Statements that apply and whether it is a Regulated Purpose Valuation
  (valuation for financial statements, listing particulars, takeovers, collective investment
  schemes, unregulated trusts, pension schemes and insurance companies)
Terms of engagement
  Identify client, purpose and subject of valuation, interest to be valued, type of property,
    and so on
  Basis, date and currency of valuation
  Status of valuer (internal, external, independent, any managed conflicts of interest)
  Source and nature of information relied upon, extent of investigations and assumptions,
    reservations, and so on
  Any consent to or restrictions on publication
  Any limits or exclusions of liability to parties other than client
  Confirmation that valuation will be undertaken in accordance with standards
  Fee basis
  Availability of complaints handling procedure
Valuation preparation
  Full or limited inspection
  Inspections
  Verification of information
  Discussions with client before draft report
  Resolution of any reservations in initial terms of engagement
  Prepare and finalise valuation
Reporting
  Identify client
  Purpose and subject of valuation and interest to be valued, type of property, and so on
  Basis, date and currency of valuation
  Status of valuer
  Source and nature of information relied upon, extent of investigations and assumptions,
    reservations, and so on
  Consent to or restrictions on publication
  Limits or exclusions of liability
  Statement of valuation approach
  Confirmation that valuation accords with standards
  Valuation (figures and words)
  Signature and date

Confirmation of valuation instruction should identify the client, the physical extent of the property and the legal interest to be valued, details and status of the valuer (including affiliation, experience and qualifications), the purpose, basis, date and reason for the valuation, scope of information supplied by the client, the extent of the inspection (if any) that will be undertaken and any caveats that need to be noted. The confirmation should also disclose any previous involvement that the valuer may have had with either the property to be valued or the client commissioning the valuation. This is required to reduce the potential for conflicts of interest. Cherry (2006) lists some of the more likely conflicts of interest that may arise:

- the valuer acts for both buyer and seller of a property in the same transaction;
- valuing for a lender where advice is being provided to the borrower;
- valuing a property previously valued for another client;
- valuing both parties' interests in a leasehold transaction.

Should such a conflict arise, the valuer must decide whether to accept the instruction depending on the specific circumstances. If the instruction is accepted the valuer must

- disclose to the client(s) the possibility and nature of the conflict, the circumstances surrounding it and any other relevant facts;
- advise the client(s) in writing to seek independent advice on the conflict;
- inform client(s) in writing that the member or member's firm is not prepared to accept the instruction unless either the client(s) request(s) the member to do so unconditionally or it is subject to specified conditions that the member has put in place as well as arrangements for handling the conflict, which the client has in writing approved as acceptable, that is, Chinese Walls (Cherry, 2006).

In addition, any assumptions, reservations, special instructions or departures, consent to or restrictions on publication and any limits or exclusion of liability to parties other than client should be noted. The fee basis and complaints handling procedure or reference thereto will also be set out.

An early task is to determine the subject matter of the valuation by way of an inspection. This draws attention to the characteristics of the locality (including the availability of infrastructure communications and other facilities that affect value) and the physical nature of the property (including dimensions and areas of land and buildings, age and construction of buildings, use(s) of land and buildings, description of accommodation, installations, amenities, services, fixtures, fittings, improvements, any plant and machinery that would normally form an integral part of the building). Floor areas are calculated in accordance with the RICS Code of Measuring Practice (see Section 2.5.2) but if drawings are supplied they must be sample-checked on site. Plant and machinery items that would normally be passed with the property are included in the valuation. Trade fixtures and fittings are normally excluded from a valuation unless the property is being valued as part of an operational entity. When valuing a standing property, particularly leasehold interests, it is essential that running costs and liability for them are identified. When valuing a development property the valuation should reflect the stage of construction that has been reached. It is acceptable to revalue a property without inspection so long as the client has confirmed that no material changes to the property or area have occurred, and subject to this assumption. Market practice suggests an inspection every 3 years for investment properties but this will vary (Cherry, 2006). Client information that is not in the public domain and that is obtained while valuing a property must be treated confidentially.

The assessment of physical factors does not involve a structural survey but a record of the repair and condition of the premises, including the decorative order, whether the property has been adequately maintained and any basic defects. The nature of the legal interest must also be ascertained including details of any leases or sub-leases, easements and other legal rights, restrictions on, say, use or further development and any improvements that may have been made to the premises by a tenant. Planning and environmental issues such as abnormal ground conditions, historic mining or quarrying, coastal erosion, flood risks, proximity of high-voltage electrical equipment, contamination (potentially hazardous or harmful substances in the land or buildings), hazardous materials (potentially harmful material that has not yet contaminated land or buildings) and deleterious materials (building materials that degrade with age, causing structural problems) must also be raised and are of paramount importance if the property is to be (re)developed, as are potential alternative uses. Because of the complexity and diversity of property interests, apparently minor legal or physical details can have a significant effect on value, such as an overly restrictive user clause in the lease or non-compliance with a fire regulation. Refer to Appendix 2A (see Appendix 2A at www.blackwellpublishing.com/wyatt) for a typical inspection checklist.

It is important to identify any potential comparable evidence, noting rents and prices achieved together with physical, legal and spatial attributes of the properties. Useful information can be obtained from online databases such as Estates Gazette Interactive (www.egi.co.uk)and FOCUS (www.focusnet. co.uk) but there is no substitute for market knowledge obtained either directly through previous valuations, through colleagues working in other departments or from contacts in other firms. The valuation itself should take account of the age, type, size, aspect, amenities, fixtures and features of the property, the tenure of the legal interest, and other significant environmental factors within the locality, the apparent general state of and liability for repair, the construction and apparent major defects, liability to subsidence, flooding and/or other risks. Particular care is needed when valuing buildings of non-traditional construction.

It is entirely appropriate to make certain assumptions when valuing a property so long as they are agreed with the client beforehand. Typical valuation assumptions are; that the property is in good condition, services are operational, there are no deleterious materials, structural defects or hazardous materials, and statutory requirements relating to construction have been met. With regard to the site it is usually assumed that it is capable of development or redevelopment with no unusual costs, that there are no archaeological remains and there is no pollution, contamination or risk of flooding. Searches of the Land Register (www.landreg.gov.uk) to verify ownership and the Local Land Charges register at the local authority to check any legal rights over the land are not normally undertaken and the valuer relies on information provided by the client, nor are detailed enquiries about the financial status of any tenant made. Informal enquiries are usually made to the local planning authority on publicly available information but it is normally assumed that no compulsory purchase powers are proposed.

As a minimum, the valuation report should identify the client, the purpose and subject of the valuation, the legal interest that has been valued and the basis on which the valuation was conducted. The dates of the inspection, the valuation and the report should be recorded together with any assumptions, conditions (such as the handling of taxation, expenses, transaction costs, goodwill, fixtures and fittings), reservations, special instructions and departures. The status of the valuer and disclosure of any previous involvement, extent of investigations and nature and source of information relied upon should also be included. The valuation amount (and the currency in which it is expressed) should be reported together with consent to or restrictions on publication, any limits or exclusion of liability to parties other than client, confirmation that valuation was undertaken in accordance with the Red Book, the basis on which the fee will be calculated, complaints handling procedure or reference thereto and the signature of valuer. When reporting the value of a portfolio of properties, if it is suspected that the value of the portfolio as a whole is different from the sum of individual property values then this should be mentioned in the report. Also, negative values must be reported separately. Negative values can occur in the case of a freehold interest where expenditure is greater than rental income or, in the case of a leasehold interest, where the rent paid is greater than the market rent or rent received (Cherry, 2006). A specimen valuation report can be seen in Appendix 2B (see Appendix 2B at www.blackwellpublishing.com/wyatt).

2.5.1 Specific valuation standards

Valuations for certain purposes are subject to additional, specific standards. In the UK the bases for valuations that are to be included in financial statements are set out in the Red Book and these are discussed in Chapter 4. Valuations may also be required for other regulated purposes. These include stock market listing particulars, takeover and merger information, for collective investment schemes, unregulated property unit trusts, financial statements of pension schemes and solvency margin calculations on insurance company assets. In the overwhelming majority of cases market value is the basis of valuation that should be employed but the Red Book also contains information on the relevant codes and requirements that must be adhered to when undertaking valuations for these purposes. In particular, where a valuer's firm has received an introductory fee or negotiated the acquisition of one or more properties for which the same client now requires a regulated purpose valuation within one year, the valuer must decline unless another firm has provided a valuation in between. Valuations for commercial secured lending are undertaken in accordance with the protocol agreed between the RICS and the British Bankers Association, which requires detailed commentary on market trends and risks and extends the general rule on disclosing conflicts to disclosure of past involvement too. This protocol will be described in more detail in Chapter 4.

2.5.2   Measurement

Given that property size is a key determinant of value, any variation in the way measurements are taken will clearly lead to valuation variance. Consistent measurement techniques are therefore required. This is achieved by making use of the RICS Code of Measuring Practice (RICS, 2001) that sets out recommended practice for the measurement of land and property.

Gross external area (GEA) is the area of a building measured externally at each floor level and includes outbuildings (which share at least one wall with the main building), loading bays and pavement vaults but excludes external open-sided balconies, covered ways and fire escapes, canopies, open vehicle parking areas, roof terraces and similar appendages. GEA is the basis of measurement for planning applications and approvals as it helps determine, site coverage and plot ratio (the ratio between GEA and site area).

Gross internal area (GIA) is the area of a building measured to the internal face of the perimeter walls at each floor level and includes loading bays and pavement vaults but excludes perimeter wall thicknesses and external projections, external open-sided balconies, covered ways and fire escapes, canopies, voids over or under structural, raked or stepped floors. GIA is a recognised method of measurement for calculating building costs and is a basis of measurement for the marketing and valuation of industrial buildings (including ancillary offices), warehouses, retail warehouses, department stores, variety stores and food superstores.

Net internal area (NIA) is the usable area within a building measured to the internal face of the perimeter walls at each floor level and includes pavement vaults and areas severed by internal non-structural walls and demountable partitions, provided the area beyond is not used in common, but excludes

- parts of entrance halls, atria, landings and balconies used in common;
- toilets, toilet lobbies, bathrooms, cleaners' rooms;
- lift rooms, plant rooms, tank rooms (other than those of a trade process nature), fuel stores;
- stairwells, lift-wells and permanent lift lobbies;
- corridors and other circulation areas which are used in common with other occupiers or are of a permanent essential nature (e.g. fire corridors, smoke lobbies, etc.);

Chapter 2

- areas under the control of service or other external authorities including meter cupboards and statutory service supply points;
- internal structural walls, walls enclosing excluded areas, columns, piers, chimney breasts, other projections, vertical ducts;
- the space occupied by permanent and continuous air-conditioning heating or cooling apparatus, and ducting in so far as the space it occupies is rendered substantially unusable;
- areas with headroom of less than 1.5 m;
- areas rendered substantially unusable by virtue of having a dimension between opposite faces of less than 0.25 m;
- vehicle parking areas (the number and type of spaces should be noted though).

NIA is the basis of measurement for the valuation of business uses, offices and shops.

Other technical definitions used in the measurement of buildings for valuation purposes include the following:

- Clear internal height: the height between the structural floor surface and the underside of the lowest point of the structural ceiling or roof. This dimension is used in the measurement of industrial and warehouse buildings.
- Cubic content: the product of the GIA and the clear internal height, used in the measurement of warehouses.
- Eaves height: internal eaves height is the height between the floor surface and the underside of the roof covering, supporting purlins or underlining (whichever is lower) at the eaves on the internal wall face. External eaves height is the height between the ground surface and the exterior of the roof covering at the eaves on the external wall face, ignoring any parapet.

Shops present particular measurement issues. The retail area of a shop is its NIA and includes ancillary accommodation formed by non-structural partitions and recessed and arcaded areas of shops created by the location and design of the window display frontage. The gross frontage of a shop is the overall external measurement in a straight line across the front of the building, from the outside of external walls or from the centre line of party walls. The net frontage is the overall external frontage on the shop line measured between the internal face of the external walls, or the internal face of support columns including the display window frame and shop entrance but excluding recesses, doorways or access to other accommodation.

A technique known as 'zoning' is used to divide up the sales area of standard shop units. It is a means of reflecting the fact that the trading area nearest to the front of the shop is most valuable. The ground floor sales area is divided into zones parallel to the frontage and to a depth of 6.1 m (20 ft). Zone A is always at the front and a maximum of three zones is usual with a 'remainder' area encompassing all that is left over. Figure 2.8 illustrates how a typical shop might be zoned. In Scotland and in parts of Oxford Street and Regent Street the zones are 12 m (30 ft) deep. We shall see in Chapter 3 how these zones are used to place more value on space at the front of the shop.

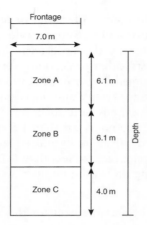

Figure 2.8 Zoning a shop.

Many properties used for leisure are valued having regard to trading potential. In these circumstances, the area of the premises may not be a factor used directly in the assessment of value. There are, however, occasions where the value is assessed or the price paid is analysed by reference to area and it is recommended that GIA is used for these types of properties (RICS, 2001).

In practice, most measuring up is undertaken using metric units but areas and rents per unit of area are often quoted and advertised in imperial units. This rather confusing and sometimes error-inducing situation has arisen because most surveyors find the calculation of areas and volumes much easier to perform in metres, centimetres and millimetres than they do in feet and inches. That said, the outcome of the calculations is an area of square metres or a rent per square metre and, for some reason, these metrics are harder to envisage spatially than square feet or a rent per square foot. Maybe it is because the imperial unit is smaller – a square foot of office space is sufficient room for a waste paper basket – that makes it easier to comprehend. After all, it is always amusing to know that office occupiers in the West End of London are paying up to £100 each year to place a litter bin on the floor!

Key points

- Valuation procedures are regulated in the UK at the national and international level by a long-established set of standards. These standards are continuously monitored by professional bodies and are revised on a regular basis. It is essential therefore that valuers keep themselves up to date.
- The valuation standards do not concern themselves with methods but regulate the procedures surrounding the initial instruction, terms of engagement, valuation preparation and reporting. Specific valuation standards regulate certain types of valuations.
- Accurate measurement of a property is fundamental to valuation and the RICS Code of Measuring Practice (RICS, 2001) provides detailed guidance on accepted de facto practice for measuring commercial premises.

Notes

1. In 1776 Smith (1723–1790) published 'Inquiry into the Nature and Causes of the Wealth of Nations' that helped create the academic discipline of economics.
2. To avoid confusion, adjectives are often added to describe value (market value, existing use value, investment value, rateable value, and so on) but market value is the focus of most valuations.

References

Adair, A. and McGreal, S. (1987) The application of multiple regression analysis to valuation, *Journal of Valuation*, 6, 57–67.

Adair, A., Berry, J. and McGreal, S. (1996) Hedonic modelling, housing submarkets and residential valuation, *Journal of Property Research*, 13, 67–83.

Appraisal Institute (2001) *The Appraisal of Real Estate*, 12th edition, The Appraisal Institute, Chicago, IL, USA.

Ball, M., Lizieri, C. and MacGregor, B. (1998) *The Economics of Commercial Property Markets*, Routledge, London, UK.

Baum, A. and Crosby, N. (1995) *Property Investment Appraisal*, 2nd edn, Routledge, London, UK.

Card, R., Murdoch, J. and Murdoch, S. (2003) *Law for Estate Management Students*, 6th edn, Oxford University Press, Oxford, UK.

Cherry, A. (2006) *A Valuer's Guide to the Red Book*, RICS Books, London, UK.

Fisher, I. (1930) *The Theory of Interest*, Macmillan, New York, USA.

Fraser, W. (1993) *Principles of Property Investment and Pricing*, 2nd edition, Macmillan, Basingstoke, Hampshire, UK.

Gordon, M. (1958) *The investment, financing and valuation of the corporation*, R. D. Irwin, Homewood, IL, USA.

IPF (2005) *Understanding Commercial Property Investment: A Guide for Financial Advisers*, 2005 edition, Investment Property Forum, London.

IVSC (2005) *International Valuation Standards*, 7th edn, International Valuation Standards Committee, London, UK.

RICS (2001) *Code of Measuring Practice – A Guide for Surveyors and Valuers*, 5th edition, RICS Books, London, UK.

RICS (2003) *RICS Appraisal and Valuation Standards*, 5th edition (as amended), Royal Institution of Chartered Surveyors, RICS Business Services Ltd, Coventry, UK.

Mill, J. S. (1909) *Principles of political economy*, Augustus M Kelly, Fairfield, NJ, USA.

Rees, W. and Hayward, R. (2000) *Valuation: Principles into Practice*, 5th edn, Estates Gazette, London.

Sayce, S., Smith, J., Cooper, R. and Venmore-Rowland, P. (2006) *Real Estate Appraisal: From Value to Worth*, Blackwell Publishers, Oxford, UK.

Chapter 2

Chapter 3
Valuation Methods

3.1 Introduction

There are three internationally recognised methods of property valuation and they are all based on the principle of market comparison. They are (1) sales comparison; (2) income capitalisation; and (3) replacement cost. Using the sales comparison method, the valuer examines the recent sales of comparable properties and uses this market intelligence to help estimate a value. Income capitalisation considers the net income that a property might generate, typically in the form of rent, and this income is capitalised using an appropriate yield (see Section 3.3) or by discounting the projected cash-flow at a suitable target rate of return (see Chapter 5). Both the rent and yield will be estimated using comparable evidence. The replacement-cost method considers the possibility that, as a substitute for the purchase of a given property, one could construct another property that is either a replica of the original or could offer comparable utility. In practice, the approach also involves an estimate of depreciation for older or less functional properties where the estimated cost of a new replacement is likely to exceed the price that would (hypothetically) be paid for the subject property (IVSC, 2005). Building costs, depreciation rates and land values are all estimated by referring to comparable evidence.

In the UK, these three internationally recognised methods are supplemented by two more methods, the profits method and the residual method, but, again, it should be pointed out that in applying all these methods the principle of comparison is fundamental. The profits method is used to value specialised properties that are usually sold as operational entities such as pubs, clubs, hotels and petrol stations. With non-specialised property (shops, offices, factories, warehouses, etc.) there is normally sufficient trading activity and homogeneity of asset within each market sector to observe price levels without having to interpret underlying economic fundamentals of the business – price is determined by comparison. But specialised properties are more heterogeneous and there are fewer transactions to call upon for comparison,

Table 3.1 Valuation methods

	Development	Occupation	Investment
Standard property	Residual method	Investment (Income Capitalisation) method using an estimated imputed rent	Investment (Income Capitalisation) method using an actual or estimated rental income
Specialised property – trade-related	Residual method	Profits method	Profits method
Specialised property – no market	Cost method (no development value)	Cost method	Cost method

so use of the comparison method is more difficult. Therefore the valuer needs to use a method that addresses the underlying fundamentals of that property so that its value can be determined by reference to its wealth-producing qualities – its contribution to business profit and analysis of the property as a business asset. In the absence of sufficient trading activity and in circumstances where it is not possible to determine the financial contribution that the property makes to the business, the replacement cost will become the principal form of valuation. The residual method is used to value land for development purposes and usually takes the form of a valuation of the completed development using the income capitalisation method from which all costs of the development are then deducted, leaving a residual land value. The method is a bit like an investment valuation and replacement (development in this case) cost valuation rolled into one. The choice of method depends on the purpose of the valuation and the type of property that is to be valued, and an attempt at categorising these is made in Table 3.1.

3.2   Comparison method

The principle of comparison is based on the economic concept of substitution- that a knowledgeable and prudent person would not pay more for a property than the cost of acquiring an equally satisfactory substitute. This implies that, within a suitable time frame, the values of properties that are considered to be close substitutes in terms of location, utility and desirability will tend to be similar, and the lowest price of the best alternative tends to establish market value. The principle of comparison underpins all valuation methods but it is also a valuation method in its own right. A property may be valued by comparing it to similar properties for which recent price information is available. Comparable properties are selected on the basis of their **elements of comparison** which include the key transaction information such as the date, price paid, market rent (MR) and yield, as well as the determinants of value that were described in Chapter 2 such as size, location, use, age, condition and tenure. Value-significant differences between each comparable and the subject property must be reconciled before price information from the former provide reliable evidence of the value of the latter. This reconciliation can be undertaken qualitatively by the valuer, who would have experience and knowledge of the local market, or a quantitative technique can be used to weigh comparable properties, isolate differences in the elements, quantify these differences and adjust the values accordingly. Typically, a combination of qualitative and quantitative approaches would be employed. Procedurally, the comparison method involves the following steps:

- Collect evidence of transactions and eliminate those not conducted at **arm's length** (between parent and subsidiary companies, for example).
- Determine which transactions are suitable for adjustment having regard to their comparability with the subject property. The geographic extent from which comparables can be selected depends on the type of property and the state of the market. Comparables yet to transact or beyond a suitable time-frame should be used with caution (Appraisal Institute, 2001).
- Select the elements of comparison.
- Compare the transactions on the basis of these elements, and make adjustments where necessary.
- Reconcile comparison elements to provide an indication of value for the subject property (taking care to ensure that any adjustments made to the comparable evidence reflect the likely reactions of market participants).

The comparison method is predicated on comprehensive and up-to-date records of transactions and is therefore a reliable method in an active market where recent evidence is available. The method's reliability is limited when market conditions are volatile or when valuing specialised properties with less market evidence. The prices paid by owner-occupiers of commercial property will provide evidence of the capital value of freehold or long-leasehold interests and, if a sufficient quantity of such capital transactions can be obtained, this would be good comparable evidence of capital values. Purchasers of property investments usually concentrate on the property's income-producing characteristics. Therefore, rental value and yield comparisons are essential for valuing commercial property investments. The comparison method is also used to help value specialised trading property, as we shall see later in this chapter, and is useful for valuing auxiliary facilities such as car parking spaces and land use that is ancillary to other business accommodation such as storage land.

3.2.1   Sources of data

Sources of data include databases of surveying firms, data publishers and the government. Surveying firms or property consultants in the UK typically offer consultancy and agency services, and the latter can provide an up-to-date and readily available source of transaction information for valuers working in the same firm. Moreover, valuers and their agency colleagues tend to share transaction information on an informal basis, and this provides a great deal of market knowledge on which to base valuation assumptions. Much of this information is not released into the public domain at the transaction level by the surveying firms themselves. Instead they prefer to release only aggregate information. As an example of what is publicly available from property consultants, CBRE publish, each quarter, rent and yield information on the main market sectors for 11 cities across the UK. Information covers prime rent and yield estimates, stock availability, average lease length and the length of typical rent-free periods offered by landlords. Although surveying firms do not publish individual transaction details, publishers and specialist data providers such as Estates Gazette (a weekly property magazine) and FOCUS (an online information house) do compile details of individual market transactions, and Table 3.2 provides an example of market transaction information that is published in the Estates Gazette. The data are obtained from the firms involved in negotiating the agreed transaction price either on behalf of the vendor or purchaser (or landlord or tenant), or the information is gleaned from other sources where deals are reported. Unfortunately, much of the detail necessary for valuation purposes is missing, and it is nearly always necessary to contact the agent(s) involved in the transaction to request more detailed information. This is almost certainly intentional as a means of maintaining the informal network of transaction information exchange. Some surveyors specialise in auctioning commercial property, and transaction results from auctions can provide very useful information on, typically, secondary property, as it is this type of property that tends to be sold at auction. Table 3.3 provides an example of auction results published in the Estates Gazette. IPD provides aggregated information about market

Table 3.2 Example of market transactions (deals) reported in the Estates Gazette.

Office: sale	
Address	Staffordshire Technology Park
Sale price	£3.4 million
Total floor space	2 323 m^2 (25 000 ft^2)
Vendor	Gladman Developments
Vendor's agent	King Sturge
Purchaser	Stafford and Rural Homes
Notes	The building is to be used as Stafford and Rural Homes headquarters
Office: new letting	
Address	46 Colebrook Row, London N1 8AF
Rental	£400 000 pa
Total floor-space	1 672 m^2 (18 000 ft^2)
Lease terms	10-year lease
Lessor	Camden Properties
Lessor's agent	HB Surveyors & Valuers and Pilcher Hershman
Lessee	Jacques Vert
Lessee's agent	DTZ

Continued

Table 3.2   (continued)

Office: new letting

Address	18 The Martletts, Crawley, West Sussex, RH10 1ES
Rental	£156 000 pa
Total floor-space	323 m^2 (3 477 ft^2)
Lease terms	10 year lease
Lessor	Sun Life Assurance Society
Lessor's agent	Savills
Lessor's asset manager	AXA Real Estate Investment Managers
Lessee	Card Factory
Lessee's agent	Fawley Watson Booth

Factory: assignment of lease

Address	Victoria Industrial Estate, Robimatic House, 19 Victoria Gardens, Burgess Hill, East Sussex RH15 9NB
Rental	£230 000 pa
Industrial space	2 712 m^2 (29 195 ft^2)
Office space	421 m^2 (4 533 ft^2)
Total floor-space	3 133 m^2 (33 728 ft^2)
Lease terms	11-year lease
Assignor	IMI
Assignor's agent	Stiles Harold Williams (Landlord's agent: Howell Brooks)
Assignee	Time 24
Assignor's agent	Vail Williams

Source: Estates Gazette, 29 July 2006.

Table 3.3   Example of auction results.

Auction by Strettons on 10 July 2006 in London:

- 39 Balaam Street, London E13, freehold terrace shop, 350 ft^2, first floor upper part (305 ft^2), development potential, vacant, £218 000.
- Digbyland Business Centre, 71 Digby Road, London E9, freehold industrial estate, 0.27 acres, arranged as 13 industrial units, one let, 12 ground rents, £135 000.

Auction by Fox and Sons on 12 July 2006 in Eastbourne:

- Towner Art Gallery & Local History Museum, Borough Lane, Eastbourne BN20, freehold former manor house, 2 285 m^2, two floors, attic and basement, office/residential, accommodation, development potential, parking space, let/vacant, £950 000.

Source: Estates Gazette, 29 July 2006.

capital values, rental values and yields in the prime investment market, as shown in Table 3.4.

Government sources of property transaction information include the Land Registry and the Valuation Office Agency (VOA). The Land Registry reports the price paid or initial annual rent agreed on individual freeholds

Table 3.4 Capital and rental values per square metre and yield on as end 2004: by market segments.

	Weighted average capital value (£/m²)	Weighted average ERV (£/m²)	Weighted average equivalent yield (%)	Weighted average initial yield (%)
Standard shops	4 498	268	5.9	5.2
Central London	9 505	539	5.7	4.9
Rest of London	4 930	271	6.0	5.3
South East and Eastern	3 460	214	6.1	5.5
Rest of UK	4 081	234	6.0	5.3
Shopping centres	4 305	270	6.4	5.5
Intown	3 584	237	6.5	5.6
Out of town	8 883	557	5.8	5.2
Retail warehouses	3 128	189	5.8	4.9
Retail parks	3 202	187	5.7	4.8
Fashion parks	5 458	321	5.4	4.4
Other retail warehouses	2 552	160	6.1	5.2
Dept/variety Stores	2 025	131	6.2	5.2
Supermarkets	2 515	145	5.7	5.0
Other retail	2 877	200	6.4	5.8
Standard offices	2 837	217	7.2	6.4
Central London	4 503	320	6.8	6.1
Rest of London	2 307	185	7.5	6.8
Inner South Eastern	2 447	182	7.7	7.2
Outer South Eastern	1 630	139	8.3	7.1
Rest of UK	2 052	157	7.6	6.5
Office parks	2 612	187	7.6	6.4
London and South Eastern	2 726	196	7.5	6.3
Rest of UK	2 291	167	7.6	6.6
Standard industrials	697	55	7.7	6.7
London	1 045	79	7.2	6.3
Inner South Eastern	1 052	81	7.5	6.5
Outer South Eastern	678	56	7.9	6.8
Rest of UK	516	43	8.1	6.9
Distribution warehouses	754	53	7.1	6.5
Other property	1 803	128	6.4	5.0
Leisure	1 701	123	6.7	6.0

Source: IPD UK Digest (2005).

and leasehold transactions of 6 years or more, and the VOA publishes aggregate market information which can provide a useful background commentary. The VOA has also published estimates of prime retail yields in 550 shopping centres throughout England on a quarterly basis since 1994 in its Property Market Report (www.voa.gov.uk) and the figures for January 2005 are shown in Figure 3.1. The yields are based on government valuers' interpretation of transactions (rents and prices) that have taken place in the relevant market. The yields relate to a hypothetical modern standard-sized

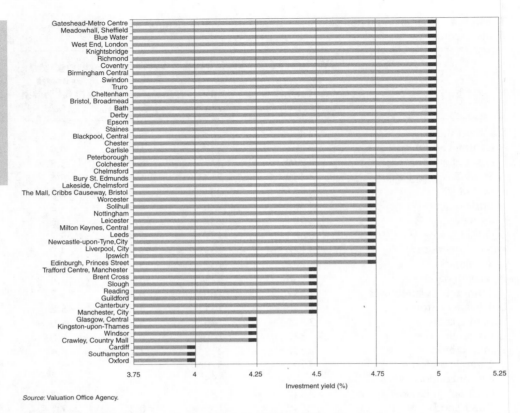

Source: Valuation Office Agency.

Figure 3.1   Retail yields, January 2006 (Valuatiion Officae Agency).

shop unit[1] in the highest rented position in the town centre (the prime yield). A comparative analysis like this, conducted on a regular basis, can give an indication of how the viability of retailing in a town centre is changing.

The VOA also report rents for the main property market sectors. These are based on opinions of valuers for properties of the types described in Table 3.5.

So far transaction information has been discussed in a rather general way, but, as can be seen from reported transactions such as those shown in Table 3.2, commercial property transactions can take several forms; they can be freehold sales (which reveal evidence of capital values and yields) or new lettings (which reveal evidence of rental values). And there are also other types of transaction that can be used to provide evidence of MR. These include renewals of existing leases, rent review settlements, assignments, arbitration awards sale and leasebacks. Sayce *et al.* (2006) provide a useful ranking of the usefulness of these sources of comparable evidence for valuation purposes: the best evidence is obtained from open market lettings that are conducted at arm's length, then lease renewals (from which the tenant can walk away although the significant costs in doing so should be borne in mind) and lastly rent reviews (where both parties have a contractual obligation under the lease). If the comparable is a lease renewal, this is usually negotiated by professionals and agreed on similar terms to the previous

Table 3.5 VOA property market information, property descriptions.

Shops
(a) Shops in prime positions in principal shopping centres
(b) Shops in good secondary off peak positions in principal shopping centres
(c) Modern, purpose built, non-food warehouse units of approximately
     2500–5000 m² in edge-of-town locations with car-parking

Offices
(a) Town centre location, self contained suites over 1000 m² in office blocks erected in
     last 10 years with good a standard of finish including a lift and good, quality fittings
     to common parts, limited car parking available
(b) As (a) but in the size range of 150–400 m²
(c) Self-contained suites in size range 50–150 m² in converted former Georgian/Victorian
     or similar houses of character usually just off town centre, good quality conversion,
     best quality fittings throughout with central heating and limited car parking

Industrial
(a) On an industrial estate, of modern construction but not high-tech design and heated
     by free standing heaters
     (i)   Small starter units (25–75 m²), steel framed, concrete block or brick construction,
            often built in terrace layout and let on weekly terms
     (ii)   Nursery units (150–200 m²), steel framed on concrete base, concrete block or
            brickwork to 2 m with metal PVC covered cladding above, eaves height 3.75–4.5 m
            with lined roof, limited or no office content and common parking and loading areas
     (iii) Industrial/warehouse units of approximately 500 m², of a similar construction to
            (ii) but with an eaves height 4.3–5.5 m and 10–15% office content, detached on
            own site with private parking and loading facilities
     (iv)   Industrial/warehouse units of around 1000 m² with same specification as (iii) but
            an eaves height up to 7.6 m
(b) Units only found in certain areas of the country as they are converted from nineteeth
     century multi-floor ex-mill or similar building of 4–5 storeys with brick construction
     with tile or slate roof, units of around 150 m² with heating from central piped
     water system, electric goods lift to upper floors and sprinklers to all levels, tenant
     responsible for internal repairs and insurance

Source: VOA.

lease, but it is important to note whether the value of any improvements that the tenant may have made to the property was disregarded when the level of rent under the new lease was agreed. Under legislation, which we will discuss in more detail in Chapter 4, the value of a tenant's improvements may be disregarded subject to certain conditions. The rent agreed at review will reflect the terms of the rent review clause in the lease and it is important to consider these terms in detail. Chief concerns:

- The timescale for operation of the rent review and the precise terms on which it should take place, including the interval between each review (the rent review period);
- whether the review of the rent is upward-only (this is the market norm);
- whether there is an assumption that the property is vacant and to let for the purposes of determining the rent;

- assumptions regarding the user clause (a lease term that may restrict the use of the premises);
- assignment (**alienation**) provisions; and
- whether the value of tenant's improvements should be disregarded.

The rent review clause in the lease will also state how disputes over the amount of reviewed rent should be resolved. Assignments, where the current tenant sells (assigns) the lease to a new tenant, do not involve a reassessment of the rent passing (contract rent) but may involve a premium if there is a profit rent, or a reverse premium if the property is over-rented. As a consequence, they are regarded as secondary or indirect evidence of MRs. If a rent at lease renewal or at a rent review cannot be agreed by the two parties and is determined by a third party, then this provides relatively weak evidence of MR. At arbitration the arbitrator must weigh up the evidence supplied by expert advisors who are appointed by the parties to the dispute. Contrastingly, if an independent expert is called in to resolve the dispute, more reliance may be placed on personal judgement. Disputes that end up in a law court often do so in order to resolve a legal matter or require an interpretation of a point of law and can be far removed from the open market.

3.2.2   Comparison metrics

Suitable comparison metrics are required to assist the comparison process by eliminating the need to make adjustments for size differences, although only comparable properties within a similar size range to the subject property should be selected. For commercial properties that are let, rents are expressed as an annual figure per square metre except for standard shop units where a measurement unit based on the zoning procedure described in Chapter 2 is used. For example, the MR of an industrial property with a gross internal area (GIA) of 325 m^2 needs to be estimated. A comparable property (arm's length transaction, similar age, condition, location, lease structure and design) has a GIA of 350 m^2 and was recently purchased by an investor for £135 000. It was subject to a new 15 year lease with 5 yearly, upward-only rent reviews at a rent of £12 200 per annum. Analysis of the comparable property reveals that the rent paid was equivalent to £34.86 per square metre, and the initial yield on the investment purchase was 9%. This information can be used to estimate the MR of the subject property as follows:

Area (m^2)	325
× Rent (£/m^2)	<u>34.86</u>
Estimated rental value (£)	11330

Car-parking spaces may either be separately valued on a unit rent per space basis or, more usually, their value will be implied in the overall rent per square metre that is applied to the main floor-space.

Another example of how the comparison method can be applied to a more unusual property is given by Rees and Hayward (2000): in estimating the rental value of a car showroom and ancillary accommodation, Rees and

Hayward suggest that there is a relationship between showroom rents and rents in off-centre retail areas; typically the rent on ancillary office space is a half to two thirds of the rent for showroom space. The rental value of workshop space would be comparable to rents for workshops in the area, and the annual rental value of one car stance should approximately relate to the average retained profit on one vehicle. The rental valuation might be set out as follows:

	Area (m²)	Rent (£/m²)	Annual rent (£)
Showroom	300	120	36 000
Sales office	30	60	1 800
General office	100	60	6 000
Reception area	20	40	800
Workshops	600	30	18 000
Parts store	20	30	600
Mezzanine floor	50	15	750
Rental value of buildings			63 950
Uncovered car stances	No. 25	400	10 000
Car-parking spaces	No. 40	100	4 000
Estimated rental value (£)			77 950

In Section 2.5.2 of Chapter 2 it was shown how the area of a standard shop unit is divided into zones as a way of placing extra weight on the rental value of space at the front of the premises and to reflect the fact that the value of sales space declines as distance from the front increases. In Figure 2.8, the shop has a frontage length of 7 m and a depth of 16.2 m. The ground floor would be divided into zones as follows:

Zone	Frontage length (m)	Depth (m)	Actual area (m2)	Area ITZA (m2)
A	7.00	6.10	42.7	42.7
B	7.00	6.10	42.7	42.7/2 = 21.35
C	7.00	4.00	28.0	28.0/4 = 7.00
			113.4	71.05

To weight the space at the front of the shop more highly the area of zone A is kept the same but the area of each subsequent zone is 'halved back'. This process derives an area 'in terms of zone A space' or ITZA for short. Looking at the example above, the area ITZA for zone A is the actual area, the area of zone B is halved and the area of zone C is halved again (i.e. quartered). Any remaining space beyond zone C might be halved again (i.e. divided by eight) but the magnitude of this fraction may vary depending on any special features of the remaining area. The calculation of an area ITZA allows a 'zone A' rent per square metre to be a standard metric for comparison purposes that can be multiplied by the area ITZA to calculate the annual rent for a shop. If we consider the example above to be a useful comparable and we discover that the MR is £40 000 per annum, this equates to £563 for each square metre of shop space when it is expressed ITZA. If we zone the property that is being valued, this zone A rent per square metre can be used to estimate MR. Sales space on floors other than the ground floor is considered to be less valuable and is expressed as a small fraction of the area ITZA, perhaps a sixth or a tenth. There is not much demand for sales space above first floor level in a standard shop unit, but the value applied will depend upon the ease with which the other floors can be reached by customers (facilitated, perhaps, by escalators and lifts or stairs at the front of the shop) and the ease with which goods can be transported to these floors. Ancillary space such as storage is even less valuable and may be expressed as a smaller fraction of the area ITZA or as a nominal rent per square metre. Office space that is ancillary to the sales area may also be expressed as a fraction of the area ITZA or may be related to rents for similar office space in the locality.

Of course, not all shops are 'standard'. A typical frontage-to-depth ratio is 1:2.5 or 1:3, Shop A in Figure 3.2. Shops with a much higher ratio, Shop B, for instance, may warrant a reduction to the valuation because although the zone A space gives display prominence there is relatively limited space for the retailer to stock goods for sale. Similar adjustments may be made if the shop is an unusual shape such as Shop C which has a masked area towards the rear of the premises (a masked area is an area made less prominent by, say, an L-shaped layout or features such as pillars getting in the way of displays or split levels). If the shop has a return frontage (where a shop is positioned on a corner and fronts two roads or pedestrian flows, Shop C in Figure 3.2) it is usual to either zone from both frontages if both provide good pedestrian flow, or zone from the prominent frontage and make an end allowance

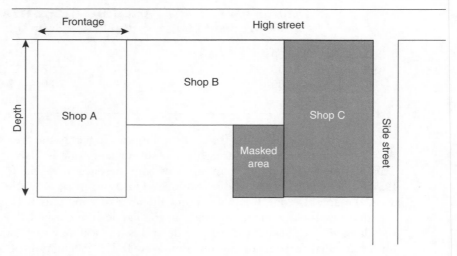

Figure 3.2   Shop shapes.

(say a 5–15% addition to the zone A rent) if warranted, bearing in mind that an excessive return can adversely affect the layout of sales space. The size of the end allowance will depend on the nature of the return frontage: is it a back street, can the property be accessed from it, what is the security like? Some shops, in a shopping centre, for example, may have frontages on two floors. Table 3.6 presents an example of a shop with complex floor areas and illustrates how this might be handled when estimating a MR. It can be seen that the valuation may be subject to end allowances including deductions for abnormal size.

Because shoppers appreciate the convenience of a well laid out and tightly packed shopping area, the rents that retailers are prepared to pay decline quite rapidly with increasing distance from the prime (most accessible) shopping location in an urban area. In valuation terms, the prime location is often referred to as the 100% prime position and zone A rents of neighbouring shops may be related to this position by expressing them as a percentage of 'prime'.

Finally, with regard to shops, many are let as 'shells'. In other words, their internal fittings are excluded, and the landlord often grants a short (say, 3 month) rent-free period to enable the incoming tenant to fit out the shop. Care must be taken when selecting comparables to ensure these fit-out periods are not confused with rent-free periods that may be granted as an incentive to take occupation, and to ensure that any measurements taken when the property was a shell are suitably adjusted or re-measured when calculating the net internal area (NIA) for valuation purposes.

Table 3.6 Example calculation of shop rent.

Floor	Description	NIA (m²)	Area ITZA (A) (halving back NIA) (m²)	Zone A rent (£/m²)	Rent (Area ITZA * Zone A rent/m²) (£)
Ground floor	Zone A	30	30 (A)		
	Zone B	30	15 (A/2)		
	Zone C	30	7.5 (A/4)		
	Remainder	20	2.5 (A/8)		
	Masked area	4	0.5 (A/8)		
	Total area ITZA		55.5	400	22 200
End adjustment	Rear access	Add 5% of ground floor rent			1 110
First floor	Sales	100	10 (A/10)		
Second floor	Office	90	6 (A/15)		
Third floor	Store	80	4 (A/20)		
Basement	Sales	80	8 (A/10)		
	Store	10	0.5 (A/20)		
	Total area ITZA		28.5	400	11 400
End adjustment	No lift	Deduct 10% of total rent			(3 471)
Estimated MR					31 239

Certain types of leisure property, which are normally valued with regard to their trading potential, may be compared using specific units of comparison too. For example, if sufficient comparable evidence is available, a capital or rental value per hotel room (inclusive of dining and conference facilities), per cinema seat, per tent or caravan pitch might be determined. Similarly, it might be possible to estimate a price per square metre or hectare for development land if a sufficient quantity of land sales has taken place.

3.2.3   Comparison adjustment

Because each property is unique adjustments need to be made to allow comparison to take place. Chapter 2 set out the determinants of property value: location, physical attributes such as size, layout and configuration, quality and condition of accommodation and legal factors such as ownership type and lease terms. These elements of comparison need to be quantified, adjusted and reconciled in the comparison method of valuation.

A quantitative approach would be to compare two or more transactions in order to derive the size of the adjustment for a single value factor. Ideally, two sales will be identical apart from the characteristic being measured, but this is rare and usually a series of 'paired' comparisons are made to isolate the effect of a single factor. Each comparable may be weighted depending on the number of adjustments applied, the total adjustment in absolute terms, the difference between positive and negative adjustments, any large adjustments made or any other factors that suggest more or less weight should be applied. Mathematically, the adjustment process is presented in Table 3.7 for establishing MR, but the process would be the same for estimating a capital value or an all-risks yield (ARY).

When analysing rents that have been agreed on comparable properties, it is important to consider the contractual terms contained in the lease. These might include payment of a premium, grant of a rent-free period, contribution towards fitting-out the premises, nature of the user clause, the way in

Table 3.7   Adjustment to elements using the comparison method of valuation.

	Comp. a	Comp. b	Comp. c	Comp. n
Rent/m^2	$£R_a$	$£R_b$	$£R_c$	$£R_n$
Elements				
Location	$£(+/-)$	$£(+/-)$	$£(+/-)$	$£(+/-)$
Physical description	$£(+/-)$	$£(+/-)$	$£(+/-)$	$£(+/-)$
Sale date	$£(+/-)$	$£(+/-)$	$£(+/-)$	$£(+/-)$
Sale conditions	$£(+/-)$	$£(+/-)$	$£(+/-)$	$£(+/-)$
Lease terms	$£(+/-)$	$£(+/-)$	$£(+/-)$	$£(+/-)$
and soon	$£(+/-)$	$£(+/-)$	$£(+/-)$	$£(+/-)$
Net adjustment	$£(+/-)_a$	$£(+/-)_b$	$£(+/-)_c$	$£(+/-)_c$
Adjusted rent/m^2	$£R_a + £(+/-)_a$	$£R_b + £(+/-)_b$	$£R_c + £(+/-)_c$	$£R_n + £(+/-)_n$

which rent is reviewed and possible exclusion from security of tenure provisions of the 1954 Landlord and Tenant Act. The details of these terms will be expanded upon in later chapters; for the time being, it is important to know that the comparison method is a means of reflecting the value implications of these terms in a valuation. In a landlord–tenant relationship, it is usually the tenant who is responsible for all repairs (internal and external) and insurance costs, and a lease that places financial responsibility for these costs on the tenant is known as a **full repairing and insuring** (FRI) lease. This reflects the relatively strong bargaining position that landlords have had in recent years and have thus been able to negotiate lease terms that are favourable to them. Recently, the bargaining positions of both parties have become more balanced, but there is no evidence to suggest that tenants have been able to pass on repair liabilities to landlords in great numbers. If the tenant occupies part of a property, perhaps sharing common parts (such as the reception, car park, lifts and corridor space) with other tenants, the cost of repairs and insurance is usually split between the tenants in the form of a service charge. The charge may be apportioned in relation to the floor-space occupied or rent paid by each tenant.

The aim of the comparison adjustment process is to derive an **effective rent** for each comparable after all these adjustments have been made. The effective rent is the contract rent plus the annual equivalent of capital expenditure on qualifying alterations or improvements by the tenant, less the annual equivalent value of any rent-free period or other financial contributions to expenditure by the landlord. The way in which some of these elements of comparison are translated to an annual equivalent sum is described in Chapter 4. For now, consider an example of how differences in repair and insurance lease terms might be reflected. As stated above, most leases require the tenant to take responsibility for internal and external repairs and insurance of the property for the duration of the lease. However, if the lease requires the landlord to take financial responsibility for these costs then adjustments might be made to the gross rent to arrive at a net rent as follows:

- *Repairs*: reduction of say 15% of the gross rent (10% for external repairs, 5% for internal repairs).
- *Insurance*: reduction of say 2.5% of the gross rent.
- *Management*: reduction of say 10% of the gross rent.

For example, a first floor office suite of 1000 m^2 has just been let at £150 000 per annum. The landlord is liable for maintaining the structure and common parts and for insuring the building. A service charge covers the cost of heating and lighting. The net rent to the landlord might be calculated as shown in Table 3.8. The landlord's liability in this case amounts to £30 per square metre.

It is quite usual for regular expenditure on management, repairs and services to be deducted from gross rental income to arrive at net income but irregular expenditure on, say, refurbishment may be handled differently, by adjusting the cash-flow at the appropriate time perhaps.

Table 3.8 Gross to net rent.

Annual rent (£)	150 000	
Area (m^2)	1 000	
Rent per square metre (£/m^2)		150.00
Less adjustments for		
External repairs at, say, 10% of the gross rent	15.00	
Internal repairs of common parts at 2.5%	3.75	
Insurance at 2.5%	3.75	
Management at 5%	7.50	
Making a total deduction of 20% of gross rent		30.00
Net (adjusted) rent per square metre (£/m^2)		120.00

Table 3.9 Comparison valuation using quantitative and qualitative approaches.

	Comp. A	Comp. B	Comp. C	Comp. D	Comp. E	Subject
MR (£)	£67 000	£75 000	£66 000	£80 000	£83 200	—
Elements						
NIA (m^2)	100	90	95	115	130	125
MR/m^2	£670	£830	£694	£609	£640	
Management costs	—	–5%	–5%	—	–5%	
Repair liability	—	–5%	–10%	—	–5%	
Insurance liability	—	–2.5%	—	—	–2.5%	
Age allowance	+5%	–5%	—	—	–5%	
Net quantitative adjustment to MR/m^2	+5%	–17.5%	–15%	—	–17.5%	
Adjusted MR/m^2	£704	£685	£590	£696	£528	
Condition	Average	Average	Average	Average	Average	Average
Ratio of parking space to NIA	Average	Average	Average	Poor	Good	Good
Location	Superior	Inferior	Average	Superior	Inferior	Superior
Net qualitative adjustment	–ve	+ve	–ve	–ve	+ve	—

In the absence of sufficient data to allow a quantitative approach, comparison elements may be expressed in qualitative terms such as 'inferior' or 'superior'. Reconciliation involves consideration of the strengths and weaknesses of each element. The valuer uses judgement to determine the direction and magnitude of the effect that each element has on value and assesses its relative importance. When this has been done for each factor and for every comparable, the net adjustment for each is resolved. A qualitative approach is popular because it reflects the imperfect nature of the property market, but it is usual to combine quantitative and qualitative approaches when using the comparison method. Table 3.9 provides an example of how this might be done when estimating a MR. The inclusion of NIA helps determine comparability in terms of size, so it is best not to calculate MR per square metre straight away. Comparables A and D appear to be very strong and should probably attract the greatest weight when reconciling these comparables to derive an estimate of MR for the subject property.

Wiltshaw (1991) argues that the comparison method is statistically flawed, primarily because of the small number of comparable transactions used in many valuations, and as the number of comparables decreases relative to the number of comparison elements to be adjusted, it increases the likelihood of statistical insignificance. Nevertheless, the principle of comparison is central to property valuation. If sufficient transaction data were available, it would be possible to use multiple regression analysis, but this is rare in practice, although automated valuation models that use such techniques are increasingly being used for mass appraisal of residential property.

Key points

- The comparison method utilises transaction data generated by the market and is based on a rational approach that compares characteristics and adjusts for any differences. The approach is less reliable when data are scarce.
- Complex income producing properties are harder to analyse due to the possible existence of special circumstances. For example, a landlord may accept a lower rent from a tenant who renews his lease, and incentives offered by the landlord such as a rent-free period and incentives offered by tenants such as a premium must be handled carefully to ensure that a rational and defensible adjustment is made. Other dangers include transactions that are not at arm's length.
- The principle of comparison is fundamental to all methods used to value commercial properties: estimates of MRs, yields, expenses, land values, construction costs and depreciation may be derived using comparison techniques.

3.3.   Investment method

The investment method is used to value properties held as investments. The owner of an investment property passes occupation rights to a tenant by way of a lease. The tenant pays rent to the owner (landlord), and the level of rent is determined by the supply of and demand for that type of property in the occupier market. To the landlord, the rent represents the income return on the investment in the property, so its capacity to keep pace with or exceed the rate of inflation is critical to its investment value. Mathematically, the rent is simply a cash-flow, and therefore the investment value of the property may be determined by calculating its present value. The actual rent specified in the lease and currently paid is known as the rent passing or **contract rent,** and the rent that a property would normally command in the open market as indicated by rents paid for comparable space near to the valuation date is known as the **MR.** An estimate of MR can be made using comparison techniques described in Section 3.2. The investment cash-flow is usually in the form of rental income for freehold and leasehold interests plus a reversionary capital value in the case of freeholds. Marshall (1920) was the first to expound methods of capitalising urban rental income as a means of pricing property investments. He focused on the scenario whereby landowners let sites on long ground leases, for 99 years say, and stated that the

> capitalized value of any plot of land is the actuarial 'discounted' value of all the net incomes which it is likely to afford, allowance being made on the one hand for all incidental expenses, including those of collecting the rents, and on the other for its mineral wealth, its capabilities of development for any kind of business, and its advantages, material, social and æsthetic, for the purposes of residence.

The calculation of the present value of the cash-flow is often referred to as capitalisation and, because rent is a regular income return, calculation of present value involves the use of present value of £1 pa formula described in Chapter 2. To estimate the present value of a property investment the valuer needs to know the net income (the income receivable after deductions for any repairs, insurance, services, rates, head rents and other rent charges), the period for which the income will be received and the yield. This information can be obtained from the lease or, if the property is empty, from comparable evidence.

Ball *et al.* (1998) point out that, unlike equities and bonds, property investments are heterogeneous and thinly traded. As a result, historically, property was treated separately from other investment markets with distinct valuation or pricing techniques. These techniques centred on deriving ARYs from comparable evidence which were then used to capitalise current flows and estimates of rental income. This contrasts with techniques used in other investment markets where discount rates and income growth expectations were estimated separately and links to other financial markets and to the wider economy were more explicitly considered. So, although traditional property valuation techniques can be derived from the principles of financial mathematics, the links are not obvious, and comparison with other asset classes is difficult. Having said this, the situation is changing and, at the present time, there are two recognised approaches to valuing a property using the investment method: income capitalisation using an ARY and discounted cash-flow (DCF) using a target rate of return or discount rate. Both calculate the present value of future economic benefits; the former is merely a simplification of the latter. Income capitalisation involves dividing either the contract rent or MR by the ARY to calculate a capital value. The magnitude of the ARY is estimated from comparable evidence of similar investment transactions. Any future growth in economic benefits (either rental income or capital value) is accounted for or implied by the choice of yield. The approach is therefore 'growth-implicit' in that it does not explicitly project the cash-flow beyond current contract rent or estimate of MR. DCF, on the other hand, requires an explicit forecast of the cash-flow over a predefined time horizon of, say, 5–15 years. The cash-flow may consist of a rental income plus a reversion or resale value and is discounted at a suitable rate, known as the target rate of return or discount rate. In this chapter, we focus on income capitalisation using an ARY and leave DCF until Chapter 5. It is important to note, however, that despite criticism that income capitalisation tends to be backward-looking because of its reliance on historical comparable evidence (see Ball *et al.*, 1998, for example), the approach still involves forecasting – it is just that future expectations are encapsulated in the yield choice. Indeed, it could be argued that because the choice of ARY is based on information that can be obtained directly from the market it is a more reliable investment valuation method – a market valuation should be based on market-derived data. Consequently, income capitalisation is widely used to value properties with stable, fairly predictable income flows and with ample comparable evidence to hand. However, problems arise with income capitalisation when properties differ markedly from one another (Baum and Crosby, 1995), and this is of growing concern as lease structures for the main property investment sectors become increasingly diverse.

In income capitalisation, the relationship between the price and rent paid on a comparable property is expressed as a yield. Valuers analyse the current and anticipated supply and demand for property similar to the one being valued, analyse rents and prices of comparable investment transactions, calculate their yields, derive a suitable ARY for the subject property and use it to capitalise its actual or estimated rent. Income capitalisation therefore has comparison at its heart and does not attempt to analyse the worth of a property investment from first principles. An investor may be willing to pay more than market value if the property satisfies requirements specific to that investor (a gap in an investment portfolio, for example), but if this sort of decision-making is not reflected in the market then it should not influence an opinion of market value. Instead, this is a quantification of worth to an investor, known as appraisal, and is discussed in Chapter 7.

Property investments may be freehold or leasehold, but the overwhelmingly majority are freehold because of their much greater potential for income and capital growth and their lower risk profile. Lean and Goodall (1966) and Fraser (1993) both provide excellent summaries of the investment characteristics of the main types of freehold property investment. A freehold in possession (the interest of an owner-occupier where there are no sub-interests) is a pure equity interest which affords the owner a perpetual right to the full benefits of the property. For a business, this is the right to the profit obtainable from undertaking business activity on the premises without the liability to pay rent. The notional annual return from this interest, known as the **imputed rent**, is the estimated MR of the property. For a freehold acquired as an investment (where the property is let) the equity extent of the freehold depends on the lease terms and, in particular, the frequency with which the rent is reviewed to MR. For example, a long lease without review is a fixed income investment whereas an annually reviewed turnover rent is an equity investment. The market norm is a review of rent every 5 years, usually upward-only. This offers a significant degree of income security but which is being eroded as leases become shorter and break options more frequent. A fixed income freehold property investment (where the property is let on a long lease at a fixed rent) is often referred to as **freehold ground rent** and is less common nowadays. They were common until the 1960s and typically took the form of a lease of a development site for a term ranging from 99 to 999 years at a very low rent with no provision to revise the rent during the lease. Such investments tend to have higher yields than equity investments owing to their lack of growth potential. Their yields are similar to yields on undated bonds but somewhat above to reflect their comparative illiquidity. As the end of a freehold ground lease approaches the yield falls in anticipation of reversionary value. When the value of the freehold ground rent for the remaining term plus the value of the reversion exceed the value of the freehold ground rent in perpetuity, the reversion is affecting value. From this point the investment will exhibit equity investment characteristics because the reversionary MR can be affected by rental growth prospects and the like. In more recent years, rent review clauses have been introduced into freehold ground rents, and these introduce a further equity element. Most business properties are let on leases with 5-year reviews and are effectively equity investments whose investment characteristics are broadly similar to shares albeit with a more staggered (5 yearly) income growth pattern. Both are growth investments which are influenced by the profitability of underlying business, although property investment return is more dependent upon the use to which the property is put rather than the specific trade of the occupier.

Depending on the timing of the investment acquisition a freehold property investment might be **rack-rented** or **reversionary**. A rack-rented property is one which is let at the current MR while a reversionary freehold property investment is one where the property is let below MR but with a reversion (usually through a rent review or lease renewal) to MR in the future. The next two sections consider the valuation of these freehold property investments in turn.

3.3.1 Valuation of rack-rented freehold property investments

For a property to be rack-rented at the valuation date it must have either been let or been subject to a lease renewal or rent review so recently that the contract rent is assumed to be the MR. Alternatively the property may be vacant at the valuation date, and a MR is estimated together with an adjustment to the yield to reflect the fact that the property is empty or a void period can be assumed. For example, value the freehold interest in a shop that was recently let at a rent (net of non-recoverable running costs) of £100 000 per annum. Analysis of recent transactions for similar premises reveals that initial yields average 8%. The net annual rent of £100 000 is receivable in perpetuity[2] and, if we assume that we need make no adjustment to the yield obtained from comparable evidence to derive an ARY to value the property, we can capitalise the MR at the ARY using Equation 2.23 from Chapter 2 (in which the ARY is represented by y):

$$V = \frac{MR}{y} = \frac{£100\,000}{0.08} = £1\,250\,000$$

The valuer might adjust the ARY obtained from comparable evidence, if the property is vacant or let on unusual lease terms such as a very short lease.

As we know from Chapter 2 the inverse of the ARY is a multiplier known as the years' purchase (YP), so called because it represents the number of years over which the net income must be received in order to recoup the present value. Mathematically, the YP is the equivalent of the Present Value of £1 pa receivable in perpetuity and, conventionally, is multiplied by the net MR (from now on we will dispense with the word 'net') to determine the total present value or, simply, the value of the property. The valuation would therefore be set out as follows:

MR (£)   100 000
YP in perpetuity @ 8%   12.5000
Valuation (£)   1 250 000

In practice, purchase costs should be deducted from the valuation. These would comprise stamp duty at 4% for any agreed sale price over £500 000 (for other rates, see Chapter 1), agent's fee of around 1% of sale price, legal fees amounting to approximately 0.5% of sale price and VAT on these fees at 17.5%. However, because these are pretty standard they are not presented in this valuation or in subsequent valuations throughout this book.

As we know from Equation 2.22 in Chapter 2, the formula above can be rearranged to derive initial yields from comparable evidence where the MR and price paid (P) are known:

$$y = \frac{MR}{P}$$

For example, a modern factory was recently let at a rent of £150 000 per annum and the freehold has just been sold for £2 250 000. What is the initial yield from this investment?

$$y = \frac{MR}{P} = \frac{£150 000}{£2 250 000} = 6.67\%$$

In fact, the initial yield method is the name often given to income capitalisation for rack-rented properties. It is perhaps worth noting at this point that, although current market practice is to assume that the rent is received annually in arrears, as the above formula does, because rent from commercial property is usually received quarterly in advance in the UK, the true initial yield y_q in this example can be obtained by adjusting the yield obtained in the above equation using Equation 2.32 in Chapter 2:

$$y_q = \frac{1}{\left(1-(y_a/4)\right)^4} - 1 = \frac{1}{\left(1-(0.0667/4)\right)^4} - 1 = 6.96\%$$

The income profile of a typical rack-rented property investment is illustrated in Figure 3.3. At the beginning of a new lease the property is let at the MR or, if the property is empty, an estimate of MR is derived from

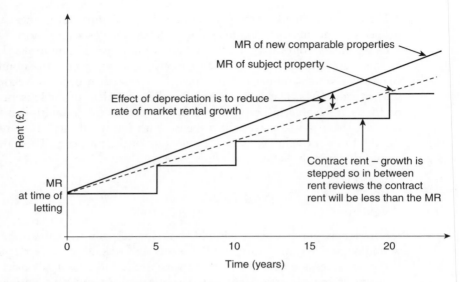

Figure 3.3 Income profite of a rack-rented property investment.

comparable evidence, and it is assumed that this rack-rent is receivable in perpetuity. Over time, the MR of equivalent new properties will increase (the solid line in Figure 3.3), but the MR of the subject property – which is getting older – will not keep pace (the dashed line). The actual rent received by the investor rises in steps under a typical UK lease arrangement to the MR of the subject property every 5 years (the stepped solid line). The effect of rent being fixed for periods is to increase the stability of capital values. Rising rental incomes since the 1950s and the system of rent reviews now in place has meant that income from property investments has rarely fallen, in contrast to dividend income from shares. Only a sustained fall in rents (such as the one that took place in the London office market in the early 1990s) would lead to reduction in rents, but even here investors are protected to a certain extent by **upward-only rent reviews.**

3.3.2 Valuation of reversionary freehold property investments

In a rental growth market not all investment properties are let at MR at the time of the valuation. Often the contract rent is not the current MR because it was agreed some time ago, usually when the lease began or at the last rent review, but sometimes because a premium was paid and the rent was reduced to reflect this. The income from a reversionary freehold comprises two elements; a contract rent secured by the lease contract which is usually prevented from falling by upward-only rent reviews, and a potential uplift or reversion to a higher MR at the next rent review or lease renewal. The value of this potential reversion should be reflected in the price the investor pays. Theoretically, according to Baum and Crosby (1995), the growth potential of reversionary investments where the term is less than the normal rent review period of 5 years is greater than for a rack-rented property because the first rent review will be in less than 5 years' time. However, it is rare for reversions to be valued at a yield lower than the ARY for equivalent but rack-rented freeholds – the market tends to regard reversionary investments less favourably because the reversionary MR is merely an estimate and thus more risky. Fraser (1993) argues that with a reversionary investment the value impact of the reversion becomes greater as it draws nearer – immediately after a rent review the capital value growth rate tends to be less than the rental growth rate but as the reversion draws nearer, it tends to exceed it. Thus investors purchasing reversionary investments anticipate three elements of return: current income, capital gain deriving from rental growth and capital gain deriving from the passage of time to reversion uplift. The latter is in effect rental growth from earlier years (not yet received because of 5-year rent reviews) being stored up and released as capital gain as the reversion approaches. The arbitrage method of valuation, described in Chapter 5, builds on this concept.

In practice, three approaches are used to value reversionary investments, and they are (1) term and reversion; (2) core and top-slice; and (3) equivalent yield. The first two split the rental income into two components and capitalise them at different yields and the last one capitalises the current and reversionary income components at a unified 'equivalent' yield.

3.3.2.1   Term and reversion

The contract rent (also known as the term rent or rent passing) is capitalised until the point at which it reverts to MR. Then the MR (known as the reversionary rent in this case) is capitalised in perpetuity, but this capital value is deferred from now until the point at which it is received. These two capital values are then added together. This is shown diagrammatically in Figure 3.4.

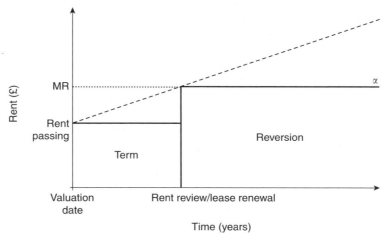

Figure 3.4   Term and reversion valuation.

Mathematically, the income streams are valued as follows:

$$V = (t \times \text{YP for term}) + (m \times \text{YP in perpetuity} \times \text{PV for term})$$

$$= \left[t \times \left(\frac{1 - (1/(1+y_t)^n)}{y_t} \right) \right] + \left[m \times \frac{1}{y_r} \times \frac{1}{(1+y_r)^n} \right] \quad\quad [3.1]$$

where
t = contract rent for term
YP = years purchase (PV £1 pa)
m = MR
n = period to rent revision
y_t = term ARY
y_r = reversion ARY

For example, a factory is currently let at £250 000 per annum on a lease with 4 years unexpired. The MR is £300 000 per annum, and the ARY is estimated to be 9%. A valuation of the property is set out below:

Term rent (£)	250 000	
YP 4 years @ 8%	3.3121	
		828 025
Reversion to MR (£)	300 000	
YP perpetuity @ 9%	11.1111	
Deferred 4 years (PV £1 for 4 years @ 9%)	0.7084	
		2 361 331
Valuation (£)		3 189 356

A valuation figure of this magnitude would usually be rounded to the nearest thousand pounds. The future reversionary rent which is usually capitalised at an ARY based on evidence from rack-rented comparable properties, while the term rent may be capitalised at a slightly lower yield. The conventional rationale for this adjustment is that the term rent is regarded as more secure and is normally in the region of 0.5–2% below the reversion yield. This logic might have been appropriate in an economy with negligible inflation and rental growth (the UK before the 1960s, for example), but in a growth economy, if the rent is fixed significantly below the MR for the length of the term, the loss in real terms can be significant. The yield used to capitalise this term income should, therefore, be more in line with yields on fixed income investments suitably adjusted for risk. In fact, the fixed term income is overvalued by capitalising it at a yield that implies growth – an error that is countered by an under-valuation of the reversion because the MR receivable on reversion is not inflated at any sort of growth rate. Greaves (1972) argued that, because the rent on reversion has growth potential it could be capitalised at a yield below that applied to the term.

A word of caution regarding the term and reversion approach is that the use of variable rates can sometimes mean that a higher value is placed on the longer reversion – something that is clearly counter-intuitive.

Bowcock (1983) demonstrated this by valuing two reversionary investments let at £100 per annum but one with a review to £105 in 5 years' time and the other in 10 years' time:

Property 1				**Property 2**		
Term rent (£)	100			Term rent (£)	100	
YP 5 years @ 9%	3.8897			YP 10 years @ 9%	6.4177	
		388.97				641.77
Reversion to				Reversion to		
MR (£)	105			MR (£)	105	
YP perpetuity				YP perpetuity		
@ 10%	10			@ 10%	10	
PV £1 5 years				PV £1 10 years		
@10%	0.6209			@10%	0.3855	
		651.97				404.82
Valuation (£)		1040.93		Valuation (£)		1046.59

In practice, valuers would adjust the yields to reflect their views of income security (quantified in terms of the difference between contract rent and MR) and the risk associated with the period until reversion. Baum and Crosby (1995) suggest that the term and reversion approach is good for valuing properties let on long fixed terms without rent reviews prior to the final reversion, adopting a high yield on the term to reflect the fixed income, based on bond yields but adjusted to reflect additional property risk, the prospect of future reversion (with growth) and the quality of the tenant.

3.3.2.2   Core and top-slice

The core and top-slice or layer approach capitalises the contract rent (core or bottom slice) in perpetuity, and the top-slice rent (also known as the incremental rent or uplift), which is the difference between the MR and the contract rent, is also capitalised in perpetuity but deferred until the rent review or lease renewal. These capital values are then added together. This is shown diagrammatically in Figure 3.5.

Usually, the lower risk, contracted element of the rent is capitalised at an ARY based on yield evidence from comparable rack-rented property investments and the riskier, top-slice element receivable at the next rent review or lease renewal is capitalised at a higher yield. Mathematically, the valuation would be as follows:

$$V = (c \times \text{YP into perpetuity}) + ((m - c) \times \text{YP in perpetuity} \times \text{PV for term})$$

$$= \left[c \times \frac{1}{y_c} \right] + \left[(m - c) \times \frac{1}{y_{ts}} \times \frac{1}{(1 + y_{ts})^n} \right] \qquad [3.2]$$

$$= \frac{c}{y_c} + \frac{m - c}{y_{ts}(1 + y_{ts})^n} \qquad [3.3]$$

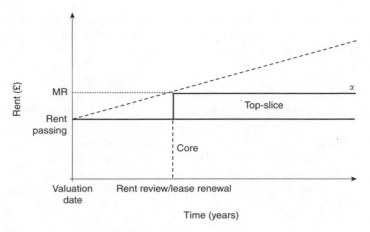

Figure 3.5   Core and top-slice valuation.

where
c = contract (core) rent in perpetuity
y_c = core yield
y_{ts} = top-slice yield

Using the same example,

Core: contract rent (£)	250 000	
YP in perpetuity @ 8%	12.5000	
		3 125 000
Top-slice: uplift to MR (£)	50 000	
YP perpetuity @ 10%	10.0000	
Deferred 4 years (PV £1 for 4 years @ 10%)	0.6380	
		319 000
Valuation (£)		3 444 000

As with the term rent in the term and reversion approach, the yield used to capitalise the core rent implies growth where there is none, thus overvaluing this component, and the top-slice is undervalued by capitalising the current rather than projected estimate of the reversionary MR (Greaves, 1972).

The rationale for dividing the income into these two layers is that the core rent is assumed to extend into perpetuity on the basis that there is little likelihood of the rent falling below the rent passing because of upward-only rent reviews and rental growth prospects. Whereas the top-slice is more risky since it is based on an estimate of MR and, because it is the top-slice, an error in this estimate would propagate as an increased error in top-slice value (Baum and Crosby, 1995). In other words, the top-slice is highly geared. For example, assume a MR estimate of £500 000 per annum was 10% over the actual MR of £450 000 per annum. If the rent passing was £400 000 per annum, the top slice would be £100 000 per annum in our original estimate but £50 000 per annum actually – an error of 50%. So the geared nature of the top-slice means that it is sensitive to error in MR estimates, but it does give valuers the opportunity to raise the top-slice yield, if they believe the

MR estimate is very suspect (Baum and Crosby, 1995). The approach is rather lopsided because not only does the top-slice have to deal with gearing, it also contains all the rental growth because the core element of the rent is fixed in perpetuity. So the valuer might feel justified in applying a lower yield if it is felt that the rate of rental growth will be particularly high.

The core and top-slice approach is not very good at valuing property investments let on short leases and with break clauses (Baum and Crosby, 1995) but can be adapted to value an over-rented property (where the contract rent is higher than the current estimate of MR) so that a higher yield can be used for the **overage** (until it ceases) as it is considered to be at a higher risk. There is still a risk of double-counting growth because the core income is fixed but capitalised using a growth-implicit yield. We shall return to the valuation of over-rented property investments in Chapter 5.

Despite the fact that both the term and reversion and core and top-slice approaches may produce acceptable market valuations, a significant drawback in the eyes of investors is that different yields are used to capitalise different components of income. This makes comparison with yields from other investments difficult and can lead to different valuations if yield adjustments between the two approaches are not reconciled – this brings us neatly to the third and final approach to valuing reversionary property investments.

3.3.2.3 Equivalent yield

The equivalent yield is a single ARY reflecting the growth potential and risks associated with the investment as a whole, rather than separate components of income: the mathematical problems associated with adjustments to yields in the above methods are eliminated (Baum and Crosby, 1995). An example of an equivalent yield valuation is given below:

Term rent (£)	750 000	
YP for 3 years @ 6%	2.6730	
		2 004 750
Reversion to MR (£)	1 000 000	
YP perpetuity @ 6%	16.6667	
Deferred 3 years (PV £1 3 years @ 6%)	0.8396	
		13 993 361
Capital value		15 998 111

The main advantage of a single equivalent yield is that it enables comparison with yields on rack-rented property investments and, indeed, the equivalent yield is usually selected in practice after analysing comparable evidence of similar rack-rented investments (Sykes, 1981). In most circumstances, the equivalent yield of a reversionary investment is slightly higher than the initial yield of a comparable rack-rented investment. It is also possible to calculate the equivalent yield of a reversionary property investment that has recently been sold. Essentially, the equivalent yield is an internal rate of return or IRR (a concept that we will come back to in Chapter 7 when we discuss appraisal) which will discount the term and reversion (or core and top-slice) income components in terms of their current rental values. In other words, no attempt is made to explicitly incorporate estimates of future rental growth in the calculation beyond the reversion.

Using the now familiar example from above, the term and reversion valuation of which is repeated below for convenience, if this property was acquired at the valuation figure, the initial yield would be 7.84% (£250 000/£3 189 356) and the reversion yield would be 9.41% (£300 000/£3 189 356).

Term rent (£)	250 000	
YP 4 years @ 8%	3.3121	
		828 025
Reversion to MR (£)	300 000	
YP perpetuity @ 9%	11.1111	
Deferred 4 years (PV £1 for 4 years @ 9%)	0.7084	
		2 361 331
Valuation (£)		3 189 356

In terms of cash-flow this investment generates four annual payments of £250 000 and then (ignoring growth in the cash-flow because it is handled in the yield) £300 000 per annum in perpetuity. So the equivalent yield is calculated by working out the growth-implicit internal rate of return (IRR) that equates this cash-flow to the purchase price of £3 189 356. This can be done using the IRR function on a spreadsheet as follows:

Year	Cash-flow description	Cash-flow
0	Purchase price	−3 189 356
1	Rental income	250 000
2	Rental income	250 000
3	Rental income	250 000
4	Rental income	250 000
5-perpetuity	Reversionary rent of £300 000	300 000 into perpetuity
IRR		8.95%

When this equivalent yield (growth-implicit IRR), which has been rounded to two decimal places, is input into the valuation above as a check the resultant valuation is shown below:

Term rent (£)	250 000	
YP 4 years @ 8.95%	3.2433	
		810 820
Reversion to MR (£)	£300 000	
YP in perpetuity deferred 4 years @ 8.95%	7.9299	
		2 378 972
Valuation (£ small discrepancy due to rounding)		3 189 791

Alternatively it is perfectly possible to use a spreadsheet trial and error function such as 'goal seek' in Excel to find the equivalent yield given different income component yields in the term and reversion or core and top-slice approach. This is done by using the goal seek function to set the equivalent yield valuation figure to same figure obtained using the term and reversion approach (or core and top-slice approach) by changing the equivalent yield used. Alternative, pre-spreadsheet methods of calculating the equivalent yield of a reversionary property investment are shown in Appendix 3A (see Appendix 3A at www.blackwellpublishing.com/wyatt).

When the period to reversion is short (less than 5 years) most of the value of a reversionary property investment is contained in either the reversion component of a term and reversion approach or the core of the core and top-slice approach, and so the equivalent yield will always be very close to the yield used to capitalise these income components. Over time, the initial yield and the equivalent yield revealed by the analysis of transactions will grow together and apart as lease lengths vary and market rental growth produces and destroys reversionary potential. Figure 3.6 shows changes in yields for all property in the IPD Index between 1981 and 2003, and the marked difference between the two can be seen throughout the 1980s when inflation was much higher than it is now. Since the recession in the early 1990s inflation has remained low and rent review periods standardised on a 5-year pattern. This means that the differences between contract and MRs are much less now, and therefore the difference between initial and equivalent yields is much less. Indeed, during the recession of the early 1990s, Central London offices became over-rented, and those properties let to tenants unlikely to default were regarded as better investments than new lettings, producing lower equivalent yields than initial yields, as can be seen from Figure 3.7.

3.3.3 Valuation of leasehold property investments

There must be at least two legal interests in a property to create a leasehold investment; perhaps a head-tenant leases the property from the freeholder

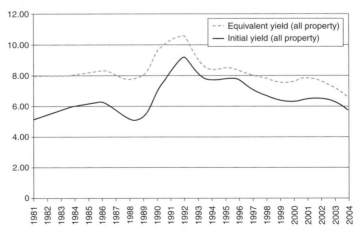

Figure 3.6 Initial and equivalent yields for all property: 1981–2004 (IPD UK Property Digest 2005).

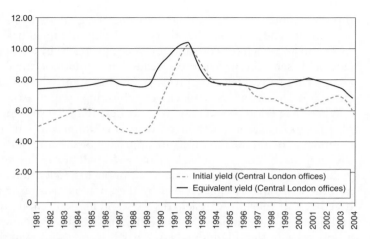

Figure 3.7   Initial and equivalent yields Central London offices: 1981–2004 (IPD UK Property Digest 2005).

through a head-lease, paying a head-rent, and sublets to a sub-tenant by a sub-lease and receives a sub-rent. Assuming the rent received from the sub-tenant is greater than the rent paid to the landlord, the head-tenant receives a **profit rent,** and if the head-lease is assignable, this profit rent may have a market value.

The freehold investments that were described in Sections 3.3.1 and 3.3.2 produce a perpetual income return – this is an important characteristic that they have in common. The cash-flow is usually in the form of a MR, reversionary and other incentives issues aside. Income return is possible for as long as the land is capable of economic use, and the capital value may be realised at any time at least equivalent to the value of the land but usually enhanced by whatever buildings have been constructed on the land. Leaseholds, on the other hand, are a much more diverse group of investment assets and generally a less popular form of property investment. A leasehold investment is terminable – the interest no longer exists once the profit rent has ceased, and therefore the original capital outlay is lost, and the investment return is in the form of income only. The income is more sensitive to the level of and changes in the MR of the property than is the case for an equivalent freehold – the profit rent is a geared top-slice form of income (Baum and Crosby, 1995; Sayce *et al.*, 2006). Indeed, if the sub-tenant stops paying rent, the head-tenant (i.e. the leasehold investor) will still have to pay the head-rent to the landlord – a situation that would not occur if the investment interest was a freehold. As the head-lease nears the end of its term it will be harder to sub-let the property for the 'fag-end' of the lease. Also, complex patterns of profit rent can occur if revisions to the rent received and rent paid are at different times and this complexity cannot be handled by making adjustments to the ARY. It is even possible for the profit rent to become negative when the contract rent exceeds the MR and, particularly in these situations but in general also, the quality of the tenant, and especially the ability to pay rent, is critical in determining risk. Being a head-leasehold interest the investor may have repair, insurance and other liabilities under the terms of the lease as well as restrictions over the way that the interest may be transferred. These constraints can be inconvenient, costly and consequently affect value. Some or all of these liabilities can be passed on to the sub-tenant under the terms of the sub-lease, but this is still a management cost, and the constraints remain nonetheless. All of this adds to the costs and risk of a leasehold investment interest.

Due to the relative unattractiveness of leasehold investments, valuations are less frequently undertaken, but where they are required they are more difficult than freeholds. Lease terms and termination dates, the gearing characteristics caused by the size of the profit rent compared to the head rent, and repair, insurance and other liabilities under the terms of the lease will all vary. This means that the range of yields and capital values revealed by analysis of comparable evidence will be very diverse. But valid leasehold yield comparisons can only be made between leasehold investments where the remaining terms and other income characteristics are similar, and this severely restricts the amount of comparable information that might be available to support a yield choice. To get around this problem, the conventional method of valuing leasehold investments was to capitalise the profit rent at a yield derived from freehold investments, which tend to be more commonplace and homogeneous than leasehold investments. To justify the use of freehold yields as a basis for the valuation of leasehold investments, valuers used to capitalise the profit rent at a **dual rate**. This comprised a remunerative rate (ARY) derived from freehold transactions of comparable properties (but increased to reflect the greater risk associated with a profit rent[3]) which was used to capitalise the profit rent; and an accumulative rate or sinking fund designed to recoup the original capital outlay at the end of the lease term so a similar leasehold investment could be purchased *ad infinitum* – thus creating, in theory at least, the equivalent of a freehold interest. The approach ensures that a leasehold investor receives a return *on* the capital outlay throughout the lease term at the remunerative rate and a return *of* the capital by the end of the term. To ensure there is very little risk attached to the recovery of the original capital outlay, it is assumed that some of the annual income from the leasehold investment is reinvested in a sinking fund that offers a low, safe accumulative rate. Although this will almost certainly recoup the original outlay (return of capital) it reduces the amount of income actually received (return of capital).

In Chapter 2, Equation 2.27 presented a version of the PV £1 pa formula that contained both a return on capital (a remunerative rate) and an accumulative (or sinking fund rate). This formula is repeated here:

$$\text{PV £1 pa} = \frac{1-(1+r)^{-n}}{r} = \frac{1}{r+\text{SF}} = \frac{1}{r+\left[s/((1+s)^n-1)\right]}$$

where r is the leasehold rate (the remunerative rate) derived from yields obtained on comparable freehold investments and s is the sinking fund or the accumulative rate. This is the formula for a dual rate PV £1 pa (YP) separating, as it does, the remunerative and accumulative rates. Incidentally, the dual rate YP is compatible with the single rate YP when the remunerative rate r and accumulative rate s are the same: that is,

$$\frac{1}{r+(s/(1+s)^n-1)}=\frac{1-(1+r)^{-n}}{r}$$

Conventionally, if the investor is a taxpayer then tax is also payable on the return received from the sinking fund, so the dual rate YP must be adjusted to allow the sinking fund to accumulate at a net-of-tax rate. For example, where an annual sinking fund is £5000 per annum and the gross of tax accumulative rate is 6% per annum the interest earned after 1year is £5000 × 6% = £300. With tax deducted at 40% this is reduced to 60% of £300, that is, £180. £180 is only 3.6% of £5000. The gross accumulative rate of 6% has been reduced to a net rate of 3.6%. The solution is to apply a tax adjustment factor of $(1-t)$ to the gross rate, where t is the tax rate. Tax is also payable on the profit rent received, and so the sinking fund has to be set up using income remaining after tax has been paid. To ensure the net of tax sinking fund still replaces the initial outlay it needs to be grossed up. The effect of tax on a sinking fund is thus twofold: tax is levied on the interest accumulated in the sinking fund – to allow for this a net accumulative rate must be used, and tax is levied on the income from which the sinking fund is drawn – a grossing up factor must be applied to the sinking fund. The formula for a dual rate YP which incorporates these tax adjustments to the sinking fund is therefore as follows:

$$YP=\frac{1}{r+\left(SF\times(1/(1-t))\right)}=\frac{1}{r+\left(\left[s/((1+s)^n-1)\right]\times1/(1-t)\right)} \qquad [3.4]$$

where income is received quarterly in advance the formula is

$$YP_{\text{quarterly advance}}=\frac{1}{4\left[1-\left(1/\sqrt[4]{1+r}\right)\right]+4\left[1-\left(1/\sqrt[4]{1+s}\right)\right]\Big/\left[(1+s)^n-1\right][1-t]} \qquad [3.5]$$

where r is the remunerative rate and s is the accumulative or sinking fund rate.

For valuation purposes it is useful to divide leasehold property investments into two types: those with fixed profit rents and those with variable profit rents.

3.3.3.1 Valuation of fixed profit rents

These tend to take the form of short periods of profit rent between rent reviews or where the lease is short. As with freehold investment valuations, before the profit rent is capitalised all irrecoverable expenses must be deducted to arrive at a net profit rent. If the profit rent is fixed during the term Equation 3.4 can be applied directly, assuming that rent is paid annually in arrears.

For example, value the net profit rent of £25 000 pa from a head-lease that has a remaining term of 4 years. The leasehold yield (remunerative rate) is assumed to be 9% and the sinking fund (accumulative rate) is 4%. Income tax is payable at 40%. Inputting these figures into Equation 3.4, the profit rent is valued as follows:

$$PV = £25\,000 \times YP = £25\,000 \times \frac{1}{0.09 + \left(\left(0.04/(1+0.04)^4 - 1\right) \times \left(1/(1-0.04)\right)\right)}$$

$$= £25\,000 \times 2.0726 = £51\,815$$

Conventionally, the YP is looked up in valuation tables (see Davison, 2002) or can be calculated using a calculator or spreadsheet. However, when the YP multiplier is derived, the valuation may be set out in the conventional format thus:

Profit rent (£)   25 000
YP for 4 years @ 9% and 4% (40% tax)   2.0726
Valuation (£)   51 815

This valuation provides a return on capital at 9% and a return of capital at 4% (adjusted for tax), and this can be shown as follows:
The annual sinking fund to replace £12 000 in 4 years @ 4% per annum,

$$SF = £51\,815 \times \frac{r}{(1+r)^n - 1} = £51\,815 \times \frac{0.04}{(1+0.04)^4 - 1} = £51\,815 \times 0.2355 = £12\,202$$

Grossed up to allow for tax on original income of £25 000:

$$£12\,202 \times \frac{1}{(1-t)} = £12\,202 \times \frac{1}{(1-0.4)} = £20\,337$$

The grossed up annual sinking fund of £20 337 deducted from the annual profit rent of £25 000 leaves £4663 per annum, a 9% return on £51 815.

Another way of looking at this is that a 9% annual return *on* £51 815 is £4663 (*r* in the formula). £25 000 less £4663 is £20 337, and this represents the annual investment into the tax-adjusted sinking fund to ensure the return *of* capital. From Equation 2.11 in Chapter 2 we know that the future value of £1 pa is

$$FV\ £1\ pa = \frac{(1+r)^n - 1}{r}$$

Substituting *r* for the net-of-tax sinking fund rate of 4% and multiplying this formula by the annual sinking fund amount we get back to the capital outlay as follows:

$$£20\,337 \times \left[\frac{(1+0.04)^4 - 1}{0.04} \times (1-t)\right] = £20\,337 \times [4.2465 \times 0.6] = £51\,816$$

One danger with the dual rate YP approach is to imply an effective gross return on the sinking fund that is greater than the remunerative rate. For example, a 7% leasehold yield and a 4% sinking fund with tax at 50% would imply that the investor would be better off (initially at any rate) putting the money in the sinking fund rather than purchasing the leasehold investment. The profit rent must grow at a rate sufficient to compensate for investing at 7% *gross* of tax rather than 4% *net* of tax. Notwithstanding this word of caution, there are many criticisms of dual rate YP approach to the valuation of leasehold property investments. Perhaps the most fundamental criticism is the use of freehold yields to derive leasehold yields. Can leasehold investments really be compared to freehold investments, even for similar properties in similar locations? The initial yield derived from a recently transacted freehold investment reflects its perpetual nature and its income and capital growth prospects. Adjusting such a yield to arrive at a suitable yield to capitalise a terminable, possibly fixed profit rent would seem irrational to many. Greaves (1972) points out that when using the dual rate YP approach, the sinking fund only recoups original capital outlay and ignores inflation and capital growth – both of which are inherent in the property investment market. Incorporating tax adjustments is not normally undertaken with other valuation methods. Indeed, tax is not paid by some investors such as pension funds and charities so the tax deductions will significantly under-value leasehold investments in the eyes of these investors (Lean and Goodall, 1966; Baum, 1982). It is difficult to justify the dual rate YP approach when most investors do not take out sinking funds and certainly not on a property-by-property basis. Instead, investors provide for reinvestment in a general, portfolio sense. Also, where a leasehold investment is made with borrowed funds, sinking funds at low rates may be lower than the interest rate charged by lenders. So investors would be better off paying back the debt rather than investing in a sinking fund.

An alternative to the YP (dual rate) approach is the YP (single rate) approach, with or without tax adjustment. In this case, it is assumed, implicitly, that the sinking fund accumulates at the remunerative rate. In other words, the sinking fund earns as much as the investment itself. When a single rate is used, a smaller sum is put aside into the sinking fund than when dual rate is used because it will accumulate at a higher rate of return. Consequently, the net income after the sinking fund deduction will be higher when a single rate is used (Lean and Goodall, 1966). However, risk to capital is lower when dual rate is used as its replacement through a lower risk sinking fund and income is more secure because there is less possibility that more money will be needed to shore up the sinking fund as it is so low risk. So, with lower income and capital risk, the investor may be willing to accept a lower dual rate leasehold yield (remunerative rate) than when single rate is used. In practice, whatever approach is adopted, the valuations should be the same, and this occurs when the YPs are the same. For example, ignoring tax for a moment, the dual rate YP for 4 years at 9% leasehold yield and 4% sinking fund is 3.0723. To obtain the same YP using a single rate requires a leasehold yield of 11.46%. But, as Baum and Crosby (1995) note, even the YP (single rate) relies on comparison, and good leasehold comparisons will always be difficult to find. The practical solution has been to base the YP (single rate) on yield evidence derived from freehold comparables with an additional risk margin but, bearing in mind the rather different investment characteristics of freehold and leasehold property investments, this is not an ideal solution. An alternative is to use the YP (single rate) based on yields derived from non-property investments such as bonds (Baum and Crosby, 1995). Fraser (1993) argues that if the MR and head rent (and hence the profit rent) are fixed for the whole term, the yield would be similar to long-dated gilts plus a risk premium to reflect default risk and terminable nature of interest – remember that gilts return the capital invested. A final alternative is to use a cash-flow technique, and this will be examined in Chapter 5.

3.3.3.2   Valuation of variable profit rents

A profit rent may vary if the head-rent is fixed, and the sub-rent varies, perhaps because the sub-lease contains rent reviews. Essentially, the head rent is a fixed deduction from a growth income. Variable profit rents tend to be for longer periods of say 10 or more years and can be for very long periods. Referring back to the freehold ground rents described at the beginning of Section 3.3, the head-leasehold interest in such an arrangement would take the form of a variable profit rent. The head-tenant could develop the site and let the property at an occupation rent (containing rent reviews) far in excess of the fixed ground rent. Fraser (1993) explains that if the head-rent is a significant proportion of the sub-rent then gearing becomes an issue. Basically, the profit rent will grow at a faster rate than the market-based sub-rent and, it should be noted, at a faster rate than rental growth from a comparable freehold. The precise rate of growth will depend on the ratio of head-rent to sub-rent (the income-gearing ratio); the higher the head-rent proportion (higher income-gearing ratio) the greater the growth rate of the profit rent. A leasehold investment where the sub-rent is reviewed regularly and the head-rent is reviewed at the same time to a fixed proportion of the MR is an equity-sharing relationship as both freehold and leasehold interests are equity investments.

A long ground lease (more than 50 years remaining) can be very similar in its income growth characteristics to a freehold investment over much of its life. Figure 3.8 illustrates this. The lines track the capital values of two investments over a period of 50 years; the upper line is a freehold with a current MR of £100 000 per annum and a rental income growth rate of 5% per annum. The rent is projected every 5 years and capitalised at an ARY of 8%. So in year 0 the current MR of £100 000 per annum is capitalised at 8% giving a capital value of £1 250 000 and in year 25 it is £100 000 compounded at 5% per annum for 25 years capitalised at 8% giving £4 232 944. Because this investment is a freehold the capital value will keep rising exponentially in perpetuity as long as the growth rate and yield assumptions hold. The leasehold investment takes the form of a long (50 year) head-lease where the head-rent is fixed at £10 000 per annum of the whole term and is sub-let at the MR of £100 000 and, like the freehold, this sub-rent is predicted to grow at an average of 5% per annum. So the value of the long leasehold now is £100 000

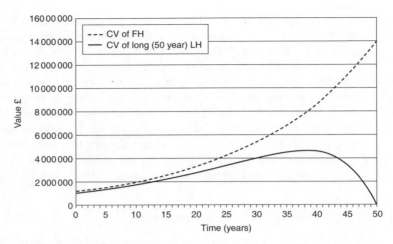

Figure 3.8   Freehold and leasehold capital.

less £10 000 giving a profit rent of £90 000 per annum capitalised at 8% for a fixed term of 50 years (assume same as freehold yield for simplicity) giving a capital value of £1 101 014. In year 25 the profit rent would have grown to £328 635 (£100 000 compounded at 5% per annum over 25 years less fixed ground rent of £10 000), and this is capitalised at 8% over the remaining 25 years of the lease giving a capital value of £3 508 110. However, towards the end of the lease term the capital value of the long lease drops dramatically.

But how do we value variable profit rents? The most popular way is to deduct the ground rent from the income to arrive at a net figure for capitalisation. In a multi-tenanted property a proportion of ground rent may be deducted from each tenant's gross income and the apportionment of ground rent may be calculated as a percentage of each tenant's rental value, as a percentage of each tenant's floor area, shared equally between tenants or as a percentage of the rent paid by each tenant. The YP (single rate) approach, with or without tax adjustment, can be used to capitalise the net profit rent subject to the same caveats as mentioned above. Using this approach, growth in the profit rent is implicitly handled in the ARY. For example, a leasehold shop is held on a head-lease with 12 years unexpired at a fixed rent of £10 000 per annum with no further rent reviews. The property is sublet for the remainder of the head-lease term (less 1 day) at a current rent of £30 000 per annum with 5 year rent reviews. The MR is £35 000 per annum. Rack-rented freehold shops sell at initial yields averaging 6%.

Rent received (£)	30 000
less rent paid (£)	10 000
Profit rent (£)	20 000
YP for 2 years @ 8%	1.7833
Term value (£)	35 666

Reversion to MR (£)	35 000	
less rent paid (£)	10 000	
Profit rent (£)	25 000	
YP for 10 years 8%	6.7101	
PV for 2 years @ 8%	0.8573	
Reversion value (£)		143 814
Valuation (£)		179 480

An alternative approach is to calculate the capital value of the ground rent separately and then deduct this amount from the capital value of the tenant's profit rent (from which the ground rent had not been deducted).

Fraser (1977) argues that it is wrong to compare yields from freehold investments with those from leaseholds with geared terminable profit rents because the income growth patterns will be different. For the profit rent from a long leasehold to be comparable to the MR from a freehold investment it needs to be for a long term and the head-rent should be fixed and significantly below MR (known as a ground rent or peppercorn rent). Alternatively the head-lease should contain reviews to a small fraction of the MR payable under the sub-lease which should contain regular, 5 year rent reviews to market levels. The yield that could be used to capitalise this type of investment might then be comparable to freehold yields but higher to reflect terminable nature of the investment, increased management and possible maintenance liability that the landlord might face. As the lease term nears termination increasing capital depreciation (see the rapid decline in capital value of the long lease-hold interest in Figure 3.8) means a leasehold investment bears little comparison to other types of investment and any supposed relationship between freehold and leasehold yields becomes tenuous. The problem with valuing variable profits at a single growth-implicit rate is that it is too simplistic. It becomes more rational to forecast profit rent over the lease term using a DCF approach, and we shall look at this in Chapter 5.

3.3.3.3   Investment method case study – valuation of an edge-of-town office building

A pension fund requires a valuation for accounting purposes. The property is located on a business park 5 miles north of the city of Bristol. It is 1 mile from a junction on the national motorway network, 1.5 miles from Bristol Parkway station – from which London is one and a half hours by train. The business park comprises 38 acres of landscaped grounds. The property consists of two storeys of open plan office space with the following NIAs: ground floor 721 m^2, first floor 717 m^2, giving a total NIA of 1438 m^2.

The accommodation includes a spacious reception area with first floor balcony, suspended ceilings with recessed lighting, raised floors with a 150 mm clear void, double glazed opening windows and gas-fired central heating. There is parking for 83 cars. The property was let 2 years ago to the regional property division of a large national bank on a 15 year lease that requires the landlord to be responsible for all repairs and insurance and is subject to upward-only rent reviews every 5 years on standard terms. There is also a service charge to cover the landlord's costs of landscaping, estate lighting and associated services. The current rent is £27000 per annum. You are aware of a recent letting on the business park of a similar property in all respects except that it has air conditioning. The rent was £26450 per annum, and the lease was on FRI terms. Analysis of this recent letting suggests a rent of £18.50 per square metre. You decide to reduce this to £17.50 per square metre to reflect the fact the subject property does not have air-conditioning. Therefore 1438 m^2 at £17.50 per square metre gives a MR for the subject property of £25165 per annum on FRI terms. The comparable property was sold by the developer to an investor for £330625 providing an initial yield of 8%. The valuation of the pension fund's property is set out as follows:

Gross term rent[a]	27000	
Less external repairs @ 10% gross rent (£)	2700	
Less insurance @ 5% gross rent (£)	1350	
Less management @ 5% gross rent (£)	1350	
Net rent (£)	21600	
YP 3 years @ 7%[b]	2.5771	
		55665
Reversion to MR (£)	25165	
YP perpetuity @ 8%[c]	125000	
Deferred 3 years[d] (PV £1 for 3 years @ 8%)	0.7938	
		249700
Valuation (£)		305365

[a]This is the rent receivable until the next rent review.
[b]The rent is capitalised at a yield that reflects the security of this income (the tenant is paying a rent less than market value and is therefore less likely to default). To reflect this, the yield obtained from the comparable evidence is reduced to 7% for the capitalisation of this income stream.
[c]Evidence of the 'growth implicit' yield is obtained from the comparable property.
[d]This capitalised income stream is receivable in 3 years' time.

Key points

- The yield describes ratio of income to capital value and is used to compare investments because yields are often comparable for similar types of property in the same area. The unit of comparison for rack-rented freeholds is the current rental income yield (initial yield) and for reversionary investments it is the equivalent yield. A **running yield** follows changes in income as a result of rent reviews, rent steps, cost changes and so on.

> ## Key points (continued)
>
> - The value of an investment depends on expected rental income and the yield. Capital value is very sensitive to changes in yield. The yield used to capitalise property investments is known as the ARY, and it is based on the initial yields derived from the analysis of recent transactions of comparable property investments.
> - The inverse of the yield is known as the YP: a multiplier used to compare different investments by stating how many years need to pass until the income received equals the capital value.
> - With freehold property investments there is a limit (based on land value) to any loss that may be incurred but for leaseholds a decline to nil value must eventually be suffered (Baum, 1991).
> - A leasehold interest can only have investment value if it produces income through a profit rent and is assignable. The conventional method of valuing leasehold investments was to convert the terminable interest (mathematically at least) into the equivalent of a freehold investment – the use of yields derived from freehold investments could then be justified. Valuers now tend to look much more closely at the nature of the cash-flow from a leasehold investment before applying a yield or yields.

3.4   Profits method

The comparison and investment methods of valuation are used to value properties for which there is an adequate supply of comparable evidence on which to base capital value, rental value and yield estimates. Not all types of property are in this happy situation, and the three remaining methods that are introduced in this chapter, although relying heavily on comparable evidence wherever possible for certain components within the valuations, adopt rather different approaches. Yet all three are based firmly on the economic principles described in Chapter 1, as we shall see.

The first of the three methods is the profits method, and this is used to value properties that are typically held as part of a business and where special characteristics of the property itself are central to the capacity of the business to generate profit. Such 'trading' properties might be regarded as specialised either because they are purpose built, owner-occupied or have some monopoly value due to their unique location, legal status or planning permission. Consequently, the attributes of the property with regard to the business operating therein are more important than the flexibility of the property for change of use. Typical properties that enjoy some element of trading monopoly are licensed premises, petrol stations, golf courses, airports, car parks but other types of 'specialised trading property' (RICS, 2003) may include hotels, garden centres and many recreational facilities such as cinemas and theatres. These properties are valued having regard to their estimated future trading potential. For most types of commercial property, valuers do not need to determine the profitability of the business undertaken in the property in order to estimate a rent because they are able to examine comparable rents agreed and yields obtained in the market. But market evidence of rental values and capital values of trade-related properties is often difficult to acquire in the local area because this type of business is usually sold as a going concern to an owner-occupier and within, because of the specialist nature of these types of properties. Having said this, it may be possible to make comparisons within trades on a wider geographical scale, perhaps examining profit made per hotel bedroom or nightclub floor, for example.

So, with the possible exception of certain leisure properties such as pubs, hotels and entertainment complexes, evidence of comparable market transactions is limited. Even when evidence is available, properties may be sold as a group and individual property values are difficult to isolate. Specialised trading properties are not usually held on a leasehold basis because of the significant investment in fixtures, fitting, furniture and equipment; consequently, there is not much rental evidence. Having said this, Rees and Hayward (2000) note that an expanding leisure industry has led to more rental evidence, but it is important to consider differences between properties such as lease length (which is typically longer for leisure properties) and user clauses (which are often more restrictive than those found in standard commercial leases due to specific planning permission or licensing for the trade). Improvements and fit-outs are often more expensive and more frequently undertaken than on standard commercial premises, and therefore it is particularly important to check how tenants' improvements are dealt with at rent review. Some small businesses such as a hotel, guest house or pub might attract purchasers willing to pay a price that includes a non-pecuniary return as well as capitalised financial income because it represents a lifestyle or location that they desire.

Specialised trading properties are valued on the basis of their potential net profit adjusted to reflect the trading of a reasonably efficient operator. Further guidance can be found in the RICS Red Book (RICS, 2003) in 'Guidance Note 1 – Specialised Trading Property Valuations and Goodwill'. The profits method values the property by isolating a portion of the available profit as rent for the premises in which the business takes place. It is therefore based on two economic assumptions: (1) the business makes a profit and (2) rent is a surplus paid out of this profit. It is also assumed that the current trading activity represents the optimum use of the property and that the business is efficiently run.

The first step then is to estimate a reasonably maintainable annual profit generated by the business by referring to income, expenditure and the operator's capital. Typically, these figures will be reported in the company's annual accounts, the previous 3–5 years of which are analysed to identify a fair, maintainable profit from a reasonable operator. It is wise to examine profit over several years because profit in any single year may be due to exceptional circumstances. Audited accounts are to be preferred but should not necessarily be accepted at face value. It should be borne in mind that profit and loss accounts may be prepared for various purposes and when using them to estimate reasonably maintainable profit, it is important to

Chapter 3

consider whether the business has more than one property. This is because consolidated accounts may not apportion expenditure on marketing, training, accountancy, depreciation, cyclical repairs or management expenses for head office premises between each property. It is also necessary to consider whether the salary or remuneration of the proprietor of an owner-occupied business is included and the effect of any additional revenue such as tips in the case of licensed premises. An inspection of the business identifies likely sources and amounts of income and expenditure, and provides a basis for comparison with the accounts. The valuer should look for any unusual items and conditions. Purchases and working expenses (including wages, repairs, insurance, rates, running costs, marketing, printing and stationery, depreciation allowance, and so on but excluding rent, mortgage payments or any interest on capital invested) are then deducted to arrive at an adjusted net annual profit or what is now referred to as earnings before interest, tax, depreciation and amortisation (EBITDA). Operators of small-scale and family-run businesses may use some personal items and capital to run the business, and these costs may not be reflected in the annual accounts; these costs should be identified and added to the working expenses. Such items might include interest payments on personal loans used to support the business, depreciation of property and reduced wages to family members. However, if the market for the business in question generally encompasses family-run employees then this should be acknowledged (Rees and Hayward, 2000). If the information in the accounts does not contain sufficient detail the company should provide trading information on a property-by-property basis for current and previous years, perhaps including receipts, if necessary, and percentages of gross turnover allocated to individual income and expenditure sources.

The next step is to use the adjusted profit to determine a capital value of the property, and there are two ways of doing this. The first is to capitalise the adjusted net annual profit at a suitable yield derived from market evidence. The second is to assume that a percentage of the adjusted net profit is retained by the business operator as remuneration for risk and operation and for interest on any capital invested in the business such as fixtures, consumable stock and cash[4.] The remainder (conventionally between 40% and 60% with a more precise figure derived from comparison to similar businesses) is assumed to be paid as rent. This notional rent is then capitalised at a discount rate obtained from the market or a multiple of marketable annual earnings (like a YP) to arrive at a capital value. This second approach is known as **dual capitalisation,** and Rees and Hayward (2000) argue that the rationale for splitting the profit into two elements is that rent provides a more secure return than business profit and can be capitalised at an appropriate (lower) property yield. Either way, the profits method is summarised in Table 3.10.

The property valuation is undertaken under the assumption that the business will, at all times, be effectively and competently managed, operated and promoted and that it is properly staffed, stocked and capitalised. The property to be valued usually includes all plant, machinery, fixtures,

Table 3.10   Profits method of valuation.

	Gross turnover
−	Cost of sales
=	Gross profit
−	Working expenses
=	Net profit
−	Remuneration to operator
−	Interest on capital invested, stock and consumables
=	Adjusted net annual profit
Then either	(1) Capitalised earnings approach (or single earning multiplier): capitalise adjusted net profit at an appropriate freehold or leasehold yield.
	(2) Dual capitalisation approach: Apportion adjusted net annual profit between rent and profit, then capitalise this notional 'annual rent'
=	Valuation

furniture, furnishings, fittings and equipment associated with the business and assumes that they are working and owned outright. A sinking fund should be set up to cover periodic replacement of these items, and therefore the annual payment into this fund should be deducted, as should a (notional) return on capital invested in the business, thus ensuring that profit emanates solely from the property (Rees and Hayward, 2000). Also included in the valuation is the market's perception of trading potential which includes transferable goodwill (such as existing and renewable licences, permits, consents, registrations, certificates, advanced bookings and order books). Moreover, freeholds are often offered for sale with the benefit of a trade inventory. Personal goodwill and consumable stock are excluded from the valuation. The valuation can reflect development or redevelopment potential, if the market would assume that possibility. For example, there may not be planning permission, but it is recognised as likely 'hope value' in the market.

Before we look at some examples of valuations that use the profits method, a word of caution is necessary. Because of the specialised nature of the businesses concerned, valuers tend to specialise in the valuation of properties used for particular trades. Some valuers may concentrate on the valuation of licensed premises such as pubs, clubs, restaurants and casinos, and others may specialise in the valuation of hotels, guest houses or care homes. The over-riding requirement for any valuer agreeing to value a specialised trading property is to have adequate knowledge and experience of the relevant business sector operating from the property. Three case studies are provided below. Marshall and Williamson (1996) cover the legal and valuation principles and methods of valuing all sorts of leisure property including caravan parks, cinemas, bingo clubs, night clubs, ten-pin bowling centres, hotels, garden centres, golf courses, pubs and restaurants. For cables and telecommunication installations, see Chapter 8 of Askham (2003).

It should be borne in mind that specialised trading properties can be of interest to conventional property investors and to business operators, and the rate of

Profits method case study A – valuation of a hotel

A 50-bed hotel in Bournemouth has an average annual occupancy of 50% and charges, on average, £70 per room per night. To value this property, first, use the comparison method to check whether £70 is a reasonable price and whether the occupancy rate is satisfactory compared to other hotels in the area. The data in Table 3.11 have been extracted from the accounts and the next step is to ensure that all sources of revenue are covered. The premises are held on a freehold basis, and the hotel is part of a small chain and must contribute towards head office overheads. The valuation is set out below:

Table 3.11 Information extracted from hotel accounts.

Income		Expenditure	
Accommodation	£638750	Purchases during the year	£45000
Bar	£45000	Wages	£200000
Restaurant	£25000	Utilities	£3500
		Laundry and cleaning	£2500
Stock		Business rates	£36000
Value on 1 Jan	£105000	Advertising	£1000
Value on 31 Dec	£95000	Contents insurance	£1250
Value of fixtures, fittings,	£250000	Repairs and renewals	£2500
furniture and equipment		Building insurance	£1000
		Repairs to building[a]	£1500
		Mortgage[b]	£1250
		Contribution to HQ costs	£2000
		Operator's remuneration	£50000

[a]These are regarded as on-off repairs and not an annual expenditure.
[b]Not regarded as a typical business expenditure and therefore excluded.

Gross turnover

Accommodation: £70 × 365 days × 50 rooms × 0.5 (£)		638750	
Bar (£)		45000	
Restaurant (£)		25000	
			708750
Cost of sales			
Purchases (£)		−45000	
Adjustment for depreciation in value of stock (£)	1 Jan: £105000 31 Dec: £95000	−10000	
			−55000
Gross profit (£)			653750

Profits method case study A – valuation of a hotel   (continued)

Less working expenses			
Wages (typically 30–35% of turnover) (£)		−200 000	
Utilities (£)		−3500	
Laundry and cleaning (£)		−2500	
Rates (£)		−36 000	
Advertising, stationery, telephone, postage, etc. (£)		−1000	
Contents insurance (£)		−1250	
Annual sinking fund for repairs and renewals (£)		−2500	
Building insurance (£)		−1000	
Contribution to HQ overheads (£)		−2000	
			−249 750
Net profit (£)			404 000
Less estimate of operator's remuneration (£)			−50 000
Less interest on operator's capital (£)			
Furniture, fixtures, fitting and equipment (FFFE)	−250 000		
Stock (average)	−100 000		
Cash (1 month's working expenses)	−21 000		
		−371 000	
Capitalised @ 10%		0.10	−37 100
Adjusted net profit (£)			316 900
(1) *Capitalised earnings valuation*			
YP in perpetuity @ 10%			10
Property valuation (£)			3 169 000
(2) *Dual capitalisation valuation*			
Estimate of MR @ 50% of adjusted net profit (£)			158 450
YP in perpetuity @ 5%			20
Property valuation (£)			3 169 000
If the business is to be sold as a going concern the trade inventory is usually included so the following items might be added when valuing the business:			
Furniture, fixtures, fitting and equipment (£)			250 000
Stock (average value) (£)			100 000
Cash (£)			21 000
			371 000
Total value of business (£)			3 540 000

return that these groups of purchasers require may be different. For the former it may relate to the perceived risk of the market and specific asset and the return that can be achieved on alternative investment assets. For the latter the rate of return may relate to the return required from the business as a whole, taking into account any mortgage and equity requirements for the type of property being valued. Consequently, the yield at which rent or the YP and which profit is capitalised should be chosen with these distinct markets in mind.

The profits method is also used to value care homes (see Sidwell, 1991, for example) with the comparison method as a check (recent sales or per registered bed multiplier in the locality). An adjusted net profit of around 25–30% of turnover for a nursing home and 35% for a less staff intensive residential home would be expected. The YP typically ranges from 4.75 to 6.25 depending on the location and quality of home, and it is particularly important to look at the quality of the catering facilities, staff costs, agency fees and medical charges.

Profits method case study B – valuation of a public house

Public houses are labour intensive, intricate businesses and subject to the demands of a fickle clientele. There are several types of purchaser including breweries, caterers/retailers, investors and owner-occupiers. As a consequence, variations of the profits method are often used depending on the type of likely purchaser. For a pub that is owned by an investor (a brewery, for example) and operated by a tenant publican, income is typically generated by three revenue streams: wholesale (beer, liquor and maybe food); retail (food and other sales) and the 'tied' rent. For a freehold pub (a freehouse) profits are derived from essentially two sources: retail sales (beer, liquor and food) and machine income. By analysing the income and expenditure streams, a net adjusted profit can be determined which is then divided between remuneration for the tenant and rent to the landlord. The rent can then be capitalised to determine a capital value. If the pub is held on a lease then the YP typically ranges between 1 and 2, and if the pub is held freehold, the YP is typically between 5 and 8. A pub may also be valued by reference to 'barrelage', and this enables the valuer to estimate likely turnover and profit without recourse to a full accounts approach. If a pub lease is terminating in the short-term, it may be worth considering the reversion to capital value rather than a revised lease rent. The profits method is also used to value nightclubs, the approach is similar to pubs but with an additional risk premium owing to the threat of licence revocation and the fickle nature of the market. Normally a YP between 3.5 and 5.5 of net adjusted profit is applied. If the pub, club or other licensed premises is let to a tenant with a strong covenant, it may be possible to value the property as an investment by capitalising the MR. The difficultly is in establishing the appropriate yield at which to do so. The term rent may be regarded as relatively secure, but the reversion may require a little more thought in terms of alternative use value, flexibility of the space, quality of the building and location. For some types of licensed premises in certain locations, an investment market is firmly established, but the profits method remains primary valuation method.

Profits method case study C – valuation of a petrol station

Petrol stations may be attached to car dealers and motorway services, found on supermarket sites, along main trunk roads and in other urban and suburban locations. They can be broadly classified as those with large throughput (of *acquisition* interest to oil companies) and those with less throughput (of *supply* interest to oil companies). Outlets tend to be; owned and operated by major oil companies, owned and operated by a dealer or retailer or owned by a major oil company (who also supplies fuel) and operated by tenant (who pays a 'tied' or low rent to the oil company). A valuer should therefore first classify the petrol station by throughput and tenure, and then analyse the capital values and throughput figures of comparable outlets to determine a scale of capital values per litre of throughput, effectively a comparative sales approach. Table 3.12 provides an example.

Then a more detailed examination of factors that influence the ability to trade can be undertaken such as the volume of passing traffic, average 'turn-in', size of average petrol purchase and so on. Great care must be exercised in adjusting throughputs of comparable petrol stations when reconciling them with the subject property. The trading potential of a specific station may depend upon many factors in addition to petrol sales, and it is important that these are taken into account. The retail element of the petrol station sales is now very significant on many sites, and opening hours and range of goods are being extended to meet growing consumer demand in this respect.

If the valuer believes the petrol station is one that an oil company might be interested in acquiring, the valuer will capitalise the throughput at a standard rate using a scale such as the one in Table 3.12 and capitalise the additional facilities, such as shop, car-wash, and so on separately. If the throughput is such that an oil company would only be interested in supplying fuel then the calculations will differ. Let us consider an example of a petrol station that is currently owned and occupied by an independent retailer and fuel is supplied by an oil company. The property is an owner-occupied, self-service petrol station located on a busy trunk road to the north west of Bristol. The road has good visibility, a 40-mph speed limit and average traffic volumes of 30 000 vehicles per day. The station has a turn-in rate of 4% from the near-side average of 16 000 vehicles per day plus 120 vehicles per day cross over from the other side

Table 3.12 Variation in capital values of petrol stations depending on throughput.

Annual throughput (litres)	Capital value per litre (pence)
2 273 000	16.50
2 727 600	19.80
3 182 200	24.20
3 636 800	26.40
4 091 400	26.40
4 546 000	26.40
5 682 500	27.50
13 638 000	29.70

Profits method case study C – valuation of a petrol station   (continued)

of the road. This produces an average of 640 customers from the nearside plus 120 'crossovers'. Estimating an average purchase of 20 liters, this equates to 15 200 liters per day or approximately 5 138 000 liters per annum on a 6.5-day week basis. Other facilities include a forecourt shop and a car wash. The petrol station is one that would, therefore, attract acquisition interest from the oil companies and is valued as if this class of purchaser would be in the market.

Forecourt (£):	1 387 260
5 138 000 L pa @ capital value of say 27 pence per litre	
(see Table 3.12)	
Shop (£)[a]:	6500
50m² @ £130 m²	
Car wash (£): @ one-third of net profit[b]	13 000
	19 500
YP in perpetuity @ 10%[c]	10
	195 000
Valuation (£)	1 582 260

[a]Shops and car washes are usually valued with regard to the forecourt throughput. In this example, comparable shop sales have been analysed on a capital value per square metre basis. £1 per 40 000 liters has been applied to produce the figure of approximately £130 per square metre. Alternatively, the retail element might be valued using a profits basis, taking the shop rent to be say 15–20% of net profit, but, as shop size increases, the profit per unit of floor area decreases as the good range is extended to include items with lower profit margins (Rees and Hayward, 2003).

[b]A fully equipped car wash is estimated to cost £75 000 to build, and, with a gross return of £50 000 per annum and running costs of £10 000 per annum, this leaves a net return of £40 000 per annum. It is assumed here that an oil company landlord would probably estimate one-third of the net profit as rent, equating to approximately £13 000 per annum.

[c]Oil companies are not institutional property investors so a 'common' yield, typically between 7% and 10%, is used to capitalise annual (non-fuel) income. Analysis of capital sales has shown the relationship between annual values and capital values to be pretty consistent.

Key points

- The valuation of specialised trading properties requires specialist skill. Only a few examples of the diverse range of trading properties that require use of profits method to value them have been given here.
- There is a heavy reliance on accounts and other financial information about the business and also reliance on expertise to value goodwill element of the business.
- Attention should be focused on two things. First, the adjustment of the costs to bring net profit back to a point where there is no regard to the individual operator – the business is assumed to be run by an averagely competent operator. And second, the selection of an appropriate capitalisation rate (yield) or capitalisation factor (YP).

3.5   Residual method

Land has value because it offers utility and therefore attracts a derived demand. The actual value of a particular piece of land (or site) will depend on not only on its current or existing use but also on its potential use and the anticipation of development rights – often referred to as **hope value** or development value. Changes in supply and demand may influence the development value of a piece of land to an extent that competition may increase the value of the land for reasons that have little to do with its current use, and it is the valuation of these potential development rights to which we now turn.

Obtaining comparable evidence of development land values is very difficult. Each site will differ widely in terms of size, condition of the site, potential use(s), design, permissible density of development, restrictions and so on, making adjustments to a standard value per hectare almost impossible. Instead, a project-based valuation approach, known as the **residual method of valuation,** is used. It is based on the assumption that an element of latent or residual value is released after development has taken place. The value of the site in its proposed state is estimated, as are all of the costs involved in the development, including a suitable level of return to the developer. If the value of the completed development is greater than its cost to build, the difference, known as the **residual value,** is the value of site. Land prices per hectare of similar sites that have recently been sold may provide a useful check.

In practice, the valuer will frequently rely on comparable evidence to assess development value and costs. In fact, for commercial development valuation, the investment method is usually employed to calculate development value. As with other valuation methods the residual method produces a snapshot valuation of the development opportunity, but it is a precursor to more rigorous techniques. Assuming the development goes ahead, the initial residual valuation is usually refined over the course of the development period using detailed cash-flow techniques which break down income and expenditure, and computer modelling may be used to assess the implications of changes in costs and expected value. We will look at these procedures in Chapter 6.

The residual method involves the estimation of a large number of cost and value-related variables, and this can lead to wide variations in site valuations as small differences in the inputs propagate to a large difference in the output valuation. Wherever possible therefore, a residual valuation should always be checked against comparable market evidence. The over-riding aim for the developer is to choose the optimum use, or uses, of the site in order to maximise value. As emphasised in Chapter 1, in any market-driven economy, it is assumed that developers seek to maximise profit and inevitably this involves identifying the sector where the permitted development will bring the highest return.

The basic equation for calculating site value is

$$
\begin{array}{ll}
 & \text{Value of completed development} \\
- & \text{Development costs} \\
- & \text{Developer's profit} \\
= & \text{Site value}
\end{array}
$$

This equation underpins the more complex valuations that are often used in practice to estimate land value (and hence how much to bid for a development site), the level of profit that may be obtained, how much lending is needed and over what time period. The residual valuation of a development site usually begins broadly at the evaluation stage and is gradually fine-tuned before the site acquisition and construction phases.

Taking a simple example, a property development company is thinking of acquiring 2 ha of cleared development land in order to construct 5000 m² of office space. Local property agents anticipate that the new space will let at an average of £130 per square metre and are confident that the freehold interest in the completed development can be sold to an investor at a price reflecting an initial yield of 8.5%. Construction costs are estimated to be in the region of £800 per square metre, and the development will take 1 year to complete. If the developer is seeking a minimum return on construction costs of 20%, what is the value of the site?

Development value:

Total constructed area (m²)	5000		
Estimated MR (£/m²)	130		
Estimated annual MR (£)		650 000	
YP in perpetuity @ 8.5%		11.7647	
			7 647 059
Less development costs			
Construction costs (5 000 m² @ £800/m²)		−4 000 000	
Profit on construction costs @ 20%		−800 000	
			−4 800 000
Site valuation (£)			2 847 059

Identification of a recently transacted comparable site will allow the site valuation to be put into a market context and confirm the viability of the proposed scheme. Now consider a more detailed example. The relevant steps of the valuation are clarified in the following section, where each numbered item is explained.

Development value:

[1] GIA (m²)	5000		
Net internal area (NIA) (m²)	3750		
[2] Estimated rent (£/m²)	150		
Estimated rental value (£)		562 500	
YP in perpetuity @ 8%		12.5	
[3] Gross development value (GDV) (£)		7 031 250	
[4] *less* disposal costs @ 2% of NDV (£)		137 868	
Net development value (NDV) (£)			6 893 382
Less **Construction Costs:**			
[5] Building costs 5000 m² @ £800/m² (£)	4 000 000		
[6] External works (£)	−80 000		
		−4 080 000	

[7] Professional fees @ 14% of building and external costs (£)	−571 200	
[8] Ancillary costs (£)	−150 000	
[9] Contingency @ 2% building, external & ancillary costs and fees (£)	−96 024	
[10] Other costs and fees:		
(a) Site Investigations, say (£)	−10 000	
(b) Planning fees, say (£)	−5 000	
(c) Building Regs, say (£)	−20 000	
(d) Bank's legal/professional fees @ 0.5% NDV (£)	−34 467	
(e) Bank's arrangement fee @ 1% NDV (£)	−68 934	
(f) Developer's legal fees @ 0.5% NDV (£)	−34 467	
Total Construction Costs (£)		−5 070 092
Less **Interest:**		
[11] on <u>half</u> total construction costs for <u>whole</u> building period @ 7% pa	−270 785	
on total construction costs and finance for void period @ 7% pa	−278 011	
Total Interest Payable		−548 796
Less **Letting & Sale Costs:**		
[12] Letting agent's fee @15% of estimated rental value (£)	84 375	
[13] Marketing (£)	5 000	
Total Letting and Sales Fees (£)		89 375
Total Development Costs (£)		5 708 263
[14] *plus* **developer's profit on total development costs @ 15%** (£)		856 239
		6 564 503
Future residual balance (Inc. profit on land) (£)		328 880
[15] *less* **Developer's profit on land costs @ 15%** (£)		42 897
Future balance (inc. interest on land and acquisition costs) (£)		285 982
[16] *less* interest on land and acquisition costs for total development and void period (PV£ 2.75 years @ 7%) (£)	0.8302	48 553
Present residual balance for land and acquisition costs (£)		237 429
[17] *less* Acquisition Costs @ 3.5% site acquisition price (£)		8 029
Residual site valuation:		**229 400**

[1] *Gross internal area.* The total internal area of the building to be developed (the area contained within the perimeter walls of the building) is termed the **GIA**, whilst the **NIA** is that part of the building on which rent can be charged and excludes corridors, plant rooms, lift lobbies, toilets and so on (see Chapter 2 and RICS, 2001). Some properties, such as supermarkets and industrial buildings are let on a GIA basis, whilst shops are zoned to reflect the higher value attached to floor area (or sales space) nearer the front of the premises. The ratio of GIA to NIA is called the **efficiency ratio**. The more efficient a building, the more space there is to charge rent on. Higher efficiency ratios lead to higher annual rentals per unit of constructed space so efficiency ratios should be maximised (e.g. open plan) without impinging unduly upon the aesthetics of the space. Here a low efficiency ratio of 75% has been used. In practice, comparable properties would be examined to determine an appropriate efficiency ratio for the design of the development in question.

GIA   = 5000 m^2
Efficiency ratio = 75%
So NIA   = 5000 × 0.75
                = 3750 m^2

[2] *Estimated rent.*   Rental value is estimated by considering rents that have been achieved on comparable properties. Rental evidence should be recent, similar and close. A net rent should be estimated that has been reduced to account for any regular expenditure such as management, repairs or insurance. It is usual to estimate current rent rather than predict the rent that might be achieved when the development is complete.

Estimated annual rent = NIA × estimated rent/m^2
                     = 3750 m^2 × £150/m^2
                     = £562 500

[3] *Gross development value*   **Gross development value (GDV)** is the price for which the completed development could be sold. For commercial property, GDV is calculated by undertaking an investment valuation based on the capitalisation of expected annual rent at an appropriate ARY. In this example, an investment valuation of the freehold interest in the development is as follows.

GDV = Estimated annual rent/yield
    = £562 500/0.08 = £7 031 250

[4] *Disposal costs.*   Costs of disposal or refinancing of the investment interest in the completed development have to be deducted from the GDV. In the case of a sale to an investor, these disposal costs will include agent's fees for marketing the scheme and negotiating sale terms, plus legal charges. If the completed development is to be retained as an investment it will usually need to be refinanced (converting the short-term development loan into a long-term debt), and it is assumed that the lender will charge an arrangement fee together with the costs of a valuation of the investment. A percentage deduction is therefore made from GDV to reflect these costs and to arrive at a net development value (NDV). A disposal fee of 2% of NDV has been assumed here.

NDV = GDV/(1 + 0.02)
    = £7 031 250/1.02
    = £6 893 382

[5] *Building costs.*   Building costs are usually estimated by a quantity surveyor, but an approximation can be gained by reference to recent contracts for similar developments. For example, reference may be made to the standard listing in building price books such as Spon's Architects and Builders Price Book (Davis, Langdon and Everest, 2004). These sources contain overall figures for construction costs (but excluding external works and professional fees) based on GIA but adjusted depending on the geographical region in which the development is located. It is usual to use current cost estimates and assume that cost inflation will match rental growth over the development period. Having said this, it is worth noting that construction contracts vary; they may be agreed on a 'rise and fall' or 'fixed price' basis. A building contractor who agrees to a fixed price contract is likely to charge a higher price because risk exposure is greater; £800 per square metre is the estimated building cost in this example

$$\begin{aligned} \text{Building costs} &= \text{building cost/m}^2 \times \text{GIA} \\ &= \text{£800/m}^2 \times 5000 \text{ m}^2 \\ &= \text{£4\,000\,000} \end{aligned}$$

[6] *External works.*   **External works** might include demolition, access roads, car parking, landscaping, ground investigations or other costs associated with the development that are in addition to the unit price building cost estimated above.

[7] *Professional fees.*   **Professional fees** are usually agreed as a percentage of the construction costs, but may be a fixed sum. Marshall and Kennedy (1993) found that a typical total for fees averaged 14.5%; Table 3.13 shows a representative breakdown of these fees:

The appropriate fee level depends on the type and location of the development. Total professional fees of 14% of construction and external costs have been assumed here.

$$\begin{aligned} \text{Professional fees} &= (\text{building costs} + \text{external costs}) \times 14\% \\ &= \text{£4\,080\,000} \times 0.14 \\ &= \text{£571\,200} \end{aligned}$$

Table 3.13 Typical professional fee levels.

Professional	Fee as a % of building costs
Architect	5–7.5
Quantity surveyor	2–3
Structural engineer	2.5–3
Civil engineer	1–3
Project manager	2+
Mechanical and Electrical consultants	0.5–3

[8] *Ancillary costs.*   **Ancillary/**miscellaneous **costs** might include planning fees, building regulation fees, insurance and other, more minor, incidental costs.

[9] *Contingency fund.*   The **contingency allowance** is a reserve fund to allow for any increase in costs. As construction costs are the single largest sum after land, any inflationary effect is likely to have a significant impact on costs. If the economy is particularly volatile, a cautionary approach is to apply the contingency allowance to *all* costs, including finance costs, but this will depend on the perceived risk of the project. Marshall and Kennedy (1993) found that the contingency fund is generally set at 3–5% of building costs, professional fees (and sometimes interest payments) but the figure varied depending on the nature of site (restrictive site, subsoil etc.) and the development project itself.

$$\begin{aligned} \text{Contingencies} &= (\text{building costs} + \text{external works} + \text{misc. costs} + \text{fees}) \times 2\% \\ &= (£4\,000\,000 + £80\,000 + £150\,000 + £571\,200) \times 0.02 \\ &= £96\,024 \end{aligned}$$

Generally, the longer the development period and the more complex the construction of the building, the higher the risk of unforeseen changes, therefore, the higher the contingency allowance.

[10] *Other costs and fees.*   Depending on the level of detail required from the residual valuation, estimates for various additional costs and fees can be included.

[11] *Development period.*   The total development time needs to allow for obtaining planning consent, preparing drawings and so on. This is sometimes referred to as a **lead-in period**. In other words, it precedes the construction phase. Finally, there may be a period of time between completion of the development and occupation by a tenant, including a possible rent-free period, and this is referred to as a **void period**. During a void period, interest is payable on *all* costs, so any extensions to this time period will significantly increase the amount of loan finance incurred. In Figure 3.9 we assume a lead-in period of 6 months, a construction phase of 18 months and a void period of 9 months.

The time-line is important as interest payments depend on the duration of the loan. A lender will charge interest at the bank base rate for lending plus a

Figure 3.9   Development time-line.

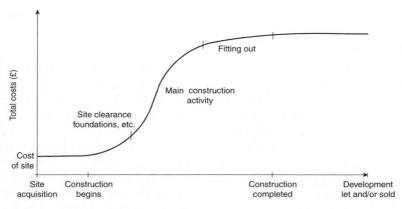

Figure 3.10   Build-up of costs over time.

return for risk. The magnitude of the risk premium will depend on the status of developer, the size and length of loan and the amount of collateral the developer intends to contribute.

Interest payments on money borrowed to fund construction usually accrue monthly but are rolled up over the development period and paid back when the development is let or sold. Rather than calculating the interest charges on a monthly basis, an approximation (for the purposes of the residual valuation) is obtained by calculating the annual interest on half of the costs over the construction period. This is a rudimentary method of reflecting the fact that costs start off low, peak in the middle and tail off towards the end of the period, illustrated in Figure 3.10.

In other words, interest is not paid on the full amount over the entire building period, assuming a straight line rather than an S-shaped build-up of construction costs, illustrated in Figure 3.11.

Detailed cash-flow projections are essential once the project is under way in order to incorporate changes in revenue and costs, and particularly so for **phased developments**.

Interest accrued on money borrowed to purchase the site, construct the property and hold over any void period is calculated separately. The calculation of the amount of interest incurred on money borrowed to purchase the site is incorporated in the final stages of the residual valuation because it is based on the figure we are trying to estimate, namely site value. Here we incorporate interest on the construction costs over the construction and void periods.

Because interest payments are rolled up until completion, the interest is compounded over this period. In this example, a base rate of 6% per annum plus a risk premium of 1% per annum has been used, giving a short-term finance rate of 7% per annum. So interest accrued during the construction period is calculated by compounding half of the total construction costs over 1.5 years @ 7% per annum interest:

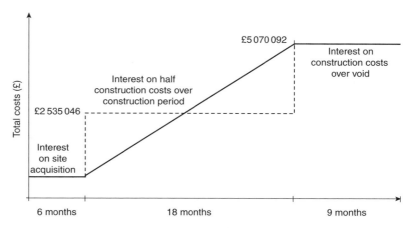

Figure 3.11 How interest is calculated.

$$= (£5\,070\,092/2) \times [(1 + 0.07)^{1.5} - 1]$$
$$= £2\,535\,046 \times 0.1068$$
$$= £270\,743$$

Sometimes interest on professional fees is calculated separately by compounding the amount over two-thirds of the building period. This helps reflect the fact that such fees tend to be incurred early on in the development, during the planning and design phase and hence interest will be incurred for a longer period of time. Alternatively, and more frequently, these days given the ubiquity of spreadsheets, a simple cash-flow would be constructed to reflect the probable timing of costs and fees on, say, a quarterly basis.

Interest accrued during the void period is calculated by compounding the total construction costs and interest rolled up during the construction period over 0.75 years (9 months) at 7% per annum interest.

$$= (£5\,072\,092 + £270\,743) \times [(1 + 0.07)^{0.75} - 1]$$
$$= £5\,342\,835 \times 0.0521$$
$$= £278\,113$$

It can be seen that approximately the same amount of interest has accrued in a void period of 9 months as over a construction period of 18 months. That is why it is very important to keep the length of any void period to a minimum.

[12] *Letting fee.* The **letting fee** covers both agent fees and legal fees. The fee that a letting agent charges is usually calculated as a percentage of the estimated MR. Here 15% of the estimated rental value has been used because it is assumed that two agents have been instructed to jointly market the development – the agent who successfully lets the scheme will receive the fee. The fee level is negotiated in practice and may well be lower than this, of course. If just one agent is marketing the completed scheme (known as a sole agency instruction) the fee would certainly be lower at, say, 5% or 10% of the estimated rental value.

$$\text{Letting fee} = \text{estimated annual rent} \times 15\%$$
$$= £562\,500 \times 0.15$$
$$= £84\,375$$

[13] *Marketing cost.*   The cost of marketing may be entered as an estimated figure. It would cover items such as advertising, opening ceremony, brochure design and production. The scale would obviously depend on the nature of the development.

[14] *Developer's profit on construction costs.*   Developer's profit is the reward for initiating and facilitating the development and is dependent upon the size, length and type of development, the degree of competition for the site and whether it is pre-let or sold before construction is complete (a for-head sale). The profitability of a development will, of course, vary. It is often argued that the profit margin obtainable from residential development is usually lower than from commercial because of the relatively competitive nature of the house-building industry. What can be confidently stated is that property development is perceived as more risky than investment in completed and let properties. Consequently, the required return will be higher than these 'standing' property investments. Marshall and Kennedy (1993) suggested that most developers calculate profit as a percentage of costs, typically ranging between 15% and 17%. Here we calculate developer's profit at 15% of costs.

$$\text{Developer's profit on construction costs} = £5\,708\,263 \times 15\%$$
$$= £856\,239$$

[15] *Developer's profit on land costs.*   The acquisition of the site is a development cost just like any other cost. The equation below shows how developer's profit on site cost is calculated.

$$\text{Developer's profit on site costs} = \text{future residual balance} - [\text{future}$$
$$\text{residual balance}/(1 + 15\%)]$$
$$= £328\,880 - (328\,880/1.15)$$
$$= £42\,879$$

[16] *Interest on site costs.*   Assuming the site was purchased by the developer at the start of the development, interest on site costs must be paid over the total development period. To do this the figure calculated thus far must be discounted to determine its present value at the short-term finance rate of 7% over the total development period. Even if money is not borrowed to fund site purchase or construction the opportunity cost of funds used should be reflected in the valuation, and the lending rate is a good proxy for the opportunity cost of capital.

$$\text{Interest on site and site acquisition costs} = £285\,982 \times$$
$$\{[1/(1 + 0.07)^{2.75}] - 1\}$$
$$= £48\,553$$

[17] *Acquisition costs.*   **Acquisition costs** must be deducted to leave the net amount remaining for purchase of the site. These acquisition costs usually include legal costs, tax (Stamp Duty and VAT), valuation and agents' fees plus any pre-contract investigations such as soil surveys, environmental impact assessments and contamination reports.

$$\text{Site value} = \text{residual balance}/(1 + 3.5\%)$$
$$= £237\,429/1.035$$
$$= £239\,398$$

The final figure is the residual site value and represents the maximum amount that should be paid for the site, if the proposed development was to proceed and all of the valuation assumptions held true.

Key points

- The residual method is based on a very simple economic concept – that the value of the land is calculated as a surplus remaining after all estimated development costs have been deducted from the estimated value of the completed development.
- Difficulties and valuation variance arises when estimating values of all the input variables because small errors in each can lead to large variation in value.
- In practice, the residual method is first employed in its simplest form and then the complexity level increases as development plans crystallise.

3.6   Replacement cost method

The replacement cost or contractor's method is used to value specialist properties that are seldom sold because there is no clear market demand. Consequently, there is little or no comparable evidence. A property might be specialist because its use requires it to be constructed in a particular way, including highly production-specific manufacturing plants such as chemical works and oil refineries; public administration facilities such as prisons, schools and colleges, hospitals, town halls, art galleries and court facilities; and transport infrastructure such as airports and railway buildings. Or the property might be specialised by virtue of its size or location such as an extensive research and development facility in a remote location – ideal for a company's specific requirement but with little or no demand in the open market.

The method is employed when the existing uses of these sorts of properties need to be valued for corporate disclosure (reporting the value of property assets in company accounts), purposes for business rates for compulsory purchase and compensation. The method is also used to estimate the replacement cost for insurance valuations. However, when these sorts of properties are offered for sale, perhaps because they are no longer required for their current use, the primary market is likely to be for alternative uses. A recent example is the sale of obsolete telephone exchanges.

When using the replacement cost method to value specialist properties for corporate disclosure it is usually called **depreciated replacement cost** (DRC).

The value is essentially a deprival value of the property to the owner. If the replacement cost value is significantly different from the market value of an alternative use for which planning permission is likely to be forthcoming, both should be reported in the company accounts.

The method does not actually calculate a market value. Instead, it calculates a replacement cost for the improvements that have been made to the land, typically in the form of buildings and ancillary man-made land uses such as car parks and the like. It is therefore fundamentally different from the valuation methods described so far. Because of an almost complete lack of comparable market transaction information the method seeks to estimate replacement cost rather than exchange price. It does not produce a market valuation (value-in-exchange) as such because cost relates to production rather than exchange, and it is often regarded as the method of last resort for this reason. The method involves assessing the value of the land in its existing use and adding the replacement cost of the building, adjusted for age and obsolescence. Mathematically, the method can be stated as follows:

Cost of new building (either an identical property or a modern equivalent)
− Disability allowance due to age and/or obsolescence
= Capital value of building
+ Value of land
= Value of property

The market value of the site is estimated by referring to evidence of comparable transactions in the land market. According to Plimmer and Sayce (2006), in the absence of better evidence, or where the building exists on a site of exceptionally high value, it may be appropriate to assume a notional replacement site, within the same locality and which is equally suitable for the existing use. Such an approach is particularly appropriate where, historically, city centre locations were preferred for uses such as local government offices, prisons and hospitals, but which now tend to locate on more peripheral, lower value sites.

Construction costs should be based on a modern equivalent building rather than an identical replacement because it will be more cost-effective. Plimmer and Sayce (2006) suggest that the land and the buildings should be valued as at the same date, an instant build in other words, as this avoids the difficulties of backdating costs during what could be a lengthy construction period. If the building is listed then the cost of replacing it with a facsimile will need to be estimated. Estimates of construction costs can be obtained from professional cost estimators (quantity surveyors), cost manuals (such as Spon's Architects and Builders Price Book (Davis, Langdon and Everest; updated each year)), builders and contractors. The cost of a new building will include the construction cost, site facilities (car parking, landscaping etc.), services, planning, building regulation fees, contingencies, fees and so on. The building cost should be adjusted to include professional fees and finance costs, the latter usually being borrowed on variable rate loans.

There are several methods of calculating a depreciation allowance to reflect the age of the building valued and any obsolescence that it might be suffering from. Obviously, such an allowance will depend on the building age and the changing requirements of the user. Essentially, it is a subjective judgement. One approach is to adopt a 'straight line percentage deduction' based on the proportion of estimated remaining economic life. If refurbishment takes place then the economic life of the building might be extended. Another method is the 'reducing balance'. This works by applying a fixed annual depreciation rate. For example, if the building cost £1 000 000 and the fixed annual depreciation rate is 10%, the value of the building at the end of the first year is £900 000. With the same rate of depreciation in subsequent years, the value will reduce to £810 000 at the end of the second year, £729 000 in the third year, and so on. This method allows for greater depreciation in the early years, and value of the building is never completely written off. Alternatively, a sinking fund may be set up that requires an annual investment to replace the capital value of the building at the end of its estimated economic life (see Equation 2.14 in Chapter 2).

The following two examples illustrate how the replacement cost method is used in practice.

Replacement cost method case study A – valuation of an owner-occupied property for accounts purposes

A purpose-built industrial property with an estimated life of 90 years with 16 years remaining has a floor area of 2500 m^2 and a site area of 0.8 ha. The current value of this property needs to be estimated for inclusion in the company accounts.

Land	0.8 ha @ £200 000[a] per ha (£)		160 000
Building	modern replacement cost including fees @ £300/m^{2b} (£)	750 000	
	Less depreciation @ 74/90 years = 82% (£)	−615 000	
			135 000
Estimated DRC (£)			295 000

[a]Figure obtained from comparable evidence of land sales
[b]Figure obtained from building cost information services such as price books.

Replacement cost method case study B – valuation for insurance purposes

These are also known as **reinstatement valuations** and are undertaken on behalf of lenders, normally in conjunction with a market valuation but are also undertaken for insurers and insurance brokers, property owners and occupiers. A reinstatement valuation provides for a similar property as at the date of the valuation or at the commencement of insurance policy cover and should be carried out at least every 3 years. In the case of insurance valuations, the site is assumed to continue in existence despite whatever disaster may have affected the buildings thereon. Consequently, it does not include a valuation of the land.

Replacement cost method case study B – valuation for insurance purposes (continued)

Furthermore, if the insurance policy provides for a replacement 'new' property (a 'new-for-old' policy as it is known) then no deduction should be made to reflect deterioration and obsolescence.

Building cost[a] ($£/m^2$)	1250	
Building area[b] (m)	500	625 000
Less obsolescence[c] allowance (% building cost)	25%	(156 250)
Less deterioration[d] allowance (% building cost)	15%	(93 750)
Reinstatement value of existing property		375 000

[a]Building costs can be broken down into component parts and based on a quantity surveyor's 'bill of quantities'
[b]Building area can also be broken down by use
[c]Obsolescence may affect different parts of building at different rates
[d]Depreciation also can vary according to type of structure

   For further information on the cost approach to valuation, see Connellan and Baldwin (1993).

Key points

- The replacement cost method is used to value properties that very rarely trade in the open market, and therefore there is little or no evidence of comparable market prices on which to base value estimates.
- As a valuation method it is generally regarded as a 'method of last resort' because it does not really produce an estimate of market value, at least not of the building component anyway.
- The method does, however, have wide application in the valuation of public and private sector specialised property assets for accounts purposes, and it is also used to estimate building reinstatement costs for insurance purposes.

3.7   Summary

Every valuation is prepared for a particular purpose, and this purpose, together with the type of property that is being valued, determines the appropriate method or methods. Market value is an estimate of exchange price so it should not be surprising that the best way of estimating market value is examining evidence of prices paid in the market for comparable properties in the recent past. The comparative method is therefore the most reliable; there is no substitute for market evidence. But no two properties are the same so the process of comparison will inevitably involve some adjustment of comparison elements. Where no evidence exists recourse must be made to another method, and it is wise to use more than one method to provide a check. Table 3.14 is an attempt to map valuation methods onto various property types. It is not intended to present an exhaustive list, just a sense of which method might be appropriate when valuing a particular type of property. This chapter has presented a fairly detailed picture of the conventional methods of valuing property in the UK. Contemporary methods and techniques offer enhancements and pose challenges to these methods, and these will be examined in the next three chapters in relation to the main property market sectors.

Table 3.14   Property types and valuation methods.

Property type	Valuation method(s)	Comparison elements
Retail		
Standard shops		Frontage, sales floors, storage, shape, rear access, service charges (shopping centres)
Large shops		
	Comparison or	Main sales area, storage/stock area, foyer,
Large food-based stores	investment	special sales and preparation areas, restaurant, concessions/shops in store, garden centre, office/staff areas, kitchens, loading areas, mezzanine, parking, petrol
Retail warehouses		sales area, storage, ancillary areas, parking
Offices		
Traditional offices	Comparison or	Air-conditioning, suspended ceilings, raised
Business parks	investment	floors, reception area, single or multiple occupier, heating, lighting
Serviced offices		
Industrial		
Factories	Comparison or	Loading area and facilities, floor loading, eaves
Warehouses	investment	height, clean areas, offices, gantries, H&S equipment, power, air conditioning, heating
Licensed		
Public houses and clubs	Profits	Parking, nature of trade, hours, sales mix, special endeavours
Hotels	Profits or comparison (£/bed)	Number of beds, ensuite, tariff, % occupation, facilities (bar, restaurant, health club) in relation to size, function facilities
Restaurant	Profits or comparison (£/cover)	Planning and licensing consents, hours, restrictions, goodwill, FFE, trading name/ franchise value, HQ costs if part of chain, fit-out costs
Fast food (high street)	Comparison or investment	
Leisure		
Cinemas		Screens, fitting out, size of auditoria, shop
Theatres and concert halls	Profits or comparison (£/seat)	units, confectionary sales, shows per day, food and drink facilities
		Capacity, seasonality, grant use, flexibility of space

Chapter 3

Table 3.14   (continued)

Property type	Valuation method(s)	Comparison elements
Leisure		
Bingo, snooker, bowling, casinos	Profits or comparison if standard building	Capacity
Night clubs		
Amusement arcades		
Sports halls/grounds		Exclusivity, surface, clubhouse, lighting
Golf courses	Profits	Exclusivity, quality of club, shop, variety/ quality of course, seasonality, waiting list, fees.
Guest houses		
Chalet parks		
Caravan sites	Profits or comparison (£/ pitch)	
Garden centres		
Horticultural		
Betting shops	Profits	
Leisure pools, centres and parks	Profits, comparison or DRC	Pool, flexibility of hall, quality of changing rooms
Motor		
Motor Trade		
Petrol stations	Profits	Forecourt sales, shop sales, hours, customer accounts, credit card sales, agency sales, canopies, toilets, parking, supply agreement details, non-forecourt buildings and car sales land
Car parks	Profits or comparison	% occupation at peak/non-peak times, proportion of upper deck spaces, pricing policy, seasonal factors, manned/P&D/free, permit-holder spaces, limited time parking, access, layout, headroom, lifts, walkways
Aviation		
Airport hangers	DRC	
Airport shops	comparison or investment	
Airfields	DRC	
Institutional		
Town halls	DRC	
Cemeteries/crematoria		
Schools and libraries	DRC or comparison if not specialist build	
Museums and galleries		Income, exclusivity, flexibility of space
Hospitals	DRC	Proportion of open wards to private rooms, number of theatres, outpatients' clinics, consulting rooms, non-renumerative facilities

Table 3.14   (continued)

Property type	Valuation method(s)	Comparison elements
Nursing homes	DRC, profits or comparison if not specialist build	
Public conveniences		
Fire stations	DRC	
Utilities		
Places of worship	DRC or comparison if not specialist build	
Miscellaneous		
Quarries, gravel pits	DRC, profits (licence for extraction) or comparison ($£/m^3$)	
Radio masts/aerials	comparison or	
Lock up garages	investment	

Chapter 3

Notes

1. A standard shop is taken to have a 6.1 m frontage, 18.3 m depth and 30 m^2 of storage or staff accommodation, and is let on lease terms that require the tenant to be responsible for all repairs and insurance.
2. It is assumed that, even though freehold property investments are let on leases of say 5, 10, 15 years or whatever, the property will re-let on expiry of current lease. Therefore, rent can be regarded as perpetual. This assumption might be altered if redevelopment or the like is planned, in which case a discounted cash-flow is more able to handle these sorts of cash-flow details – see Chapter 6.
3. The remunerative rate for leasehold investments is typically 1–2% above comparable freeholds to reflect the top-slice nature of profit rent, the dual contractual burden suffered by leaseholder, risk of dilapidations expenses inherited from previous tenants (Baum and Crosby, 1995), also to reflect the poor marketability of the interest and the cost of managing a sinking fund and purchasing another investment at the end of the lease.
4. This is personal and not transferable.

References

Appraisal Institute (2001) *The Appraisal of Real Estate*, 12th edn, The Appraisal Institute, Chicago, USA.

Askham, P. (2003) *Valuation: Special Properties and Purposes*, Estates Gazette, London, UK.

Ball, M., Lizieri, C. and MacGregor, B. (1998) *The Economics of Commercial Property Markets*, Routledge, London, UK.

Baum, A. (1982) The enigma of the short leasehold, *Journal of Valuation*, 1, 5–9.

Baum, A. (1991) Property Futures, *Journal of Property Valuation and Investment*, 9, 3.

Baum, A. and Crosby, N. (1995) *Property Investment Appraisal*, 2nd edn, Routledge, London, UK.

Bowcock, P. and Harker, N. (1983) The valuation of varying incomes, *Journal of Valuation*, 1, 4, 363–376.

Connellan, O. and Baldwin, R. (1993) The cost approach to valuation, *Journal of Property Valuation and Investment*, 11, 1.

Crosby, N. (1986) The application of the equated yield and real value approaches to market valuation: the logic of techniques and the analysis of comparables, *Journal of Valuation*.

Davis, Langdon and Everest (eds) (2004) *Spon's Architects' and Builders' Price Book*, Taylor and Francis, London, UK.

Davison, A. (2002) *Parry's Valuation Tables,* 12th edn, Estates Gazette, London, UK.

Fraser, W. (1977) *The Valuation and Analysis of Leasehold Investments in Times of Inflation*, Estates Gazette, London, UK, Issue 244, 15 October, 197–203.

Fraser, W. (1993) *Principles of Property Investment and Pricing*, 2nd edn, Macmillan Basingstoke, Hampshire, UK.

Greaves, M. (1972) *Discounted Cash Flow Techniques and Current Methods of Income Valuation*, Estates Gazette, London, Issue 233, 2147–2151 and Issue 233, 2339–2345.

IVSC (2005) *International Valuation Standards*, 7th edn, International Valuation Standards Committee, London, UK.

Lean, W. and Goodall, B. (1966) *Aspects of Land Economics,* Estates Gazette Ltd, London, UK.

Marshall, A. (1920) *Principles of Economics,* 8th edn, Macmillan, London, UK.

Marshall and Kennedy. (1993) Development valuation techniques, *Journal of Property Valuation and Investment*, 11, 1.

Marshall, H. and Williamson, H. (1996) *The Law and Valuation of Leisure Property*, 2 nd edn, Estates Gazette, London, UK.

Plimmer, F. and Sayce, S. (2006) Depreciated Replacement Cost – Consistent Methodology? Proceedings of the XXIII FIG Congress, Munich, Germany, 8–13 October 2006.

Rees, W. and Hayward, R. (2000) *Valuation: Principles into Practice*, 5th edn, Estates Gazette, London, UK.

RICS (2001) *Code of Measuring Practice – A Guide for Surveyors and Valuers*, 5th edn, RICS Books, London, UK.

RICS (2003) *RICS Appraisal and Valuation Standards*, 5th edn (as amended), Royal Institution of Chartered Surveyors, RICS Business Services Ltd, Coventry, UK.

Sayce, S., Smith, J., Cooper, R. and Venmore-Rowland, P. (2006) *Real Estate Appraisal: From Value to Worth*, Blackwell Publishers, Oxford, UK.

Sidwell, A. (1991) The valuation of nursing and residential homes, *Journal of Property Valuation and Investment*, 9, 4.

Sykes, S. (1981) Property valuations: a rational model, *The Investment Analyst*, 61, 20–6.

Wiltshaw, D. (1991) Valuation by comparable sales and linear algebra, *Journal of Property Research*, 8, 3–19.

Chapter 4
Property Occupation Valuation

4.1   Introduction

A lot of money is tied up in commercial property. The Government estimates that commercial, industrial and other non-domestic property is worth approximately £625 billion and the Investment Property Forum (IPF) estimates that around £400 billion is in the private sector, representing 34% of total business assets (IPF, 2005). But not all firms are able, or indeed want, to purchase the property that they intend to occupy. Many of those firms that do own the properties that they occupy will have financed the acquisitions by borrowing money, perhaps secured against the value of the properties themselves. It is estimated that 64% of commercial property is owner-occupied in the UK, and most of these will be debt financed. Other firms prefer to rent their properties from owner-investors. Being able to lease a property rather than purchase it means that the occupier does not have to finance its acquisition, and the firm has greater flexibility to move when the property is no longer suitable. The ownership of property, where occupation is transferred to a tenant, is a form of investment, the financial return from which must be sufficient to compensate for the effort of owning the property and leasing it out. Consequently, valuations for investors and valuations for occupiers are two sides of the same coin, and the investment side will be considered in the next chapter.

The split between occupation and ownership is personified by the landlord–tenant relationship where, in general terms, the landlord owns a freehold interest in a property and the tenant owns a leasehold interest in the same property. The legal relationship can be more complicated than this with head-leaseholds, sub tenants, over-riding leases and the like, which can lead to complex situations where legal advice may be needed to identify the various interests in a single building before any valuation can be tackled. Valuations are required by the owners and occupiers within this landlord–tenant relationship to determine the level of rent that should be paid (the rental value) at the commencement of a new lease, at rent reviews during a lease, at the renewal of an existing lease and to determine the amount of any compensation payments that might be payable to the tenant by the landlord at the end of the lease or at its renewal. Moreover, occupiers – whether tenants or owner-occupiers – may require capital valuations of their property assets for inclusion in company financial statements. If a business operator wishes to purchase a property he may well do so using debt finance, and the lender will require a capital valuation of the property if it is going to be used as collateral for the loan. These are probably the most common reasons for valuers being asked to conduct rental and capital valuations of commercial property from an occupation perspective, but there are other reasons too: rental and capital valuations of properties are required by Government for tax purposes; capital valuations are required when business property is to be compulsorily acquired or when compensation payments are due; and insurance companies require capital valuations of business premises that they insure. This chapter will look at each of these.

4.2 Rental valuations at lease commencement, rent review and renewal

In this section, we are concerned with the assessment of rental value at the commencement of a new lease, at a rent review or at the renewal of an existing lease. Usually, this is a matter of gathering and adjusting comparable evidence from recent lettings of similar properties in the locality using the comparison method of valuation (see Chapter 3). However, the increasing diversity of lease contracts means that this process is no longer as straightforward as it sounds, as French *et al.* (2000) put it,

> In the late 1990s the business environment experienced substantial structural change and tenants began to demand bespoke leases to suit their particular occupational requirements. This led to a plethora of different lease contracts, as tenants require shorter leases, the ability to expand and contract, break clauses and upwards/downwards rent reviews. The market is now as diverse as it was uniform.

This structural change in the business environment was caused initially by an over-supply of commercial property (office space in London in particular), but then there was a shift in the organisational structure of businesses in all sectors. In the office sector, changing working practices were brought about by increased use of IT such as hot-desking, home-working and peripatetic office use; outsourcing of not only non-core or peripheral business but also management of property and estates; increased use of serviced offices and other ways of using accommodation over short time periods. All of this has had a profound effect on the conventional lease contract and has also shortened the economic life of many commercial buildings owing to the early onset of obsolescence. Many of these buildings are otherwise physically sound and have found new uses such as residential apartments.

In the retail sector, internet shopping, home delivery and the perception of shopping as a leisure activity has changed occupier requirements. In the industrial (factories and warehouses) sector, these retail trends have led to an increased demand for large shed-style warehousing facilities and, in cases where manufacturing does take place in the UK, the automation of production has meant that factory requirements can be highly specified.

Up until the end of the 1980s, standard leases in the UK were 20–25 years long with all repair and insurance liabilities imposed on the tenant, either directly or through a service charge in a multi-let property. Most leases provided for upward-only rent reviews every 5 years. Tenants had the right to renew their leases under the Landlord and Tenant Act 1954 and could usually assign or sub-let any unexpired lease term with the landlord's consent, which could not be unreasonably withheld. Until 1996, tenants had a continuing liability for lease terms after assignment. In 1996, this liability was removed, but, as a partial compromise, landlords were given greater scope for refusing to allow an assignment. Where assignment is permitted, the landlord can require the outgoing tenant to guarantee the lease obligations of the incoming tenant (Crosby *et al.*, 1998). Much of this conventional lease structure remains intact, but there has been a significant reduction in average lease length, and the number of leases with break options has increased. Tenants now want a choice of flexible lease contracts, or **flexi-leases**, that allow them to respond quickly to changing business circumstances. Evidence of this can be found in the Strutt & Parker/IPD Lease Events Review, 2005. The review was based on analysis of 55 000 tenancy records that appeared in the IPD UK Databank both at the end of 2003 and 2004. Table 4.1 shows that the overall percentage of leases that were renewed was 30% when weighted by rental value – a lower rate was found for offices in the city of London. In the retail sector, small- and medium-sized enterprises (SMEs[1]) had a lower renewal rate than large multiples, but even these were more likely to renew than large companies in the office and industrial sectors. SMEs typically sign shorter leases: according to the BPF/IPD Annual Lease Review, 2004, the average lease signed by SMEs in 2003 was for 5 years (including new

Table 4.1 Lease expiry and break events in 2004.

	By number	By rental value
Lease expiries		
Renewed (%)	41	30
Re-let (%)	24	22
Vacant at year-end (%)	35	48
Break clauses		
Not exercised (%)	75	70
Exercised and re-let (%)	8	7
Exercised and vacant at year-end (%)	16	23

Source: Strutt & Parker/IPD (2005).

lettings and renewals) whereas for large companies it was 9.5 years. Of leases that contained break clauses, 30% were exercised in 2004; but this hides significant variation at the sector level: for offices the rate was 36%, for retail it was 18% and for industrial property it was 25%. The propensity of tenants to exercise break options has steadily increased over the past decade, but this is mainly due to the office sector. The average void period at the end of 2004 was 15.3 months, pulled upwards by the office sector where 16.1 months was the average. For retail it was 13.5 months and for industrial property it was 15.1 months. In the retail sector the smallest or least valuable units tended to have longer voids whereas in the industrial sector the smallest units had the shortest voids.

Landlords sometimes offer incentives to tenants under flexi-lease arrangements as a means of attracting them to a particular property. In the subsections that follow, the financial impact on *rental value* of typical incentives are considered. In Chapter 5, the *capital value* implications are considered. In each case the valuer is trying to estimate the **effective rent** that is being paid, and this comprises the actual **headline rent** plus the annual equivalent of any capital expenditure for the acquisition of the interest and expenditure on alterations or improvements made by tenant less the value of any incentives (such as rent-free periods and other capital contributions) made by the landlord. It is important to remember that cost does not always equate to value and therefore not all expenditure need be amortised – each item must be considered carefully.

4.2.1   Rent-free periods

A rent-free period refers to a fixed length of time within the term of a lease during which no rent is paid. If a rent-free period is offered to a prospective tenant as an incentive to take occupation of a particular property and such an incentive is not regarded as standard practice for the property type and location in question, then a valuer may wish to calculate the market rent of the property assuming no incentive was granted. It should be borne in mind that it is common, especially in the case of retail property, for a landlord to grant a short (say 3–6 months) rent-free period for fitting out the premises. If this is the case, and the tenant is not trading from the premises during the 'fitting-out period', then the financial benefit to the tenant (or financial loss to the landlord) as a result of granting such a fitting-out period should be ignored when estimating the market rent. What we are concerned with here is when a landlord offers a more substantial rent-free period as a way of inducing a tenant to take occupation of the property. To determine the financial effect of a rent-free period on the market rent it is necessary to spread or amortise the capital value of the rent that is actually paid, known as the headline rent, over a period that includes the rent-free period. In effect the landlord is attempting to maintain a headline rent so that at rent review the landlord can make the case for a revision to market rent which includes the financial value of the incentive. Also, declaring a headline rent rather than the effective rent can be beneficial in terms of bank lending ratios if debt has been used to help finance the purchase of the property investment and, in the case of long leases and an occupier of high quality, it may assist in raising the valuation of the asset (Sayce *et al.*, 2006).

The period over which this headline rent is amortised has a significant effect on the calculation of the effective rent and there may be additional risk to the tenant if upward-only rent reviews are present. This is best illustrated using an example: a retail unit has been let on a 15-year lease with 5-year upward-only rent reviews at a headline rent of £200 000 per annum. A rent-free period of 1.5 years was given, 6 months of which is a normal fitting-out period. Assuming that the incentive is written off over the period to the first rent review and ignoring the time value of money the effective rent would be calculated as follows:

Headline rent (£)	200 000	
× number of payments actually received	3.5	
Capital received (£)		700 000
Divided by number of payments normally received		4.5
Annual equivalent or effective rent (£)		155 556

Incorporating the time value of money at a discount rate of 10% (unsecured borrowing rate[2]), the effective rent would be as follows:

Headline rent (£)	200 000		
YP 3.5 years[a] @ 10%	2.8365		
PV 1.5 years[b] @ 10%	0.8668		
Capital received (£)		491 736	
Divided by YP 4.5 years[c] @ 10%		3.4877	
		140 991	
Divided by PV 0.5 years @ 10%		0.9535	
Annual equivalent or effective rent (£)			147 867

YP = years purchase; PV = present value.
[a]Because £200 000 is received for 3.5 years, assuming the market rent overtakes the headline rent at the first rent review in year 5.
[b]Because the first rent payment is not received until the 1.5-year rent-free period has expired.
[c]Because the cash-flow up until the first rent review typically consists of 4.5 years of rent when an initial 6 month fitting-out period is the norm.

The effective rent can also be calculated using the goal-seek and net present value (NPV) functions on a spreadsheet. The easiest way to do this is to calculate the total present value of the headline rent over the period to the first rent review. This has been done in the rental valuation below using the NPV function[3] to sum the present values of the annual rent payments, remembering that no rent is received in year 1 and only 6 months' rent is received in year 2. The total present value in this case is £493 695. Next, set up another valuation where a first guess at the effective rent is input, remembering that these are equal payments except that, in this case, the initial 6 month fitting-out period reduces the annual rent by half. The goal-seek function can then be used to equate the total present value of the headline rent with the total present value of the effective rent by changing the amount of effective rent. The effective rent differs slightly from the valuation above due to rounding.

Year	Headline rent (£)	Effective rent (£)
1	0	73 990
2	100 000	147 979
3	200 000	147 979
4	200 000	147 979
5	200 000	147 979
Yield	10%	10%
NPV	£493 695	£493 695

By writing off the value of the incentive over the first 5 years of the lease, the rental valuation above assumed that the effective rent for this property will be overtaken by the market rent at the first rent review in 5 year's time. In other words, the financial benefit of the rent-free period will not be felt after this time. If it is considered that the headline rent will continue to be the contract rent after the first rent review because the market rent for this property has not grown sufficiently to overtake the headline rent and the rent review is upward-only, the following rental valuation might be appropriate where it is assumed that the incentive is written off over the whole lease term. Ignoring the time value of money the rental valuation would be as follows:

Headline rent (£)	200 000
× number of payments actually received	13.5
Capital received (£)	2 700 000
Divided by number of payments normally received	14.5
Annual equivalent or effective rent (£)	186 207

Incorporating a 10% discount rate the valuation would be as follows:

Headline rent (£)	200 000	
YP 13.5 years @ 10%	7.2382	
PV 1.5 years @ 10%	0.8668	
Capital received (£)	1 254 814	
Divided by YP 14.5 years @ 10%	7.4892	
	167 550	
Divided by PV 0.5 years @ 10%	0.9535	
Annual equivalent or effective rent (£)		175 721

Using the goal-seek and NPV functions on a spreadsheet, the rental valuation below calculates the same effective rent except for a small rounding difference.

Year	Headline rent (£)	Effective rent (£)
1	0	87 866
2	100 000	175 732
3	200 000	175 732
4	200 000	175 732
5	200 000	175 732
6	200 000	175 732
7	200 000	175 732
8	200 000	175 732
9	200 000	175 732
10	200 000	175 732
11	200 000	175 732
12	200 000	175 732
13	200 000	175 732
14	200 000	175 732
15	200 000	175 732
Yield	10%	10%
NPV	£1 256 753	£1 256 753

Clearly, when it comes to rent review or lease renewal negotiations a shorter amortisation period favours the tenant and a longer one the landlord, but, in reality, these two rental valuations might be regarded as a minimum and a maximum. Crosby and Murdoch (1994) suggest a means of checking the veracity of each extreme by calculating the growth rate that needs to be applied to the market rent for it to overtake the headline rent by the first rent review, the second rent review, and so on until the end of the lease. So, for the value of the incentive to be written off by the first rent review, the rent of £147 867 per annum must increase to above £200 000 per annum in 5 years. This would take an annual growth rate of 6.23%, calculated as follows:

$$£147\,867 \times (1+r)^5 = 1200000$$
$$(1+r)^5 = \frac{200\,000}{147\,867} = 1.3526$$
$$(1+r) = \sqrt[5]{1.3526} = 1.06227$$
$$r = 0.06227(6.23\%)$$

Over the whole lease term, the rent of £175 721 per annum must increase to above £200 000 per annum in 15 years, and this would take an annual growth rate of 2.62%. This sort of explicit growth rate analysis can be used to help decide the period over which the value of the incentive should be amortised prior to estimating the effective rent being paid by the tenant.

4.2.2 Premiums and reverse premiums

A **premium** is a consideration by a tenant to a landlord for the grant or renewal of a lease on favourable terms. The consideration is usually financial but can be non pecuniary such as the carrying out of repairs or improvements. Favourable terms might be a reduced rent, less frequent rent reviews, a percentage based rent at review (say 80% of the market rent – known as a geared review), landlord taking responsibility for repairs or insurance (i.e. not FRI) or a wider user-clause. The benefit of a premium to a landlord is a cash-flow where a capital sum is received early and the benefit to the tenant will be an immediate profit rent. A premium may also be paid by the assignee when a lease is assigned and there is a profit rent available because the contract rent is below the market rent. When there is great demand for a property, such as prime retail, tenants may pay **key money** to secure the property – effectively a premium in addition to rent. This key money should be treated as the capital value of additional rent and amortised over the period for which future occupation is assumed (perpetuity in some cases) and added to the contract rent. Because a premium is different from key money it is important that the valuer determines the reason for the payment of a capital sum when valuing a property where one has been paid or when using a comparable with one. It is important for the valuer to determine whether the capital sum was payment for fixtures, fittings and equipment, whether it was for a monopoly position for a certain trade (key money) or whether it was a payment in lieu of a rent saving (premium).

A premium, then, is nothing more than capitalised rent; so, if we assume that there is a normal situation where the tenant pays the landlord a market rent, the size of any premium that might be paid will clearly depend on how much reduction from the market rent the tenant receives. In effect, the landlord is 'selling' part of the market rent, and the tenant is 'buying' it in the form of a profit rent. To calculate a premium, the agreed rent reduction (profit rent) should be capitalised. For example, a property is let on a lease with 4 years remaining at a rent of £12 500 per annum. The current market rent is estimated to be £15 000 per annum. If the tenant assigns the lease, what premium should be paid by the assignee to compensate for the profit rent? Capitalising the profit rent over the 4 years,

Profit rent (£)	2500	
YP 4 years @ 10%[a]	3.1699	
Premium (£)		7925

[a]Risk-free rate plus a return for risk, lack of growth and illiquidity.

With no discounting, the premium would simply be £10 000 (£2500 × 4). Once again, goal-seek and the NPV function on a spreadsheet can be used to equate the total present value of the market rent over the first 5 years with the total present value of the premium and contract rent over the same time period.

To calculate the market rent when a premium has already been agreed, amortise the premium over the period of the benefit. For example, at the start of a

Year	Premium + contract rent (£)	Effective rent (£)
0	7925	£0
1	12500	15000
2	12500	15000
3	12500	15000
4	12500	15000
Yield	10%	10%
NPV	47548	47548

new lease with 5-year rent reviews the tenant agrees to pay a rent of £10 000 per annum plus a premium of £11 750. What is the effective or market rent?

Contract rent (£)		10 000
Premium (£)	11 750	
Divided by YP 5 years @ 15%	3.3522	
Annual equivalent of premium (£)		£3505
Effective rent (£)		13 505

Similarly, using goal-seek and NPV spreadsheet functions,

Year	Premium/headline rent (£)	Effective rent (£)
0	11 750	0
1	10 000	13 505
2	10 000	13 505
3	10 000	13 505
4	10 000	13 505
5	10 000	13 505
Yield	15%	15%
NPV	45 272	45 272

If a premium is to be paid at some point in the future, the amount should be discounted at a low rate because the tenant has a contractual obligation to pay it and therefore the risk from the landlord's perspective is low.

Sometimes a lease might specify that at each rent review the rent is reviewed to a proportion of market rent; in other words, the tenant receives a discount in the form of a profit rent at each review. A premium might be paid to compensate the landlord for offering such an incentive. For example, a tenant pays a premium of £10 000 at the start of a 10-year lease where the rent is reviewed to 70% of market level in year 5. The initial contract rent is £5000 per annum, but what is the effective rent of this property?

Effective rent for first 5 years (£)	x
Less contract rent for first 5 years (£)	-5000
Profit rent (£)	$x - 5000$
YP 5 years @15%	3.3522
	$3.3522\,x - 16\,761$
Effective rent for second 5 years (£)	x
Less contract rent at review (£)	$0.7\,x$

Profit rent (£)	0.3x
YP 5 years @ 7%[a]	4.1002
PV 5 years @ 7%	0.7130

$$0.8770\ x$$

Capital value of profit rent $4.2292x - 16\,761$

Premium to landlord should exactly compensate for the profit rent to tenant, therefore;

£10 000 = 4.2292 x – 16 761

x   = 6 328

Thus effective rent (£) = 6 328

[a]All-risks yield because of growth potential at rent review.

Algebraic solutions like these are easily transferred to a spreadsheet on which the goal-seek function may be used to solve for x. It may be necessary to consider the value of premiums and associated profit rents from both the landlord and tenant's viewpoints. The values will differ if different yields are used to amortise the rent reduction and the actual amount of premium may therefore require a negotiated settlement in practice.

A **reverse premium** is a capital payment usually made by an assignor of a lease to induce the assignee to take occupation. This situation may arise in a depressed market where the supply of accommodation exceeds demand and the current rent exceeds the market rent; the property is thus **over-rented**. If the lease contains upward-only rent reviews and the difference between the contract rent and the market rent is significant, the property may remain over-rented for some time. The assignor of a lease on a property that is over-rented will need to pay a reverse premium to the assignee equivalent to the capital value of the overage rent. For example, a property was let 2 years ago on a 10-year lease with an upward-only rent review in the fifth year at a contract rent of £250 000 per annum. The tenant wishes to assign the lease but is aware that the current market rent for the property is £235 000 per annum. What size of reverse premium should the assignor pay the assignee? This is calculated by determining the size of the overage rent (£15 000 per annum in this case) and then deciding over how long this overage rent would be paid for, bearing in mind that the rent review is upward-only and the future level of market rent will not be known. If we assume that market rental growth for this property will be negligible over the remaining term of the lease, we can capitalise the overage for 8 years at a yield based on fixed income investments suitably adjusted for risk. A relatively high yield of 12% has been used here to reflect the over-rented nature of the interest.

Contract rent (£)	250 000	
Market rent (£)	235 000	
Overage (£)	15 000	
YP 8 years @ 12%	4.9676	
Reverse premium (£)		74 514

Note that this time, using the goal-seek and NPV functions, the reverse premium is an expenditure incurred by the assignor and appears as a negative sum.

Year	Market rent (£)	Reverse premium/ contract rent (£)
0	0	−74 515
1	235 000	250 000
2	235 000	250 000
3	235 000	250 000
4	235 000	250 000
5	235 000	250 000
6	235 000	250 000
7	235 000	250 000
8	235 000	250 000
Yield	12%	12%
NPV	1 167 395	1 167 395

If a valuer is seeking to use a property on which a reverse premium has been paid as comparable evidence, the market rent of the property is calculated by deducting the annual equivalent of the reverse premium from the contract rent. Using the example above, assume the tenant assigned the lease and paid a reverse premium of £75 000 to the assignee. Assuming the rent review is upward-only the market rent is calculated as follows:

Contract rent (£)		250 000
Reverse premium (£)	75 000	
Divided by YP 8 years @ 12%	4.9676	
		15 098
Market rent (£)		234 902

This brings us back to the £235 000 per annum with a small rounding error. Using the goal-seek and NPV functions:

Year	Reverse premium/ contract rent (£)	Market rent (£)
0	−75 000	0
1	250 000	234 902
2	250 000	234 902
3	250 000	234 902
4	250 000	234 902
5	250 000	234 902
6	250 000	234 902
7	250 000	234 902
8	250 000	234 902
Yield	12%	12%
NPV	1 166 910	1 166 910

4.2.3 Capital contributions

A capital contribution is a financial payment by a landlord to induce a tenant to take occupation and usually takes the form of a financial payment but may also be for fitting out, taking financial responsibility for an existing lease or some other non-pecuniary contribution. In lieu of making such a capital contribution, the landlord would expect to receive a rent from the tenant in excess of the market rent. The calculation of the effective rent of a property where a capital contribution has been made and a headline rent has been paid is conducted by applying the same principles as for rent-free periods and reverse premiums: determine the amount of the contribution and the length of the amortisation period (typically to a rent review or to the end of the lease). For example, a landlord offers a tenant £100 000 to induce occupation under a new 15-year lease with 5-year rent reviews at a rent of £300 000 per annum. Amortising the capital contribution over the period to the first rent review:

Headline rent (£)		300 000
Capital contribution (£)	100 000	
Divided by YP 5 years @ 10%	3.7908	
		26 380
Effective rent (£)		273 620

Using the goal-seek and NPV functions,

Year	Capital contribution/ headline rent (£)	Effective rent (£)
0	–100 000	0
1	300 000	273 620
2	300 000	273 620
3	300 000	273 620
4	300 000	273 620
5	300 000	273 620
Yield	10%	10%
NPV	1 037 236	1 037 236

Amortising the contribution over the whole lease produces a market rent of £286 853 per annum.

4.2.4 Stepped rents

Stepped rents are a series of rent reviews at intervals more frequent than the standard 5-year pattern. Normally the rent is reviewed to pre-agreed sums, but this need not necessarily be the case. Stepped rents can help the tenant's cash-flow at the start of a lease, if the initial rent is less than the market rent, but the final rent might be higher. In cases where a stepped rent is paid, it may be necessary to determine the effective rent so that the transaction can be used as comparable evidence. This is done by calculating the present value of each stepped rent and then calculating the annual equivalent of the sum of these present values over the period of the incentive. For example, a property has just been let on a 15-year lease with 5-year rent reviews at a rent of £200 000 in year 1, £225 000 in year 2, £250 000 in year 3, £275 000 in year 4 and £300 000 in year 5. After year 5 the rent reverts to the market level. Assuming an all-risks yield of 9%, the capital value (sum of the present values) of these stepped rents is as follows:

Year	Rent (£)	PV £1	PV (£)
1	200 000	0.9174	183 480
2	225 000	0.8417	189 383
3	250 000	0.7722	193 050
4	275 000	0.7084	194 810
5	300 000	0.6499	194 970
Capital value (£)			955 693

This figure is then amortised over the period to the first rent review when the stepped rents end and the market rent is payable.

Capital value (£)	955 693
Divided by YP 5 years @ 9%	3.8 897
Annual equivalent or effective rent over first 5 years (£)	245 698

Using goal-seek and NPV functions the same effective rent is calculated (with a slight rounding difference):

Year	Stepped rent (£)	Effective rent (£)
0	0	0
1	200 000	245 705
2	225 000	245 705
3	250 000	245 705
4	275 000	245 705
5	300 000	245 705
Yield	9%	9%
NPV	955 706	955 706

As the tenant is paying £300 000 per annum in year 5, and this is greater than the current estimated market rent of £245 700 per annum, the tenant must take a view on whether rental growth over the next 5 years will mean that the market rent at that time will exceed £300 000 per annum. If it does not, and the lease provides for upward-only rent reviews, the property will be over-rented at this point.

4.2.5   Short leases and leases with break options

So far, the pricing of lease terms has necessitated comparison with the market rent payable on a lease on 'standard terms'. The problem nowadays is that the concept of a standard set of lease terms is hard to define, and this is mainly due to the shortening of leases and the increasing use of break clauses. In many other countries, where there are active commercial property investment markets, lease lengths are typically shorter than in the UK and increasing cross-border investment activity has led to pressure in the UK for lease lengths to fall (into line). Also, internationalisation of business and changing business practice has led to pressure from tenants in the UK for shorter leases with more flexible terms (Baum, 2003). Other reasons are highlighted by Sayce *et al.* (2006): Stamp Duty Land Tax, introduced in 2003, makes the amount of tax payable proportional to lease length; adoption of international accounting standards throughout the EU in 2005 has changed the way occupational leases are reported in accounts; and Government has pressed (without legislation so far) for shorter more flexible leases. Tenants have shorter business time horizons, and flexi-leases avoid over-commitment of financial resources and allow for possible expansion plans. These pressures have led to a reduction in lease length since 1990, mainly between 1990 and 1995. Shorter leases are not evident across all sectors though. Because retailers, particularly those in prime locations, are paying high rents to secure a trading location, on which they often spend a lot of money fitting out to a corporate brand image, they are keen to remain there and build up goodwill. Consequently, longer leases or leases that provide security of tenure are preferable. Baum (2003) found evidence that retail warehouses were typically let on longer leases of 20–25 years and that, across all sectors, longer leases were to be found in prime locations, on high value properties let to major companies.

Most break clauses now coincide with 5- and10-year review dates, but the period of notice that the tenant is required to give and the penalty payment (if any) for exercising the break option do vary, the latter typically between 6 and 12 months of rent. Also, there might be more than one break opportunity, the break option may be tenant-only (usual), landlord-only (very rare) or landlord and tenant activated and the break may or may not coincide with a rent review although most do now (the alternative is a break within first 3 years, known as a short-term break, and these tend to be a feature of less valuable properties). Because of the diversity of break option terms, cash-flow uncertainty tends to be greater with a break clause than with a short lease (McAllister, 2001). It should also be noted that securing a break clause in a lease often requires the tenant to pay a rent in excess of the market rent, so if the break option is not exercised, the total cost of the lease to the tenant will be higher than if there was no break clause and a market rent was paid.

Flexi-leases are not popular with institutional landlords who are looking for long-term cash-flow security. Because only a minority of tenants exercise a break option, short leases are regarded as being more damaging to investment asset value than break clauses. Lenders to property investors are also resistant to flexi-leases because banks place high importance on unexpired lease terms in their risk management procedures, and the observed yield damage on leases less than 10 years (or 15 years in some sectors) unexpired can be seen as a rational outcome of financing criteria (Baum, 2003). In a market where upward-only rent reviews are almost universal, a flexi-lease offers not only an opportunity to vacate the property but also an opportunity to negotiate a downwards adjustment of rent. If a tenant vacates at the end of a short lease or at a break opportunity the landlord will incur a set of fixed and variable costs. Fixed costs will include fees for finding a new tenant, and variable costs will include management and maintenance costs while the property is empty, loss of rent until a new tenant is found and the cost of any other incentives that might need to be offered (McAllister, 2001). The magnitude of these variable costs will depend on the length of the void period. It should not be forgotten that the landlord may be better off in the long run if the rent agreed on a new lease is higher than the rent under the old lease and if the penalty payment made by the tenant more than compensates for the costs incurred or if the property is re-let to a tenant of a higher quality. On the plus side Baum (2003) notes that flexi-leases may lead to faster letting and reduce the need for rent-free periods. In short, a flexi-lease granted at a headline rent, together with penalty payments, may easily compensate for the risk of incurring voids and re-letting costs.

How do valuers estimate the financial impact of short, breakable leases? Baum (2003) found that the most popular valuation adjustment for short leases (say less than 5 years) and leases with break options in a similar time frame was the inclusion of a rent void, but one which did not reflect the 'true' expected costs of the void. Instead, it was moderated to reflect an estimated probability of the tenant breaking or not renewing. If it was certain that the tenant would exercise the break option or not renew the lease then a full void allowance was included. For breaks, the notice period and penalty payment would be factored in (i.e. a long notice period and big rent penalty would neutralise void allowance). When valuing shopping centres in which units are let on short leases, the valuer would build in a running void assumption into the cash-flow based on the average void rate and expected average void period. In Table 4.2, adapted from Baum (2003), the expected mean rent impacts of variations from a standard 15 year lease with 5 year rent reviews and a 3–6 month rent-free period are listed. It should be noted that the impact will vary from sector to sector and is dependent on building and location quality.

Baum (2003) found that, at rent review, the assumption of a long lease was regarded as onerous and often attracted a 2.5–3% rent discount for hypothetical unexpired terms longer than 15 years. But in the opposite case, where the unexpired lease term was assumed to be short, landlords were unable to achieve an uplift in rent. Also, the only occasion where the existence of a break clause in a lease was found to affect the rent at rent review was when the landlord had an option to break, and this led to a rent discount.

A higher rent to compensate for the break option or short lease might be agreed, but the level of the headline rent and the length of time over which it should be amortised will depend on views about rental growth over the lease term because, under a standard lease with upward-only rent reviews, the rent cannot fall, whereas with a break the tenant could vacate. It will also depend on the size of the penalty payment. The level of this higher rent might be calculated by first valuing the flexi-lease with a rent void and maybe a higher all-risks yield too, then valuing the same property assuming standard lease terms and finally equating the capital values of each by adjusting the rent

Table 4.2   Rent impact of lease variations.

Lease variation	Mean rent impact (%)
Review 1 break	10.45
Review 2 break	6.60
All rent review break	17.00
5-year lease	15.23
10-year lease	7.00
10-year lease with 5-year break	16.40
3-year reviews	−3.79
Two way rent reviews	6.25
RPI lease	5.80

Source: Baum (2003).

reserved for the first 5 years (French, 2001) using the goal-seek function on a spreadsheet. For example, calculate the rent that should be paid for the first 5 years of a 10 year flexi-lease which has a break option and a rent review in year 5. It is assumed that there is a 6 month void at the break after which the rent reverts to the market rent, and there is a 1 year void at the end of the lease (to cover marketing and any rent-free period granted) after which the property reverts to a standard lease.

Term 1 rent (£)	x	
YP 5 years @ 6%	4.2124	
		$4.2124x$
Term 2 rent (£)	300 000	
YP 4.5 years @ 6%	3.8442	
PV 5.5 years @ 6%	0.7258	
		837 036
Reversion to market rent on standard lease	300 000	
YP perpetuity @ 6%	16.6667	
PV 11 years @ 6%	0.5268	
		2 634 005
Valuation (£)		$3 471 041 + 4.2124x$

Now assume that the standard lease arrangement for this property is a 15-year lease with 5-year upward-only rent reviews let at a market rent of £300 000 per annum. The capital valuation would be as follows.

Market rent (£)	300 000	
YP perpetuity @ 6%	16.6667	
Valuation (£)		5 000 000

If we finally assume that the capital value of the property subject to the flexi-lease and the standard lease arrangement should be the same we can state that

$$£3 471 041 + 4.2124x = £5 000 000$$
$$x = £362 966$$

Using goal-seek and NPV spreadsheet functions

Year	Market rent (£)	Headline rent
1	£300 000	£362 621
2	£300 000	£362 621
3	£300 000	£362 621
4	£300 000	£362 621
5	£300 000	£362 621
6	£300 000	£150 000
7	£300 000	£300 000
8	£300 000	£300 000
9	£300 000	£300 000
10	£300 000	£300 000
11	£300 000	£0
12	£300 000	£300 000
13	£300 000	£300 000
14	£300 000	£300 000
15	£300 000	£300 000
Yield	6%	6%
NPV	£2 913 675	£2 913 675

So the initial contract rent under the flexi-lease terms must be set £62 966 per annum above the £300 000 per annum market rent to compensate for the estimated voids. Of course, there may be other adjustments to make such as factoring costs of the voids or raising the all-risks yield on the flexi-lease, but the valuer must be careful to avoid double counting the financial implications of flexi-terms. Some may argue that the rent at the break point in the flexi-lease might not drop to £300 000, but the tenant would undoubtedly exercise the break to ensure the rent is the market rent (although this may incur costs), and also, Baum (2003) found that the courts did not impose a premium rent for short (less than 5 years) unexpired terms.

Two difficulties arise, the first is finding a suitable comparable that is let on standard lease terms – an increasingly difficult prospect given the diversity of lease terms that now exists, the second is dealing with uncertainty in the cash-flow. Uncertainty arises because it is not known whether (1) a break option will be exercised or (2) a short lease will be renewed. But the uncertainty does not end there: how long will a rent void be, how much will re-letting costs be, will there be a downward movement in rent at the break or lease end (which, in turn, will depend on the rate of rental growth and length of time until the break or the end of the lease)? To reflect this uncertainty the valuation approach described above can be enhanced by assuming various outcomes with associated probabilities, calculating a weighted average flexi-lease capital value and then equating that to the capital value under standard lease terms. These probabilities can be obtained from previous cases, but the individual circumstances of the subject property, the tenant and the economic environment at the time of the valuation must be considered too. For example, the likelihood that a tenant might exercise a break or not renew a lease may depend on the amount of financial penalty, the expected cost of dilapidations, the amount spent on fitting out the premises, the availability of alternative premises, estimated relocation costs, growth or contraction of the tenant's business and expected rental growth (Baum, 2003). Some of the ways that uncertainty might be quantified using probability are examined in Chapter 5 when we look at these issues from the landlord's perspective.

4.2.6   Turnover rents

Increasingly, when landlords want to participate in the underlying potential profitability of the tenant's business in addition to the rent that they receive, turnover rents are encountered. In the UK, these are becoming increasingly popular in the case of individual shop units located in modern shopping centres, airports and other transport termini and are sometimes found in high street retail and petrol stations. A turnover rent provides a landlord with the opportunity to participate more directly in the equity of the tenant's business through a rent that is reviewed annually. Landlord's management costs are likely to be higher than for rack-rented properties, but they provide the landlord with an incentive to maintain and enhance rental growth more directly than with 5-year rent reviews. They tend to be favoured where comparables are either difficult to obtain (perhaps because the units are in a new development) or the landlord does not wish to share rental information with all the tenants in a centre. The level of rent generated by a turnover rent structure is dependent upon the performance of the shopping centre and on the success of individual retailers. With regard to the centre as a whole, tenant mix is important and the provision of loss-leading leisure facilities can increase retail trade, as can public areas and food courts. In shopping centres, anchor tenants may be subject to beneficial turnover percentages to reflect their contribution to the success of the centre as a whole (Sayce *et al.*, 2006). Indeed the landlord of a shopping centre is aware of the trading activity of all tenants and can try to actively manage the centre in order to optimise turnover. Information on the performance of the centre as a whole may also indicate the optimum time to refurbish.

With regard to individual retailers, the most common turnover rent arrangement is a minimum base rent (often a percentage of the market rent of the property, say 75–80%, and usually subject to 5-yearly rent reviews) plus an additional rent based on a percentage of the turnover of the business (usually calculated with reference to annual audited accounts). The concept is a reflection of Ricardian rent theory – rent is paid out of the surplus revenue after other costs and normal profit have been deducted. Comparable evidence helps determine the level of base rent and select the appropriate percentage for turnover. The percentage of turnover paid to the landlord is determined by the profit margins obtainable from different trades and by the level of base rent – the lower the base rent the higher the percentage applied to turnover. Indeed, in the case of airports, the turnover percentages are much higher, and a base rent is not paid. Food sales from supermarkets trade on large volumes but narrow profit margins whereas jewellery is very much the opposite. Typical percentages of turnover payable as rent on top of a base rent are shown in Table 4.3 but the percentage can depend on covenant strength as much as trade type. It may be necessary to vary the turnover percentage for different types of sales sold in the same shop because, for example, tobacco sales from a newsagent include a large amount of tax. It is also important to check the user-clause, especially in shopping centres where they may be a tenant-mix policy.

A turnover rent is usually derived from a percentage of turnover net of VAT, sales to staff (staff discounts), returned goods, goods traded in, defective goods, charges made by credit card companies and bad debts. The percentage applied to turnover is usually fixed for the term of the lease, but there may be provisions for variations to take account of changes in use, occupation or longer-term changes in retailing practice and profitability. Turnover lease terms can be complex, requiring a minimum trade performance level, notional turnover if closed for several days, restrictions that only allow assignments to similar trades, for example. A clause may be inserted into the lease allowing the landlord to terminate the lease contract if a certain level of turnover is not attained during a specified period. The tenant will normally try to cap the turnover rent at say 120% of the market rent, and the ability to reduce this to a lower percentage will depend on the covenant strength of the tenant.

McAllister (1996) found that the most common type of turnover lease in the UK is where the tenant must pay either a market rent *or* a turnover rent, whichever is highest. A stepped base rent plus a turnover rent is where the base rent increases annually to levels specified in the lease. Sometimes the turnover element disappears at the first rent review and is therefore a method of attracting new tenants. In terms of capital value, an all-risks yield may be used to capitalise the base rent, but a higher yield (selected intuitively) is often used to capitalise the turnover rent because, it is argued, it will vary annually and perhaps quite markedly. It is difficult to accurately predict turnover, so capitalisation is usually of current turnover with an assumption that it will continue. The use of a higher yield on the turnover rent will reduce the capital value in comparison to a rack-rented property. This is one reason why base rents account for 75–80% of the total rent and why

Table 4.3 Typical percentage of turnover paid as rent.

Trade	Percentage of turnover payable as rent
Grocers	1.5
Department store	1–3
Supermarkets	1–2
Variety stores	2–4
Furniture	5
Restaurant	6–12
Electrical	5–9
Fashion	7–15
Books, sports	8
Shoes	9–13
Leather, jewellery	9–13

pure turnover rents are rare. Investment value could be enhanced by providing for reversion to rack-rent at some point in the future. Because of the caution with which turnover rents are treated by investors it can be more difficult than usual for developers of shopping centres to secure necessary funding.

An example of a capital valuation of a shop subject to a turnover rent appears below. The base rent is 80% of the market rent for this type of property, and the turnover rent is calculated as 5% of net turnover.

Base rent @ 80% market rent (£)	80 000	
YP perpetuity @ 8%	12.5	
		1 000 000
Turnover rent @ 5% turnover (£)	20 000	
YP perpetuity @ 10%	10	
		200 000
Valuation (£)		1 200 000

Key points

- As far as rented commercial property is concerned, different businesses require different types of accommodation and, increasingly, a single firm requires a range of accommodation types. The differentiation occurs along physical and legal lines; in other words more customised space and more flexible leases, known as flexi-leases. This has significant implications for valuation.
- In an ideal world all leases of commercial property would be on the same terms, and estimating rental value would simply be a case of making adjustments to reflect differences in location, physical attributes and unexpired term. But whereas in the past leases were fairly standard and comparison fairly straightforward, it is now necessary to identify the main features of flexi-leases and their scope for variation. These centre on lease length, incentive arrangements such as break clauses, rent-free periods and reverse premiums and rent revision arrangements such as stepped rents or turnover rents. There may be other arrangements too, such as a non-standard rent-review pattern or a first review that is sooner or later, but the valuation principle is the same.
- The scarcity and variability of rental value evidence means that valuers find it difficult to analyse, adjust and apply data from what may appear to be physically comparable properties but which differ because of flexi-lease arrangements. This all sounds pretty hopeless, but it must be remembered that valuation is all about quantifying economic benefits or costs financially in terms of rental or capital value. With this in mind, any flexi-lease arrangement that is made in lieu of rent paid should be reflected in the valuer's estimate of rental and capital value. This typically involves amortising any financial benefit received by the occupier in place of rent over a period that has regard to the estimated life of the benefit, the lease term and rent review provisions in the lease contract.

> **Key point** (continued)
>
> - A lot of the flexi-lease arrangements can be regarded as short-term cash bonus to the tenant at the expense of increased rent later (similar to unsecured borrowing), and the financial impact can be modelled in a spreadsheet and using 'goal-seek' to determine effective rent by changing various input variables. But flexi-leases can lead to a more uncertain cash-flow than a standard lease, and the valuer needs to be able to reflect this uncertainty in the rental value. This will be examined in Chapter 5.

4.3   Capital valuations at lease end and lease renewal

4.3.1   Landlord and tenant legislation

In the UK, there is a substantial body of legislation and case law – known as landlord and tenant law – that governs the legal relations between parties to a lease. Key statutes that regulate business tenancies and affect their valuation are described below.

The Landlord and Tenant Act 1927 (as amended by Landlord and Tenant Act 1954 Part III): This statute requires the landlord to compensate a tenant who leaves at the end of a lease for 'qualifying'[4] improvements made during the lease. Shops, for example, are quite likely to have been subject to tenant's improvements – perhaps a staircase or an escalator was constructed at the front of the shop (in the valuable Zone A area) to entice shoppers to venture up to the first floor. Landlord's consent is normally required before the improvements can qualify but, under the Landlord and Tenant Act 1988, this consent cannot be unreasonably withheld. The amount of compensation is calculated as the lesser of the value added as a result of the improvements or the cost of the improvements at the lease termination date. The value added must relate to the intended use, so no compensation is payable if the property is to be demolished. If the tenant renews the lease, then the value of the improvement is disregarded (deducted) from the estimated market rent for a period of 21 years. Assuming the improvements qualify for compensation, the initial valuation problem is determining the extent to which they impact on value.

The Landlord and Tenant Act 1954 Part II (as amended by the Law of Property Act 1969): This statute provides business tenants with security of tenure by allowing the original lease term to continue but subject to certain grounds that the landlord can establish to regain possession. The occupying tenant is entitled to automatic continuance of the original lease until terminated in accordance with the Act, that is, as a result of some positive action by either party, usually the serving of a notice. The tenant's interest is assignable and therefore valuable. In addition to the right of automatic continuance the landlord or tenant can apply for new lease. Where a new lease is granted to the existing tenant, the rent payable is normally the market rent but disregarding the effect on rental value of the fact that the tenant or predecessors in title have been in occupation, any goodwill from the existing tenant, qualifying improvements for a period of 21 years[5] and any licences that belong to the tenant in respect of licensed premises. In practice, the quantification of the financial effect of these 'disregards' on market rent is very difficult. The tenant may continue to pay the existing rent beyond the end of the lease known as 'holding over' but, while the terms of the new lease are being agreed, the landlord or the tenant can apply for an **interim rent**. This is determined under the Act and, in most cases, it will be equivalent to the initial rent under a new lease. Where there is no new lease, the interim rent will be the rent that the courts find reasonable on the basis that the property is let on a yearly tenancy. Case law has established that this works out at approximately 75–80% of the existing market rent. Landlords could try and have an 'upward-only penultimate day review' drafted into the lease to ensure that the interim rent is not less than the rent passing.

If the parties cannot agree to the terms of the new tenancy, then the courts are able to grant the tenant a new lease of up to 15 years on expiry of the existing lease at the market rent assuming similar terms as the original lease. The prospective landlord and tenant can agree in writing to 'contract out' of (exclude themselves from) the provisions of the 1954 Act, but the lease must be for a fixed term and the landlord cannot contract out of disturbance compensation liability if lease is longer than 5 years. Baum (2003) notes that contracting out occurs only occasionally but is more prevalent in the case of secondary and tertiary properties and may be increasing as landlords try to avoid renewals of short leases. Baum also found that, at lease renewal, tenants who secure a short lease do not pay a rent premium nor is a rent premium paid if a break clause is inserted. But, as with rent reviews, there is precedent suggesting that a landlord's option to break leads to a rent discount.

The landlord is entitled to counter the tenant's application for a new lease by establishing one of seven grounds for possession prescribed by the Act. If the landlord regains possession on the grounds that the rent for the property would be increased if let as a whole, redevelopment is intended or the property is required for own occupation, then the tenant is entitled to 'disturbance compensation' for loss of **goodwill**. The amount of disturbance compensation that is payable is calculated as a multiple of the **rateable value** of the property – a higher multiplier is used if the business has been in continuous occupation for the past 14 years or more.

Two examples will help illustrate the impact of some of the legislative points described above on the valuation of business property.

Example 1

A factory is held on a 15-year lease with 5 years left at a contract rent of £5000 per annum. The tenant carried out qualifying improvements 4 years ago which increased the market rent by 20%. The cost of these improvements today would be £7500. The market rent, including the value of the improvements, is £10000 per annum, the rateable value of the property is £12000 and the all-risks yield for investments in this type of property is 8%. Value the landlord's interest in the property assuming:

> ## Example 1   (continued)
> (a) he tenant vacates on termination of the existing lease;
> (b) a new 10-year lease with a rent review in year 5 (with a clause that states that the value of improvements is disregarded) is granted to the existing tenant on expiry of the current lease;
> (c) the landlord repossesses the property at the end of the existing lease for own occupation;
> (d) the landlord repossesses the property at the end of the existing lease for redevelopment and the site value is estimated to be £100 000.

The tenant has the right to two types of compensation if required to vacate the premises at the expiry of the existing lease:

- Disturbance compensation at twice the current rateable value of the premises. This equates to £24 000.
- Improvements' compensation at the lesser of the cost of the works or value added. The cost (as at the valuation date) is £7500 and the value added is calculated as the capital value of the increase in rent resulting from the improvements.

Increase in market rent (£)	1000[a]	
YP perpetuity @ 8%[b]	12.5	
Capital Value of improvements (£)		12 500

[a] 20% of the £5000 contract rent.
[b] All-risks yield.

Cost therefore prevails as improvements' compensation.

But these are future liabilities of the landlord, and it is important to consider changes in amounts (e.g. a rating revaluation, inflation in building costs). Here it is assumed that the rateable value remains constant and building costs rise at 3% per annum.

(a) *Valuation assuming the tenant vacates on termination:*

Term (contract) rent (£)		5000	
YP 5 years @ 7%[a]		4.1002	
			20 501
Reversion to market rent (£)		10 000	
YP in perpetuity @ 8%		12.5000	
PV £1 5 years @ 8%		0.6806	
			85 075
			105 576
Less cost of improvements (£)	−7500		
Inflated over 5 years @ 3% pa	1.1593		
		−8695	
PV £1 5 years @ 7%[b]		0.7130	
			−6199
Valuation (£)			99 377

[a] Term yield based on all-risks yield of 8% but reduced to reflect security of term rent.
[b] Cost of improvements has been discounted at same rate as term rent was capitalised.

(b) *Valuation assuming a new lease is granted at end of lease:*   It is helpful to sketch a timeline and mark important dates as in Figure 4.1. It is easier to spot when the rent reduction in respect of improvements runs out. In this case the tenant benefits from a rent reduction for 20 years that reflects the value added by the improvements, after which the rent reverts to the market rent including the value added by the improvements.

Capital value of first 5 years' rent (as above) (£)		20501
Subsequent 15 years rent (£)	8000[a]	
YP 15 years @ 8%	8.5595	
PV 5 years @ 8%	0.6806	
		46605
Final reversion market rent	10000	
YP in perpetuity @ 8%	12.5000	
PV £1 20 years @ 8%	0.2145	
		26813
Valuation (£)		93919

[a]This is the market rent of £10000 less 20% to reflect value added by tenant's improvements.

(c) *Valuation assuming the landlord repossesses at the end of current lease for own occupation:*

Value (as (a)) (£)		105576
Less improvements (as (a)) (£)	−6199	
Less disturbance; 2 x RV	−24000	
	−30199	
PV £1 5 years @ 7% [a]	0.7130	
		−21532
Valuation (£)		84044

[a]This discount rate should reflect the risk of an increase in improvement compensation and disturbance compensation may increase if there is a rating revaluation.

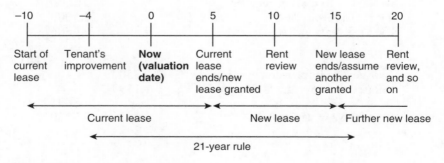

Figure 4.1   Events timeline.

Chapter 4

(d) *Valuation assuming the landlord repossesses at end of existing lease for redevelopment:* The landlord must have owned the property for at least 5 years to regain the property at the end of the lease. There is no compensation for improvements because their value to the landlord will be zero in the case of redevelopment. In practice, few tenants receive compensation under the 1927 Act due to the negating impact of dilapidations.

Term (contract) rent (£)	5000	
YP 5 years @ 7%[a]	4.1002	
		20501
Reversion to site value (£)	100000	
Less disturbance; 2 x RV	(24000)	
	76000	
PV £1 5 years @ 7%[b]	0.7130	
		5488
Valuation (£)		74689

[a]Term yield.
[b]This is a relatively low yield to reflect attractive of redevelopment potential.

Example 2

The tenant of a shop in a prime position holds a 15 year internal repairing (IR) lease granted 11 years ago at a current rent of £24000 per annum. Six years ago the tenant obtained consent to carry out improvements costing £60000. The current freehold all-risks yield is 6%, the market rent on full repairing and insuring (FRI) terms is £50000 per annum, £5000 of which can be attributed to the improvements made by the tenant. The rateable value of the premises is £50 000, and building cost inflation is averaging 10% per annum. Value the current interests of the landlord and tenant assuming:

(a) The landlord will get permission for his own occupation at the end of the lease;
(b) The tenant will continue in occupation under a new lease with a typical rent-review pattern.

As in the previous example, disturbance compensation is twice the rateable value, producing a figure of £100000. Compensation for improvements is estimated as the lesser of the cost of or value added by the improvements:

Value added by improvements (£)	5000	
YP perpetuity @ 6%	16.6667	
		83333
Cost of improvements (£)	60 000	
Inflated at 10% pa over 6 years	1.7716	
		106296

The value added produced the lower figure in this case.

(a) *Valuation assuming the landlord gets permission for his own occupation at the end of the lease:*

- Valuation of the landlord's interest

Term (contract) rent (£)	24 000	
Less external repairs @ 10% of market rent on FRI terms (£)	−5000	
Less insurance @ 2% of market rent on FRI terms (£)	−1000	
Net income (£)	18 000	
YP 4 years @ 5%	3.5460	
		63 828
Reversion to market rent on FRI terms (£)	50 000	
YP perpetuity @ 6%	16.6667	
PV £1 4 years @ 6%	0.7921	
		660 085
Less disturbance compensation (£)	−100 000	
Less improvements compensation (£)	−83 333	
	−183 333	
PV £1 4 years @ 5%	0.8227	
		−150 828
Valuation (£)		573 085

- Valuation of the tenant's interest

Market rent on FRI terms (£)	50 000	
Plus external repairs (£)	5000	
Plus insurance (£)	1000	
Market Rent on IR terms (£)	56 000	
Less rent paid (£)	−24 000	
Profit rent (£)	32 000	
YP 4 years @ 10%[a]	3.1699	
		101 437
Plus compensation (as above) (£)		125 216
Valuation (£)		226 653

[a]Risky, terminable, non-growth investment.

(b) *Valuation assuming the tenant will continue in occupation under a new lease with a typical rent review pattern:* Figure 4.2 illustrates the timeline.

- Valuation of the landlord's interest

Term net income (as above) (£)	18 000	
YP 4 years @ 6%	3.4651	
		62 372
Reversion to market rent on IR terms, excluding improvements (£)[a]		
– Market rent on FRI terms, excluding improvements	45 000	
– *Less* external repairs (calculated as above)	−5 000	
– *Less* insurance (calculated as above)	−1000	
	39 000	
YP 15 years @ 6%[b]	9.7122	

PV £1 4 years @ 6%	0.7921
	300 028

Reversion to market rent on IR terms, including improvements (£)	
– Market rent on FRI terms, including improvements	50 000
– *Less* external repairs (calculated as above)	–5 000
– *Less* insurance (calculated as above)	–1 000
	44 000
YP perpetuity @ 6%	16.6667
PV £1 for 19 years @ 6%	0.3305
	242 367
Valuation (£)	604 767

[a]Under the 1954 Landlord & Tenant Act the terms of the new lease will be based on the terms of the existing lease.
[b]This yield may be reduced below the freehold all-risks yield to reflect security afforded to a tenant occupying on IR terms, but the unattractiveness of an investment returning a non-market rent for 15 years may counter this. Consequently, the yield remains at 6%.

- Valuation of the tenant's interest

Profit rent (as above) (£)	32 000
YP 4 years @ 10%	3.1699
	101 437
Reversion to profit rent equal to the increase in market rent made by improvements at lease renewal (£)	5000
YP 15 years @ 9%[a]	8.0607
	40 304
Valuation (£)	141 741

[a]Growth potential due to possible rent reviews in sub-lease, so yield is based on freehold yield plus leasehold risk premium.

4.3.2 Surrender and renewal of leases

Sometimes a tenant may wish to surrender the current lease before its term has expired in order to preserve goodwill attached to a particular location or remove future uncertainty surrounding the terms of a new lease. If the

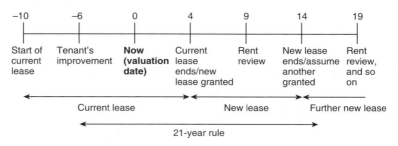

Figure 4.2 Events timeline.

landlord agrees to accept the surrender of the current lease for the grant of a new one then the capital value of any profit rent that the tenant was entitled to should be reflected as a rent reduction or some other financial benefit under the terms of the proposed lease. Valuations are undertaken to ensure that neither the landlord nor tenant jeopardise their existing financial positions. This is achieved by calculating the capital value of each party's present and proposed interests in order to determine the rent that should be reserved under the proposed lease. In practice, a negotiated settlement between the landlord and tenant's positions usually takes place and the impact of landlord and tenant legislation strengthens the tenant's bargaining position in a 'surrender and renewal' situation.

For example, a tenant wishes to surrender the remainder of an existing lease in return for the grant of a new, longer one. The present lease has 3 years to run with no review, and the rent passing is £20 000 per annum. The estimated market rent is £27 000 per annum, and comparable evidence suggests that the current all-risks yield for freehold investments in similar properties is 10%. The landlord is willing to accept a surrender of the current lease and grant a new 15 year lease with rent reviews every 5 years. The rent that should be reserved for the first 5 years of the proposed lease is calculated by valuing the landlord's and tenant's interests under the present and proposed terms:

Valuation of the landlord's present interest:

Term (contract) rent (£)	20 000	
YP 3 years @ 9%	2.5313	
		50 626
Reversion to market rent (£)	27 000	
YP perpetuity @ 10%	10.0000	
PV£1 3 years @ 10%	0.7513	
		202 851
Valuation (£)		253 477

Valuation of the landlord's proposed interest:

Let new rent be (£)	x	
YP 5 years @ 9%	3.8897	
		$3.8897x$
Reversion to market rent (£)	27 000	
YP perpetuity @ 10%	10.0000	
PV£1 5 years @ 10%	0.6209	
		167 643
Valuation (£)		$167\,643 + 3.8897x$

If the landlord is to be in the same financial position under the proposed terms as under the present terms then

$$167\,643 + 3.8897x = 253\,477$$
$$x \text{ (new rent)} = £22\,067$$

Valuation of the tenant's present interest:

Market rent (£)	27 000
Less Contract rent (£)	−20 000
Profit rent (£)	7000
YP 3 years @ 12%[a]	2.4018
Valuation (£)	16 813

[a]This is the freehold all-risks yield adjusted upwards to reflect the additional risk and relative unattractiveness of a short leasehold investment.

Valuation of the tenant's proposed interest:

Market rent (£)	27 000
Less new rent (£)	−x
Profit rent (£)	27 000 − x
YP 5 years @ 12%	3.6048
Valuation (£)	97 330 − 3.6048x

Assuming the value of the tenant's present interest should equal the value of the proposed interest

$$97\,330 - 3.6048x = 16\,813$$
$$x \text{ (new rent)} = £22\,336$$

A single figure is usually negotiated that lies somewhere between the two rental values estimated from the landlord and tenant perspectives. In fact, in nominal cash-flow terms, the rent forgone by the landlord is the same as the profit rent gained by the tenant; the only reason different rental values are calculated is because the yields are different. This means that transferring the valuation to a spreadsheet is very straightforward, and that the value impact of yield selection can easily be modelled. In practice, the agreed amount will depend on the relative bargaining strength of the parties.

Key points

- Legislation has a considerable influence on valuations undertaken in connection with the termination and possible renewal of business leases. It is essential that valuers have a full understanding of the relevant statutes and their impact on rental value.
- Conventionally a number of these types of valuations were undertaken from the perspective of the landlord and the tenant, the difference in value often resulting from the different yields that were used to capitalise income. Nowadays, the use of spreadsheets enables a more straightforward approach where various yields and other variables can be trialled and their impact on rental value measured.

Chapter 4

4.4   Capital valuations for financial reporting

Commonly referred to as asset valuations, these relate to the valuation of an occupier's property assets for inclusion in financial statements such as company accounts, stock exchange prospectuses, City Code documents for take-overs and mergers, the property assets of pension funds, unit trusts and life funds and Government requirements under Insurance Company Regulations. Asset valuations almost invariably end up in the public domain and may relate to very large amounts of money. Consequently there is a need for tight control, and accounting standards regulate this process. In the UK, valuers must refer to international and national valuation standards and guidance when undertaking valuations for financial reporting purposes. The situation is rather complicated at the moment because there are different accounting standards in place around the world, but there is a concerted effort to consolidate these to a single worldwide standard. The International Accounting Standards Board (IASB) publishes International Financial Reporting Standards (IFRS) but has also adopted the body of standards issued by its predecessor the International Accounting Standards Committee (IASC), and their standards continue to be designated as International Accounting Standards (IAS). Publicly listed companies in the UK (and in the European Union as a whole) must publish consolidated financial statements that conform to IFRS but, at the moment, private companies in the UK can elect to adopt UK Generally Agreed Accounting Procedures (GAAP) instead of IFRS. As a consequence, Practice Statement (PS) 3.6 of the Red Book (RICS, 2003) states that valuations for financial statements shall be in accordance with IFRS, but if a valuation is required to comply with UK GAAP then the Financial Reporting Standards (FRS) published by the Accounting Standards Board (ASB) take precedence. The ASB intends to amend its UK FRS to converge with IFRS, but the process is slow and ongoing and not due to complete until 2008. In the meantime, valuers have to cope with various sets of standards and guidance, learn to cross refer and reconcile them where required to, where possible and where appropriate.

As was discussed in Chapter 2, the International Valuation Standards Committee (IVSC) publishes International Valuation Standards (IVSC, 2005) and, within these standards, International Valuation Application 1 (IVA 1) explains the principles that apply to the valuation of property assets prepared for use in financial statements and related business accounts. UK valuation standards (RICS, 2003) refer to IVA 1.

What does all this mean as far as valuing a property asset for financial statements is concerned? The following sub-section deals with the international financial reporting standards that came into force in 2005 before considering the existing national standards that are applicable in the UK.

4.4.1   International financial reporting standards

The first step is to classify property assets as either **operational** (subclassified as **non-specialised** or **specialised**) or **non-operational** (subclassified as held for future development, investment or surplus). Public sector assets are categorised as operational, non-operational, infrastructure and community. The classification of assets determines which IFRS or IAS applies and the basis of valuation that should be adopted.

IAS 16: Property, Plant and Equipment prescribes the accounting treatment for operational property assets. Initially they are to be reported at cost but subsequently they can be reported either at cost (less accumulated depreciation and any accumulated impairment losses) or at a revalued amount (less subsequent accumulated depreciation and any accumulated impairment losses). The revalued amount is the **fair value** at the date of revaluation. The choice of reporting measurement must be applied consistently to an entire class of property. According to international valuation standards (IVSC, 2005 – IVA 1), where a business entity adopts the fair value revaluation option, valuations of property assets should be undertaken on a market value basis. This would be carried out using market evidence for non-specialised property or using a depreciated replacement cost (DRC) method for specialised property, and examples of these methods are given in Section 4.4.3. In addition to standard report content, under IAS16 the valuation should also report the extent to which the value was determined by reference to observable prices in an active open market or was estimated using other techniques (Cherry, 2006). UK valuation standards (RICS, 2003; Appendix 3.2) note some ambiguity at the moment as to whether the market value of an operational property should be estimated assuming that it is sold as part of the continuing enterprise in operation (what is referred to in the UK as **existing use value**) or assuming that it is to be sold in isolation after removal of the enterprise in occupation. The latter basis is market value and would include possible alternative uses. At the moment, the RICS recommends that two valuations are carried out and any significant difference between existing use value and market value is reported to the client. Whichever basis of value is used, valuations should be repeated with sufficient regularity to ensure that the figure reported in the financial statement (the 'carrying amount') does not differ materially from that which would be determined using fair value at the balance sheet date (IVSC, 2005).

If the property assets are held as investments[6] then *IAS 40: Investment Property* prescribes the appropriate accounting treatment. As with operational property, investment properties are initially recognised at cost but subsequently they can be reported either at cost (less accumulated depreciation and any accumulated impairment losses, as prescribed by IAS 16) or at fair value (but this time without any deduction for subsequent accumulated depreciation and any accumulated impairment losses). The measurement model must be applied consistently to all investment property. According to IVA 1 (IVSC, 2005) valuations of investment property under IAS 40 should be conducted on a market value basis, regardless of whether the entity chooses the cost or fair value model. Under IAS 40, the report should indicate whether the value was supported by market evidence or was heavily based on other factors because of the nature of the property and lack of comparable market data (Cherry, 2006). Investment properties reported at fair values will have their revaluation gains and losses transferred directly to the profit and loss account (unless they reverse previous losses that have been shown against equity). Under present UK GAAP, these are shown in the Statement of Total Recognised Gains and Losses (STRGL) but not in the profit and loss account.

IFRS 3: Business Combinations prescribes the financial reporting treatment when one company merges with or acquires another. Market value is regarded as the appropriate basis on which to value all property assets.

IAS 36: Impairment of Assets prescribes the procedures that a business must apply to ensure that its assets are appropriately depreciated so that they are carried at no more than their **recoverable amount**. We can see from the above that operational property assets need to be depreciated regardless of whether they are reported at cost or value, and investment properties must be depreciated when they are reported at cost. The depreciable amount of an asset is allocated systematically over its useful life, and depreciation is applied on a component basis. That is to say, each part of an item of property with a cost that is significant in relation to the total cost of the item is depreciated separately. At each balance sheet date businesses must review whether a property is impaired in some way. If it is, then the reported amount (either historic cost or earlier valuation) should be depreciated to the recoverable amount, which is the higher of its **value-in-use** (the present value of future cash-flows expected from an asset) or fair value less costs to sell (equivalent to market value less reasonably anticipated selling costs) (IVSC, 2005). The recoverable amount is determined for each individual asset. However, if the asset does not generate cash inflows that are largely independent of those from other assets, it may be determined for the cash-generating unit to which the asset belongs. A cash-generating unit is the smallest identifiable group of assets which generates cash inflows that are largely independent of the cash inflows from other assets or groups of assets. For the purpose of impairment testing, goodwill acquired in a business combination is allocated to each of the cash-generating units, or groups of cash-generating units, which are expected to benefit from the synergies of the combination.

Under IAS 17: Leases, a lease is classified as an operating lease or a finance lease. Operating leases are time-limited arrangements, where the rent paid can be regarded as payment for a temporary right to use the asset (RICS, 2003). The leased assets are accounted for on the balance sheet of the lessor, and the lessee merely presents the periodic (annual) rental payments in the profit and loss statement, with future rent liabilities that are due over the contractual term of the lease disclosed in the notes to the accounts. Broadly speaking, a finance lease is one that transfers substantially all of the risks and rewards of ownership of an asset to the lessee, even though he is not the legal owner; for example, where the rent payable under a lease is a set of instalments for the purchase of the leased asset including interest payments (RICS, 2003). Its capital value thus appears on the balance sheet of the lessee as an asset net of any depreciation and impairment with the corresponding rent payments due over the remaining term of the lease capitalised[7] and shown as a liability (Brett, 2004).

Operational leasehold interests may be classified as finance leases, but most will be classified as operating leases. Where leasehold interests in property are treated as investments, they must be accounted for as finance leases, reported at fair value and valued on a market value basis as any other leasehold investment would. On the liabilities side of the balance sheet, the total present value of the rent payments that the tenant is committed to make over the term of the lease is reported. But, as Brett (2004) points out, this raises a valuation problem: the liability to pay rent has already been allowed for in the valuation of the leasehold interest as a balance sheet asset. So, to avoid double-counting this liability, the present value of rents due under the lease should be added to the valuation figure for the leasehold that appears on the assets side of the balance sheet in order to arrive at the reporting amount. For example, a property investment company owns a long leasehold interest with 40 remaining on the lease. A fixed ground rent of £10 000 per annum is payable. The leasehold interest is valued at £2m, but this value reflects a liability to pay the ground rent. The present value of the remaining ground rent payments is £133 000 assuming a discount rate of 7%. The company must report this liability, but, on the assets side, it must report the value of the leasehold interest (£2 million) plus the present value of the remaining ground rent payments (£133 000). So the carrying amount (balance sheet asset value) of £2 133 000 is not the market value of the leasehold interest but an accounting value that might correspond more closely to what the property would be worth if it were a freehold with vacant possession, that is, the leasehold interest had been merged with the freehold (Brett, 2004).

Under *IFRS 5: Non-current Assets Held for Sale and Discontinued Operations* surplus property assets must be identified and accounted for individually or as a group to be disposed of together. IVA 1 (IVSC, 2005) states that either the individual market values of surplus property assets or the market value of the group as a whole to be disposed of in a single transaction should be reported and separately noted if different. *IAS 2: Inventories* states that the net realisable value (NRV) of properties held for sale in the ordinary course of business should be reported where NRV is the market value less sale costs.

4.4.2   UK financial reporting standards

UK financial reporting standards still apply to UK companies that are not publicly listed and which elect to use UK GAAP. UK GAAP includes, but is not limited to, Statements of Standard Accounting Practice (SSAP) and FRS issued by the ASB and its predecessors. In order to illustrate how these standards apply, we will consider a typical set of UK company accounts which comprise a balance sheet, profit and loss account, director's report and chairman's statement. UK FRS require the balance sheet to provide a true and fair view of the capital value to the business of tangible fixed assets which include land and buildings, plant and machinery, fixtures, fittings, tools and equipment, payments on account, assets in the course of construction

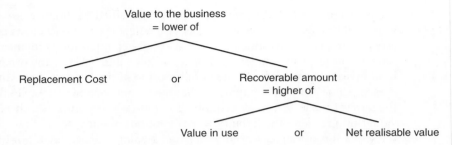

Figure 4.3   Reporting the value of tangible fixed assets (ASB, 1999).

and investments. A rational business would purchase such assets if they believed that the economic benefit (its value-in-use) was going to be greater than the economic cost. It is not appropriate for company accounts to record the value-in-use of an asset as this would reflect future economic benefits that have not yet been realised. Instead, it is reasonable to record the net replacement cost of the asset, in other words, the economic loss that would be suffered by the business if deprived of the asset – its deprival value. However, if the asset is impaired in some way[8] so that its recoverable amount is actually less than the replacement cost then the company accounts should record the remaining economic benefit that can be derived from the asset either from its continued use (value-in-use) or from its sale (NRV). This logic is presented diagrammatically in *FRS 15: Tangible Fixed Assets* (ASB, 1999) and is reproduced in Figure 4.3. IAS 2 (see above) also requires inventories (assets and resources) to be reported at the lower of cost or NRV.

As far as property assets are concerned, in the great majority of cases there will be no need to provide for impairment, and the replacement cost of property assets will be reported. In undertaking replacement cost valuations the 'going concern' assumption is key and it is essential to ensure the valuation can be supported by the potential profitability of the company. If the valuation is for a public body the assumption is that it is subject to the prospect and viability of the current occupation and use. As is the case with international financial reporting standards, companies generally have the freedom to choose whether to report replacement cost as the historic cost (i.e. purchase price, historic valuation or cost) or to regularly revalue them. If a company opts for the latter approach, the requirement is for a full valuation of each asset every 5 years and an interim valuation in year 3, plus additional interim valuations in intervening years where there has been a material change in value. Alternatively there are provisions for rolling valuations.

In the case of investment properties, the current value, and changes in current value, are of prime importance rather than a calculation of systematic annual depreciation. *SSAP 19: Accounting for Investment Properties* therefore requires investment properties to be included in the balance sheet at their open market value, but without charging depreciation. As with international standards, investment properties are thus treated differently from operational property assets, which are subject to depreciation charges to reflect, on a systematic basis, the wearing out, consumption or other loss of value of the asset required by FRS 15. If the business is planning to continue using the asset, its value will normally be the net current replacement cost which is the existing use value for non-specialised owner-occupied properties, DRC for specialised owner-occupied properties and market value for properties that are either surplus to requirements or held as an investment.

All companies (except property investment companies) are required to depreciate the value of fixed assets that have a limited economic life over the life of those assets (property investment companies are required to value their fixed assets annually) and the annual profit and loss account contains a charge in respect of the amount of depreciation suffered in any one accounting year. The figure on which the depreciation charge allocated to the profit and loss account is based is known as the **depreciable amount**. Freehold land is not normally liable to depreciation unless it has a limited economic life such as mineral-bearing land or land subject to a time-limited planning permission. But the buildings that are sited on freehold land and leasehold property interests are wasting assets and liable to depreciation. To arrive at the depreciable amount, the reported value of the property asset must be apportioned between wasting and non-wasting elements – ostensibly between the building(s) and the land respectively – so that the depreciable amount can be allocated to the wasting element. The depreciable amount is then calculated by either deducting the value of the land in its existing use from total cost/value of the asset or by making an assessment of the replacement cost of the buildings net of any depreciation. To calculate the depreciation charge the depreciable amount is divided by the number of years of remaining economic life. Because of the difficulty in estimating lives of buildings it is common to adopt bandings of say, 10–30 and 30–50 years.

4.4.3   Methods of valuing property assets for financial reporting purposes

The methods of valuation described in Chapter 3 are used to value property assets for financial reporting purposes. The existing use value or market value of a non-specialised office property may be estimated using the investment method, a chain of hotels (specialised trading properties) may be valued using the profits method and specialised properties for which there is no market are valued using the replacement cost method but on a DRC basis.

Existing use value is essentially net replacement cost, 'the least cost of purchasing the remaining service potential of the asset at the date of valuation' (ASB, 1999). It is assumed that a replacement property would be identical to the subject property in terms of location, size, specification, configuration, age, state of repair and so on. So a good starting point will be the market value of the actual property (RICS, 2003). The key differences between market value and existing use value are that the latter assumes potential alternative uses are disregarded, the buyer is granted vacant possession of parts occupied by the business, all parts of the property are required by the business and any parts occupied by third parties are valued subject to that occupation (Cherry, 2006). The Red Book (RICS, 2003) gives the following examples of circumstances in which existing use value may differ from market value:

- where an occupier is operating with a personal planning consent that could restrict the market in the event of the owner vacating;
- where the occupier holds the property under a lease and there are lease covenants that impose constraints on assignment or alternative uses;
- where a property is known to be contaminated but the continued occupation for the existing use is not inhibited or adversely affected, provided there is no current duty to remedy such contamination during the continued occupation;
- where an industrial complex is overdeveloped and the extra buildings have either a limited market value, or detract from the market value, but would need to be replaced to fulfil the service potential to the business;
- where the existing buildings are old and so have a limited market value, but would have a higher replacement cost to the business;
- where the property is in an unusual location or oversized for its location, with the result that it would have a very low market value, but where the cost of replacing the service potential would be significantly greater.

Depreciated replacement cost is an application of the replacement cost method of valuation used to assess the market value of specialised property assets for financial reporting purposes where market evidence is limited. The approach is described in *GN 8 – The Cost Approach for Financial Reporting – (DRC)* published by the IVSC (2005). It is the current gross reproduction or replacement cost (GRC) of the building(s) less an allowance for depreciation plus the market value of the land in its existing use taking into account the constraints, if any, on use imposed by the existing buildings and other improvements made to the land. The RICS Red Book adds supplementary guidance (RICS, 2003, Appendix 3.1 DRC) suggesting that the extent of land to be included in a DRC valuation should be agreed in advance as some might be surplus or retained for future expansion. It also suggests that planning permission for existing use or relevant range of uses prevailing in the locality should be assumed if the existing use is very specialised. Land value should be assessed by reference to the cost of purchasing a notional replacement site that would be equally suited to the existing use. In terms of building costs the Red Book advises that they should include everything necessary to complete the construction fit for existing use as at the valuation date. If the buildings are of architectural or historic interest and protected by legislation then the cost of actual reinstatement should be included in the GRC. If the buildings are not legally protected then the valuer must decide where the property falls along a spectrum between simple modern alternative and reinstatement of existing.

If the subject building is not new then its replacement cost is usually based on the cost of a replacement new building but with a reduction for depreciation. Depreciation in value can result from physical deterioration of the building and the onset of obsolescence. The causes and impact of depreciation are examined in more detail in Chapter 6. For accounting purposes, physical deterioration is usually allowed for by applying a 'depreciation factor' to the estimated cost of a replacement new buildings The depreciation factor is the ratio between the estimated remaining life of the existing building and the full economic life of a new equivalent building (RICS, 2003). This is shown in below:

(remaining economic life/full economic life) × replacement cost = depreciated amount   [4.1]

For financial reporting purposes most buildings are assumed to have an economic life of 50 years but a valuer may regard the depreciation factor to be higher or lower (and hence the lifespan of a building to be shorter or longer) after taking into account its type and construction, its use, specification, degree of specialisation and whether any capital investment has extended the life of the building (RICS, 2003). For leasehold interests the remaining economic life should be the lower of the unexpired term of the lease or the remaining economic life of the asset (RICS, 2003). The valuer should also consider the impact of legislation on the use of the building, including Health & Safety Regulations, Fire Regulations and access for the disabled. The impact of obsolescence on property value is an altogether much harder thing to quantify because it refers to the effect on value caused by buildings becoming outdated or outmoded rather than simply wearing out. The RICS (2003) suggests that *functional* obsolescence (where a building is no longer wholly fit for purpose) should be considered in two parts of the valuation. First, in terms of replacement building cost: has the size, type and design of the existing building become obsolete? If so the cost of a replacement building may be quite different and would help quantify the impact of obsolescence at the scale of the entire building. Second, at the scale of the internal layout, have the specification and configuration of the building become obsolete? Structural columns and internal walls that restrict the movement of goods within an industrial building or the layout of an office floor or retail unit might affect value and would be effectively handled by adjusting the depreciation factor applied to the replacement cost of the existing building. Great care is needed to avoid double-counting the financial impact of obsolescence, and the valuer should determine the extent to which the building's disabilities affect the efficient use of the building by the company.

If there is a material difference between the existing use value or DRC of a property asset and its market value (which, you will recall, can include alternative use) then the valuer must report market value if it is clearly identifiable and likely to produce a higher value. Where a potentially more valuable alternative use is uncertain, or is speculative, the valuer should indicate that the market value may be higher without necessarily providing a figure.

Example 1

The valuation of a non-specialised owner-occupied property asset.

Example 1   (continued)

A single-storey factory with a gross internal area (GIA) of 1000 m^2 is owned and occupied for industrial use. The premises were built 17 years ago when it was estimated that the economic life would be 50 years. The market rent of the factory is estimated to be £25 000 per annum on FRI terms. Planning permission has been granted to redevelop the whole site as 2000 m^2 GIA of new industrial floor-space for which there is a ready leasehold market. It is estimated that the works, which could commence immediately, would be completed within 1 year and that the finished scheme would let at approximately £40 per square metre on FRI terms. Costs, including building, financing and fees, are estimated to be £220 per square metre. Analysis of recent freehold investment transactions suggests a 9.5% initial yield. Value these premises for inclusion in the occupier's company accounts.

Estimated market rent (£)	25 000	
YP perpetuity @ 9.5%	10.5263	
Existing use value (£)		263 158

This figure will appear in the balance sheet. The depreciable amount in respect of the wasting element of the existing use value is calculated by estimating the GRC of the building and then depreciating this cost to arrive at a net replacement cost. The impact of depreciation can be estimated in several ways: straight line depreciation, declining balance (fixed percentage) and sinking fund replacement. By far the most common approach (and the one that is used here) is the straight line method where the future economic life of the building will be divided by the total life expectancy of a modern equivalent.

GRC (1000 m^2 × £220/m^2) (£)		220 000	
Age (years)	17		
Estimated economic life (years)	50		
Depreciation factor	33/50	0.66	
Net replacement cost (NRC) (£)			145 200

The market value, which will include alternative use value (also known as 'hope' or redevelopment value) is estimated by looking at the figures relating to the redevelopment of the site. It was suggested that a letting could be achieved at £40 per square metre on a building twice as large as the current one. This is likely to mean that the market value of the property of existing is considerably different to its existing use value, so it needs to be reported. A simple residual valuation would suffice. Because the property is industrial, both building costs and rental value are estimated on a GIA basis. Assuming a 1 year building period the valuation might be as follows.

Estimated market rent on 2000 m^2 @ £40/m^2 (£)	80 000	
YP perpetuity @ 8.5%	11.7647	
Gross development value (£)		941 176
Less:		
Estimated demolition costs (£)	−10 000	
Building costs on 2000 m^2 @ £220/m^2 (£)	−440 000	
Agent and legal fees @ 1.25% GDV (£)	−11 750	
Developer's profit @ 20% of demolition and building costs and fees costs (£)	−92 350	
		−554 100
Residual balance (£)		387 076
Less		
Interest on land and acquisition costs @ 8.5% pa (£)		−32 901
Acquisition costs @ 4% residual balance (£)		−15 483
Residual value (£)		338 692

Example 1   (continued)

This figure would be included in the valuer's report since it is significantly different from existing use value.

Example 2

The valuation of a specialised owner-occupied property asset.

The property is a fully utilised sports centre, held by the current occupier on a lease-hold interest with 32 years remaining on the lease. The majority of the buildings that comprise the sports centre were constructed in 1979 but in 1990 a swimming pool was added to the centre. Because of the age of the premises and its piecemeal expansion, configuration is poor, and it is expensive to maintain. The flat roofs on the 1979 buildings need renewing at an estimated cost of £169 000. The 1.2 ha site is surrounded by good quality owner-occupied residential property and current residential land values are estimated to be in the order of £1 200 000 per hectare, but for the existing use they are estimated to be in the region of £250 000 per hectare. Demolition and site clearance costs are currently estimated to be £900 000.

Because of the specialised nature of the premises a DRC valuation is appropriate. The GRC is the cost of erecting a modern equivalent building, allowing for depreciation. The depreciation allowance is, once again, estimated using the straight line method.

Description	Date built	Life expectancy of a modern equivalent	Life expectancy of expected building as at 2006	Estimated GRC (£)	Depreciation factor	Net replacement cost (£)	Value (£)
Main sports centre building	1979	50	23	8 000 000	23/50	3 680 000	
Less replacement of flat roofs						−169 000	
Swimming pool extension	1990	40	24	2 000 000	24/40	1 200 000	
DRC of buildings							4 711 000
Plus value of land: 1.2 ha @ £250 000/ha							300 000
Valuation							5 011 000

The alternative use value of £540 000 should also be brought to the attention of the finance director. This value is based on a residential land value of £1 200 000 per hectare less demolition and site clearance costs of £900 000.

> ### Key points
>
> - As far as international accounting standards are concerned, the IVSC advises that, in all cases, when valuing a property asset, market value is the appropriate basis. But the devil is in the detail.
> - Slowly but surely there will be parity between UK and international financial reporting standards. In fact, UK standards have provided companies with a choice between reporting property assets at cost or value for some time so the merger will not be too onerous. There will of course be implications for companies as the international standards take effect and these are very well documented by Brett (2004).

4.5   Valuations for loan security

One of the underlying principles of valuation for financial reporting is the assumption of the continuation of the business; such an assumption does not apply to valuations of properties that are going to be used as security for a loan (IVSC, 2005). Loan security valuations might be required for property that is owner-occupied, held as an investment or going to be redeveloped or refurbished and, in the UK, such valuations are regulated by the RICS (2003), specifically, UK Practice Statement 3.1. This is a protocol that has been agreed between the RICS and the British Bankers Association and which must be followed unless the client requests departure. The protocol deals with conflicts of interest; does the valuer have a current or recent fee-earning involvement with the property to be valued, with the borrower, prospective borrower or any party connected to the transaction for which the lending is required. Under Practice Statement 3.7 of the Red Book the RICS states that valuations for lending purposes undertaken by its members shall be in accordance with International Valuation Standard *'IVA 2: Valuation for Lending Purposes'*. It also deals with matters of enquiry; the valuer should enquire if there has been a recent market transaction or provisionally agreed price and practicable enquiries as to details should be made. The valuer should also request that if such matters arise before the loan is finalised then the valuation should be referred back for further investigation (Cherry, 2006).

In the overwhelming majority of cases valuations of commercial property for secured lending purposes will be conducted on the basis of market value or, in some cases, market value with special assumptions. These special assumptions may relate to the completion of a development or refurbishment, a new letting on specified terms, a restricted period in which to sell the property or the grant of planning permission for a particular use. The valuation should also include comment on potential demand for alternative uses. Existing use value is not a consideration here and owner-occupied properties should be valued on the basis of vacant possession. This does not preclude the owner as part of the market but does require that any special advantage of the owner's occupancy, which may be reflected in the value of the business, be separated from the value of the property. This is done because, in the event of default on the financial arrangements, security for the loan can be realised only by a change in occupancy (IVSC, 2005). Partly as a result of this, specialised properties, which by definition have limited marketability and derive value from being part of a business, may not be suitable as separate security for loans. If they are offered as security individually or collectively they should be valued assuming vacant possession (IVSC, 2005). Because specialised trading properties are valued with regard to the maintainable profit of an operational business, when valuing them for lending purposes the valuer should notify the lender of any significant difference in value that may result if the business was to close, the inventory removed, licenses/certificates, franchises or permits removed or placed in jeopardy, the property vandalised or other circumstances that may impair future operating performance (IVSC, 2005). The valuer may also wish to note any specific circumstances that might put the business's profitability at risk, given that the profits method relies on an assumption of adequate profitability.

Valuations that are based on replacement cost are used for specialised properties which are not bought or sold and are not often used for secured lending purposes but use is made of this basis to calculate the cost of physical reinstatement for insurance purposes, which is a requirement of commercial mortgages. Development properties can be valued using the residual method under the assumption that the construction work is complete, but it is important to consider market movements between the valuation date and estimated completion date (IVSC, 2005). Cherry (2006) also notes that the valuation should be based on current estimates of costs and value rather than projections to the likely end of the development period and that the following additional matters should be reported:

- a comment on costs and contract procurement;
- a comment on viability of the proposed project;
- an illustration of sensitivity to assumptions made;
- implications on value of any cost overruns or delays.

The valuer should also indicate whether plans and costs have been provided by an architect and quantity surveyor respectively.

As well as the usual matters that must be included in a valuation report, and described in Chapter 3, other matters relevant to a loan security valuation include the marketability of the property, potential demand for alternative uses, valuation methodology adopted, details of significant comparable transactions relied upon, suitability of the property as security for mortgage purposes and environmental or economic designation. There will be more specific matters depending on the type of property being valued; the valuation of an investment property, for example, would require consideration of the covenant strength of the tenant or tenants.

Sayce *et al.* (2006) argue that the substantial increase in the number of investors using a combination of equity and debt finance to fund the acquisition of property will lead to a shift away from the use of income capitalisation as a way of valuing property investments and towards more cash-flow based valuations. The latter, which will be examined in Chapter 5, allow the lender calculate various ratios that are used to help make the lending decision, including loan-to-value and debt service ratios. Also, income capitalisation does not provide information on potential gearing in the debt and equity returns.

4.6   Valuations for tax purposes

4.6.1   Capital gains tax

Capital gains tax (CGT) was introduced in 1965 as a means of taxing capital gains made by individuals and trustees on the disposal of assets (which includes properties), after having set off any losses incurred within a tax year. Companies are subject to the same tax regime under the name of Corporation Tax. CGT is only paid on disposal of an asset if a 'chargeable gain' was made in the preceding financial year. This is calculated by taking the sale proceeds and deducting the original cost, acquisition fees, any enhancement expenditure, disposal fees and an allowance for inflation over the period for which the asset was held, known as an 'indexation allowance'. The first part of the chargeable gain is exempt for individuals (half for trustees), but the exact amount varies from year to year. The process of calculating the amount chargeable to CGT is illustrated in Table 4.4.

In most cases, where the disposal is by way of an open market sale, the disposal proceeds are the amount actually received for selling the asset. But sometimes the market value may need to be estimated if the sale was not made at arm's length or was a gift. The Taxation of Chargeable Gains Act, 1992 (TCGA 1992) defines market value as the price for which those assets could be sold on the open market with no reduction for the fact that this may involve an assumption that several assets are to be sold at the same time. Certain costs are allowable (deductible) such as those associated with the acquisition of the property, including professional and legal fees. Enhancement expenditure is permitted as an allowable deduction so long as it is reflected in the state or nature of the property at the time of disposal, thus excluding improvements which have worn out by the time the property is disposed of. Disposal costs are also allowable and these, like acquisition costs, include professional and legal fees and any other costs reasonably incurred in marketing the property, including the cost of a valuation and any apportionment for CGT purposes. If the 'gain before indexation' is negative this 'loss' may be offset against other gains made in the same or in future tax years. 'Roll-over relief' is available where proceeds from a disposal are used to acquire another asset for use in the same business and 'retirement relief' is available where the individual is 50 or over. Stock-in-trade is not regarded as capital for CGT purposes so property companies' developments are not subject to CGT (Rees and Hayward, 2000). Certain disposals are exempt including transfers between husband and wife and gifts to charity. Also, certain organisations are exempt from CGT including charities, local authorities, friendly societies, scientific research associations, pension funds and non-resident owners (Johnson *et al.*, 2000).

Table 4.4 Procedure for calculating CGT.

Disposal proceeds or sum received from assets	After allowing for reliefs which reduce the figure to be treated as proceeds. Sometimes market value is used instead of the actual proceeds
Less allowable costs	If this is a negative number, then you have made a loss, which may be an allowable loss
=Gain before indexation	
Indexation allowance	For inflation, up to April 1998, may not create or increase a loss
= Indexed Gain	
Other reliefs	For example, business asset roll-over relief, retirement relief
= Chargeable gain	For each asset individually
Sum total chargeable gains	Total of all the chargeable gains in the tax year.
Allowable losses	Losses in the tax year and unused losses carried forward from earlier years
Chargeable gains after losses	
Taper relief	A relief that reduces a chargeable gain after losses according to how long you held the asset. Taper relief is applied separately to each chargeable gain.
Tapered chargeable gains	
Annual exempt amount	£8800 for the tax year 2006–2007
= Amount chargeable to CGT	

Source: HMRC.

Because the capital value of properties tends to appreciate over time, on the 31 March 1982 special 'rebasing' rules were introduced to ensure that, for properties acquired on or before that date, only the increase in capital value after that date is taken into account when working out the chargeable gain. An election can be made to apply these rebasing rules so that the original acquisition costs of all properties held on 31 March 1982 is disregarded completely and, instead, the market values at that date can be used to calculate the chargeable gain. If no such election is made, the charegable gain for each property held on 31 March 1982 must be calculated using both their market value at that date and their original acquisition cost. Then

- if both calculations show a gain, the smaller of the gains is the chargeable gain;
- if both calculations show a loss, the smaller of the losses is the allowable loss;
- if one calculation shows a gain and the other shows a loss, there is neither a chargeable gain nor an allowable loss.

Between 31 March and 6 April 1998, an 'indexation allowance' adjusts the chargeable gain to take account of the effects of inflation by giving an allowance equal to the amount by which the value of the property would have risen on a monthly basis if its value had kept pace with inflation, as measured by

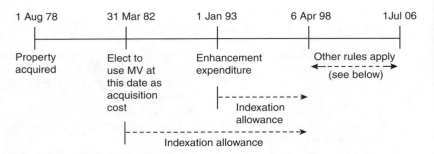

Figure 4.4   Events timeline.

the increase in the retail price index (RPI). The indexation allowance is based on the increase in the RPI between the month in which the property was acquired or, for subsequent expenditure, the month in which the expenditure on the property was incurred, or March 1982 if that is later, and the month in which the property was disposed of, or April 1998 if that is earlier. For example a property was purchased in August 1978, refurbished in January 1993 and disposed of in July 2006. A timeline is presented in Figure 4.4.

To help calculate the indexation allowance, the Government provides a table of 'indexation factors' which can be used to calculate the rise in the RPI between the month in which expenditure was incurred on the property and April 1998. These indexation factors are shown in Table 4.5.

First of all, it is necessary to determine which month the expenditure (either acquisition or enhancement) took place and locate the relevant indexation factor. This is then multiplied by the expenditure amount to give the indexation allowance which can be deducted from the chargeable gain. For example, a property was purchased in March 1992 for £100 000 and sold in June 1999 for £500 000. The indexation factor to be used for a property acquired in March 1992 is 0.189. Multiplying this by £100 000 gives an indexation allowance of £18 900 and the indexed capital gain is calculated as follows:

Proceeds (£)	500 000
Less cost (£)	−100 000
Gain before indexation (£)	400 000
Less indexation allowance (£)	−18 900
Indexed gain (£)	381 100

If the property was owned at 31 March 1982 and no election has been made to rebase, the indexation allowance is calculated on the greater of either the total cost incurred up to 31 March 1982 on that property (including its initial acquisition price) or the value of the property at 31 March 1982. If an election has been made for rebasing, the indexation allowance is calculated on the value of the property at 31 March 1982. If part of a property is disposed of then only part of the costs of the property can be deducted when working out the gain or loss. The indexation factor is multiplied by the part of the cost that can be deducted, not by the whole of the cost of the

Table 4.5 Indexation factors.

Year	Jan	Feb	Mar	Apr	May	Jun	Jul	Aug	Sep	Oct	Nov	Dec
1982			1.047	1.006	0.992	0.987	0.986	0.985	0.987	0.977	0.967	0.971
1983	0.968	0.960	0.956	0.929	0.921	0.917	0.906	0.898	0.889	0.883	0.876	0.871
1984	0.872	0.965	0.859	0.834	0.828	0.823	0.825	0.808	0.804	0.793	0.788	0.789
1985	0.783	0.769	0.752	0.716	0.708	0.704	0.707	0.703	0.704	0.701	0.695	0.693
1986	0.689	0.683	0.681	0.665	0.662	0.663	0.667	0.662	0.654	0.652	0.638	0.632
1987	0.626	0.620	0.616	0.597	0.596	0.596	0.597	0.593	0.588	0.580	0.573	0.574
1988	0.574	0.568	0.562	0.537	0.525	0.525	0.524	0.507	0.500	0.485	0.478	0.474
1989	0.465	0.454	0.448	0.423	0.409	0.409	0.408	0.404	0.395	0.384	0.372	0.369
1990	0.361	0.353	0.339	0.300	0.283	0.283	0.282	0.269	0.258	0.248	0.251	0.252
1991	0.249	0.242	0.237	0.222	0.213	0.213	0.215	0.213	0.208	0.204	0.199	0.198
1992	0.199	0.193	0.189	0.171	0.167	0.167	0.171	0.171	0.166	0.162	0.164	0.168
1993	0.179	0.171	0.167	0.156	0.153	0.153	0.156	0.151	0.146	0.147	0.148	0.146
1994	0.151	0.144	0.141	0.128	0.124	0.124	0.129	0.124	0.121	0.120	0.119	0.114
1995	0.114	0.107	0.102	0.091	0.087	0.085	0.091	0.085	0.080	0.085	0.085	0.079
1996	0.083	0.078	0.073	0.066	0.063	0.063	0.067	0.062	0.057	0.057	0.057	0.053
1997	0.053	0.049	0.046	0.040	0.036	0.032	0.032	0.026	0.021	0.019	0.019	0.016
1998	0.019	0.014	0.011									

property. It should also be noted that an indexation allowance can reduce or eliminate gains which are chargeable to tax, but for disposals on or after 30 November 1993, the indexation allowance cannot be used to turn a gain into a loss or to increase a loss.

On the 6 April 1998, taper relief replaced the indexation allowance for individuals and trusts. Taper relief reduces the gain by a percentage that is dependent on whether the property is a business or non-business asset and the number of whole years for which it is held. The chargeable gain is reduced by the relevant taper reduction, as shown in Table 4.6.

For example, a property was acquired on 1 June 1999 for £150000 and sold on 1 July 2005 for £250000. It was a non-business asset throughout the period of ownership, and there are no allowable losses. The chargeable gain before taper relief is therefore £100000 (disposal proceeds of £250000 less allowable costs of £150000). The property was held for 6 whole years so the amount of the chargeable gain that remains chargeable after taper relief is £80000 (£100000 × 80%). Where a non-business asset was acquired before 17 March 1998 and is owned on 5 April 1998 then a bonus year is added to the period of ownership after the 5 April 1998. Where property interests have merged or divided and the property disposed of derives part of its value from an earlier asset the qualifying holding period may be extended. For example, a leasehold interest is acquired on 8 January 1995 and the freehold interest of the same (physical) property is acquired on 4 February 2000; the lease being extinguished by merger with the freehold. The freehold is then disposed of on 31 March 2006.

Table 4.6 Taper relief.

Business asset (used for the purpose of a trade, profession or vocation)		Non-business asset (generally, let property is a non-business asset)	
Number of whole years in the qualifying holding period	Gain remaining chargeable (%)	Number of whole years in the qualifying holding period	Gain remaining chargeable (%)
Less than 1	100	Less than 1	100
1	50	1	100
2 or more	25	2	100
		3	95
		4	90
		5	85
		6	80
		7	75
		8	70
		9	65
		10 or more	60

As the value of the freehold is derived to some extent from the extinguished lease the qualifying holding period begins on 6 April 1998, and there are 7 whole years between that date and the date of disposal. In addition, as this is a non-business asset, the property is treated as having acquired before 17 March 1998 and qualifies for the bonus year.

For business assets acquired before 6 April 1998 and disposed of after that date there will be an indexation allowance up to 6 April 1998 and then taper relief thereafter up to the disposal date. For example, a property was acquired on 10 July 1985 for £100000 and sold on 8 September 2002 for £1 000000. It was a business asset and there are no allowable losses. The chargeable gain before taper relief is £829 300 (disposal proceeds of £1 000000 less allowable costs of £100000 and an indexation allowance to April 1998 of £70 700). From 6 April 1998 the property was held for 4 whole years (there is no bonus year for business assets disposed of on or after 6 April 2000). Therefore, the amount of the chargeable gain that remains chargeable is £207 325 (£829 300 × 25%).

If a disposal is made where only *part of the property* was used as a business asset during the relevant period of ownership, then the chargeable gain must be apportioned between the gain on the business asset and the gain on the non-business asset. The property will qualify for business asset taper relief on one part and non-business asset taper relief on the other and the amount of each relief is calculated using the full qualifying holding period. Consider the following example of a property acquired on 1 December 1994 and sold on 31 March 2006 making a gain of £20000 on the sale. In the period of ownership falling after 5 April 1998, 80% of the property was used by the owner as a shop and the remaining 20% of the property was let as a furnished flat. There are 7 whole years in the qualifying holding period for a business asset and 8 years for a non-business asset (seven complete years and the bonus year). In calculating taper relief the overall gain needs to be apportioned between business and non-business use. For business use the gain is £16 000 (£20 000 × 80%) and the qualifying holding period is 7 years so 25% of this part of the gain will be chargeable, that is, £4000. For the non-business use the gain is £4000 (£20 000 × 20%) and the qualifying holding period is 8 years, so 70% of this part of the gain will be chargeable, that is, £2800. The aggregate chargeable gain is therefore £6800.

Now consider a property acquired on 16 March 1995, sold on 5 April 2006 making a gain of £20 000 on the sale and used only *part of the time* as a business asset. The property was a business asset until 5 April 2002 and then it was empty until the sale date with the gain during this latter period being treated as arising on the sale of a non-business asset. Again, the property will qualify for business asset taper relief on one part and non-business asset taper relief on the other and the amount of each relief is calculated using the full qualifying holding period. There are 7 whole years in the qualifying holding period for a business asset and 8 years for a non-business asset (7 whole years and the bonus year). During the period of ownership between 6 April 1998 and 5 April 2006, the property was used for business purposes 50% of the time (6 April 1998 to 5 April 2002) and for non-business use (empty) for the other half (6 April 2002 to 5 April 2006). Therefore, the chargeable gain on the period while the property was a business asset is £10 000 (£20 000 × 50%) and on the period while the property was empty is also £10 000 (£20 000 × 50%). So £10 000 of the gain qualifies for business asset taper relief appropriate to a qualifying holding period of 7 years, meaning that 25% of this part of the gain will be chargeable, that is, £2500. £10 000 of the gain qualifies for non-business asset taper relief appropriate to a qualifying holding period of 8 years, meaning that 70% of this part of the gain will be chargeable, that is, £7000. The aggregated chargeable gain is therefore £9500.

The grant of a lease is regarded as a part disposal of a property asset and is liable to CGT. The way that the liability is calculated depends on the duration of the lease, classified as follows:

- A long lease (more than 50 years duration remaining) granted out of a freehold or long leasehold interest.
- A short lease (50 years or less remaining) granted out of a freehold or long leasehold interest.
- A short lease granted out of a short leasehold interest.

The duration of a lease for CGT purposes will normally be the time remaining until expiry of the current lease term but can also be affected by any provision in the lease allowing the landlord or the tenant to give notice to terminate the lease or by a provision allowing the tenant to extend it. Once the statutory rules have been applied to a part disposal of a property, they have to be applied to subsequent disposals.

- Grant of a long-lease out of a freehold or long leasehold interest.

To calculate the gain arising from the grant of a long lease out of a freehold or long leasehold interest, any allowable expenditure (apart from the costs of disposal) is apportioned between the freehold reversion (or head-leasehold interest retained) and the lease granted. This is done by applying the fraction $A/(A + B)$ to the allowable expenditure where A is the premium or consideration received and B is the value of the interest retained plus the value of the right to receive the rent under the lease. For example, on 30 June 1988, the freehold interest in a property was purchased for £150000. On 30 June 2005, the landlord granted a 75 year lease of the property for a premium of £200000. A ground rent of £5000 per annum was due under the lease. The landlord incurred legal fees of £3000 on the grant of the lease. The value of the freehold reversion at 30 June 2005 was £30000, and the value of the right to receive the rent was £70000. The landlord's allowable expenditure is as follows:

$$£150\,000 \times A/(A + B) = £150\,000 \times \frac{200\,000}{200\,000 + (30000 + 70000)}$$

$$= £100\,000$$

The chargeable gain accruing to the landlord on granting the long lease is then calculated as follows:

Premium received (£)	200 000
Less apportioned cost, from above (£)	−100 000
Less legal fees (£)	−3 000
Unindexed gain (£)	97 000
Less indexation up to April 1998, £100 000 × 0.525 (£)	−52 500
Chargeable gain, subject to taper relief (£)	44 500

- Grant of a short lease out of a freehold or long leasehold interest.

The calculation is the same as for the grant of a long lease except that part of any premium received for the grant of a short lease is chargeable to income tax, calculated as 2% for each year of the term other than the first, so this taxed amount must not be subject to CGT too. This is achieved by leaving it out of the numerator A in the $A/(A + B)$ fraction but including it in A in the denominator. For example, on 6 April 1986, a freehold shop was acquired for £200000. On 6 April 2005, the landlord granted a 15-year lease with 5-year rent reviews for a premium of £50000 and an initial rent of £9000 per annum. The estimated market rent at the time of disposal was £12000 per annum and the yield was 6%. The calculation of chargeable gain can be broken down into several steps:

(a) Part of premium subject to income tax:

2% of premium (50 000 × 2%)	1 000
× (15 − 1) years	14
	14 000

(b) Part of premium subject to CGT:

Whole premium	50 000	
Less amount chargeable to income tax	−14 000	
		36 000

(c) Calculation of value of retained interest plus value of right to receive rent under the lease:

Term rent (to first rent review)	9 000	
YP 5 years @ 6%	4.2124	
		37 912
Reversion to market rent	12 000	
YP in perpetuity @ 6%	166 667	
PV £1 5 years @ 6%	0.7473	
		149 460
		187 372

(d) Applying the part disposal formula $A/(A + B)$ to apportion the allowable expenditure:

$$£200 000 \times \frac{£36 000}{£50 000 + £187 372} = £30 332$$

(e) Calculation of chargeable gain

Disposal proceeds (£)	36 000
Less allowable expenditure (£)	−30 332
Unindexed gain (£)	5 668
Less indexation allowance up to	−20 171
April 1998, £30 332 x 0.665 (£)	
Chargeable gain (loss), subject to	−14 503
taper relief (£)	

If a capital loss arises, as in this case, it may be restricted in some circumstances but this is generally where the services of an accountant rather than a valuer are called for!

■ Grant of a short lease out of a short leasehold interest

Where a premium is paid for a short sub-lease granted out of a short head-leasehold interest (i.e. a remaining term of less than 50 years) only that part of expenditure on the head-lease that will waste away over the period of the sub-lease can be set against the premium received (Johnson *et al.*, 2000). Basically, the short head-lease is treated as a wasting asset, and the chargeable gain is reduced by a 'depreciation allowance' calculated as follows:

Reduced gain (reduced acquisition price)

= original acquisition cost x YP 6% for years remaining at disposal
  ―――
  YP 6% for years remaining at aquisition

During a lease, if a capital sum is received instead of rent in exchange for its assignment, surrender or for a variation or waiver of some of the lease terms, it is chargeable to CGT. An assignment or surrender of a lease may be treated as a complete disposal of that leasehold interest whereas a variation or waiver of lease terms may be treated as part disposal.

So it can be seen that where part of a property interest is disposed of, it is necessary to apportion allowable expenditure on the property between the part sold and the part retained in order to calculate the gain or loss arising. The statutory rules for doing this require a valuation of the part retained. In order to avoid the need for doing this, it is usually acceptable to treat the part disposed of as a separate asset from the part retained; any fair and reasonable method of apportioning part of the allowable expenditure to the part disposed of will be accepted. To determine the value of the property retained the value of the part disposed of is deducted from the total value of the property interest. For example, part of a property which was acquired in 1975 is sold in 2005 for £50 000 and the costs of disposal were £2000. The market value at 31 March 1982 of that part was £20 000. The gain before indexation using the alternative basis is

Sale proceeds (£)	50 000
Less market value at 31 March 1982 (£)	−20 000
Less costs of disposal (£)	−2000
Gain before indexation (£)	28 000

If the alternative basis is not used it would be necessary both to value the whole property at 31 March 1982, and to value the whole of the property retained at the date of the sale.

If the part disposal is small and if certain conditions[9] are met, it is possible to claim that it should not be regarded as a disposal and that the consideration received should instead be deducted from the allowable cost of the rest of the property. On a later disposal, or part disposal, of the remaining property, only the reduced expenditure is taken into account in calculating any subsequent gain or loss.

In summary, property valuations may be required to calculate the gain or loss arising when a property interest is disposed of. The main circumstances in which valuations are required are where the property was owned at 31 March 1982, the disposal was not an open market sale, or there has been a disposal of part of a property and the alternative basis for calculating the allowable cost is not being used.

4.6.2   Inheritance tax

The Inheritance Tax Act 1984 requires Inheritance Tax (IHT) to be paid at a rate of 40% on the transfer value (net of costs and CGT) of a person's estate held at death, on certain lifetime gifts and some transfers in and out of trusts. The value of these transfers is calculated by reference to the reduction in value of the remaining estate and in most cases this is the same as the value of the transferred estate. The reduction in value is estimated by valuing the transferor's estate before and after the transfer. For example, John owns two small prime shop units in Oxford Street, together they are worth £1 million, but individually each is worth £300 000. John leaves one of the units to his daughter. The gift for the purposes of IHT is the 'loss to John's estate', in other words, £1 million less £300 000. So a valuation is required to measure the loss in value of the transferor's estate, and this will usually be the market value of the property assets transferred plus the IHT due at the time of the transfer. The valuation date is the date of transfer and with regard to transfers on death the exact valuation moment is that immediately before death. No reduction is made to the valuation due to the sale of the estate 'flooding the market' but if a higher price is achievable by selling in smaller lots then this can be assumed (Johnson *et al.*, 2000).

Inheritance Tax is payable in cases where the transfer value is over the threshold of £285 000 (2006/7 tax year). Certain (generally low value) gifts are exempt, including those made between husband and wife, those not exceeding £3000 in any tax year, maintenance payments, wedding gifts, small gifts to many people, and gifts out of income tax. Of more relevance to property are gifts to UK based charities, registered housing associations, qualifying Parliamentary political parties, national museums, universities, The National Trust and certain other bodies.

If an outright gift is made to someone during the estate-owner's lifetime it is a 'potentially exempt transfer' and will only become chargeable to IHT if the transferor dies within 7 years of making the gift. An outright gift is one in which the transferor does not retain any benefit or value. A gift with reservation of benefit is one that is not fully given away so that either the person getting the gift does so with conditions or restrictions attached, or the person making the gift retains some benefit. Where this happens to gifts made on or after 18 March 1986, the assets are included in the estate but there is no 7-year limit as there is for outright gifts. To complicate matters even more a gift may begin as a gift with reservation but some time later the reservation may cease. For example, if an estate-owner gives a shop to his child but continues to run his business there rent-free, that would be a gift with reservation. If after 2 years the transferor starts to pay a market rent, the reservation ceases. The gift becomes outright at that point and the 7-year period runs from the date the reservation ceased. Conversely a gift may start as an outright gift and then become a gift with reservation.

If, during an estate-owner's lifetime, a gift is made to a company or to certain types of trust (known as discretionary trusts) the gift is immediately taxable at a rate of 20%. If the transferor then dies within 7 years of making an immediately taxable gift, tax will be due at 40% of the amount exceeding the minimum threshold and credit will be given for the tax previously paid at 20%.

Table 4.7 Taper relief on potentially exempt transfers.

Number of years between the gift and death	Tax charged reduced by
0–3	No relief
3–4	20%
4–5	40%
5–6	60%
6–7	80%

So, when a transferor dies, all potentially exempt transfers made in the 7 years before death become chargeable transfers but are subject to 'taper relief'. If the total chargeable value of all the gifts made between 3 and 7 years before death is more than the taxable threshold at death, then taper relief will apply. The relief reduces the amount of tax payable on a gift – it does not reduce the chargeable value of the gift. The reductions are shown in Table 4.7. Any immediately chargeable gifts made in those 7 years are also taken into account.

Consider the following example of Mr X who dies in July 2006 leaving an estate of £850 000 to D but who also made the following lifetime transfers:

Date	Value of gift (£)	Recipient
October 1999	200 000	A
September 2000	250 000	B
January 2005	100 000	C

The tax payable on the gifts, ignoring exemptions, is calcuated as follows:

Date	Value of gift	Amount of threshold used	Taxable balance
October 1999	£200 000	£200 000	£0
September 2000	£250 000	£85 000	£165 000
January 2005	£100 000	Nil	£100 000
		£285 000	

There is no IHT to pay on the gift to A as it is below the taxable threshold. IHT on the gift to B is £66 000 (£165 000 taxed at a rate of 40%). As Mr X died more than 5 but less than 6 years after the date of the gift, taper relief reduces the tax payable by B by 60% to £39 600. IHT on the gift to C is worked out as £100 000 at 40% = £40 000. As this gift is within 3 years of the death, no taper relief is due. The entire value of the estate left to D is taxed at 40% as the threshold has been used up.

4.6.3   Business rates

Business rates or, more formally, national non-domestic rates (NNDR) is the property-based tax system in England and Wales used to raise revenue for the provision of local services. Business Rates are levied annually on individually occupied non-domestic premises. These separately occupied units of business accommodation are legally defined as **hereditaments** and the amount, of tax due from each occupier is based on an assessment of the annual 'rateable' value of the hereditament occupied. The rate payments are collected by Billing Authorities who, in general, are the local authorities. The amount of tax payable is calculated by multiplying the **rateable value** of the hereditament by the appropriate national uniform business rate (UBR) multiplier set by the Government on 1 April each year (43.3p for 2006/6 but reduced by 0.7p for hereditaments with a rateable value less than £15 000 (£21 500 for hereditaments in Greater London). Under the current NNDR list or rating list, which was effective from 1 April 2005, a hereditament is valued to its annual rateable value as at 1 April 2003. This date is known as the antecedent valuation date. The rateable values in the rating list are reassessed every 5 years.

The Valuation Office Agency (VOA) is the Government agency charged with producing and maintaining the rating list. A rateable value is assigned to each hereditament of which there are some 1.7 million in England and Wales. Market transactions provide evidence of rents actually being paid, and these are analysed and adjusted into line with the definition of rateable value so that these 'beacon' properties provide a good indication of the level of values as at the antecedent valuation date. Then every hereditament will be assessed on the basis of the adjusted rental evidence and put into the rating list. There is also a central list which deals with hereditaments that are, generally in the form of a network throughout the country such as property owned by the Water Companies and other utilities, national oil pipelines and so on.

Rating legislation comprises the Local Government Finance Act 1988 and Local Government Act 1989 (as amended). The definition of Rateable Value under Paragraph 2(1) Schedule 6 of the Local Government Finance Act 1988 is

> The rent at which it is estimated the hereditament might reasonably be expected to let from year to year if the tenant undertook to pay all usual tenant's rates and taxes and to bear the cost of the repairs and insurance and the other expenses necessary to maintain the hereditament in a state to command that rent.

The definition is based on the concept of a hypothetical property that is vacant and available to rent on an annual tenancy with a reasonable prospect of continuance. The valuation must account for all possible bids, and it is assumed that the landlord and tenant are commercially prudent yet reasonably minded and the premises are in a reasonable state of repair for the type of property, location and tenant. As a consequence of this latter assumption, the impact on value of any disrepair is normally ignored because the tenant is assumed to maintain the hereditament.

The extent of the hereditament is determined by four rules; it must be

- capable of separate occupation;
- a single geographical unit that is contiguous or otherwise functionally essential;
- in single use;
- in a single definable position.

The rateable occupier is not defined by statute, instead the meaning is deduced from case law, but there are four essential ingredients. Occupation must

1. Be *actual*, and this includes an intention to occupy at some time in the future.
2. Be *exclusive*, difficulties arise where several parties have rights of occupation, see, for example, *Westminster City Council v Southern Railway Co and Others, 1936* where shops, offices, kiosks, bookstalls and showcases on Victoria Station were held to be in separate, exclusive occupation of the traders.
3. Be *beneficial*, in other words, occupation must be of value or benefit. It is not necessarily the actual occupier who must pay a rent but the 'hypothetical tenant'. The rental value should reflect the actual use or an alternative use if, under the same mode of occupation, planning permission could be obtained and no structural alterations were required.
4. Have a *degree of permanence*, builders' huts or caravans are not sufficiently permanent. Hereditaments that exist for at least a year are usually regarded as sufficiently permanent under the '12 month' rule.

To help the VOA value 1.7 million hereditaments it has the legal right to inspect premises and gather occupation details. In particular, it can issue notices to all business occupiers in England and Wales requiring information for rating purposes which each recipient must supply within 21 days. This information includes a description of accommodation, details of any rent paid, whether outgoings are included in the rent, whether the rent includes other items such as fixtures, fittings and services, details of rent review provisions and so on. The information received is analysed, the rent adjusted to correspond with the definition of rateable value and used together with all other information obtained to keep the current rating list up-to-date and assist in the compilation of the next one. The billing authorities help in the preparation of the list to the extent that they have a responsibility to inform the VOA of any changes occurring in their areas which require an amendment of the rating list. Such things would involve the construction or alteration of property, or the change of use of property – in fact those changes which would normally be apparent from the granting of planning permissions or the approval of work by Building Control Officers. A new or altered property becomes rateable after the local authority serves a 'completion notice', and this can be served up to 3 months before the expected completion date. When new properties are constructed or when properties are amalgamated or split, this causes reassessments, and these will be based on values as at the antecedent valuation date. This continues to be the case for all new assessments until a new list comes into force. Creating a level of values at a particular historical date is known as 'having regard to the tone of the list'. The publication of a new list triggers the ratepayer's right of appeal, should he or she disagree with either entry of the hereditament in the list, the extent of the hereditament assessed, the description of the hereditament or more particularly, the value ascribed to it.

The problem is, of course, that circumstances change through the years so that, although we might be attempting to value our shop at the antecedent date when the location was a peaceful village, at the time of valuation the shop may be in the midst of an expensive suburb. Conversely, a particular shopping street might now be worth less in value due to physical changes in the neighbourhood – the building of a shopping centre for instance. Such problems are dealt with in Local Government Finance Act, 1988, Schedule 6, paragraphs 5, 6 and 7, whereby certain matters have to be taken into account when a property is valued as at a particular date for entry in the list. These are

(a)   matters affecting the physical state or physical enjoyment of the hereditament;
(b)   the mode or category of the occupation of the hereditament;
(c)   the quantity of minerals or other substances in or extracted from the hereditament;
(d)   matters affecting the physical state of the locality in which the hereditament is situated or which, though not affecting the physical state of the locality, are nonetheless physically manifest there;
(e)   the use or occupation of other premises situated in the locality of the hereditament.

Occupation of part of a hereditament is deemed to be the same as occupation of the whole, but if the occupier can establish that there is no intention to reoccupy the vacant part it may be separately assessed. Separate provision is made to apportion the rateable value where part of the hereditament is vacant for only a short period.

Rateable hereditaments include most shops, offices, factories, warehouses, workshops, schools, hospitals, universities, places of entertainment, hotels, pubs, town halls, sewage farms, swimming pools, and so on but there might be rating relief for certain occupiers such as charities. Some properties are used for both domestic and non-domestic use, and these 'composite' hereditaments require an apportionment of tax liability between business rates and council tax, and each element is valued having regard to the benefit of the other. Certain premises are exempt from business rates, and these include agricultural premises, fish farms and fisheries, places of religious worship, parks and property used for the disabled.

Methods of assessment are synonymous with valuation methods described in Chapter 3, namely, rental comparison, profits and replacement cost (usually referred to as the contractors' method in the context of business rates) with the addition of either statutory or nationally agreed formulae for the valuation of certain specialised properties such as hospitals. The focus as far as rating is concerned is on rental value (as a basis for the assessment of rateable value) rather than capital value.

4.6.3.1 Rental comparison

The most widely used valuation method for business rates purposes is rental comparison, where schedules of contract rents are prepared, based on rents devalued on a zoned basis for shops or in terms of a main space for office and industrial space. Evidence of contract rents can be obtained from a number of sources, the best being market rental transaction evidence close to the antecedent valuation date. Evidence may also be derived from rent reviews and lease renewals, but such evidence is considered secondary to market transactions. The comparison method can be difficult to apply when there is a lack of market evidence or where the transaction involved specific arrangements including rent-free periods, stepped or turnover rents, premiums, break options, capital contributions, non-standard repairing and insuring obligations or other incentives. The rent may also include the use of other facilities or may be below normal market levels if it is for a unit in a new development such as an anchor tenant. A typical rental valuation for a retail property which, in this case, is zoned on the basis of normal 6.1 m (20 ft) zones, is as follows:

Description	Area (m²)	Fraction of zone A	Unit value (£/m²)	Value (£)
Ground floor				
Zone A	26.5	A	900	23 850
Zone B	25.4	A/2	450	11 430
Zone C	15.6	A/4	225	3 510
Storage	10.3	A/10	90	927
First floor				
Storage	60.7	A/20	45	2 732
Site				
Car parking spaces	3 no.		£400 per space	1 200
Rateable value (£)				43 649

It is possible for a range of factors to add value (in the form of an end allowance) to the basic assessment, including return frontages to shops, air conditioning and car-parking spaces. The valuer may also consider that a quantum allowance should be applied where a property is exceptionally large compared to comparable evidence and a prospective tenant bidding on the property would reduce the rental bid on the basis of the large amount of space being taken. A reverse quantum allowance is the opposite, where a particularly small property value added to its basis assessment. This is known as the 'kiosk' effect. Disability allowances can apply where, for example, a property suffers from some form of geographical or functional factor which would reduce the likely rental bid from a prospective tenant. Temporary allowances are applied, as their name suggests, to situations where a temporary change in the property or its physical location warrants (usually) a reduction in the rateable value. Once the factor causing the temporary allowance has been removed, then the assessment will be reinstated to its full (but not necessarily the same) value.

Most properties have a rental market upon which evidence can be drawn, and therefore it is possible to use this information to arrive at an assessment of rateable value. However, there are hereditaments which do not have ready letting market and therefore need to be valued using alternative methods.

4.6.3.2 Profits method

There are various types of specialised trading property which we have discussed in Chapter 3, such as public houses, bowling alleys, night clubs, cinemas and hotels, for which comparable evidence of rents can be very hard to find. In such cases, the trading figures will give some idea as to how much 'profit' the hereditament makes and hence what it can afford to pay in rent (and thus rates). The method requires the valuer to make adjustments to the accounts to bring them into line with the definition of rateable value. The turnover is adjusted to reflect the cost of purchases and working expenses. This yields the net profit which is referred to as the 'divisible balance' for rating purposes and is apportioned between the profit or return to the occupier and rent to the owner, just like dual capitalisation. The division between the two will vary according to the perceived risk of the business; higher the risk, the higher the operator's required return (Marshall and Williamson, 1996). An example of a profits method valuation of a hotel for rating purposes is given below. The trading figures are those that pertain to the hereditament at the antecedent valuation date and are exclusive of VAT.

Turnover (gross receipts from rooms, bar, restaurant) (£)	1 600 000
Less purchases (£)	−300 000
Equals gross profit (£)	1 300 000
Less working expenses (wages, utilities, stationery, marketing, insurance, vehicles, rates, etc., repair and maintenance of property, repair and renewal of furniture, fixtures, fittings and equipment) (£)	−700 000
Equals net (trading) profit or divisible balance (£)	600 000
Less	
Interest on tenant's capital (FFFE, stock, cash) (£)	−40 000
Return (normal profit) to operator/tenant (£)	−200 000
Equals rent to landlord (on which the rateable value is based) (£)	360 000

As discussed in Chapter 3, care is required when deriving information from the accounts. Usually, valuers will consider the accounts figures drawn from the 3 years leading up to the valuation date and arrive at a fair maintainable trade (the expected trade that the reasonably minded operator would derive from the property and business). Therefore, abnormally large amounts of expenditure in any single year may be written down over a number of years to arrive at a figure for the fair maintainable trade. The rent to the landlord is equivalent to the rateable value. Actual rates paid should be deducted as part of the working expenses so that the bottom line is equivalent to the rent only (see *Thomason v Rowland (VO) (1995) RA 255*).

In place of a full profits method valuation as noted above, it is possible to draw up relationships between other figures in the accounts, between gross receipts (turnover) and rent (as a proxy for rateable value), for example. Thus, a reasonably run hotel might expect that the percentage of gross receipts paid as rent to be in the region 20%. This short-cut technique is known as the 'shortened profits method'. A formula based on some other method may also be used to value certain hereditaments, such as hotel price per bedroom or bed-space. When the profits method is used to value a hereditament, the valuation will include all plant and machinery used in the business operation. For instance, if a fuel storage depot is valued on a profits basis any rateable plant in the hereditament simply goes to make up the profit – tanks, security fencing, fire protection equipment and the like all help to produce the profit – if they were not there, the enterprise would either not operate or not be so profitable.

4.6.3.3   Contractor's method

Any hereditament that cannot be valued by rental comparison and not, in itself, showing a profit will be dealt with using the contractor's method. It is regarded as the method of last resort and is applied to properties which do not usually let in the open market such as schools, universities, petrol chemical works, hospitals, light houses, clinics, town halls and fire stations. The assessment is derived from cost information rather than rents or profits.

In the case of new buildings the method is fairly easy to employ because building costs close to the antecedent valuation date can be examined. But when valuing older buildings an adjustment needs to be made to reflect probable depreciation in value as a result of deterioration and obsolescence. In such cases, the method starts to become unreliable as there is no ready market information to help ascertain what reductions should apply.

The contractor's basis involves estimating the current cost of replacing the hereditament with a functionally equivalent building at the antecedent valuation date, including any rateable plant and machinery, and deducting an allowance for age and obsolescence. The value of the site, cleared but with all services available for the existing use, will then be added to the replacement building cost. An adjustment may then be made, usually by applying a percentage reduction, to allow for general difficulties with the hereditament such as a confined site or poor access. The capital value thus produced will then be brought to an annual equivalent by applying a decapitalisation rate appropriate to the rating list in question. These rates may be set by Government and vary depending on type of property. The final stage is to 'stand back and look' at the valuation, taking account of any items or matters not already considered. For example, the economic health of an industry, business or organisation could be reflected.

Consider a large county hospital built in the 1970s and valued using the contractor's method:

Cost of new buildings totalling $15\,487\,\mathrm{m}^2$ @ £1 150/m² (£)	17 810 050
Less 23% depreciation allowance for age and obsolescence (£)	−4 096 312
Plus value of land totalling 5 ha for existing use @ £250 000/ha (£)	1 250 000
Subtotal (£)	14 963 739
Decapitalise (multiply) capital value at rate of say 3.67%	× 0.0367
Stand back and look; reflect on buildings in poor	549 169
run down area, say, RV (£)	500 000

Wherever possible it is useful to use more than one method to assess rateable value: the contractor's method for an 'awkward' building with rental comparison applied to those buildings within the hereditament have been let at market rents. A seaside pier might be valued using the profits method for the fairground element, contractor's method on the non-profit making elements and rental comparison for the kiosks.

Key points

- As far as CGT is concerned, for most properties, the gain on disposal will usually be restricted to the gain since 31 March 1982 for properties acquired before that date or the date of acquisition for properties acquired afterwards. Generally, a valuation is required to estimate the market value of the asset on the disposal date if the disposal was not at arm's length. A valuation might also be required to estimate the market value on the 31 March 1982 for rebasing the gain and calculating the indexation allowance. For part disposals, property valuations may be required of the part disposed of (A) and the part retained (B).
- Market valuations are required for IHT purposes when there is no evidence of an open market sale of the transferred estate. This might be because the transfer was by way of a gift or some other means that does not fit the description of an 'arm's length' transaction.
- The maintenance of the rating list by the VOA is a monumental task. Every rateable hereditament in England and Wales must be assessed every 5 years and, in between these valuations, appeals and changes to the list are constantly taking place. The rateable values are, essentially, market valuations with some specific assumptions so there is plenty to keep the valuer busy here.
- a For detailed examples of property valuations for CGT and IHT purposes see chapter 8 of Rees and Hayward (2000). Refer to Bond and Brown (2006) for a detailed discussion of rating valuation.

4.7   Valuations for compulsory purchase and compensation

The Government and the organisations responsible for the utility networks in the UK have the legal power to compulsorily acquire property for specific purposes. This might be to build a new road, a wind farm or a nuclear power station for example. Freehold, leasehold and equitable interests (such as a mortgagee) in property can be compulsorily purchased by these 'acquiring authorities'. Should a property owner be affected by such an acquisition, compensation can be claimed for any land taken, for injurious affection (severance) caused and for disturbance. The legal basis of the right to claim compensation in these respects can be found in the Land Compensation Act 1961 (LCA61), the Compulsory Purchase Act 1965 (CPA65) and the Land Compensation Act 1973 (LCA73), as amended by the Planning and Compensation Act 1991 (PCA91) and the Planning and Compulsory Purchase Act 2004 (PCPA04). A substantial body of case law provides legal interpretation of these statutes.

Valuers are often appointed to estimate the value of the property compulsorily acquired and to estimate any diminution in value of land resulting from either construction activity or use of the finished development (smell from a sewage works for example). The statutes mentioned above refer to their own definition of market value so, when valuing for compulsory purchase and compensation, valuers need to depart from Red Book definition of market value and follow statutory regulations instead. The guiding principle of the legislation in respect of property owners who have been affected by compulsory purchase is to ensure, financially at least, that they are restored to the position before acquisition took place. Denyer-Green (2005) provides a detailed discourse of the statutory framework and case law that has built up around compulsory purchase and compensation; here we investigate the material from the valuer's perspective.

Despite the simple equitable principle of compensation for loss suffered there is complexity in the way that the legislation requires this compensation to be calculated and the way that the courts have interpreted the legislation. The owner of an interest being compulsorily acquired is entitled to compensation equivalent to the value of the land being acquired. Where the owner retains some land and its value drops, he is entitled to be compensated for this drop whether it is caused by severance of the two parts of land or by injurious affection to the retained land (Denyer-Green, 2003). An owner will also be entitled to losses that are a consequence of being compelled to vacate the land, known as disturbance (Denyer-Green, 2003). The following sections consider these various situations in which compensation will be payable, known as 'heads of claim', but, in many cases, owners of property interests will be entitled to more than one 'head of claim'. It should also be noted that although it is common practice to talk about *land* being acquired or the value of *land* being affected by compulsory acquisition and public works, the legislation and therefore valuation rules apply to property interests in general.

4.7.1 Compensation for land taken

The acquiring authority sets out the nature and extent of the property interest to be acquired in a 'notice to treat' which may be served on owners of all property interests except holders of periodic tenancies of a year or less. Where a tenant has a contractual or statutory right to renew a lease that right will form part of the value of his leasehold interest (Johnson *et al.*, 2000), but the leasehold interest should be valued on the basis of the earliest termination date (Denyer-Green, 2003). The appropriate date for assessing the value of the interest to be acquired is the earlier of the date when the acquiring authority takes possession of the land or the date when the values are agreed. When compensation is assessed by the Lands Tribunal, the valuation date is the last day of the hearing, if possession has not already been taken by then.

Section 5 of the LCA61 sets out six valuation rules governing compensation for land that has been compulsorily acquired and further qualifications to these rules are contained in the Act. Essentially, the property owner is entitled to compensation equivalent to the price that the land would sell for in the open market assuming there had been no compulsory acquisition. The valuation should therefore be to market value and incorporates the assumption that the seller is willing to sell despite the rather obvious fact that this is not the case! It can be difficult to obtain evidence of market values if the compulsory purchase order (CPO) has been around for a while because the impending development may have blighted values in the area.

Development value may be considered alongside existing use value but, in many compulsory purchase cases, an impending acquisition will mean that no planning permission for development will be forthcoming (Denyer-Green, 2003). Therefore, it is necessary to make certain planning assumptions so that an accurate assessment of development value can be made. LCA61 (as amended) states that the following can be assumed:

- Existing planning permission.
- Permission for the acquiring body's proposal for the land being taken but ignoring any value attributable to the 'wider scheme'.
- Planning permission in accordance with an allocation in the Local Development Framework.
- Planning permission for development specified in Certificate of Appropriate Alternative Development (hypothetical planning permission).

PCA91 provides for compensation where permission for additional development is granted after acquisition of land but within 10 years of the acquisition completion date, the amount being the difference between the compensation paid and the amount which would have been paid assuming the permission was in force at the time (Denyer-Green, 2003).

Marriage value can also be taken into account when estimating market value. For example, if the area that connects the road to the development land in Figure 4.5 is being compulsorily acquired in order to provide access to the development land behind, the owner is entitled to a percentage of the

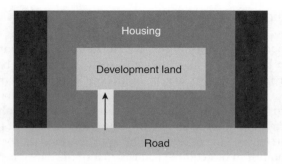

Figure 4.5   Development value.

development value of development. This principle was laid down in the land-mark case of *Stokes v Cambridge Corporation (1961)* and in that case, the proportion was one-third. If the development land is being acquired too but can only be developed if satisfactory access can be provided, the market value will be the full development value less the estimated cost of acquiring the necessary additional land (Denyer-Green, 2003).

The effect on value of the scheme underlying the acquisition is disregarded by the operation of the following statutory (a) and (b) and judicial (c) rules (Denyer-Green, 2003):

(a)   Section 6 and Schedule 1 of the LCA61 for certain 'defined' schemes; no account should be taken of any increase or decrease in value due only to development under the acquiring authority's scheme – the 'no scheme' world.

(b)   Section 9 of the LCA61; any loss in value due to the threat of acquisition (blight) must be ignored.

(c)   The 'Pointe Gourde Principle': compensation cannot include an increase in value which is entirely due to the 'scheme' underlying the acquisition. Problems arise when there is more than one CPO and when there is an evolving large-scale development such as a new town. Johnson *et al.* (2000) provide a good example of the difficulty valuers face here; when valuing land which is to become part of a new town and which is surrounded by new town development, the valuer must decide what would have happened had there been no new town scheme. He may assume, for example, that permission would have been granted for out-of-town offices but cannot assume infrastructure built as part of the new town development unless he can prove that such infrastructure would have been developed even without the new town. This would normally be very difficult to show.

Section 7 of the LCA61 states that any increase in the value of contiguous land of the same owner shall be offset against the compensation payable for the land taken.

Market value does not include enhanced value attributable solely to the use proposed under a scheme for which compulsory acquisition of the land is required. This enhanced value is not part of market value because it is not an element the owner could have realised in the market. Also, no value can be attributed to illegal uses. If there is no market on which to base an estimate of existing use value then the basis of valuation is 'equivalent reinstatement' unless development value is higher. Because the acquisition is compulsory the owner has the right to disturbance compensation and certain other payments in addition to the value of the land acquired.

Johnson *et al.* (2000) suggest that the methods employed to estimate the value of the property that is compulsorily acquired are no different from those that adopted in other market valuations, just subject to the above rules. In most cases, the valuation is likely to be on an existing use basis using the comparison or investment method. Care must be exercised when selecting comparable evidence because transactions would have taken place in the 'scheme' world. If the valuer feels that the scheme has influenced the evidence obtained from these comparables then they may need to be adjusted to give a value in the 'no scheme' world. Marshall and Williamson (1996) note that the basic thrust of the legislation is to ensure that the acquiring authority is not required to pay for any benefit which its own scheme creates whilst ensuring that the claimant does not lose out if the scheme causes a drop in value of the interest acquired.

4.7.2   Severance and injurious affection

4.7.2.1   Compensation where part of an owner's land is acquired

Where only part of an owner's property is taken, the CPA65 allows compensation for severance of and injurious affection to the part retained. Compensation for severance is based on the reduction in value of the retained land, which need not be contiguous but must be in the same ownership and functionally related. While a drop in value due to severance is fairly easy to explain, injurious affection to the retained land is slightly harder to envisage. Essentially, it is injury or damage caused by construction works, including disturbance for having to vacate premises. But it also covers any diminution in value caused by subsequent use of the works. To estimate these figures, a valuer would value the land as it was before the CPO and then value the same land on completion of the works. The difference between the before and after valuations represents the drop in value. If the value of the land taken is then deducted from difference between the before and after valuations, this gives the compensation for severance and injurious affection. For example, the market value of a property before the acquiring authority's scheme was £250 000 and afterwards it is £200 000, compensation is therefore £50 000. If the market value of the land taken is £30 000 then the loss in value of retained land due to severance and injurious affection is £20 000.

Now consider a more detailed case. A local authority wishes to substantially redesign access to an industrial estate in preparation for its expansion. To enable this, it has served a CPO on the industrial unit at the entrance to the estate, giving notice of the planned acquisition of part of its land. Once the redesigned access is complete in 3 years' time, the unit will benefit from improved access arrangements plus additional storage land. The tenant of the unit has 8 years remaining on a 15-year FRI lease with 5-year upward-only rent reviews. The current rent is £100000 per annum, the (no scheme) market rent for the whole unit is estimated to be £120000 per annum and for the retained part after severance it is £80000 per annum. Injurious affection caused by carrying out of works will reduce the market rent of the retained land to £70000 per annum, but it is estimated that its market rent will rise to £90000 per annum once the works are complete. The local authority has stated that it will pay for the new access and storage land. Compensation for the landlord and tenant are assessed as follows:

Landlord's interest

- Before' valuation

Term rent received (£)	100000	
YP 3 years @ 8%	2.5771	
		257710
Reversion to market rent (£)	120000	
YP perpetuity @ 8%	12.5	
PV £1 3 years @ 8%	0.7938	
		1190700
'Before' capital value (£)		1448410

- After valuation

Term rent (100 000 × 80 000/120 000)[a] (£)	66 667	
YP 3 years @ 8%	2.5771	
		171808
Reversion to market rent (£)	90000	
YP perpetuity @ 8%	12.5	
PV £1 3 years @ 8%	0.7938	
		893025
'After' capital value (£)		1064833

[a]This calculation determines the *current* rent for the retained part using the evidence of *market* rents for the retained part and the whole.

Therefore the drop in value resulting from part of the land being acquired and from injurious affection is the difference between the before and after valuations, £1448410 – £1064 833 = £383577. The following calculation determines the value of land taken only:

Term rent lost (100 000 – 66 667) (£)	33333	
YP 3 years @ 8%	2.5771	
		85902
Reversion to market rent lost	40000	
(120 000 – 80000) (£)		
YP perpetuity @ 8%	12.5	
PV £1 3 years @ 8%	0.7938	
		396900
Capital value of land taken (£)		482802

Therefore, compensation for severance and injurious affection (betterment in this case) is £383 577 – £482 802 = -£99 225. In other words, the value of the land taken (£482 802) is reduced by the capital value of the enhancement to the unit resulting from the works, that is, an increase in market rent from £80 000 to £90 000 per annum on reversion, when capitalised into perpetuity at 8% deferred 2 years, produces a betterment (or improvement in capital value) of £99 225.

Tenant's interest

- Before valuation

Market rent of whole unit (£)	120 000	
Less contract rent (£)	–100 000	
Profit rent (£)	20 000	
YP 3 years @ 10%	2.4869	
Valuation (£)		49 738

- After valuation

Market rent of retained part (£)	70 000	
Less contract rent for retained part	–66 667	
(100 000 x 80 000/		
120 000)[a] (£)		
Profit rent (£)	3 333	
YP 3 years @ 10%	2.4869	
Valuation (£)		8 290

[a]Calculated as above.

Therefore the value of the land taken plus injurious affection is £49 738 – £8290 = £41 448. Separating these two amounts can be undertaken as follows:

Value of land taken

Profit rent (20 000 – (20 000 × 80 000/120 000))	6 667	
YP 3 years @ 10%	2.4869	
Valuation (£)		16 580

Therefore, compensation for severance and injurious affection is £41 448 – £16 580 = £24 868.

In cases like the one above, where part of a property subject to a lease is taken, the rent needs to be apportioned between the part taken and the part left, and this was done in the ratio of rental value of the part retained to the rental value of the whole. In cases where only a small part of a property is taken, a nominal apportionment of, say, £1 per annum on land taken may be agreed. The tenant then continues to pay full rent under the lease for the remainder of the term but receives full compensation for loss of rental value from the acquiring body while the landlord is compensated for injury to his reversion (Johnson *et al.*, 2000).

The CPA65 provides the owner with an option to require the acquiring authority to purchase the whole property and the success of such a request depends on whether there has been a material detriment to the retained property. LCA73 requires whole proposed works to be taken into account (including those off-site) when assessing detriment.

4.7.2.2 Compensation where no land is taken

Property owners can also claim compensation where none of their land is taken. There are two ways in which this can be done: under Section 10 of the CPA65, compensation can be claimed for execution of works and under Part 1 of the LCA73, compensation can be claimed for use of public works.

Section 10 of the CPA65 provides for compensation, even where no land is taken, for execution of works where rights of access, light and support are taken. To successfully claim compensation for injurious affection caused by execution of works, four rules must be satisfied. These are known as the 'McCarthy Rules' because they resulted from a House of Lords decision in the case of *Metropolitan Board of Works v McCarthy (1874)*:

(a)   The works must be authorised by statute.
(b)   If the works were not authorised by statute the injury caused would be actionable at law (as a nuisance).
(c)   The injury arises from a physical interference with some right which is attached to the land and which has a market value. In cases where the interference is temporary a decrease in rental value is sufficient to sustain a claim even where the capital value, after conclusion of the works, is unaffected (Denyer-Green, 2003).
(d)   The injury must be caused by execution of works, not subsequent use.

The usual measure of compensation is the reduction in value of the affected land attributable to the injury that gave rise to the claim (Marshall and Williamson, 1996).

Part 1 of the LCA73 provides a code for compensation for use of public works such as roads, airports, and so on. Owners of affected land have a right to claim compensation (referred to as making a 'Part 1 Claim') for the reduction in value of their interest caused by certain physical factors, namely, noise, vibration, smell, fumes, smoke, artificial lighting or the discharge of any substance subject to reasonably foreseeable future intensification of the use (Johnson *et al.*, 2000). The claimant must own the freehold or leasehold interest in a property, the latter having at least 3 years remaining and a rateable value of £29 200 or more (2005 rating list). The basis of compensation is the diminution in the existing use value of the interest and, in most cases, the practical approach to the valuation is to estimate a 'no scheme world' value of the affected property and then make a judgement as to the percentage depreciation that can be attributed to the physical factors (Denyer-Green, 2003). Compensation can be reduced if the compensating authority mitigates the effects. For a detailed analysis of compensation where no land is taken, see Chapter 4 of Askham (2003).

4.7.3   Disturbance compensation

The owner of a compulsorily acquired property has the expense of finding
new accommodation and moving. As we have seen compensation for land
taken is based on a definition of market value that assumes the seller is a
'willing' seller, but this is clearly not the case, and loss is suffered as a result of
being dispossessed and having to find new business premises. The compulsory
purchase legislation recognises this and a business occupier can claim either
the costs of relocation (including removal costs, loss of stock, new stationery,
and loss of goodwill) or the cost of winding up the business, known as 'total
extinguishment'. In most cases the business occupier will only be granted
relocation costs but a sole trader aged 60 or over in a property with a rateable
value of £29 000 or more (as at the 2005 rating list) has a statutory right to
opt for total extinguishment. Disturbance compensation is usually payable
in respect of any item that is not too remote and is a natural and reasonable
consequence of the acquisition of the owner's interest. The amount of disturbance compensation is normally calculated by valuing existing fixtures from
the perspective of an incoming tenant in the same line of business plus, if the
business is to be extinguished, the loss on forced sale (the difference between
value to an incoming tenant and the price achieved on sale) (Johnson *et al.*,
2000). Additional payments for owners of business property were introduced
by the PCPA04: a 'basic loss payment' is payable to all owners and is the
lower of 7.5% of the value of the interest or £75 000; and an 'occupier's loss
payment' is payable to owners who have been in occupation for a year or
more and is the greater of 25% of the value of the interest up to a maximum
of £25 000. Also, an investor landlord who has had an interest acquired can
claim for the costs of reinvestment in another UK property within 1 year of
the date of entry. Finally, the LCA73 authorises disturbance *payments* to
claimants in cases where disturbance *compensation* is not payable because
the claimant has not had an interest compulsorily acquired but has been dispossessed. This situation would arise if the acquiring authority compulsorily
acquired a freehold interest subject to a short lease. The authority is unlikely
to renew the lease, so a disturbance payment is made to cover reasonable
removal expenses and, where relevant, loss sustained for the business having
to quit the land (Johnson *et al.*, 2000).

4.7.3.1   Case study

Mrs Brown is the tenant of a shop (ground and upper floors) which is to be
compulsorily acquired by a local authority for use as a public open space. Mr
Brown has lived in the upper part and run a bakery on the ground floor for
the past 5 years. He pays a rent of £70 000 per annum for the whole property
on an internally repairing and insuring (IRI) lease with 10 years unexpired.
The market rent of the property is £100 000 per annum, of which £60 000
per annum can be attributable to the shop part. The rateable value of the
shop is £40 000. The net profit for the last financial year was £180 000 after
deducting rent of £70 000, mortgage interest of £10 000, repairs of £5000
and rates of £20 000, all relating to the whole building. The previous 2 years'

unadjusted net profits have been £160 000 and £170 000 but remuneration to the owner (who works full-time for the business) and her husband (who works half-time) has not been deducted. Mrs Brown is 62 years old and does not wish to buy another business. Prepare a full claim for compensation.

Land taken (Rule 2, Section 5, LCA61)

Market rent (£)	100 000	
Plus landlord's expenses;		
▪ External repairs (£)	5000	
▪ Insurance (£)	5000	
IRI rental value (£)	110 000	
Less rent paid (£)	−70 000	
Profit rent (£)	40 000	
YP 10 years @ 8%	6.7101	
Valuation (£)		268 404

Disturbance (Rule 6, Section 5, LCA61): The claimant is over 60 years old so a claim for total extinguishment under S46 of the LCA73 stands. The average of the last 3 years' earnings is taken as the best evidence of profitability.

Net profit (£)		170 000
Mortgage interest (£)		10 000
Repairs for upper part, say (£)		1 000
Less (hypothetical) part-time assistant (£)		−40 000
Less profit rent in respect of shop part, say (£)		−30 000
Less interest on capital:		
▪ fittings (£)	15 000	
▪ stock (£)	5 000	
▪ cash (£)	3 000	
Total capital	23 000	
Amortised at 8%	× 0.08	
		−1 840
Adjusted net profit (£)		109 160
Capitalised in perpetuity at a target rate return of 20%		5
Value of goodwill (£)		545 800
Additional items[a]:		
▪ Sale of fittings to acquiring authority (£)		10 000
▪ Notification to suppliers (£)		1 000
▪ Loss on stationery (£)		1 000
▪ Disconnection of services (£)		500
▪ Removal costs (£)		3 000
▪ Finding new living accommodation (£)		4 000
▪ Home loss (£)		5 000
Disturbance ompensation (based on total extinguishment) (£)		570 300

[a]Business is a bakery, so there is no forced sale of stock.

4.7.4   Planning compensation

Compensation may also be paid to property owners when certain planning decisions are made.

4.7.4.1   Revocation, modification and discontinuance orders

The Town and Country Planning Act, 1990 (TCPA90) provides for compensation if a planning permission that was previously granted is revoked, modified or discontinued by a local planning authority. The order must be made before building or other work is completed or before a change of use has taken effect (Johnson *et al.*, 2000). Compensation covers abortive expenditure and loss or damage directly attributable to the order, including a drop in property value, calculated in accordance with Section 5 of the LCA61 (i.e. a before-and-after valuation to reveal the difference between the market value of land with the benefit of the planning permission and with the permission revoked or modified (Johnson *et al.*, 2000)). The Planning (Listed Buildings and Conservation Areas) Act 1990 provides for compensation on the same basis as the TCPA 1990 but in respect of loss caused by the refusal, revocation, modification or the grant of conditional listed building consent or by the issue of a Building Preservation Notice.

4.7.4.2   Purchase notices and blight notices

Under the TCPA90, where planning permission is refused or granted subject to conditions or where a local planning authority serves a revocation, modification or discontinuance order or refuses, modifies or grants a conditional listed building consent, this may entitle the owner to serve a Purchase Notice as an alternative to a compensation claim as described above (Johnson *et al.*, 2000). The property owner must serve the notice on the local authority within 1 year of the planning decision requiring it to purchase the property interest and prove that the property is incapable of reasonable beneficial use. Once the purchase notice is confirmed, the acquiring authority is deemed to have served a notice to treat and normal compulsory purchase rules apply (Marshall and Williamson, 1996).

Similarly, planning proposals which could eventually involve compulsory acquisition may well depreciate the value of affected property or even render it valueless. As a result, under certain circumstances (for business property, where the rateable value is £29 200 or less), the owner-occupier can compel the acquiring authority to purchase the property by serving a Blight Notice. The owner must be able to show that reasonable efforts to sell the property were unsuccessful except at a price substantially lower than might reasonably be expected in a market without the threat of compulsory acquisition.

4.7.5   A note on CGT and compensation for compulsory acquisition

If a property is compulsorily acquired the compensation is subject to CGT in the normal way, but there are some special rules. These determine the date of disposal, provide for some small disposals not to be treated as a disposal, allow for any gain arising to be rolled-over against the acquisition of a new property in certain circumstances and provide for an apportionment of the compensation between its constituent factors.

Where land is compulsorily acquired, the disposal date is the time at which the compensation for the acquisition is agreed, or otherwise determined. Where the compulsorily acquired land is part of a larger holding and the following conditions are satisfied, it is possible to claim that the compensation received should not be regarded as a disposal, but that it should instead be deducted from the allowable expenditure on the entire holding. On a later disposal, or part disposal, of the remainder of the holding only the reduced expenditure is taken into account in calculating any subsequent gain or loss. The conditions are as follows:

- the holding is not a wasting asset (i.e. a lease with 50 years or less to run);
- the market value of the land is small compared to the value of the entire holding;
- no steps were taken to sell any part of the holding.

For example, the freehold of a property was purchased for £200 000 in 1989. A small strip of the land is acquired by compulsory purchase for £8000 in 1993. A claim is made for the disposal to be disregarded for CGT purposes. The remaining property is sold for £250 000 in 2005. There is no gain or loss on receipt of the compensation, and the gain before indexation on the sale in 2005 is as follows:

Sale proceeds (£)	250 000
Less original cost (£)	−200 000
Plus compensation (£)	8 000
Gain before indexation and taper relief (£)	58 000

If a new property is purchased the gain made on receipt of compensation can be rolled over and deducted from the cost of the new property, subject to two main conditions:

- no steps have been taken to sell any part of the holding;
- the new land cannot include a dwelling-house that is or may become the owner's sole or main residence.

For example, land purchased for £50 000 in April 1991 was compulsorily acquired for £80 000 in May 2005. The compensation is used to buy more land costing £100 000 and the owner claims that the gain should be rolled over. The gain is as follows:

Compensation (£)	80 000
Less cost (£)	−50 000
Less indexation to April 1998 (£)	−11 100
Gain (£)	18 900

The allowable cost of the new land thus reduces by £18 900 from £100 000 to £81 100. If the new land becomes a wasting asset within 10 years (typically a lease which on acquisition has 60 years or less to run), the rules are modified. They are also modified where only part of the compensation is used to acquire new land.

In law, compensation for compulsory purchase is a single sum, but for tax purposes it is apportioned between its constituent factors and is taxable accordingly. The categories for which compensation may be received are for the land itself, for disturbance and for severance or injurious affection. Compensation for disturbance may include several items, and the tax treatment varies accordingly. The most common elements are compensation for losses on stock and loss of profits (taxed as income), compensation for loss of goodwill (chargeable to CGT), compensation for expenses (set against those expenses), and any remaining amounts are chargeable to CGT, if they derive from chargeable assets. Compensation for severance or injurious affection is calculated by reference to the fall in the value of land retained caused, and this is treated as giving rise to a part disposal of that retained land. Any resulting gain or loss is calculated in the normal way, subject to the rules for small disposals referred to above.

Key points

- Valuation for compulsory purchase is a complex area of valuation work where valuation economics is considerably influenced by the large body of statutes and case law. Valuers working in the private sector on behalf of property owners and valuers representing the Government and other acquiring authorities may be requested to provide opinions of market value or, with sufficient knowledge and experience, to negotiate compensation claims on behalf of either party.
- Although the law is complex two fundamental points are worth reiterating. First, market value is central to the assessment of compensation for land taken and diminution in market value is central to the assessment of compensation for severance and injurious affection. Second, market valuations must be undertaken in the 'no scheme world' – a concept that lends itself more to theoretical understanding than practical application!

4.8 Valuation of contaminated land

Some sites may be contaminated as a result of their previous use. These are referred to as 'brownfield' sites and valuers have mandatory responsibility to report on contamination impact where suspected. International valuation standards, in the form of *IVS GN 7 – Consideration of Hazardous and Toxic Substances in Valuation* (IVSC, 2005) states that the existence of such deleterious materials must be reported, together with the way they have been dealt with. The valuation of contaminated sites adds a level of volatility to the valuation. Perhaps unsurprisingly, it is very difficult to find comparable evidence to help value a contaminated site because the variability of location-specific contaminants and resultant severity and extent of contamination will often lead to wildly different estimates of impaired value. The accepted approach, in the likely absence of comparable evidence, seems to be the 'cost to correct' approach. Indeed, IVS GN 7 states that where impairment is present, the valuer should value as if it had been removed and identify the cost of remediation where possible. So the value of the site is equal to its value in good condition (unimpaired) less the cost of rectifying the impediment and a deduction for stigma. The cost of remediation would be based on the quantification of factors identified in an environmental impact assessment (EIA) or a land quality statement (LQS). It is important to note that valuers must understand what an EIA entails in order to give meaningful advice, including an interpretation of cost implications. Stigma is the value impact of potential risk and uncertainty surrounding the future use of a contaminated site, even though the contamination may have been removed. In practice, the valuation impact of stigma is accounted for by either adjusting the yield or making an end allowance but attempting to quantify the 'unquantifiable' carries significant risks! No matter how well sites are treated, problems of stigma may remain.

By way of example, a valuation is required of a freehold factory situated on contaminated land. The current freeholder has legal responsibility for the contamination. The current rent is £800 000 per annum and the 15-year lease has 2 years remaining. The current tenant does not intend to renew the lease and remediation is deemed necessary. An EIA suggests a £2 000 000 remediation cost and a period of 1 year in which to complete the work. The all-risks yield for uncontaminated comparable property investments is 9.5%. The current market rent is £850 000 per annum.

Term rent (£)	800 000	
YP 2 years @ 9.5%[a]	1.7473	
		1 397 840
Reversion to market rent (£)	850 000	
YP perpetuity @ 10.5%[b]	9.5238	
PV £1 for 3 years @ 10.5%[c]	0.7412	
		6 000 184
		7 398 024
Less remediation costs:		
■ clean-up costs	−2 000 000	
■ finance @ 8% for 6 months[d]	−78 461	
■ cost of EIA, say	−9 000	
■ cost of LQS, say	−5 000	
Total	−2 092 461	
PV £1 for 2 years @ 8%[e]	0.8573	

Valuation (£)   −1 793 867
                                                  5 604 157

[a]Although the security of a term rent below market rent would normally attract a reduction from the all-risks yield, in this case, because of the contaminated state of the site, the yield has not been reduced.
[b]The all-risks yield has been increased by 1% to reflect stigma.
[c]Discounting the reversionary value over 3 years builds in the 1-year clean-up period.
[d]It is assumed the clean-up costs are debt-financed at 8% per annum, but the costs are spread evenly over the year (i.e. interest only paid on total cost over 6 months).
[e]Costs are deferred until the end of the current lease at the finance rate of 8% (it is assumed money can be invested at the same rate that it can be borrowed).

The adjustment to the all-risks yield to account for uncertainty at re-letting due to possible residual contamination and stigma is very subjective, and it might be argued that an explicit end allowance would be more accurate. This is because the effect of a unit adjustment to the all-risks yield will have a greater effect on property investments that are valued at lower yields than those valued at higher yields. For example, take two investment opportunities; a factory in the north of England and a shop in the West End of London, both valued at £500 000 and both requiring the same expenditure on remediation:

	Factory		**Shop**	
Unimpaired valuation				
Income (£)	500 000		250 000	
YP perpetuity @ 10% (factory)/5% (shop)	10		20	
Valuation (£)		5 000 000		5 000 000
Impaired valuation				
Income (£)	500 000		250 000	
YP perpetuity @ 11% (factory)/6% (shop)	9.0909		16.6667	
		4 545 455		4 166 667
Less Remediation costs, say		−1 000 000		−1 000 000
Valuation (£)		3 545 455		3 166 667
Reduction in value		29%		37%

Ceteris paribus the shop suffers a much greater depreciation in value. One solution is to adjust the yield proportionately, say an increase of 10%, would mean an impaired yield for the factory of 11% and 5.5% for the shop, thus producing the same diminution in value for the shop and factory.

For more information on the valuation of contaminated land, see Richards (1996), Syms (1996), chapter 6 of Askham (2003) and chapter 2 of Syms (2004).

Notes

1. According to the Companies Act, 1985 these are businesses with less than 250 employees.
2. If a growth-implicit all-risks yield was used to calculate the real rental value it would imply that the gap between the headline rent and the market rent widens over the amortisation period rather than that the market rent rises. In fact, because the amortisation period is so short the rental value difference is minor.
3. The NPV function on a spreadsheet discounts each subsequent row in a cash-flow for an additional period at a specified discount rate, in this case 10%.
4. To qualify for compensation the improvements must have been made after the 25 March 1928 and not in pursuance of a statutory or contractual obligation (except that after 1954 those in pursuance of a statutory obligation will qualify).
5. The value of improvements may not be disregarded (i.e. may be included) in the rent fixed at rent reviews within this 21-year period if the lease does not mention how they should be treated (*Ponsford v HMS Aerosols Ltd 1978*). However, most leases now explicitly state that the value of any tenant's qualifying improvements should be disregarded at rent reviews.
6. Defined for accounting purposes as interests in land and/or buildings held for their investment potential.
7. The rent is divided between an interest charge (shown in the profit and loss statement) and a charge for the repayment of capital. The lessee's accounts will also usually show an annual depreciation charge on the asset.
8. *FRS 11: Impairment of Fixed Assets and Goodwill* ensures that any impairment loss is handled correctly and the development of this standard shadowed the development of IAS 36.
9. The value of the disposal does not exceed 20% of the market value of the holding, the total value of all disposals made in the year does not exceed £20 000 and the property interest is not a wasting asset (e.g. a lease with 50 years or less to run).

References

ASB (1999) Financial Reporting Standard 15: Tangible Fixed Assets, Accounting Standards Board.

Askham, P. (Ed) (2003) *Valuation: Special Properties and Purposes*, Estates Gazette, London, UK.

Baum, A. (2003) Pricing the options inherent in leased commercial property: a UK case study, ERES conference Helsiaki, June 2003.

Bond, P. and Brown, P. (2006) *Rating Valuation: Principles and Practice*, 2nd edn, Estates Gazette, London, UK.

Brett, M. (2004) *Property under IFRS: A Guide to the Effects of the New International Financial Reporting Standards*, RICS, London, UK.

Brett, M. (2004) *Property under IFRS: A Guide to the Effects of the New International Financial Reporting Standards*, RICS, London, UK.

Cherry, A. (2006) *A Valuer's Guide to the Red Book*, RICS, London, UK.

Crosby, N. and Murdoch, S. (1994) Capital valuation implications of rent-free periods, *Journal of Property Valuation and Investment*, 12, 2, 51–64.

Crosby, N., Lizieri, C., Murdoch, S. and Ward, C. (1998) Implications of changing lease structures on the pricing of lease contracts, The Cutting Edge Conference, RICS, London, August 1998.

Denyer-Green, B. (2003) *Compulsory Purchase and Compensation*, 8th edn, Estates Gazette, London, UK.

French, N. (2001) Uncertainty in property valuation: the pricing of flexible leases, *Journal of Corporate Real Estate*, 3, 1, 17–27.

French, N., Evans, M. and Atherton, E. (2000) *Flexibility: Pricing the Uncertainty*, The Cutting Edge Conference, RICS, London, September, 2000.

IPF (2005) *Understanding Commercial Property Investment: A Guide for Financial Advisers*, 2005 Edition, Investment Property Forum, London, UK.

IVSC (2005) *International Valuation Standards*, 7th edn, International Valuation Standards Committee, London, UK.

Johnson, T., Davies, K. and Shapiro, E. (2000) *Modern Methods of Valuation*, 9th edition, Estates Gazette, London, UK.

Marshall, H. and Williamson, H. (1996) *Law and Valuation of Leisure Property*, 2nd edn, Estates Gazette, London, UK.

McAllister, P. (1996) Turnover rents: comparative valuation issues, *Journal of Property Investment and Valuation*, 14, 2, 6–23.

McAllister, P. (2001) Pricing short leases and break clauses using simulation methodology, *Journal of Property Investment and Finance*, 19, 4, 361–374.

Rees, W. and Hayward, R. (2000) *Valuation: Principles into Practice*, 5th edn, Estates Gazette, London, UK.

RICS (2003) *RICS Appraisal and Valuation Standards*, 5th edn (as amended), Royal Institution of Chartered Surveyors, RICS Business Services Ltd, Coventry, UK.

Sayce, S., Smith, J., Cooper, R. and Venmore-Rowland, P. (2006) *Real Estate Appraisal: From Value to Worth*, Blackwell Publishers, Oxford, UK.

Strutt and Parker/IPD (2005) *Lease Events Review 2005*, Strutt & Pather/Investment Propoerty Databank, Landon, UK.

Syms, P. (2004) *Previously Developed Land: Industrial Activities and Contamination*, Blackwell Publishers, Oxford, UK.

Chapter 4

Chapter 5
Property Investment Valuation

5.1 Introduction

Around half of all commercial and industrial properties in the UK are held as investments, where the ownership interest is separate from the occupation interest. The landlord leases the property to an occupying tenant or tenants. Investors in UK commercial property include large financial institutions such as pension funds and insurance companies (28%), overseas investors (15%), UK listed property companies (14%), UK private property companies (15%), limited partnerships, landed estates, charities, trusts, unitised and pooled funds and private investors (23%) (IPF, 2005). The majority of commercial property investments can be placed in one of three principal sectors: retail (shopping centres, retail warehouses, standard shops, supermarkets and department stores), offices (standard offices and business parks); and industrial (standard industrial estates and distribution warehousing). Investment market sub-sectors are often defined using a combination of this sector classification and their location, 'City of London offices' or 'south west high street retail', for example. There are also several smaller sectors of the property market that attract investment interest such as leisure parks, restaurants, pubs and hotels.

Property that is typically held as an investment is valued with this purpose in mind; the valuer will capitalise the rental income produced by the property at an appropriate investment yield using the investment method of valuation, as we saw in Chapter 3. The underlying principle is to discount net economic benefits from an investment over its predicted life at a specified rate of return or **discount rate**. Chapter 2 described discounting as the process of finding the present value (PV) of expected net benefits that may be in the form of a regular income, a future capital reversion or a combination of the two (Havard, 2000). The all-risks yield (ARY) technique described in Chapter 3 is based on the assumption that there is a relationship between the price paid (capital value) and the annual return (net rental income). This chapter develops this notion more explicitly and describes a technique for valuing a property investment that involves more direct recourse to the underlying cash-flow characteristics of the investment. Before that, though, a history lesson.

Up until the 1960s landlords who wished to lease commercial properties typically did so using long leases with no rent reviews. Investment in these commercial premises was regarded as low risk. Consequently the required (or target) rate of return was closely linked to similar low-risk investments such as gilts. Conventionally a premium of around 1–2% was added to the redemption yield on long-dated gilts to account for property market risk. Long-dated gilts were used as a benchmark because property was regarded as a long-term investment. Valuation of property investments involved analysing comparable evidence to determine the appropriate yield which was, in fact, mathematically and logically equivalent to the target rate of return (TRR) (Baum and Crosby, 1995). No adjustment was made to either the yield or the rent to reflect income or capital growth because there was none. A typical investment valuation prior to the 1960s is shown below.

Market rent (MR)(£)	10 000
Years' purchase (YP) perpetuity @ 10%[a]	10
Valuation (£)	£100 000

[a]Investor's target return and therefore comparable with other investments.

After the 1960s, and a period of limited supply of new commercial and industrial property and restrictive macroeconomic policy, commercial property rents increased significantly and landlords introduced rent reviews into shortening leases so that they did not miss out on rising rents. Property became a growth investment, more like equities than fixed interest bond investments, albeit with a peculiar income pattern that goes up (usually) every 5 years (Havard, 2000). Investors were prepared to accept a lower return at the start of the investment term in expectation of higher returns later on. Property investment valuation techniques handled this change not by explicitly forecasting rental growth but by capitalising the current rent at an ARY (derived from comparable evidence) that is lower than the TRR because it implies future rental income and capital growth expectations. The gap between the two represented the expected or implied rental growth hidden in the valuation – directly analogous to the concept of a reverse yield gap between equities and bonds (Baum and Crosby, 1995). Consequently, the assumed static cash-flow is not the expected cash-flow, the yield is not the target rate and is not comparable to target or discount rates used to capitalise or value income from other investments. A typical investment valuation after the 1960s is shown below.

MR (£)	10 000
YP perpetuity @ 8%[a]	12.5
Valuation (£)	£125 000

[a]Growth implicit ARY, not the target rate and therefore not comparable with other investments.

From Chapter 3 we know that the ARY investment valuation technique relies on comparison to justify adjustments to initial yields obtained from comparable investment transactions. These adjustments account for all factors that influence investment value except those that can be handled by altering the rent such as regular/annual management and maintenance expenditure. The most important investment characteristics that need to be reflected in the ARY are income and capital risk and growth potential, but influencing these characteristics are a multitude of economic and property-specific factors including macroeconomic conditions, property market and subsector activity, the financial standing of individual tenants, property depreciation and changes in planning, taxation, landlord and tenant legislation. The ARY has to implicitly quantify these factors and the all-encompassing nature of the ARY means that capital value is very sensitive to small adjustments. In essence, a single divisor (ARY) or multiplier (YP) conceals many of the assumptions regarding choice of TRR (which includes risk) and income and capital growth expectations.

Nevertheless, the ARY approach is practical and appropriate where there is a plentiful supply of comparable market transactions providing evidence of yields, rents and capital values. But there are circumstances when it is particularly difficult to use the ARY technique to value a property investment. Problems arise when, first, comparable evidence is scarce, either because market activity is slow or the property is infrequently traded, and second, where there is greater variability in investments, meaning more variables must be accounted for in the ARY. Regarding this latter point, we saw in Chapter 4 how flexi-lease terms are creating greater diversity in property investment cash-flows, often with gaps in rental income. But, in addition to that, non-prime properties are generally more variable in terms of location, physical quality, condition or covenant and are therefore more risky. And problems arise where the property is more complicated than a simple rack-rented investment: the ARY technique is inappropriate for valuing property that is over-rented, let on short leases or produces varying rental income streams from multiple tenants. It can be especially difficult to quantify all of these factors in an ARY when comparable evidence is scarce.

Harvard (2000) notes that increasing diversity in the property investment market has undermined the ARY valuation technique because it relies heavily on comparison between relatively homogeneous investment assets and simple adjustments to comparable evidence. As a result, property investment valuation techniques have emerged that focus more explicitly on the TRR that an investor requires, the expected flow of income, expenditure and capital growth that might be expected from an investment. The discounted cash-flow (DCF) technique uses an established financial modelling technique that allows comparison between property and other forms of investment. Where information is scarce, or when an unusual property is being valued, the DCF technique assists in the consideration of income and capital growth, depreciation, timing of income receipts and expenditure payments and the TRR. Indeed, International Valuation Standards now include guidance on the use of DCF analysis for valuation in *GN9 – Discounted Cash Flow Analysis for Market and Non-market Based Valuations* (IVSC, 2005). The guidance describes how DCF analysis involves the projection of a cash-flow for an operational or development property. This projected cash-flow is discounted at an appropriate market-derived discount rate to establish PV. In the case of standing investment properties, the cash-flow is typically a series of periodic net rental incomes (gross income less expenditure) along with an estimate of reversion value anticipated at end of the projection period. In the case of development properties' estimates of capital outlay, development costs and anticipated sales income produce a net cash-flow that is discounted over the projected development and marketing periods (cash-flows from property development will be covered in the Chapter 6). The guidance note discusses the structure and components of DCF models and the reporting requirements for valuations based on DCF analysis.

5.2   A DCF valuation model

The academic case for valuing property investments by capitalising a DCF at a TRR rather than capitalising an initial income estimate at an ARY derived from comparable evidence began in the late 1960s and continues to this day. Appendix 5A (see Appendix 5A at www.blackwellpublishing.com/wyatt) lists references to papers that make this case in detail, culminating in the seminal UK text book in this field by Baum and Crosby (1995). But whatever valuation technique is employed, it must reflect the behaviour of market participants. Recourse to comparable evidence (which is generated by market transactions) whenever possible and the adoption of pricing models that are used by market participants will undoubtedly be the most reliable and consistent way of estimating market price.

The ARY technique relies on analysis of prices and rents achieved on recent comparable transactions to estimate an ARY for the subject property. The growth-implicit ARY is then used to capitalise an initial estimate of the cash flow. The DCF technique capitalises or, in the language of investment mathematics, discounts the actual or estimated cash-flow at the investor's TRR. The DCF technique requires explicit assumptions, based on evidence, to be made regarding several factors but most importantly the TRR (which should cover the opportunity cost of investment capital plus perceived risk) and expected rental income growth. When a valuer capitalises an initial rent at an ARY of, say, 8% it is done so in the knowledge that the investor is anticipating a return in excess of 8% over the period of ownership as the expectation is that rental income and perhaps capital value will increase. Essentially, the DCF technique removes the growth element from the ARY and puts it in the cash-flow. As a result, it re-establishes the relationship between the TRR required from a property investment and those required from other investments, as was the case before the 1960s when rental growth was negligible. Instead of simply capitalising the current income (actual or estimated) at an ARY, the expected cash-flow, projected over a certain period of time at a rental growth rate, is discounted at a TRR.

Of course, as we shall see, the DCF technique is not a panacea and several criticisms can be levelled at it. The selection of the discount rate or TRR is subjective and the Appraisal Institute (2001) argues that it is difficult to find market-supported estimates for the key variables in the cash-flow. It might be necessary to estimate current market rent (MR) and expected changes over the next few years. It might also be necessary to try and predict what will happen when the tenant has an option to break or when the lease needs renewing. The variation in possible lease incentives that might be offered, length of possible voids and expenditure that might be incurred is considerable. Moreover, because the DCF technique separates the value significant factors as distinct inputs into the cash-flow and even separates the discount rate into a TRR and an exit yield, the risk of double-counting the effect on value of these factors is high.

5.2.1   Constructing a DCF valuation model

The relationship between the growth-implicit ARY and the growth-explicit DCF techniques can be represented by a simple equation:

$$y = r - g \qquad [5.1]$$

where y is the ARY, r is the investor's target return and g is the annual rental growth rate.

The left side of the equation represents the growth-implicit ARY technique and the right side represents a growth-explicit DCF technique. The DCF technique separates the ARY into two elements; a rental income growth rate and a TRR; in other words, the ARY implies the rental growth that the investor expects in order to achieve the TRR. An investor accepting a relatively low initial yield from a property investment when higher yields might be available from fixed interest investments implies an expectation of future income growth. For example, an investor with a target rate of 15% who purchases a property investment for a price that reflects an initial yield of 10% would require a 5% annual growth to achieve the target rate. This simple relationship is made more complex in the UK property market because income from property investments (in the form of rent) is normally reviewed every 5 years. This means that a slightly higher annual growth rate will be required to meet the investor's annual TRR. Provided the growth rate, target return and rent review period in the DCF approach are mathematically consistent with the yield adopted in the ARY approach, the valuation will be the same. The following explains why.

Starting with the ARY approach, the present (capital) value, V of an income stream from a rack-rented freehold property investment is the pv PV £1 pa or YP (see Equation 2.18 in Chapter 2) multiplied by the annual income or MR:

$$V = MR \; \frac{1 - \left(1 \big/ \left(1 + y\right)^{n}\right)}{y} \qquad [5.2]$$

where y is the growth-implicit ARY and n is the number of years for which the rent is received. If the rent is receivable in perpetuity, that is, freehold property investment, the above formula simplifies to Equation 2.23 from Chapter 2:

$$V = \frac{MR}{y}$$

In other words, the PV is equivalent to a constant annual income capitalised at (divided by) the ARY. In the case of the DCF technique, the income stream is discounted at the investor's TRR, r, rather than the ARY. So the PV of a rack-rented freehold property investment which consists of a constant (i.e. non-growth) annual MR receivable in perpetuity annually in arrears can be expressed as follows:

$$V = \frac{MR}{r} \qquad [5.3]$$

But because the DCF technique is explicit about income growth we now need to introduce rental income growth, g, into this valuation model. Let us assume rent is receivable in perpetuity and there are annual rent reviews at which the rent is increased at the estimated long-term average annual rental growth rate, g. Assuming r, g, rental growth can be incorporated as follows:

$$V = \frac{MR}{r-g} \qquad [5.4]$$

But for most property investments rent does not grow each year. If non-annual rental growth is now introduced, the following equation represents a freehold property recently let at MR in perpetuity with 3 year reviews:

$$V = \frac{MR}{(1+r)} + \frac{MR(1+g)}{(1+r)^2} + \frac{MR(1+g)}{(1+r)^3} + \frac{MR(1+g)^3}{(1+r)^4} + \frac{MR(1+g)^3}{(1+r)^5} + \frac{MR(1+g)^3}{(1+r)^6} + \frac{MR(1+g)^6}{(1+r)^7} + \cdots + \infty$$

The above expression (which is a geometric progression) simplifies to:

$$V = \frac{MR}{r - r\left[\left((1+g)^3 - 1\right)/\left((1+r^3 - 1)\right)\right]} \qquad [5.5]$$

Rearranging Equation 2.23 we can show that $MR/V = y$ and, substituting these variables into Equation 5.5, the relationship between the ARY and DCF techniques can be shown by:

$$y = r - r\left(\frac{(1+g)^p - 1}{(1+r)^p - 1}\right) \qquad [5.6]$$

This is the property yield equation derived by Fraser (1993) and based on a rack-rented freehold property investment. It shows that y is determined by the investor's TRR, r, the annual rental growth rate, g, and the number of years between each rent review (the rent review period), p. This equation is the same as Equation 5.1 except that the annual rental growth rate g has been increased to compensate for the fact that rental growth is not actually received until each non-annual rent review.

If the property to be valued is rack-rented and the rent and review period are known, then, applying the ARY technique, the valuer only has one variable, ARY, to predict in order to value the property. If sufficient evidence is available this is straightforward. With the DCF technique there are two unknowns: the investor's TRR and the growth rate. To predict the growth rate it is necessary to compare yields on recently let comparable freehold properties with an estimate of the investor's target return for those properties. Armed with this information and rearranging Equation 5.6 an average annual growth rate can be implied as follows:

$$g = \left(\frac{(r-y)(1+r)^p + y}{r} \right)^{1/p} - 1 \qquad [5.7]$$

Where g is the annual rental growth expectation, y is the yield obtainable from comparable properties, p is the period between rent reviews in years and r is the estimated target return for properties of this type. The complexity of this formula is due to the rent review periods being greater than 1 year. If reviews were annual, the growth rate would be the target rate minus the initial yield on a rack-rented freehold property ($g = r - y$). For example, if an investor accepts an initial yield of 8% but requires an overall return of 12%, then the income must grow by 4% over the year. But with 5-year rent reviews

$$g = \left(\frac{(0.12 - 0.08)(1+0.12)^p + 0.08}{0.12} \right)^{1/5} - 1$$

$$g = 4.63\%$$

So an investor accepting an initial yield of 8% would require 4.63% per annum growth in the income, on average (compounded at each review) to achieve the target return. Figure 5.1 illustrates this.

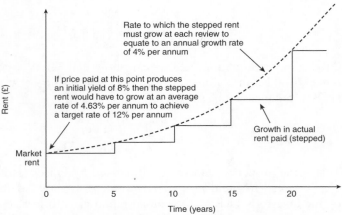

Figure 5.1   Rental growth. The figure assumes rent received in perpetuity (The figure assumes rent received in perpetuity).

Equation 5.7 is often referred to as the implied rental growth rate formula. The higher the client's target rate relative to the market-derived ARY, the better the investment must perform over the holding period to achieve the desired level of return. Comparable evidence can be used to ascertain the implied growth rate necessary to reconcile an ARY valuation with a DCF valuation (Crosby, 1990). The implied growth rate formula is constructed on assumption that property is rack-rented. *g* represents the market's expectations of future growth and is an average growth rate. In fact it is a discounted growth rate into perpetuity so *g* is influenced by expectations in the near future more than ones further away (Fraser, 1993). As an alternative it is possible to derive an explicit growth rate from direct analysis of rental growth rates prevalent in various market sectors, regions and towns. Some argue that the assumption of a stable and constant growth rate is simplistic but it can be taken to be an adequate reflection of the decision-making process of most investors. Before looking at the practical application of the DCF technique the next section will look at the input variables in more detail.

5.2.2   Key variables in the DCF valuation model

The key, value significant, variables in the DCF technique are the rent, rental growth rate, the TRR and the exit yield. Other variables include regular and periodic expenses, transaction fees and taxes, but these are determined in relation to the key variables and their estimation is relatively straightforward.

The rent must be net of any regular or periodic expenditure and the estimation of MR is undertaken in the same way as for the ARY technique described in Chapter 3. Rental growth can be separated into two components; growth in line with inflation and real growth in excess of inflation. Depreciation is the rate at which the MR of an existing property falls away from the MR of a property that is comparable in all respects except that it is (hypothetically) permanently new. The causes of depreciation, namely deterioration and obsolescence, will be discussed in Chapter 6. So, assuming constant rental growth, an annual rate of rental growth must be net of an average annual rate of depreciation. As these two components are interacting growth rates their mathematical relationship with is (Fraser, 1993):

$$g = g_m - d - dg_m \qquad [5.8]$$

Where g is the average annual rental growth rate of actual property, g_m is the average annual rental growth rate of permanently new property and d is the average annual rate of depreciation. As dg_m is usually very small the equation can be simplified to:

$$g = g_m - d \qquad [5.9]$$

A valuer may buy in or undertake research aimed at forecasting explicit rental growth rates and movements in capital values. Simple models might take the form of an historic time series of rents and capital values from which a moving average or exponentially smoothed set of values for future years might be predicted. More complex regression-based models will produce equations which identify independent variables such as GDP or other output measures, expenditure, employment, stock, vacancy, absorption and development pipeline and measure their effect on a dependent variable such as rental growth or yield (Baum, 2000). The Investment Property Databank (IPD) publishes figures for rental value growth for the properties in its databank (which, it should be remembered, are prime institutional investments in the main). Figures are published by sector, segment and region and within these broad groupings it is possible to examine the rental growth of various sectors of the property investment market and their broad location. Using these figures it is possible to get a feel for the rental growth rates of prime investment grade property. Table 5.1 shows how badly office investments in the City of London have performed recently, especially in comparison to Mid Town and West End offices and only mid-sized office space did not produce negative rental value growth in 2004. The annualised returns between 1999 and 2004 and 1994 and 2004 show that, over the longer term, things looked a little healthier but still lagged performance to the west of the City.

A similar analysis of rental growth for single-let standard shop units, shopping centres and retail warehousing reveals significant differences in performance, as can be seen from Table 5.2.

A more detailed regional and sector breakdown of rental value growth can be performed using IPD data and two examples are shown in Tables 5.3 and 5.4.

This sort of market intelligence, although not at the individual property level, paints a very useful picture of rental growth performance across the main investment sectors and locations in the UK and allows an implied rental growth rate to be verified against growth rates achieved in the market. As the tables above demonstrate, a great deal of rental growth information about prime investment property can be obtained from IPD and this information can be used to derive explicit rental growth rates depending on property type and location. It must be remembered, though, that rents can be volatile in the short-term and very little is known about depreciation rates and their effect

Table 5.1 Annual rental value growth (%).

Office investments in	Floor area (m²)				
	0–1000	1001–2500	2501–5000	5001–10000	10001+
City					
2004	−2.0	−3.4	0.0	−2.5	−1.4
1999–2004	−0.9	−1.6	−2.2	−1.8	−3.2
1994–2004	3.5	3.2	3.2	2.7	1.8
Midtown/West End					
2004	1.0	4.0	3.7	2.6	5.1
1999–2004	−0.7	0.2	0.6	0.2	1.6
1994–2004	5.0	5.3	4.8	5.2	4.3

Source: IPD.

Table 5.2 Annual rental value growth (%).

	2004	1994–2004	1999–2004
Single-let standard shops by floor area (m²)			
0–250	2.0	2.2	3.1
251–500	2.6	1.9	3.1
501–1000	3.4	2.4	3.4
1001–2000	3.0	2.5	3.8
2001+	2.3	2.7	5.2
All single-let standard shops	2.9	2.4	3.6
Shopping centres by floor area (m²)			
0–7000	3.3	3.4	3.6
7001–14,000	2.5	3.0	2.7
14,001–25,000	2.9	3.7	3.8
25,001–50,000	3.6	3.1	4.2
50,001+	4.7	3.4	6.0
All shopping centres	3.7	3.3	4.2
Retail warehouses by floor area (m²)			
0–2500	4.0	4.3	4.7
2501–5000	4.3	4.1	4.4
5001–10000	5.4	5.3	5.7
10001–15000	6.4	6.6	7.4
15001+	7.9	7.2	8.3
All retail warehouses	6.0	5.8	6.3

Source: IPD.

on rental growth prospects in the long-term. As an alternative, therefore, a long-term average expected 'market' rental growth rate can be implied from the relationship between the ARY derived from comparable evidence and the target rate on rack-rented freehold property investments. The way that this implicit growth rate can be calculated was shown in Section 5.2.1. The growth rate should be indicative of rental growth on properties regardless of whether they are rack-rented or reversionary freeholds or leaseholds (but with due care exercised in the case of geared profit rents). Also, if attempting to derive an implied growth rate from a reversionary comparable transaction it is important to bear in mind what Brown and Matysiak (2000) say in Section 5.2.3 below.

The TRR (also referred to as the **equated yield** or discount rate because it is the rate at which cash-flows are discounted to PV) should adequately compensate an investor for the opportunity cost of capital plus the risk that the investor expects to be exposed to. It is therefore a function of a risk-free rate of return and a risk premium: a higher risk premium (and thus higher target rate) would be used to discount the future cash-flow of a more risky property investment and cause its PV to reduce accordingly. It is difficult to obtain evidence of the target rate from the market but the base-line is the return from a risk-free investment. The closest available proxy for the risk-free rate is the gross redemption yield on long-dated fixed interest gilts; the

Table 5.3 Annual rental value growth (%).

	City/Mid-Town	West End	C. London Fringe	Rest of London	South East	South West	Eastern	East Midlands	West Midlands	North West	Yorks & Humber	North East	Scotland	Wales
Retails														
2004	0.7		0.5	3.8	4.9	4.9	4.9	3.5	3.7	3.9	5.2	5.0	3.0	4.4
1999–2004	2.4		2.7	4.1	4.2	3.4	4.0	3.7	4.2	3.6	3.8	3.6	2.9	3.6
1994–2004	5.7		6.4	4.4	4.2	3.6	4.8	4.4	4.4	4.3	3.9	4.8	4.1	3.8
Standard retails														
2004	0.6		0.0	2.5	2.8	5.3	2.8	3.3	2.3	2.6	5.6	3.2	1.3	2.6
1999–2004	2.2		2.7	3.2	2.4	2.9	2.4	2.4	2.3	2.3	3.4	2.6	1.0	2.3
1994–2004	5.9		6.3	3.7	2.6	2.6	2.4	3.4	2.4	3.3	3.3	3.7	3.5	3.0
Retail warehouses			*(London)*											
2004			4.4		7.4	6.8	6.9	5.8	5.4	5.9	6.1	5.6	6.1	5.4
1999–2004			5.8		6.6	6.1	6.6	6.2	5.4	6.3	4.5	5.2	4.9	4.1
1994–2004			6.1		6.1	6.7	6.5	7.4	6.8	6.5	6.1	6.7	5.2	5.4
Offices			*(London)*	*(Outer London)*										
2004	−1.7	0.4	4.6	−2.8	−2.1	1.2	0.1	−0.8	1.8	2.8	1.0	2.6	−0.1	1.7
1999–2004	−2.4	−0.7	0.6	−0.8	−2.2	2.7	1.0	0.6	2.0	2.7	1.7	2.2	1.8	0.8
1994–2004	2.3	4.0	5.0	2.3	1.3	1.0	2.5	0.9	1.4	2.0	0.5	1.5	1.5	0.3
Industrials			*(London)*											
2004			1.5		1.0	1.5	1.6	0.5	0.8	0.3	2.2	3.1	0.5	−0.6
1999–2004			3.3		2.1	1.8	2.6	1.3	1.6	2.1	1.7	1.6	1.8	2.5
1994–2004			4.1		3.1	1.7	2.3	1.6	1.7	1.6	1.0	1.5	1.5	2.4

Source: IPD.

Table 5.4 Annual rental value growth (%).

	2004	5 years	10 years
Standard shops	2.4	2.4	3.5
Central London	0.0	2.6	6.3
Rest of London	2.2	3.1	3.8
South East and Eastern	2.8	2.3	2.6
Rest of UK	3.4	2.3	3.0
Shopping centres	3.7	3.3	4.2
In-town	3.5	3.3	3.9
Out-of-town	4.5	3.4	—
Retail warehouses	6.0	5.8	6.3
Retail parks	6.5	6.1	6.7
Fashion parks	6.9	8.6	—
Other retail warehouses	4.6	4.3	4.8
Dept/variety stores	3.5	4.0	4.0
Supermarkets	3.6	2.7	2.6
Other retail	1.6	2.3	3.1
Standard offices	0.6	−0.4	2.5
Central London	1.3	−0.9	3.6
Rest of London	−1.9	−0.6	2.3
Inner South Eastern	−2.3	−2.4	1.5
Outer South Eastern	1.8	1.3	1.4
Rest of UK	1.7	2.4	1.3
Office parks	−1.9	−0.7	2.4
London and South Eastern	−2.6	−1.4	2.7
Rest of UK	−0.3	1.0	1.8
Standard industrials	1.1	2.4	2.7
London	1.6	3.4	4.1
Inner South Eastern	0.9	2.2	3.2
Outer South Eastern	1.1	2.5	2.5
Rest of UK	0.9	2.0	1.8
Distribution warehouses	1.1	1.5	1.9
Other property	1.1	1.2	2.7
Leisure	0.5	0.9	1.9

Source: IPD.

cash-flow is certain, the investment is liquid and it is cheap to manage. It thus provides a good indication of the opportunity cost of long-term investment capital – an investment time-frame or holding period comparable to property investment (Fraser, 1993). However, with an increasing prevalence of shorter leases, it might be appropriate to look to medium-dated gilts and SWAP rates as benchmark evidence for a risk-free rate of return. A risk premium is then added to this risk-free rate which should cover (Baum and Crosby, 1995):

- Tenant risk; risk of default on lease terms, particularly payment of rent but also repair and other obligations, risk of tenant exercising a break

- option or not renewing lease (higher risk if the lease is short). The level of tenant risk will depend to an extent on the type of tenant; a public sector organisation may be considered less likely to default than a fledgling private sector company.
- Physical property risk; management costs (e.g. rent collection, rent reviews and lease renewal) and depreciation. This type of risk is less acute in the case of prime retail premises because land value is a high proportion of total value, but the reverse is true for, say, small industrial units. A certain amount of physical property risk can be passed on to the tenant via lease terms.
- Property market risk; illiquidity caused by high transaction costs, complexity of arranging finance and accentuated by the large lot size of property investments.
- Macroeconomic risk; fluctuating interest rate, inflation, GDP, and so on, all affect occupier and investment markets in terms of rental and capital values and potential for letting voids.
- Planning risk; in the main, this refers to planning policy and development control. For example, Sunday trading, presumption against out-of-town retailing, promotion of mixed-use, city centre developments on previously developed land.

Baum and Crosby (1995) point out that, for valuation, it is not feasible to quantify all of these components of risk as this would need to be done for each comparable – this sort of thing is more appropriate in property investment appraisal (see Chapter 7). Instead, the valuer subjectively chooses and adjusts a target rate not at the individual property level but by grouping various property investments and examining the risk characteristics of each. By far the most frequently encountered investment type is a rack-rented freehold. Regular rent reviews mean that this is an equity-type investment that benefits from income and capital growth just as equities do, albeit with less frequent income growth participation. Whereas the return from an investment in company shares relies on the continued existence and profitability of that company, a property investment will remain even if the occupying company fails. Unlike share dividends, rent is a contractual obligation paid quarterly in advance and is a priority payment in the event of bankruptcy. After a likely rent void the premises can be re-let and perhaps used for a different purpose, subject to location, design and planning considerations. This reduces the reliance of the investment on a single business occupier, helps underpin the value of the investment and reduces risk. A freehold let on fixed ground rent has a risk profile similar to undated gilts as it generates a fixed income from a head-tenant who is very unlikely to default on what will probably be a significant profit rent. Consequently this type of property investment is very secure and risk will derive from changes in the level of long-term interest rate and inflation rather than property or tenant-specific factors (Fraser, 1993).

Some of the more general 'market' risks, such as illiquidity, tenant covenant and yield movement are best incorporated by adjusting the TRR.

Other, property-specific, risks such as regular deductions from gross rent, a depreciation rate slowing rental growth, voids and management costs can be reflected in adjustments to the cash-flow. In this way properties of the same type can be grouped together to help estimate a risk premium for a particular sector or sub-sector of the market such as high street shops or secondary industrials on the basis that properties within each sector have similar tenant risks and lease structures.

The selection of a risk premium for an individual property is therefore rather subjective but Baum and Crosby (1995) argue that a risk premium of around 2% is an appropriate rule of thumb 2% is based on historical relationship between prime property yields and gilt yields prior to reverse yield gap, although the size of the premium will vary over time and differ depending on sector.

The Appraisal Institute (2001) suggests that investors should be interviewed to obtain their views on target rates of return. If a target rate is used with an ARY to imply an average annual rental growth rate the valuation is insensitive to the level of target rate (within realistic bounds); a higher target rate implies a higher growth rate, *ceteris paribus*. Figure 5.2 illustrates the sensitivity of the capital value of a rack-rented freehold property investment to changes in the ARY and changes in the target rate. It can be seen that, particularly between 1% and 10% value is much less sensitive to changes in the target rate regardless of the growth rate and exit yield assumptions.

A property is a durable, long-term investment asset and in order to avoid trying to estimate cash-flows far off into the future, a **holding period** of between 5 and 15 years is normally specified, after which a notional sale is assumed. The length of the holding period can be influenced by lease terms, such as the length of the lease or incidence of break clauses, or by the physical nature of the property, perhaps timed to coincide with a redevelopment towards the end of the period, but the longer the period the more

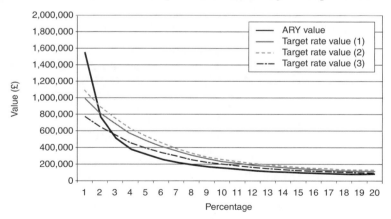

Figure 5.2 Capital value sensitivity to ARY and TRR. Capital value of £17 500 pa rental income using a range of ARYs and a range of TRR assuming a (1) rental growth at 5% pa and an exit yield after 25 years of 10%; (2) growth 5% exit yield 8% and (3) growth 3% and exit yield 8%.

chance of estimation error when selecting variables. The notional sale value or **exit value** is usually calculated by capitalising the estimated rent at the end of the holding period at an ARY. When an ARY is used to estimate an exit value it is called an **exit yield** and is usually higher than initial yields on comparable but new and recently let property investments because it must reflect the reduction in remaining economic life of the property and the higher risk of estimating cash-flow at the end of the holding period. The exit yield may reflect land values if demolition is anticipated. Prime yields tend to be fairly stable but care should be taken when choosing an exit yield, if the holding period is less than 20 years as it can have a significant impact on the valuation figure. Where an allowance has been made for refurbishment in the cash-flow during the holding period the exit yield should reflect the anticipated state of the property. The extent of depreciation also needs to be considered: for example, if the subject property is 10 years old and the appropriate market capitalisation rate is 7%, given an expectation of stable yields, the best estimate of the resale capitalisation rate after a 10-year holding period is the current yield on similar but 20-year old buildings. The effect of depreciation also needs to be considered when estimating projected rental values.

5.2.3   Applying the DCF valuation model

5.2.3.1   Rack-rented freehold property investments

A freehold property investment was let recently at £10 000 per annum (receivable annually in arrears) on a 15-year FRI lease with 5-year rent reviews. Assuming an initial yield of 8% (from comparable evidence), a target return of 12% (risk-free rate 9%, market risk 2%, property risk 1%), an implied annual growth rate (calculated in Section 5.2.1) of 4.63% and a holding period of 10 years after which a sale is assumed at an exit yield equivalent to today's ARY, the valuation of this property is shown below:

Period (years)	Rent (£)	Growth @ 4.63% pa	Projected rent (£)	PV £1 @ 12%	YP in perpetuity @ 8%	PV (£)
1	10 000	1.0000	10 000	0.8929		8 930
2	10 000	1.0000	10 000	0.7972		7 970
3	10 000	1.0000	10 000	0.7118		7 120
4	10 000	1.0000	10 000	0.6355		6 360
5	10 000	1.0000	10 000	0.5674		5 670
6	10 000	1.2539	12 539	0.5066		6 357
7	10 000	1.2539	12 539	0.4523		5 668
8	10 000	1.2539	12 539	0.4039		5 066
9	10 000	1.2539	12 539	0.3606		4 527
10	10 000	1.2539	12 539	0.3220		4 038
10+	10 000	1.5724	15 724	0.3220	12.5000	63 289
Valuation						124 986

Chapter 5

The net income in each period is discounted at the TRR to a PV and these are totalled to obtain a total PV or valuation of the subject property. Because no growth is implied in the target rate the rental income must be inflated at the appropriate times (rent reviews) over the term of the investment to account for growth. At the end of the holding period a notional sale is assumed so the projected rent of £15 724 is capitalised at an exit yield based on the current initial yield of 8% (a YP of 12.5).

Checking this answer against an ARY valuation, because the rental growth rate has been implied from the relationship between the target rate and the ARY, the answers will be the same.

MR (£)	10 000	
YP in perpetuity @ 8%	12.5000	
Valuation (£)		125 000

A rack-rented freehold is least prone to inaccurate valuation using the ARY technique. The advantage of the DCF technique is that more information is presented, use of a target rate enables cross-investment comparisons and specific cash-flow problems such as voids and refurbishment expenditure can be incorporated. DCF valuations are frequently used for complex investment properties where there may be many tenants, all with different covenant strengths, rents, lease terms and rent review dates. Comparable evidence will therefore be scarce and the number of input variables high.

5.2.3.2   Reversionary freehold property investments

As we know from Chapter 3 a reversionary property is one where the rent passing is below the MR. The valuation of a freehold reversionary interest in a retail property let at £10 000 per annum on a lease with 3 years until the next rent review and a 5-year rent review pattern is shown below. A comparable property recently let on a similar review pattern at £15 000 per annum sold for a price that generated an initial yield of 6%. It is assumed that the investor's TRR is 13% and the holding period is until the second rent review in 13 years' time.

ARY term and reversion valuation:

Term (contract rent) (£)	10 000	
YP 3 years @ 5%	2.7232	
		27 232
Reversion to MR (£)	15 000	
YP in perpetuity @ 6%	16.6667	
PV £1 in 3 years @ 6%	0.8396	
		209 900
Valuation (£)		237 132

DCF valuation: Using the implied growth rate formula (Equation 5.7), the annual growth rate implied from a target rate of 13% and an initial yield of 6% assuming 5-year rent reviews is 7.76% per annum.

Years	Rent (£)	Growth @ 7.76%	Projected rent (£)	PV £1 @ 13%	YP in perpetuity @ 6%	PV (£)
1	10000	1.0000	10000	0.8850		8850
2	10000	1.0000	10000	0.7831		7831
3	10000	1.0000	10000	0.6931		6931
4	15000	1.2512	18772	0.6133		11513
5	15000	1.2512	18772	0.5428		10189
6	15000	1.2512	18772	0.4803		9016
7	15000	1.2512	18772	0.4251		7980
8	15000	1.2512	18772	0.3762		7062
9	15000	1.8189	27284	0.3329		9083
10	15000	1.8189	27284	0.2946		8038
11	15000	1.8189	27284	0.2607		7113
12	15000	1.8189	27284	0.2307		6294
13	15000	1.8189	27284	0.2042		5571
13+	15000	2.6436	39653	0.2042	16.6667	134954
Valuation						240425

Baum and Crosby (1995) argue that, in a valuation, it is not really necessary to show cash-flow growth explicitly beyond the point at which the MR is obtained; that is more appropriate for appraisal, which we will look at in Chapter 7. Instead, a 'short-cut' DCF technique, developed by Sykes (1981) can be used. The technique discounts the term rent (which is fixed and contains no prospect of growth until the next rent review or lease renewal) at the TRR and then capitalises the rent receivable on reversion (which has been adjusted to account for any rental growth over the term period) at a growth-im. If an implied growth rate has been used then the projected rent at the reversion can be capitalised at the market yield for a rack-rented freehold. Mathematically:

$V = (c \times$ YP for term at $r) + ($inflated $m \times$ YP in perpetuity at $y \times$
    PV for term at $r)$

$$= \frac{c\left(1-\left(1/(1+r)^n\right)\right)}{r} + \frac{m(1+g)^n}{y(1+r)^n}$$ [5.10]

Where c is contract rent for term, m is the MR (net of non-recoverable running costs and ground rent), r is the TRR, y is the ARY and n is the period to next rent revision which might be the next rent review or lease renewal. The valuation would look like this:

Term (contract rent) (£)		10000
YP for 3 years @ 13%		2.3612
		23612
Reversion to MR (£)	15000	
growth @ 7.76% pa for 3 years	1.2515	
		18772
YP in perpetuity @ 6%		16.6667
PV £1 in 3 years @ 13%		0.6931
		216854
Valuation (£)		240466

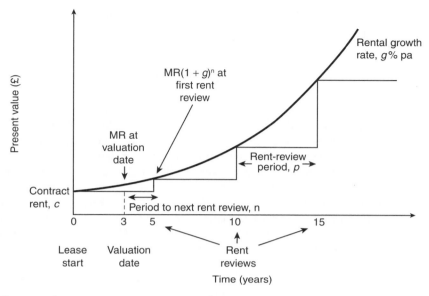

Figure 5.3   Rental growth between rent reviews.

Unlike the ARY-based term and reversion technique the short-cut DCF technique shows the correct capital values of the term and reversionary incomes and reveals the growth assumption over the term. It is explicit about the target rate and growth rate up to the first rent review, at which point the MR (which has been projected at the long-term implied growth rate) is capitalised at the ARY. For properties where the cash-flow is more complex and comparable evidence more scarce, a full DCF is perhaps more appropriate but can lead to greater variability between valuers regarding values of key input variables (Havard, 2000).

It is possible to use the implied rental growth rate formula to derive a growth rate that is implied from the ARY, TRR and rent-review period of a reversionary freehold property investment. The mathematics is a little more complex but Brown and Matysiak (2000) provide a clear explanation. Diagrammatically the situation is illustrated in Figure 5.3. The core and top-slice ARY model (with equivalent yields) for calculating the PV of this investment is adapted from Equation 3.3 in Chapter 3:

$$V = (c \times \text{YP into perpetuity}) + ((m - c) \times \text{YP in perpetuity} \times \text{PV for term})$$

$$V = \frac{c}{y} + \frac{m-c}{y(1+y)^n} \qquad [5.11]$$

Where y is the equivalent ARY and the other variables are as defined for Equation 5.10. The ARY implies growth and therefore the rent is not explicitly projected at the growth rate g. The DCF model does project rent at the growth rate but, unlike a rack-rented property, there are two periods to incorporate into the calculation; one that lasts until the first rent review and then the normal rent review period thereafter:

$$V = \frac{c\left(1-\left(1/\left(1+r\right)^{n}\right)\right)}{r} + \frac{m\left(1+g\right)^{n}}{r\left(1+r\right)^{n}}\left[\frac{\left(1+r\right)^{p}-1}{\left(1+r\right)^{p}-\left(1+r\right)^{p}}\right] \quad [5.12]$$

Where n is the period to the next rent revision and p is the rent review period. If we assume that the PVs from each model produce the same answer we can calculate the implied growth rate for a reversionary property investment. To see how this works, take an example where the ARY is 8%, the TRR is 12%, the rent review period is 5 years (for a rack-rented property investment the growth rate implied by these figures would be 4.63% per annum) but the period to next review is 2 years. The contract rent is £8 000 per annum and the current MR is £10 000 per annum. An ARY core and top-slice technique, using equivalent yields, produces the following valuation:

$$V = \frac{8\,000}{0.08} + \frac{10\,000 - 8\,000}{0.08(1+0.08)^{2}} = 100\,000 + 21\,433 = £121\,433$$

If we assume that a DCF valuation should produce the same valuation, using spreadsheet iteration in the final stage, g can be calculated as follows:

$$121\,433 = \frac{c\left(1-\left(1/(1+r)^{n}\right)\right)}{r} + \frac{m\left(1+g\right)^{n}}{r\left(1+r\right)^{n}}\left[\frac{\left(1+g\right)^{p}-1}{\left(1+r\right)^{p}-\left(1+g\right)^{p}}\right]$$

$$121\,433 = 13\,520 + \frac{10\,1000(1+g)^{2}}{0.1505}\left[\frac{0.7623}{1.7623-(1+g)^{5}}\right]$$

$$\therefore g = 0.0455 = 4.55\%$$

Therefore the implied growth rate from this reversionary property is slightly lower than from the rack-rented equivalent because the rental growth will arrive sooner due to the rent review in 2 years' time rather than in 5 years.

5.2.3.3   Leasehold property investments

Baum and Crosby (1995) argue that a leasehold property investment producing a fixed profit rent over its entire term produces a risk that is almost entirely dependent upon the quality of the sub-tenant: a cash-flow from a good quality tenant is similar to the return from a fixed income bond plus a suitable risk premium. The target rate used to discount a fixed profit rent is therefore likely to be derived from comparison to other fixed income investments such as gilts with similar maturity dates. This approach is more logical and is not based on questionable comparisons with the freehold investment market (see Chapter 3).

If the profit rent is variable then there is a gearing effect. Basically if a fixed head-rent is deducted from a sub-rent which includes rent reviews the resultant profit rent must vary by an amount greater than the variation in the sub-rent itself. The magnitude of this variability depends on the size of the fixed deduction of head-rent from the variable sub-rent and can be expressed as the income-gearing ratio. To illustrate this consider three property investments; a freehold, a leasehold where the head-rent is very similar to the sub-rent and another leasehold where the sub-rent is very much larger than the head-rent. All three investments generate an initial income of £100 000 per annum subject to annual rent reviews and rental growth is estimated to be 5% per annum. As can be seen from Table 5.5 the income from the freehold investment grows at the rental growth rate of 5% per annum. The first leasehold investment receives a £900 000 per annum sub-rent and pays a £800 000 per annum head rent, leaving £100 000 per annum profit rent. The second leasehold receives a £110 000 per annum sub-rent and pays a £10 000 per annum head rent, leaving £100 000 per annum profit rent.

Except where the head rent is a peppercorn (very low) rent, rental growth for a leasehold profit rent is greater than the rental growth on an equivalent freehold. The growth rate diminishes at each subsequent rent review and tends towards the market rental growth rate in perpetuity (Baum and Crosby, 1995). The income-gearing ratio for the first leasehold is 89% and for second it is 9%. Life becomes a whole lot more complicated as we introduce asynchronous rent reviews in the head- and sub-leases. So the way

Table 5.5   Geared leasehold profit rents.

Year	Freehold initial net income (£)	Freehold income growth (%)	Leasehold 1 initial net income (£)	Leasehold 1 income growth (%)	Leasehold 2 initial net income (£)	Leasehold 2 income growth (%)
0	100 000	—	100 000	—	100 000	—
1	105 000	5.00	145 000	45.00	105 500	5.50
2	110 250	5.00	192 250	32.59	111 275	5.47
3	115 763	5.00	241 863	25.81	117 339	5.45
4	121 551	5.00	293 956	21.54	123 706	5.43
5	127 628	5.00	348 653	18.61	130 391	5.40
6	134 010	5.00	406 086	16.47	137 411	5.38
7	140 710	5.00	466 390	14.85	144 781	5.36
8	147 746	5.00	529 710	13.58	152 520	5.35
9	155 133	5.00	596 195	12.55	160 646	5.33
10	162 889	5.00	666 005	11.71	169 178	5.31
...						
40	703 999	5.00	5 535 990	5.76	764 399	5.07
41	739 199	5.00	5 852 789	5.72	803 119	5.07
42	776 159	5.00	6 185 429	5.68	843 775	5.06
43	814 967	5.00	6 534 700	5.65	886 463	5.06
44	855 715	5.00	6 901 435	5.61	931 287	5.06
45	898 501	5.00	7 286 507	5.58	978 351	5.05
46	943 426	5.00	7 690 832	5.55	1 027 768	5.05
47	990 597	5.00	8 115 374	5.52	1 079 657	5.05
48	1 040 127	5.00	8 561 143	5.49	1 134 140	5.05
49	1 092 133	5.00	9 029 200	5.47	1 191 347	5.04
50	1 146 740	5.00	9 520 660	5.44	1 251 414	5.04

Chapter 5

that a profit rent might be expected to grow depends on the income-gearing ratio. Use of an ARY technique (even the single rate approach described in Chapter 3) is hard to justify because of heterogeneity of interests and potential complexity profit rent cash-flows. Similarly, identifying a market TRR for leaseholds with variable and geared profit rents is difficult as each investment opportunity will have unique ratios between head-rent and sub-rent leading to individual profit rent cash-flows and gearing circumstances. Furthermore, there will be differences in tenant quality and remaining lease term. The leasehold target rate must relate to the lease structure and any profit rent gearing and Baum and Crosby (1995) suggest that attention should focus on the choice of risk premium when moving from a freehold to a leasehold target rate. Other cash-flow variables such as the head-rent, rent reviews and so on can also be incorporated in the cash-flow.

Freehold investment transactions can be analysed to derive a suitable rental growth rate which can be applied to the leasehold investment cash-flow and this should be done in preference to estimating a growth rate that is implied by the relationship between target rate and ARY on a leasehold investment because of the heterogeneity of cash-flows from leasehold investments (Baum and Crosby, 1995). If the leasehold includes a head rent and sub-rent both with rent reviews at the same time and both rents are assumed to grow at the same rate, then the profit rent would grow at the same rate as the growth in MR for a freehold. But in cases where the rent reviews in the sub-lease (say every 5 years) are different to those in the head-lease (say every 15 years) the complexities are best handled by a full DCF rather than a short-cut. As an example the leasehold investment described in Section 3.3.3 of Chapter 3 will be valued again but this time using a DCF technique. Assuming a target rate of 10% and an ARY of 6% for freehold property this implies rental growth of 4.47% per annum. But the target rate at which the cash-flow from a leasehold investment is discounted must be adjusted to reflect additional risk. Here the adjustment is from 10% to 15%.

Years	Rent received (£)	Growth @ 4.47% pa	Inflated rent (£)	Less rent paid (£)	Profit rent (£)	PV @ 15%	PV (£)
1	30000	1.0000	30000	−10000	20000	0.8696	17392
2	30000	1.0000	30000	−10000	20000	0.7561	15122
3	35000	1.0913	38196	−10000	28196	0.6575	18539
4	35000	1.0913	38196	−10000	28196	0.5718	16122
5	35000	1.0913	38196	−10000	28196	0.4972	14019
6	35000	1.0913	38196	−10000	28196	0.4323	12189
7	35000	1.0913	38196	−10000	28196	0.3759	10599
8	35000	1.3578	47523	−10000	37523	0.3269	12266
9	35000	1.3578	47523	−10000	37523	0.2843	10668
10	35000	1.3578	47523	−10000	37523	0.2472	9276
11	35000	1.3578	47523	−10000	37523	0.2149	8064
12	35000	1.3578	47523	−10000	37523	0.1869	7013
Valuation							151269

Chapter 5

5.2.4   Case study – valuation of a city centre office block

You have been asked to value, for sale purposes, the freehold and head-leasehold interests in the property described below. The valuation date is the 1 April 2005. The property was constructed in 1980 and is located in the central business district of Bristol. It comprises a basement (used for storage) with five floors above (including the ground floor). Externally, notable features include glazed exterior cladding, a high quality entrance and reception area on the ground floor and a secure barrier to the car park at the rear. The office accommodation is open plan and finished to a reasonable specification (suspended ceilings and perimeter trunking but no air-conditioning or raised floors). There are two lifts serving all floors. Car parking is rather restricted due to the location of the property in the centre of the city but access to the railway station and main bus routes is good. The property is also close to the main retail area of the city. Occupying tenants can internally partition the floor-space under the terms of the leases. With regard to maintenance of the building, each occupying tenant pays a portion of the annual service charge to the landlord. The floor area that each tenant occupies is used to apportion the service charge between tenants. The service charge pays for the cleaning of common parts, general repairs, services, lighting to common parts, lifts, insurance and management. The tenants pay for their own cleaning and lighting.

5.2.4.1   Head-lease

Y is the landlord of the site which was let to Z on a 125-year-ground lease in 1988. The initial rent that was agreed was £10 000 per annum and the landlord has no responsibility for the insurance or repairs of the office building on the site. The rent payable under the ground lease is reviewed every 25 years. At each review the rent is reviewed to the existing ground rent plus 5% of the estimated market rental value of the head-lease in excess of the existing ground rent. The wording of the rent review clause in the ground-lease permits the head-lease to be valued assuming the building is vacant and to let.

5.2.4.2   Occupational sub-leases

All of the occupational sub-leases specify that the sub-tenants are responsible for all repairs and insurance (non-internal repairs and insurance payable via the service charge) and are subject to 5-year, upward-only rent reviews. Table 5.6 lists the details of the sub-leases.

Each occupying sub-tenant must pay a portion of the annual service charge, itemised in Table 5.7.

This total service charge per square metre is then apportioned between the sub-tenants on a floor area basis with a reduction of 50% for the basement store. The apportioned charges are listed in Table 5.8.

After a review of your firm's internal records and discussions with colleagues at other surveying firms in the city, three properties have recently

Table 5.6   Sub-leases.

Floor	Tenant	Use	Business	Covenant[a]	Area (m²)	Current rent (£)	Date lease commenced	Length of lease (years)
Basement	A	Store	Solicitors	Good	305	21 350	1997	15
Ground	A	Office	Solicitors	Good	251[b]	40 160	2003	10
First	B	Office	Insurance	Good	449	76 330	2005	15
Second	C	Office	Travel	Poor	449	49 390	1988	25
Third	D	Office	Surveyors	Average	449	69 595	2000	10
Fourth	E	Office	Publishers	Poor	398	55 720	1997	15
Totals					2301	312 545		

[a]The covenant describes the quality of the tenant in terms of ability to meet the terms of the lease. It is a subjective measure of the security of the income.
[b]Entrance and reception areas are on this floor.

Table 5.7   Service charge details.

Item	Cost (£/m²)
Staff	3.50
Cleaning of common parts	2.00
General repairs	5.00
Services	2.75
Lighting to common parts	1.25
Lifts	2.75
Insurance	2.75
Management	2.50
Total	22.50

Table 5.8   Service charge apportionment.

Floor	Sub-tenant	Use	Area (m²)	Service charge (£)
Basement	A	Store	305	3 431.25
Ground	A	Office	251	5 647.50
First	B	Office	449	10 102.50
Second	C	Office	449	10 102.50
Third	D	Office	449	10 102.50
Fourth	E	Office	398	8 955.00

been the subject of transactions that provide comparable evidence for your subject property:

(a)   The basement of the office building next door was recently let to the publishers (who occupy the fourth floor of the subject property) for additional archiving and general storage. The lease was agreed on standard terms for a period of 5 years at a rent that equated to £90 per square metre.

Table 5.9 Current and full rental values of the sub-leases.

Floor	Tenant	Date lease commenced	Length of lease (years)	Current rent (£)[a]	Next rent review	Current market rent (£)[b]
Basement	A	1997	15	21 350	2007	27 450
Ground	A	2003	10	40 160	2000	42 670
First	B	2005	15	76 330	2002	76 330
Second	C	1988	25	49 390	2000	76 330
Third	D	2001	10	69 595	1998	76 330
Fourth	E	1997	15	55 720	1999	67 660
Totals				312 545		366 770

[a]MR is not received until first rent review for each sub-lease.
[b]The comparable evidence of market rents for storage and office space are used to calculate the rental values for each floor of the subject property.

This provides evidence of the current MR for storage space in this type of building.

(b) The letting of the first floor of the subject property to the insurance company was recent and was agreed on standard terms. It therefore provides good evidence of the current MR for the office space. The rent agreed equates to £170/m^2.

(c) The fifth (top) floor of the office building next door was recently let on standard terms. The lease was for a term of 15 years at a rent that equates to £150/m^2. However, on inspection of this building it is noted that the lift only goes up to the fourth floor and clearly a reduction to the 'normal' MR for office space in this area has been made to take this into account.

It is decided that the comparable evidence in (c) will be classed as secondary due to the poor lift access. Thus the current MR for office space in this locality is estimated to be £170/m^2. Table 5.9 shows the current and estimated MRs for each sub-lease.

5.2.4.3 Valuation of the freehold interest

Term rent (£)		10 000
YP 8 years @ 8%		5.7466
		57 466
Reversion to MR of head-lease (£)	366 770	
less rent passing (£)	−10 000	
	356 770	
5% share of MR	0.05	
	17 839	

plus rent passing (£)	10 000	
		27 839
YP in perpetuity @ 10%		10.000
PV £1 for 8 years @ 10%		0.4665
		129 871
Valuation (£)		187 337

5.2.4.4   Valuation of the head-leasehold interest

Valuing year-by-year until the rent on each floor is reviewed to market rental value and incorporating the review of the ground rent, the valuation below has been set out as a cash-flow. Given the long length of the ground-lease (125 years) and the relatively low ground rent (currently £10 000) this interest will be valued as though it were a freehold. The difference is negligible; the YP for the remainder of the ground lease (108 years) at 11% is 9.0906 whereas the YP in perpetuity at 11% is 9.0909.

Year	Rent received (£)	Ground rent (£)	Profit rent (£)	YP in perpetuity @ 11%	PV £1 @ 11%	PV (£)
2005	312 545	10 000	302 545		0.9009	272 563
2006	319 280	10 000	309 280		0.8116	251 018
2007	337 320	10 000	327 320		0.7312	239 327
2008	366 770	10 000	356 770		0.6587	235 004
2009	366 770	10 000	356 770		0.5935	211 743
2010	366 770	10 000	356 770		0.5346	190 729
2011	366 770	10 000	356 770		0.4817	171 856
2012	366 770	10 000	356 770		0.4339	154 802
2013	366 770	27 839	338 931[a]	9.0909	0.3909	1 204 436
Valuation						£2 931 480

[a]This rent is receivable for the remainder of the ground-lease (assumed to be in perpetuity) and is capitalised at a yield of 11% but deferred 9 years.

The main decision that a valuer must make is the choice of yield. Although this long leasehold interest is, in many ways, similar to a freehold interest, it is ultimately a wasting asset and is usually not as desirable as a freehold investment. The yield should reflect such market perception as well as opportunity cost of capital, potential for growth and a return for risk taken. Yield choice is always difficult and is particularly so with interests such as this where comparable evidence is hard to obtain. In practice different yields may be applied to the capitalisation of the various rental income streams. For example, a higher yield may be adopted for the capitalisation of the reduced profit rent receivable after the review of the ground rent in 2013. Similarly, different yields may be chosen depending on which sub-tenant the rental income originates from. This may help to reflect the security value of each portion of the rental income.

Key points

- The value of an investment can be considered to be a multiple of the current rent where the multiplier is the reciprocal of the investor's required income yield (ARY valuation technique) or the PV of the expected future cash-flow (DCF valuation technique) (Fraser, 1993). Techniques vary depending on the extent to which assumptions are made explicit. For example a valuer may wish to include an explicit growth rate forecast rather than imply a long-term average from analysis of comparable evidence, or depreciation may be explicitly accounted for in the cash-flow. The problem with being more explicit is that there is greater potential for valuation variance (Havard, 2000).
- The ARY model does not explicitly reveal the total return that an investor expects; instead, future rental income is discounted (capitalised) at a rate that implies that the investor expects the income to grow in order to achieve a TRR. The DCF model involves selecting a suitable holding period, forecasting the cash flow over this period and selecting an appropriate target rate and exit yield. All of these assumptions should reflect market behaviour so valuers need to interpret activities and expectations of market participants (Appraisal Institute, 2001).
- The DCF technique is better at isolating factors affecting future income flow from those that affect the TRR required by the investor, thus allowing direct comparison with other investment opportunities. It can also deal with complexity and reveal assumptions explicitly. In cases where a property presents a non-standard pattern of income a DCF approach will usually be preferable. For example, investments with a ground lease and an occupational lease granted at different times, phased development projects or leaseholds where the head-lease has infrequent reviews and the sub-lease does not, the DCF approach provides more information and helps focus attention on fundamental characteristics that the investor will be interested in, namely income growth, depreciation, the holding period, timing of income and expenditure and the TRR. Rent tends to be subject to depreciation and capital values to obsolescence and the effect of these can be handled explicitly by adjusting the rental growth rate and exit yield or implicitly by adjusting the TRR (Sayce *et al.*, 2006).
- Choice of method is a matter of availability of evidence and complexity of the property interest being valued: use the ARY technique when investments have a standard pattern of income and rent reviews, use the DCF technique for complex interests, long reversions and short leaseholds. When valuing leasehold investments complex gearing effects are much more suited to detailed cash-flow analysis rather than simple yield capitalisation.

5.3   Valuing contemporary property investments using ARY and DCF valuation techniques

At the end of the last section the case was made for using a DCF technique to value properties with particular investment characteristics that render the ARY technique inadequate. These characteristics include properties that are over-rented, let on short leases or on leases that contain break clauses. A DCF technique might also be employed to analyse transactions where properties have not been let at MR (perhaps because an incentive such as a rent-free period or capital inducement was offered) so that they can be used as comparable evidence. In all of these cases the overriding concern to the landlord is that the financial position is adequate for the option or incentive granted. The number of property investments subject to flexi-leases is increasing and Table 5.10 shows the percentage of tenancies monitored by IPD that were over-rented and void in 2004.

Table 5.10 Over-rented and void tenancies at the end of 2004 by market segment.

Market segment	% tenancies over-rented	% tenancies void
Standard shops	18.5	7.2
Central London	25.2	9.4
Rest of London	14.7	5.9
South East and Eastern	22.0	5.8
Rest of UK	15.6	7.4
Shopping centres	17.3	6.8
In-town	17.6	7.2
Out-of-town	15.5	4.3
Retail warehouses	6.8	4.8
Retail parks	7.1	4.0
Fashion parks	6.3	5.9
Other retail warehouses	6.3	6.4
Dept/variety stores	11.6	14.7
Supermarkets	10.7	5.3
Other retail	18.6	5.0
Standard offices	38.2	15.8
Central London	44.6	16.7
Rest of London	44.7	16.1
Inner South Eastern	54.4	15.2
Outer South Eastern	35.4	14.7
Rest of UK	20.5	14.6
Office parks	43.1	16.4
London and South Eastern	52.0	20.3
Rest of UK	27.6	9.4
Standard industrials	25.3	11.6
London	19.9	9.5
Inner South Eastern	27.5	11.2
Outer South Eastern	31.5	11.6
Rest of UK	23.0	12.4
Distribution warehouses	20.4	6.0
Other property	10.1	7.1
Leisure	14.4	11.0
All retail	16.1	6.7
All office	38.7	15.8
All industrial	25.1	11.5
All property	22.8	9.7

Source: IPD UK Digest (2005).

This section looks at how ARY and DCF valuation techniques can be used to value property investments subject to flexi-leases and over-rented properties.

5.3.1   Short leases and leases with break clauses

Short leases and leases with break options, collectively referred to as flexi-leases (see Chapter 4), mean greater diversity of lease contracts and increased uncertainty for investors. Will the tenant renew the short lease? If not will there be a rent void and how long might it be? What will the lease terms be and what will be the quality of the new tenant? Will a break option be exercised? All this uncertainty creates an income risk that an investor will wish to be compensated for in terms of price paid and the expected return. McAllister (2001) argues that the capital value of a contemporary property investment is dependent upon the cost and probability of the tenant vacating, a rent void occurring or the rent dropping, and the impact on value will depend on the length of the short lease, the structure of the break clause (specifically the terms of any penalty payment), the tenant's business plan and market factors (such as rental growth prospects and the state of the lettings market).

Before flexi-leases became commonplace homogeneity of lease contracts meant that, for property investment valuation, adjustments to initial yields of comparables to reflect geographical and physical differences could be justified. But now it is much harder to find comparables and justify small but often cumulative adjustments to the ARY because of the greater variety of possible differences between the subject property and each comparable. ARY adjustment is, therefore, an over-simplification and it is difficult to quantify and support; a more explicit approach is required to illustrate the reasoning behind the assumptions (Crosby *et al.*, 1998). The DCF technique allows assumptions to be made more clearly; the financial costs (and possible benefits) associated with the exercise of a break option or non-renewal of a lease and the possible void period that may follow for example. Research has revealed errors and a lack of consistency amongst valuers when valuing flexi-leases (see McAllister and O'Roarty, 1999; Ward and French, 1997). Valuers tend to focus on the worst-case scenario and assume that there will be a rent void at the end of the (short) lease or that a break option will be exercised. This is despite the fact that if the out-going tenant had to pay a penalty fee (equivalent to several months' rent) and a new tenant was found in the meantime the landlord may actually receive an income bonus. This conservative approach tends to undervalue flexi-leases and reduce their attractiveness to investors.

Consider the following example: a modern office property has just been let on a 15-year FRI lease at a MR of £50 000 per annum with no rent reviews. There is a break option in the tenant's favour in year 5, just before the rent review (to prevent the tenant from using it as a bargaining tool). Comparable evidence suggests that rack-rented office investments let on 15-year FRI leases with 5-year rent reviews to MR sell at prices that generate initial yields of around 7%. Long-term gilts currently yield 8% and a typical property risk premium is 2%. The inclusion of a break option clearly adds a degree of uncertainty to the income that the investor would receive after year 5. Indeed, an early break will have a greater impact on capital value than a later one due to the time value of money (Havard, 2000). Possible outcomes at the break are; the tenant exercises the break and a rent void follows, the break is exercised but there is no void, or the tenant continues in occupation. Faced with such uncertainty the valuer might increase the ARY slightly on the assumption that the break will definitely be exercised (French, 2001). Here the ARY has been increased from 7% to 8%.

MR (£)	50 000	
YP perpetuity @ 8%	12.5	
Valuation (£)		625 000

If the lease had no break option and was valued using a 7% yield the capital value would be £714 286, so the yield adjustment leads to a 12.5% reduction in value. This approach is simple and benefits from a direct relationship with comparable evidence, assuming there is a sufficient amount available, but it hides a lot of assumptions (Havard, 2000). Another approach might be a modified term and reversion valuation where the ARY is adjusted by a lesser amount and a rent void is incorporated in the cash-flow after the break. The valuer needs to be sure (via market evidence) that the void duration is realistic. An advantage of this approach is that different yields can be used for the existing and new leases (Havard, 2000) but, again, only if justified by market evidence. The valuation below incorporates a void period of 1 year after the break option in year 5 and, in order to avoid double-counting, the yield has only been adjusted upwards to 7.5%. Clearly this results in a more optimistic valuation.

MR – first lease (£)	50 000	
YP 5 years @ 7.5%	4.0459	
		202 950
MR – new lease (£)	50 000	
YP perpetuity @ 7.5%	13.33	
PV 6 years @ 7.5%	0.6480	
		432 000
Valuation (£)		634 950

It is useful to look at the level of rental growth as a guide to the likelihood of the rent dropping at the time a break option might be exercised. The short-cut DCF valuation is explicit about the target rate and the growth rate and accurately values each part of the income flow in a reversionary investment. Havard (2000) argues that the target rate would probably need to be increased to reflect the added risk associated with investing in a short lease. The problem is that there are now a lot of assumptions to make and this could lead to increased valuation variance. Similarly a full (year-by-year) DCF valuation is even more explicit about assumptions and therefore may lead to even greater valuation variance; changes to each key variable (growth rate, exit yield, target rate, void period, holding period) in isolation have little impact on the valuation but taken together they do (Havard, 2000). Assuming a TRR of 10% and an ARY of 7.5%, this implies a growth rate of 2.88% per annum. A full DCF valuation of a short lease with a break clause is shown below. On a standard lease a rent of £50 000 per annum and a yield of 7.5% would produce a valuation of £666 667.

Year	Net cash-flow (£)	Implied growth rate of 2.88%	Estimated cash-flow (£)	PV £1 @ target rate of 10%	Discounted income (£)
1	50 000	1.0000	50 000	0.9091	45 455
2	50 000	1.0000	50 000	0.8264	41 322
3	50 000	1.0000	50 000	0.7513	37 566
4	50 000	1.0000	50 000	0.6830	34 151
5	50 000	1.0000	50 000	0.6209	31 046
6	0	0.0000	0	0.0000	0
7	50 000	1.1857	59 286	0.5132	30 423
8	50 000	1.1857	59 286	0.4665	27 658
9	50 000	1.1857	59 286	0.4241	25 143
10	50 000	1.1857	59 286	0.3855	22 858
11	50 000	1.1857	59 286	0.3505	20 780
11-perp.	50 000	1.3666	911 065	0.3505	319 323
Valuation (£)		13.3333			635 723

A difficulty with these modified ARY and DCF approaches is their inability to handle the possibility that the break option is not exercised (or if it is and there is no rent void). Under this assumption, in terms of the cash-flow, the flexi-lease is no different from a standard lease but because of the yield adjustment and void assumption the landlord will receive a financial bonus in comparison to a standard lease. The problem is uncertainty; the cash-flow has been made more uncertain by the flexi-lease and this uncertainty has a price. The dilemma for the valuer is trying to estimate that price. One solution to this problem is to produce a range of valuations under different scenarios; the break clause is/is not exercised, the rent void does/does not occur, a void lasts for 6 months, 1 year, and so on. This leads to a lot of valuations and, as a way of summarising the various outcomes, probabilities could be assigned to them and a weighted average 'expected' valuation calculated (French, 2001). It is possible to extend this simple 'discrete' probability analysis into a continuous probability analysis using simulation or option pricing and we will look at these approaches in Section 5.4.

5.3.2   Over-rented property investments

Over-renting occurs when the rent payable under a lease with upward-only rent reviews exceeds the MR. Some valuers value **over-rented properties** as perpetual cash flows at the passing rent when the lease is long, contains upward-only rent reviews and no break clause. Because of the higher risk associated with the element of rent that exceeds the MR, known as the **over-age** or froth, other valuers use a layer (core and top-slice) approach, using an ARY based on rack-rented freehold comparables to capitalise the core rent (which is taken to be the MR at the time of the valuation) and a fixed income yield that reflects the covenant strength of the tenant to capitalise the top-slice or 'overage'.

For example, value a property let 4 years ago at a rent of £250 000 per annum on a 15 year lease with 5 year upward-only rent reviews. The current MR is £200 000 per annum. Comparable properties have recently sold for yields averaging 6%. Medium-dated gilts are yielding 5% and the investor's TRR for this property is 11%. The ARY (core and top-slice) valuation is as follows:

Core (market) rent (£)	200 000	
YP in perpetuity @ 6%	16.6667	
		3 333 340
Top-slice (overage) (£)	50 000	
YP 11 years @ 7%[a]	7.4987	
		374 935
Valuation (£)		3 708 275

[a]Gilt yield plus a 2% risk premium.

However, there are problems with this approach: first, the core rent is capitalised at an ARY that assumes 5 years to the next review but the property is reversionary and the growth potential is closer – consequently the approach over-values the bottom layer; second, there is a lack of evidence on which to base the overage yield; and third, no attempt has been made to estimate the length of time that the property will remain over-rented. To resolve the last problem many valuers capitalise the overage for the whole period that the tenant is contracted to pay it (Crosby and Goodchild, 1992). But if, as Martin (1991) points out, the MR grows each year and the overage reduces, the MR may overtake the contract rent before the end of the lease and part of the overage is capitalised twice – the property will be over-valued. This is illustrated in the Figure 5.4.

Even if the overage is capitalised until the first rent review after the MR overtakes the contract rent a (smaller) amount of double-counting still occurs. The layer approach is unable to calculate the corresponding reduction in the overage necessary to avoid this double-counting. One way to resolve this problem is to be explicit about growth in the rental income and project the MR at a growth rate to determine when it will overtake the contract rent. This growth rate can be implied from the relationship between the chosen ARY and target rate or it can be explicitly forecast. A DCF approach can then be used to capitalise the contract rent up to this cross-over point (or the next review thereafter) at the target rate and the uplifted MR is capitalised at an ARY from the cross-over point into perpetuity, discounted for the period of waiting, at the target rate – just like a short-cut DCF.

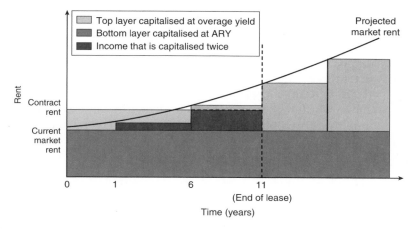

Figure 5.4 Over-rented property.

Continuing the example above, using a growth rate of 5.57% per annum, implied from the ARY of 6% and the target rate of 11%, the MR will grow to the following amounts at the next two rent reviews:

$$£200\,000 \times (1+0.0557)^1 = £211\,140$$

$$£200\,000 \times (1+0.0557)^6 = £278\,868$$

So the MR overtakes the contract rent between the first and second rent reviews and the growth-explicit short-cut DCF valuation is as follows:

Term (contract rent) (£)	250 000	
YP 6 years @ 11%	4.2305	
		1 057 625
Reversion to MR (£)	200 000	
FV 6 years @ 5.57%	1.3843	
YP in perpetuity @ 6%	16.6667	
PV 6 years @ 11%	0.5346	
		2 466 828
Valuation (£)		3 524 453

The valuation is lower than the layer approach above because the double-counting has not occurred and the use of a target rate to capitalise the term rent means that the problem of using a rack-rented ARY to value a bottom layer where the reversion is closer does not arise. A drawback of the growth-explicit DCF approach is the lack of comparable evidence to support the choice of rental growth rate and TRR which may need to be adjusted to reflect the covenant strength of the tenant, the length of the remaining lease term and the extent of the overage (Crosby, 1991). In between rent reviews rent is only subject to tenant (default) risk and if the contract rent is very high in comparison to MR for long periods (e.g. beyond the first rent review) then it is exposed to a greater degree of tenant risk. As such it may be more characteristic of a corporate bond-type investment issued by the tenant (Brown and Matysiak, 2000).

A property let at a headline rent is, in effect, over-rented and should, arguably, be valued as such. Revisiting the property described in the Section 4.2.1 on rent-free periods in Chapter 4, assume that a write-off period of 15 years (the lease term) is appropriate. This equates to a growth rate of 2.62% per annum which we can insert as an explicit growth rate into the capital valuation. If we also assume an ARY of 7% and a target rate of 10% the valuation of the freehold investment interest using a short-cut DCF technique would be as follows:

Headline rent (£)	200 000	
YP 13.5 years @ 10%	7.2382	
PV £1 1.5 years @ 10%	0.8668	
		1 254 814
Reversion to MR (£)	175 721	
FV £1 15 years @ 2.62% pa	1.4739	
YP perpetuity @ 7%	14.2857	
PV £1 15 years @ 10%	0.2394	
		885 763
Valuation (£)		2 140 577

To investigate the impact that the rent-free period has on capital value, assume the property has no rent-free period (apart from the normal fitting out period of 6 months), it is let at the real rent of £175 721 per annum (calculated in Chapter 4) and the ARY is 7%:

MR (£)	175 721	
YP perpetuity @ 7%	14.2857	
PV 0.5 years @ 7%	0.9667	
Valuation (£)		2 426 705

For the valuation of the property let at MR to equate to the DCF valuation of the property let with the rent-free period, the MR would have reduced from £175 721 to £155 002 per annum. So, because of the yield impact on capital value, incentives such as rent-free periods are preferable to reductions in the headline rent (Crosby and Murdoch, 1994).

Key points

- At the beginning of the twentieth century valuers would capitalise rent at an evidence-based initial yield. Initial yield evidence was obtained from the market and comparable to gilts plus a risk premium as there was no rental growth or inflation. By the mid-1970s rent reviews were introduced so that landlords could benefit from rising rents. The relationship between gilts and property yields was broken – property was now regarded as a growth

> **Key points** (continued)
>
> investment like equities but with a peculiar income growth pattern. A simple initial yield approach was no longer appropriate, particularly for valuations between reviews, therefore term and reversion, hardcore and top-slice and equivalent yield methods were devised.
>
> - Structural changes in the economy during the 1990s brought about by low inflation, increased uncertainty, changing business structure, developments in ICT and globalisation led to a decrease in lease lengths, increased use of break clauses and other options, plus increased use of incentives. All of this leads to more complex valuations. Investors may now be faced with two options; investing in much shorter leases with break clauses or investing in sale and leasebacks to corporate occupiers. The latter may be 25-to 35-year leases and on inflation-linked rent reviews.
> - In terms of valuation there are problems with the ARY technique when valuing properties let on flexi-leases, over-rented property and properties not let at MR due to inducements. A short-cut DCF technique solves many of the problems associated with the ARY technique and is mathematically consistent and explicit regarding the target rate and growth assumptions, at least until the first review. Its inputs are also largely derived from market evidence and should therefore produce a market valuation (Havard, 2000).
> - With a full DCF, more assumptions have to be made and reliance on simple market ratios and other information is reduced – the valuation starts to become an appraisal. Such a method may produce a wider variation of answers depending on the assumptions made. Consequently a full DCF may be appropriate when valuing complex properties with few comparables.

5.4   Advanced property investment valuation techniques for dealing with uncertainy in valuations

5.4.1   Valuation accuracy, variance and uncertainty

Because of the market imperfections and inefficiencies in the property market referred to in Chapter 1, the expertise and experience of a valuer is required to form an opinion of value based on an assessment of value-significant influences. These influences may change and therefore a valuation is not a permanent part of the property. Analysis of market data only suggests what happened in the past and it is for the valuer to interpret these data to assess current market value. Valuers do not operate with perfect market knowledge, they must follow client instructions, make judgements, analyse information and respond to different pressures when preparing a valuation and all these factors influence the final valuation figure. Values can be difficult to assess due to the heterogeneity of property and the number of transactions that occur at prices that do not represent market values. Although the profession has sought to enforce more rigorous mandatory standards and practice statements, backed by detailed guidance notes, valuations of the same property conducted by different valuers will not always be the same and the valuation(s) may not necessarily equate to the agreed exchange price. The disparity in valuations of the same property is referred to as valuation variance and the discrepancy between a valuation figure and the exchange price is referred to as valuation inaccuracy. Valuation uncertainty is a recently coined phrase used to acknowledge the fact that valuation variance and valuation inaccuracy are inevitable consequences of the valuation process and recent research has attempted to quantify the degree of uncertainty that surrounds valuation. Market conditions and the type and location of property investments will influence the degree of uncertainty. There have been a number of studies that have investigated the degree of valuation inaccuracy and extent of valuation variance that occurs in typical property investment valuations and the Royal Institution of Chartered Surveyors (RICS) has considered ways of reporting valuation uncertainty when it is deemed appropriate.

5.4.1.1   Valuation accuracy

Brown (1985) examined the accuracy of valuations by regressing valuations on exchange prices for 29 properties where the sale price and preceding valuation were known and found a high correlation between valuations and prices. In 1988 similar regression techniques[1] were applied to a much larger sample of 1442 valuations and sale prices taken from the IPD (IPD/Drivers Jonas, 1988). This study and its update (IPD/Drivers Jonas, 1990) both found that valuations and prices were highly correlated. There have, however, been criticisms of the statistical validity of the regression analysis in these studies, particularly in relation to the problem of heteroskedasticity[2] (Lizieri and Venmore-Rowland, 1991). A longitudinal study of the accuracy of valuations is now funded by the RICS and conducted using IPD data. In 2004 RICS and IPD conducted an analysis of 984 valuations and subsequent sale prices of properties in the IPD databank.[3] The overall average price-value difference was 9.5% and 79% of valuations were within 15% of sale prices (RICS, 2005). These results were similar to those achieved in the preceding 2 years of the study and it may be tempting to suggest that valuation accuracy has reached its ceiling, but the results could also be explained by the rapidly rising market conditions over the past 2–3 years and valuations, which are backward-looking, failing to keep pace. It should also be noted that the IPD databank typically contains prime assets for which market evidence might be expected to be more readily available and of a more consistent nature than for lower grade property investments where incentives might be prevalent. Force is added to this argument when the valuations are weighted by value; the variation was smaller, producing an average difference of 8.1% instead of 9.5%, suggesting that valuations of higher value properties have been closer to sale prices. Regression analysis was used to detect any bias in the data, such as a tendency to over- or under-value. According to the regression analysis of the IPD data over the past 5 years, valuers consistently under-value and there may be several explanations for this: the market value assumptions preclude bids by special purchasers, vendors may selectively dispose of properties when bids are received above the valuation figure, vendors actively 'present' properties for sale to enhance bids, the growth assumptions used in the analysis may not pick up rapid market movements, or valuers may be inherently conservative and backward-looking.

5.4.1.2   Valuation variance

Hagar and Lord (1985) conducted a small experiment on ten valuers to investigate how much their valuations of a sample of two properties varied and to test their hypothesis that the range would be ±5% around the average valuation. Actually Hagar and Lord did not calculate an average but asked a valuer with experience of valuing the two properties to perform 'control' valuations instead. Their results showed valuation variance much greater than ±5% but, due to the sample size, the results cannot be regarded as conclusive. Brown (1985) examined valuation variance by taking a sample of 26 properties which had been valued by two different firms of valuers over a 4-year period. It was found that the valuations from one firm were a good proxy for the valuations of the other and that there was no significant bias between the two firms' valuations. Hutchison *et al.* (1996) undertook research into variance in property valuation, involving a survey of major national and local firms. The average overall variation was found to be 9.53% from the mean valuation of each property. They also found evidence to suggest that valuation variation may be a function of the type of company that employs the valuer and, specifically, whether it is a national or local firm. The study revealed that national practices produced a lower level of variation (8.63%) compared with local firms (11.86%) perhaps due to the level of organisational support, especially in terms of availability of transactional information.

Over the last few years there has been a significant amount of research into the causes of valuation variance. Kinnard *et al.* (1997) found that valuers conducting valuations for lending purposes experienced significant pressure from certain types of client, especially mortgage brokers and bankers. Gallimore and Wolverton (1997) found evidence of bias in valuations resulting from knowledge of the asking price or pending sale price. Gallimore (1994) found evidence of confirmation bias where valuers make an initial valuation, 'anchor' to this estimate of value and then find evidence to support it. The initial opinion of value or asking price was found to significantly influence the valuation outcome. In a survey of 100 lenders, finance brokers, valuers and investors Bretten and Wyatt (2001) found that the majority of factors believed to cause variance related to the individual 'behavioural characteristics' of the valuer. Variance can enter the valuation process at any stage from the issuing of instruction letters and negotiation of fees through to external pressure being exerted on the valuer when finalising the valuation figure. Following the Carsberg Report (RICS, 2002) the RICS Red Book now contains strict guidelines to reduce the likelihood of external pressure and the adoption of quality assurance systems in the workplace can help maintain acceptable standards. For example, terms of engagement must include a statement of the firm's policy on the rotation of valuers responsible and a statement of the quality control procedures in place. If a property has been acquired within the year preceding the valuation and the valuer or firm has received an introductory fee or negotiated the purchase for the client, the valuer/firm shall not value the property unless another firm has provided a valuation in the intervening period.

The courts have adopted the margin of error concept (the legal manifestation of valuation variance) as a means of establishing whether a valuer has been negligent. It has been established in UK courts since the first case on this point (*Singer and Friedlander v John D Wood and Company, 1977*) that a margin of ±10% around the subsequent transaction price (or some other notion of 'correct' market value) would be permissible. Crosby *et al.* (1998) is the recognised authority on the findings that link valuation variance, margin of error and the legal position adopted by UK courts: 38 High Court valuation negligence cases between 1977 and 1998 in which the margin of error had been an issue were investigated and the authors found the majority of judgements on the size of the bracket lie at 10% (26.1%) and between 10% and 14.99% (30.4%). Three causes for this variation were suggested. First, expert witnesses are unfit to present themselves as 'experts'. Second, the margin of error principle and the 'brackets' applied are too onerous a test for negligence, indicating that the margin should be increased. Third and regarded as the most likely, is because expert witnesses are being 'influenced' to produce a valuation to suit their client's particular need. Crosby *et al.* (1998), noted that

> judges sometimes reach a finding as to the true value of the property in question which agrees entirely with the opinion expressed by one of the expert witnesses. On other occasions, the judge's ruling may fall somewhere between the figures which the opposing expert witnesses have proposed.

The 'correct' valuation is therefore arbitrary and raises concerns over the reliability of the margin of error principle as a test of negligence. It also confirms the occurrence of variance by virtue of the imprecision displayed by experts and the subsequent judgement deemed necessary by the court. The continuing adoption of the margin of error principle provides formal recognition of the inevitability of valuation variance. Crosby *et al.* (1998) concluded that

> the margin of error principle, as it is presently applied by the English courts, is lacking in any empirical basis and indeed runs counter to the available evidence. Its use as a means of establishing negligence by a valuer is fundamentally flawed.

The standard of conduct expected of a professional valuer is not onerous but the courts continually fail to examine the processes involved in the calculation of the valuation and focus instead on the outcome. The authors suggest that the margin of error should be used as an early warning rather than a test of negligence.

5.4.1.3 *Valuation uncertainty*

Guidance Note 5 of the RICS Appraisal and Valuation Manual (RICS, 2003) suggests that valuation uncertainty can arise because of the inherent features of the property, the market place or the information available to the valuer. The following are examples of where valuation uncertainty is likely to arise:

- If the location or the physical characteristics of the property are unusual;
- The property is of a type for which there is little or no comparable evidence;
- Because of the number of input variables, properties undertaken using the profits or residual methods are very sensitive to the underlying assumptions.

Despite acknowledging these cases of what the RICS terms 'abnormal uncertainty', the RICS does not see the need for a quantitative measure of the degree of valuation uncertainty that a valuer might ascribe to a valuation, such as a confidence statistic, a range, or a mean and standard deviation. Instead, the RICS considers that the single estimate valuation could be accompanied by a qualitative comment in cases where uncertainty is thought to materially affect the valuation. The comment would indicate the cause of the uncertainty and the degree to which it is reflected in the reported valuation. The valuer might also comment on the robustness of the valuation, perhaps noting the availability and relevance of comparable market evidence, so that the client can judge the degree of confidence that the valuer has in the reported figure. Only for some properties does the RICS consider it appropriate to express the valuation as a range between upper and lower limits but, if a valuer can reasonably foresee that different values may arise under different circumstances, a preferable approach would be to provide alternative valuations on the basis of special assumptions reflecting those different circumstances. On other occasions where uncertain market conditions or other variable factors could have a material impact on the valuation, it may be prudent to provide a sensitivity analysis to illustrate the effect that changes to these variables could have on the reported valuation. This will be particularly appropriate where a residual method has been used.

Rather than express valuation uncertainty qualitatively, Lizieri and Venmore-Rowland (1991) argued that a valuation should not be regarded as a single value but rather as a point estimate within a range of values. Lavers *et al.* (1996), on the other hand, found that, with regard to commercial property valuations for lending purposes, the majority of lenders wanted the valuation expressed as a single figure. French and Mallinson (2000) suggested that, as well as reporting abnormal uncertainty, being explicit about uncertainty under normal valuation conditions is also potentially very useful to clients and valuers and they list items of information which should be conveyed when reporting uncertainty: the valuation figure, range and probability of the most likely observation and any skewness in the probability distribution. This suggestion and the view of Lizieri and Venmore-Rowland was confirmed by the findings of Bretten and Wyatt (2001) who found support amongst valuers and their clients for the reporting of a valuation figure in the context of a range rather than a point estimate.

It is to these quantitative measures of valuation uncertainty that we now turn. The range of enhancements to property investment valuation approaches discussed so far presume that the future or, more accurately, valuers' expectations of the future, can be predicted with a high level of confidence. Yields, MRs, the exercising of break options and the lengths of void periods are all input as single estimates. If the future were that predictable life would be pretty boring. Fortunately it is not and we need to consider ways to reflect this in our valuation models – more so now than ever before because of the greater diversity of lease arrangements flexi-leases produce. The first thing to point out is that input variables in a valuation cannot always be selected as absolutes. We have already thought about this when considering what might happen at the end of a short lease or at a break option in a lease – something that happens more and more frequently nowadays, but there are other ways too. Some of the techniques described in the sub-sections below will be considered in greater detail in Chapter 6 when we look at development appraisal but we need to have a look at them here too because those same techniques are being applied to the valuation of existing property investments (standing investments) as well as to new developments.

5.4.2   Sensitivity analysis

Sensitivity analysis investigates the impact of uncertainty on key input variables such as rent, target rate, ARY and rental growth rate by examining the degree of change in the valuation caused by a pre-determined change in one or more of the key input variables. Usually a margin of 10–20% either side of the expected values of the key variables is tested to measure the effect on value. A more sophisticated analysis may apply more realistic variations to the key variables; for example, more upside variation in rent in a rising market. Or different positive and negative percentage changes may be applied depending on the variable; for example, plus or minus 10% for rental value and plus or minus 2% for rental growth. Sensitivity analysis does not consider the likelihood of particular outcomes and the input variables are usually altered one at a time. The technique tends to confirm what we already know; that, because the ARY is an *all-risks* yield, small movements in it lead to large shifts in the valuation, but the process does require the valuer to think about the realistic limits on shifts in the input variables and does produce a range of valuations within which the actual price would be expected to fall.

To help demonstrate how sensitivity analysis works, let's just recap on where we have got to in terms of valuing freehold rack-rented and reversionary property investments, because we will use these as a basis for what follows. Table 5.11 provides some initial input values for key variables relating to ARY and DCF valuation techniques.

Table 5.11   Key variables.

Market information	
All-risks yield (ARY)	8.00%
Market rent (£)	250 000
Explicit-growth rate	2%
Property information	
Years to reversion (term)	4
Term (contract) rent (£)	200 000
Rent-review period	5
Term and reversion method	
Term yield	7.00%
Reversion yield	8.00%
Equivalent yield method	
Equivalent yield	7.96%
Core and Top-slice method	
Core yield	8.00%
Top-slice yield	8.50%
DCF method (short-cut and full)	
Target rate of return	10.00%
Implied growth rate	2.33%
Exit yield	8.00%

The valuations below use the information provided in Table 5.11 to produce a series of single point estimate valuations. The first valuation is of a rack-rented freehold property investment.

MR (£)	250 000	
YP in perpetuity @ 8%	12.5000	
Valuation (£)		3 125 000

The next valuation uses the term and reversion approach to value a reversionary freehold property investment.

Term (contract) rent (£)	200 000	
YP for initial term of 4 years @ 7%	3.3872	
		677 442
Reversion to estimated MR (£)	250 000	
YP in perpetuity @ 8%	12.5000	
PV £1 4 years @ 8%	0.7350	
		2 296 968
Valuation (£)		2 974 411

The equivalent yield is then determined using spreadsheet interpolation ('Goal Seek' in Excel). The result is an equivalent yield of 7.96% and this yield can be fed back into the valuation as a check.

Term (contract) rent (£)	200 000
YP for initial term of 4 years @ 7.96%	3.3150
	662 995
Reversion to estimated MR (£)	250 000
YP in perpetuity deferred 4 years @ 7.96%	9.2457
	2 311 416
Valuation (£)	2 974 411

For the sake of completeness this reversionary freehold is also valued using a core and top-slice approach.

Core rent (£)	200 000
YP in perpetuity @ 8%	12.5000
	2 500 000
Top-slice: uplift to estimated MR (£)	50 000
YP in perpetuity @ 8.5%	11.7647
PV £1 4 years @ 8.5%	0.7216
	424 455
Valuation (£)	2 924 455

Then, moving from the ARY approaches to the DCF technique, the reversionary freehold is valued using the short-cut DCF approach.

Term (contract) rent (£)	200 000
YP for initial term of 4 years @ 10%	3.1699
	633 973
Reversion to estimated MR (£)	250 000
Compounded over 4 years @ 2.33% pa	1.0965
PV £1 4 years @ 10%	0.6830
YP in perpetuity @ 8%	12.5000
	2 340 481
Valuation (£)	2 974 454

And lastly the rack-rented freehold is valued using a full DCF.

Year	Net cash-flow (£)	Growth rate of 2.33%	Estimated cash-flow (£)	PV £1 @ target rate of 10%	Discounted income
1	250 000	1.0000	250 000	0.9091	227 273
2	250 000	1.0000	250 000	0.8264	206 612
3	250 000	1.0000	250 000	0.7513	187 829
4	250 000	1.0000	250 000	0.6830	170 753
5	250 000	1.0000	250 000	0.6209	155 230
6	250 000	1.1221	280 526	0.5645	158 349
7	250 000	1.1221	280 526	0.5132	143 954
8	250 000	1.1221	280 526	0.4665	130 867
9	250 000	1.1221	280 526	0.4241	118 970
10	250 000	1.1221	280 526	0.3855	108 155
10-perp	250 000	1.2591	3 934 728[a]	0.3855	1 517 008
Valuation (£)					3 125 000

[a]This is the projected rent capitalised in perpetuity at an exit yield of 8%, that is, (250 000 × 1.2591)/0.08.

We are going to concentrate on the reversionary investment first and look at the impact on the valuation of plus and minus 5% and 10% shifts in the MR estimate and the ARY estimate in the ARY equivalent yield model. We will then look at the same magnitude shifts in the target rate, MR and growth rate estimates in the short-cut DCF model. This sort of analysis can be set up on a spreadsheet and Table 5.12 shows the results of the downside or pessimistic shifts in the key variables using the ARY (equivalent yield) and Table 5.13 shows the results using the short-cut DCF.

So we can see how sensitive the valuations are to changes in these input variables. The ARY valuation is very sensitive to movements in the ARY whereas the DCF valuation is much less sensitive to changes in the target rate.

5.4.3   Scenario testing and discrete probability modelling

Scenario testing extends sensitivity analysis by taking a range of possible values for the key variables and combining them to produce a range of possible valuations. The difference between sensitivity analysis and scenario testing is that the latter examines the impact on value of changes to several variables simultaneously and therefore begins to give a more realistic representation

Table 5.12   Sensitivity analysis of reversionary freehold valuations (ARY equivalent yield).

Variable	Change (%)	Value change	Valuation	Change in valuation (%)
MR	−5	237 500	2 858 840	−3.89
	—	—	2 974 411	—
	−10	225 000	2 743 269	−7.77
	+5	8.36%	2 826 143	−4.98
ARY	—	—	2 974 411	—
	+10	8.76%	2 691 038	−9.53

Table 5.13   Sensitivity analysis of reversionary freehold valuations (short-cut DCF).

Variable	Change (%)	Value change	Valuation	Change in valuation (%)
TRR	+5	9.50	2 970 854	−0.12
	—	—	2 974 454	—
	+10	9.00%	2 967 146	−0.25
MR	−5	237 500	2 857 430	−3.93
	—	—	2 974 454	—
	−10	225 000	2 740 406	−7.87
Rental Growth	−5	2.21%	2 963 420	−0.37
	—	—	2 974 454	—
	−10	2.10%	2 953 408	−0.71

of how the key variables might respond to economic changes. It creates specific pictures (scenarios) of the future as a means of reflecting uncertainty. It is usual to test optimistic, realistic and pessimistic scenarios but special attention is paid by investors and lenders to the pessimistic scenario because, for obvious reasons, they are particularly concerned with the downside of the investment.

Let us look at the rack-rented freehold investment that has been valued using a full DCF model shown above. The rack-rent is £250 000 per annum, the target rate is 10%, the ARY (and exit yield) is 8% and the implied rental growth rate is 2.33% per annum. The valuation is £3 125 000. Now consider some discrete scenarios where the shifts in estimated MR, growth rate, ARY and exit yield shown in Table 5.14 are assumed.

This is an improvement on sensitivity analysis and allows the valuer to 'bookend' the valuation but it still does not give any idea of the likelihood that any of these discrete outcomes might actually occur. To do that we need to enter the scary world of probabilities! If we assign some measure of probability or likelihood to each scenario we could calculate a weighted average valuation. Take the three valuations in the scenario summary above, round them and add two more scenarios that fall in between the two extremes, as shown in Table 5.15. Note that neither the distribution of valuations nor the probabilities themselves have to be symmetrical about the middle or realistic valuation – in fact here we have a distribution of valuations that is skewed towards pessimism and a counter-balancing set of probabilities that are

Table 5.14   Scenario summary.

	Realistic	Optimistic	Pessimistic
Changing variables			
ARY (%)	8.00%	7.80%	8.20%
MR (£)	250 000	260 000	240 000
Growth rate (%)	2.33%	3.00%	1.50%
Exit yield (%)	8.00%	8.00%	9.00%
Valuation (£)	3 125 000	3 291 995	2 803 269

Table 5.15   Discrete scenarios with probabilities.

Scenarios	Valuations	Probability (%)	Weighted valuation (val'*n* × probability)
Pessimistic	2 800 000	2	2 800 000 × 0.02
Slightly pessimistic	3 000 000	18	3 000 000 × 0.18
Realistic	3 125 000	60	3 125 000 × 0.60
Quite optimistic	3 200 000	15	3 200 000 × 0.15
Optimistic	3 300 000	5	3 300 000 × 0.05
Weighted average valuation (£)	(Sum of weighted valuations)		3 116 000

Table 5.16 Risk and discrete probability modeling.

Property 1			Property 2		
Valuation (£)	Probability (%)	Weighted valuation	Valuation (£)	Probability (%)	Weighted valuation
2 800 000	2	56 000	−80 000	5	−4 000
3 000 000	18	540 000	2 000 000	20	400 000
3 125 000	60	1 875 000	3 500 000	50	1 750 000
3 200 000	15	480 000	3 700 000	20	740 000
3 300 000	5	165 000	4 600 000	5	230 000
Weighted average valuation (£)		3 116 000	Weighted average valuation (£)		3 116 000

skewed towards optimism. This highlights the main drawback with this type of analysis – a lack of objective market evidence on which to base selection of probabilities, even if the scenarios have been very carefully constructed.

The approach still relies on subjective assessments of scenarios and associated probabilities but the process does focus the mind on the likelihood of achieving predicted returns. For example, a prime shop property and an old factory may yield the same return but how likely is the latter to be achieved relative to the former? In other words, how risky is the return? Discrete probability modelling does not properly reflect the uncertainty or risk that might be associated with the expected cash-flows – it calculates an expected value rather than a measure of variation or uncertainty. To illustrate what this means, consider the property investment in Table 5.15 alongside another, these are named Property 1 and Property 2 in Table 5.16.

The weighted average valuations are identical and, at first glance, the most probable outcome for Property 2 is £3 500 000 compared to £3 125 000 for Property 1, but closer inspection reveals that the range (volatility) of valuations for Property 1 is £500 000 and for Property 2 it is £4 680 000 and with a 5% probability of making a loss! Clearly Property 1 is more attractive to the risk-averse investor. Such an extreme would rarely occur but it serves to make the point about the limitation of calculating a weighted average from a set of discrete outcomes.

5.4.4 Continuous probability modelling and simulation

It is unrealistic to assume a small number of discrete possible valuation outcomes. In reality there would be a range of outcomes best represented by a probability curve. If the frequency distributions or probability curves for predicted valuation outcomes for Properties 1 and 2 are assumed to be 'normally distributed' around the mean, Property 1 would have a narrower, more peaked curve indicating lower volatility whereas Property 2 would have a flatter, wider curve indicating higher volatility. Standard deviation measures this volatility; the smaller the standard deviation of a distribution the less volatile it is. See Appendix 5B (See Appendix 5B at www.blackwell-publishing.com/wyatt) for a little refresher on measures of central tendency, dispersion and probabilities.

Let's assume that we have asked 50 valuers to value Properties 1 and 2 from Section 5.4.2 and the mean valuation for Property 1 was £3 200 000 with a standard deviation of £500 000 and for Property 2 the mean valuation was £3 500 000 but with a much higher standard deviation of £1 000 000. The 'coefficient of variation' is a useful measure of volatility because it gives a percentage variance for one standard deviation either side of the mean and is useful for comparing projects whose expected values (means) are not equal. It measures dispersion relative to the mean. The coefficient of variation for Property 1 is 15.63% and for Property 2 it is 28.57%. Property 1 is less volatile by both standard deviation and coefficient of variation measures.

So far we have looked at assigning probabilities to the valuation outcomes but what about the values chosen for the key input variables? At the moment they are point estimates but could they not take one of a possible range of values with some more likely than others (Sayce *et al.*, 2006)? Would they not be better modelled as probability distributions? Now we enter a whole world of concurrent probability distributions of variables that might be correlated and our tiny little brains fail to cope with such complexity. We need computer power to help in the form of a simulation programme. Simulation enables valuers to assign probabilities to input variables in the valuation and run simulations of most likely combinations of values of these input variables in order to produce a probability distribution and associated confidence range for the output valuation. Statistics that quantitatively summarise the uncertainty surrounding the valuation output can then be calculated. Most notably these would include a mean valuation and a measure of dispersion, usually the standard deviation.

Simulation involves a series of steps:

Build a valuation model and identify key variables.   The valuation might be constructed using an ARY or DCF technique and the best estimates of the input variables are likely to be used when constructing the model. These input variables can be classified as either deterministic variables, which can be predicted with a high degree of certainty, or stochastic variables, which cannot be predicted with a high degree of certainty. Generally the stochastic variables that have a significant impact on the valuation are the ones on which simulation is likely to be run. Deterministic variables might include the rent review period, purchase and management costs. Key stochastic variables will include the ARY, MR, rental growth rate and exit yield. The TRR is unlikely to vary. When looking at flexi-leases in particular it may be wise to simulate different void periods and associated costs too.

Ascribe a range of probable values or probability distribution for each key input variable.   The key variables need to be represented as a probability distribution rather than a point estimate. A probability distribution is a device for presenting the quantified risk for the variable. Ideally the estimation of probability distributions for key variables would be based on empirical evidence but often the data are not available in a sufficient quantity to allow this. A pragmatic alternative is to gather opinions of possible values of each variable, along with their probability of occurrence, from experts. These expert opinions could then be used to select an appropriate probability function, of which there are many. The probability functions that are typically chosen are the continuous 'normal' distribution (in which case a mean and standard deviation would need to be specified) and the closed 'triangular' distribution (in which case the mode, minimum and maximum values would need to be specified). A useful characteristic of the triangular distribution is that, unlike the normal distribution, symmetry does not have to be assumed; the maximum and minimum values do not have to be equally spaced on each side of the mode. In this way the triangular distribution might offer a more realistic representation than the normal distribution if more upside or downside risk is expected.

The input variables may also be independent or dependent. An independent variable is unaffected by any other variable in the model whereas a dependent variable is determined in full or in part by one or more other variables in the model. Different degrees of interdependence can significantly affect the simulation result. It is therefore necessary to specify the extent to which the input variables are correlated. Sayce *et al.* (2006) note that significant research is needed in this area to establish an empirical base for correlation assumptions, particularly, as Byrne (1996) points out, correlations may be non-linear. This is especially pertinent in the case of development valuation, which we will look at in the next chapter, because, unlike the valuation of standing property investments, which typically involves a small number of key variables, development valuation can incorporate a large number of correlated input variables. McAllister (2001) points out that, in general, as correlation reduces, the mean and standard deviation increase, but this is not proportionate since the covariance also increases.

Run simulation.   Having selected the key variables and their probability distributions the simulation can begin. Simulation refers to the method whereby the distribution of valuation outcomes is generated by recalculating the valuation model many times, each time using different randomly sampled combinations of values from within the parameters of the probability distributions of the key stochastic variables.[4] In other words, because some values of key variables will have a greater probability of being achieved than others, the sample selection procedure ensures that these values are simulated more frequently. This simulation process determines the range and probability of the valuation outcome.

Output.   When setting up the simulation program the uncertain output variable in the valuation model would have been specified; invariably, this will be the valuation figure. The simulation results will provide information about the distribution of the output variable, including its central tendency (mean, median, mode), spread (range, standard deviation) and measures of symmetry (skewness) and peakedness (kurtosis). Regression analysis is also undertaken to rank the input variables in terms of their impact on the output valuation.

Let us look at two examples using the @RISK simulation software add-in to Microsoft Excel. The first example is a short-cut DCF valuation of a rack-rented freehold property investment recently let on conventional lease terms. Our best estimates of the key variables are an ARY/exit yield of 8%, a MR of £50 000 per annum and a rental growth rate of 2.5% per annum. An ARY valuation would produce a capital value of £625 000 and, assuming a TRR of 10%, a point estimate DCF valuation would generate a figure of £628 593 – a higher figure because the explicit growth rate of 2.5% was used instead of the rate of 2.33% implied by an ARY of 8% and a target rate of 10%.

MR (£)	50 000	
YP 5 years @ 10%	3.7908	
		189 539
Reversion to MR (£)	50 000	
Growth rate over 5 years @ 2.5%	1.1314	
	56 570	
YP in perpetuity @ 8%	12.5000	
PV £1 for initial term @ 10%	0.6209	
		439 054
Valuation (£)		628 592

We are now going to introduce some uncertainty into three key variables in the above valuation. The exit yield has a triangular distribution with a mode of 8%, a minimum value of 6.5% and a maximum of 9%. Both the MR and rental growth rate are normally distributed with a mean of £50 000 and standard deviation of £5000 in the case of the former and 2.5% and 1% respectively for the latter. Correlations between these variables are subjectively chosen and specified in Table 5.17.

The second example is an identical property but this time recently let on flexi-lease terms that incorporate a break option at the end of year 5. If we value this property using a short-cut DCF and assume a void of 1 year at

Table 5.17   Correlation matrix.

	ARY/exit yield	Market rent	Growth rate (explicit)
ARY/exit yield	1		
Market rent	−0.5	1	
Growth rate (explicit)	−0.5	0.5	1

the end of year 5 but keeping the values of all other variables the same, the valuation would be as follows:

Chapter 5

MR (£)	50 000	
YP 5 years @ 10%	3.7908	
		189 539
Void for 1 year		
Reversion to MR (£)	50 000	
Growth rate over 6 years @ 2.5%	1.1597	
	57 985	
YP in perpetuity @ 8%	12.5000	
PV £1 for initial term plus void @ 10%	0.5645	
		409 135
Valuation (£)		598 675

Clearly, uncertainty surrounds the exercise of the break option and so simulation can allow this uncertainty to be quantified by representing the length of any void period that may occur after the end of year 5 as a probability distribution, here based on a normal distribution with a mean of 1 year and a standard deviation of 1 year.

Ten thousand iterations were run and the valuation outputs from the conventional and flexi-leased properties are shown below. The optimistic skew of the exit yield distribution has increased the mean valuation of both properties approximately £15 000 above the original point estimates. In both cases the standard deviation around the mean was just under £100 000. Figure 5.5 and the skewness value in Table 5.18 reveal that both output distributions are positively skewed, the property let under standard lease terms slightly more so. This is because the exit yield, which is itself positively skewed, explains more of the variation in value of the standard let investment, as shown in Table 5.19.

The 'regression' columns in Table 5.19 report standardised regression (β) coefficients for the input variables. A coefficient of 0 indicated no significant relationship between the input and the valuation while a coefficient of +1 or

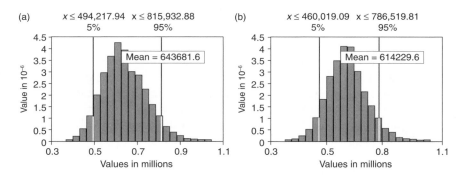

Figure 5.5 Valuation probability distributions: (a) distribution for valuation of standard lease and (b) distribution for valuation of flexi-lease.

Table 5.18 Summary statistics.

	Standard lease	Flexi-lease
Mean (£)	643 682	614 230
Std Dev (£)	98 214	99 581
Skewness	0.3573	0.3134
Kurtosis	3.1323	3.1511

Table 5.19 Sensitivity.

	Standard lease		Flexi-lease	
	Regression	Correlation	Regression	Correlation
Market rent	0.651	0.918	0.612	0.875
Exit yield	−0.314	−0.737	−0.290	−0.710
Growth rate (explicit)	0.224	0.686	−0.265	−0.220
Void period	—	—	0.247	0.681

−1 indicates a +1 or −1 change in the standard deviation of the valuation for a +1 or −1 change in the standard deviation of the input. The 'correlation' columns report Spearman's rank-order correlation coefficient which can also vary between −1 and +1. These two extremes would indicate a perfectly negative and a perfectly positive correlation respectively whereas a coefficient of 0 indicates no correlation at all. It is important to examine the signs of the coefficients to be sure that the correlation is in the right direction. If the R^2 value reported by the regression results is high the relationship between the input and output variables is linear. If the R^2 value is low the relationship is non-linear and rank-order correlation should be analysed to determine the sensitivity of the model. Remember, though, that this is an illustration and, because of the lack of evidence to support the correlations between the input variables, it should not be regarded as a practical application.

5.4.5 Arbitrage

Simulation techniques allow the impact of uncertainty surrounding key input variables to be examined. One variable was not considered to be uncertain, however, and this was the TRR. The assumption was that the investor would know what this was and would stick to it. But what if the target rate is not set in stone over the holding period for the investment? Different portions of forecast cash-flows – the rent agreed for the first 5 years and the rent agreed at the first rent review for example – may have different levels of risk and therefore different target rates (Appraisal Institute, 2001). To consider the valuation implications of this we can use an option pricing technique known as arbitrage.[6]

The arbitrage valuation technique was first applied to property investment by French and Ward (1995) and is based on the premise that each part of a cash-flow from any investment should be valued by comparing it with other assets with similar risk characteristics (Havard, 2000): think of how you might 'lay off' a bet. Like the short-cut DCF valuation technique, when applied to property, the arbitrage valuation technique adopts a term and reversion approach. But, instead of using a yield based on property risk factors to capitalise the term income, the arbitrage approach uses a low discount rate that is based on tenant risk factors. In other words the term income is regarded as comparable to income from an illiquid bond based on the tenant's default risk. The value at reversion is based upon the capitalisation of the rent at an ARY, representing a notional sale at this point. The arbitrage technique differs from the short-cut DCF technique in its approach to the deferral of this notional sale value and the rental value on which it is determined.

The short-cut DCF technique uses a constant (average) growth rate to project the MR at the review date and a single target rate to discount all cash-flows, and this can distort the risk profile into the future by putting less relative weight on distant cash-flows (Crosby, 1996). The arbitrage approach questions the appropriateness of using a single target rate and suggests that it should be based on debt and equity components of the financing package used to purchase the investment. French and Ward (1995) derive two target rates that can be used to discount the term and reversion components of a reversionary property investment. Two rates are justified on the basis that the term income is known and therefore certain, whereas future reversions must be estimated. From the tenant's viewpoint the term rent is certain over the initial term and so the financial liability is equivalent to interest payments on any fixed income loan and can therefore be valued using a discount rate appropriate for such payments. From the landlord's viewpoint an additional risk premium might be appropriate to reflect illiquidity and tenant default risk.

Consider a rack-rented freehold property investment let at £100 000 per annum and for which the ARY is 8%. From the tenant's perspective there is a contractual obligation to pay £100 000 per annum rent for the first 5 years. If the bank lending rate is 10% per annum, then

$$£100\,000 \times \text{YP 5 years @ 10\%} = £379\,079.$$

In valuing the second term the tenant is not certain of the rent in 5 years' time but needs to estimate the amount that should be invested now to provide funds to offset the rent liability when known. Arbitrage principles suggest that the tenant should find an asset with the same risk characteristics as the rent liability and then value the second term by investing in that asset at today's price. The arbitrage investment is to invest in a similar freehold and, to match the liability of the second 5-year term, the tenant would notionally invest in the proportion of the freehold which would provide the first 5 years of rent, that is, £379 079/£1 250 000[7] or 30.326% of the value of the freehold. This notional investment is 'held' for 5 years and then 'sold'.

Whatever the value of the freehold the sum realised will, assuming constant yields and rates, be sufficient to offset the financial liability of the second term. So if the tenant owns 30.326% of the freehold he would receive 30.326% of the rent each year, that is, £30 326 per annum which, when capitalised for 5 years at 10%, equals £114 961. The total cost of the investment is therefore £379 079 - £114 961 = £264 118. This process can be repeated to value subsequent terms but if, as French and Ward (1996) suggest, we assume that the arbitrage valuation must equal a more conventional valuation then we can use the following formula to derive a reversion rate known as the 'deferred capital yield' (DCY) either by iteration or by formula.

By iteration.   A conventional ARY valuation of the property, assuming an ARY of 8% and a MR of £100 000 per annum, would produce a capital value of £1 250 000. This valuation needs to be broken down to differentiate the target rates used to capitalise the known and unknown cash-flows. As before, assume a discount rate of 10% for the known rent over the first 5 years. Knowing the capital value of the cash-flow over the first 5 years (£379 080), the overall valuation (£1 250 000) and that the rent on reversion will be capitalised into perpetuity at ARY of 8%, it is possible to calculate the appropriate DCY by iteration (Havard, 2000).

Term (£)	100 000	
YP 5 years @ 10%	3.7908	
		379 080
Reversion (£)	100 000	
YP perpetuity @ 8%	12.5000	
PV £1 5 years @ 7.49%[a]	0.6967	
		870 920
Valuation (£)		1 250 000

[a] Rate obtained by iteration

By formula.

$$1 + DCY = Term \sqrt{\frac{1}{1 - (r_a \cdot YP \ term, \ r_f)}} \qquad [5.13]$$

where Term = period to revision

$$r_a = ARY$$

$$r_t = low\text{-}risk \ TRR$$

Substituting the values as above into Equation 5.11 the DCY is 7.49% (French and Ward, 1996).

To recap, the arbitrage valuation technique is based on the assumption that the value of the whole is equal to the sum of the term and reversion

Chapter 5

components. The capital value of the unknown rent after the first review is calculated by capitalising the term rent using a low-risk yield and deducting this from the total capital value of the subject property or a comparable. The resultant reversionary value can be analysed for the DCY. An arbitrage valuation thus proceeds as follows:

$$PV = (CR \times YP \text{ for term}) + (MR \times YP \text{ in perpetuity} \times PV \text{ for term})$$

$$= \left[CR \times \left(\frac{1-(1+r_t)^{-n}}{r_t} \right) \right] + \left[\frac{MR}{r_a(1+DCY)^n} \right] \qquad [5.14]$$

where

    CR = contract rent for term
    MR = Market rent
    r_t = TRR
    n = period to next rent revision

French and Ward (1996) show how the arbitrage method can also be applied to the valuation of reversionary property investments. A comparable (but this time reversionary) freehold property investment let one year ago at £80 000 per annum has been valued using a short-cut DCF technique. The target rate is 12% and the ARY is 8%, giving an implied rental growth rate of 4.63% per annum.

Term rent (£)	80 000	
YP 4 years @ 10%	3.1699	
		253 590
Reversion to MR	100 000	
PV 4 years @ 7.494%	0.7490	
YP perpetuity @ 8%	12.5000	
		936 190
Valuation (£)		1 189 780

However, the DCF approach still fails to recognise the different risk profiles of the known and unknown cash-flows. Using the DCY calculated above for the rack-rented comparable, the arbitrage valuation is

Term rent (£)	80 000	
YP 4 years @ 12%	3.0373	
		242 984
Reversion to MR	100 000	
Growth @ $(1.0463)^4$	1.1985	
PV 4 years @ 12%	0.6355	
YP perpetuity @ 8%	12.5000	
		952 058
Valuation (£)		1 195 042

This is a growth-implicit arbitrage valuation. A growth-explicit arbitrage valuation can be produced by inflating the DCY at the implied rental growth rate g (4.63%) to produce a capital yield (CY) as follows:

$$(1 + CY) = (1 + DCY) \times (1 + g) \qquad [5.15]$$
$$(1 + CY) = 1.07494 \times 1.0463$$
$$CY = 12.47\%$$

And the valuation would be as follows:

Term (£)	80000	
YP 4 years @ 10%	3.1699	
		253590
Reversion (£)	100000	
Growth @ 4.63% pa	1.1985	
YP perpetuity @ 8%	12.5000	
PV £1 4 years @ 12.47%	0.6250	
		936328
Valuation (£)		1189918

Table 5.20 compares full growth-explicit DCF valuations of the reversionary property investment assuming (1) target rates based upon arbitrage principles and (2) a constant TRR.

Table 5.20 Growth-explicit DCF and arbitrage valuations.

Year	Rent (£)[a]	(1) Arbitrage YP	PV (£)	(2) DCF YP @ 12%	PV (£)
0–3	80000	4 years @ 10% = 3.1699	253589	4 years @ 12% = 3.0373	242987
4–8	119859	5 years @ 10% discounted @ 12.47% for 4 years = 2.3687	283912	5 years @ 12% discounted @ 12% for 4 years = 2.2909	274584
9–13	150316	5 years @ 10% discounted @ 12.47% for 9 years = 1.3159	197812	5 years @ 12% discounted @ 12% for 9 years = 1.300	195399
14–18	188514	5 years @ 10% discounted @ 12.47% for 14 years = 0.7310	137823	5 years @ 12% discounted @ 12% for 14 years = 0.7376	139049
19–23	236418	5 years @ 10% discounted @ 12.47% for 19 years = 0.4061	96026	5 years @ 12% discounted @ 12% for 19 years = 0.4185	98950
24–perp	296495	Perp @ 8% discounted @ 12.47% for 24 years = 0.7441	220629	Perp @ 12% discounted @ 12% for 24 years = 0.8235	244163
Valuation (£)			1189791		1195132

[a]Growing at 4.63% per annum.
Source: French and Ward (1995).

Although the valuations are roughly the same, the values of each term differ. The arbitrage value for the first term is higher because the income is discounted at the low-risk yield of 10% rather than the uniform target rate of 12%. Then, in the arbitrage approach, subsequent terms are discounted at 12.47% rather than 12%. It could be argued that if the rent passing was significantly below MR the discount rate applied to the term could be even lower to reflect the reduced risk of tenant default. The arbitrage approach thus requires consideration of the risk profile of the term and reversion incomes. When valuing rack-rented freeholds both approaches will produce the same answers.

The arbitrage method of property valuation has not been widely adopted in practice. The selection of an appropriate target rate for the known initial term rent is subjective (French and Ward, 1996) and the technique still requires good comparable evidence, although not so much if the period to reversion is long and therefore a significant part of the rental value is capitalised at a bond rate (Havard, 2000). Simulation and arbitrage valuation techniques push the boundaries of market data analysis to the limits. That is no reason to dismiss them; rather it should act as a spur to the continued improvement of property data so that these techniques may be developed and refined.

Key points

- Valuation variance has been identified in empirical studies of valuation practice. The courts accept that a degree of variance is inevitable through the adoption of the margin of error principle. To an extent, because of the expert witness process in the courts, it is axiomatic that valuers also accept the existence of valuation variance. Indeed, Crosby *et al.* (1998) state that the margin of error principle was conceived by expert witnesses who are, by definition, experienced valuers.
- A valuation accuracy of 100% is an unattainable goal. Annual research funded by the RICS helps quantify the extent of valuation inaccuracy and demonstrates a degree of openness that is to be applauded. Only by learning more about the nature and extent of valuation inaccuracy, can methods to deal with valuation uncertainty be developed.
- Simulation is a logical extension of sensitivity analysis, scenario testing and discrete probability modelling that adds a quantitative measure of risk to a single point estimate of value. It does this by assigning probability distributions to key input variables. The drawback with this type of analysis at the moment is the lack of evidence on which to base these distributions and any correlations between them. Nevertheless, the discipline of building a 'risk aware' simulation model can lead to a deeper understanding of the nature of the property investment under consideration.
- Short-cut DCF and arbitrage approaches go some way to assigning the correct value of to various parts of the cash-flow but do not address the issue of volatility of future cash-flows.

Chapter 5

Notes

1. Ordinary least squares but this time regressing price on value, normalising for size by using price or value per unit area as last time but, unlike Brown, using these in their untransformed state rather than taking logs.
2. When using statistical techniques such as ordinary least squares regression a number of assumptions are typically made. One of these is that the error term has a constant variance. This will be true if the observations of the error term are assumed to be drawn from identical distributions. Heteroskedasticity is a violation of this assumption.
3. The valuations were adjusted for market movement between the valuation date and sale agreement date by increasing or decreasing the valuation according to movements in the IPD capital growth index for the relevant market sector. Percentage difference between valuation and sale price was found by applying the following formula: Difference = (price − adjusted valuation)/price.
4. Havard (2000) provides a useful illustration of how this process works in the case of two variables; annual rental growth rate and exit yield to which discrete probabilities have been assigned. The simulation programme randomly selects from the cumulative probability distribution for each variable. If we assume 22 was randomly selected for rental growth and 67 for the exit yield this would equate to 3% rental growth rate and an exit yield of 9.25%. These sample values are then input into an iteration of the valuation model.
5. Rank-order correlation calculates the relationship between two data sets by comparing the rank of each value in a data set. To calculate rank, the data are sorted from lowest to highest and assigned numbers (ranks) that correspond to their position in the order.
6. Arbitrage refers to the activity of market traders who compare the prices of similar assets, selling or buying to realise profits if the prices are out of line with one another. The principle is best known in foreign exchange markets.
7. Market rent of £100 000 per annum capitalised at an assumed freehold ARY of 8%.

References

Appraisal Institute (2001) *The Appraisal of Real Estate*, 12th Edn, The Appraisal Institute, Chicago, IL' USA.

Baum, A. (2000) *Commercial Real Estate Investment*, Chandos, Oxford, UK.

Baum, A. and Crosby, N. (1995) *Property Investment Appraisal*, 2nd edn, Routledge, London, UK.

Bretten, J. and Wyatt, P. (2001) Variance in commercial property valuations: an empirical study, *Journal of Property Investment and Finance*, 19, 3, 267–282.

Brown, G. (1985) Property investment and performance measurement: A reply, *Journal of Valuation*, 4, 1, 33–44.

Brown, G. and Matysiak, G. (2000) *Real Estate Investment: A Capital Market Approach*, FT Prentice Hall, Harlow, Essex, UK.

Byrne, P. (1996) *Risk, Uncertainty and Decision-making in Property Development*, 2nd edn; E. and F. N. Spon, London, UK.

Crosby, N. (1990) The practice of property investment appraisal: reversionary freeholds in the UK, *Journal of Property Valuation and Investment*, 9, 109–122.

Crosby, N. (1991) Over-rented freehold property valuations, *Journal of Property Valuation and Investment*, 10, 517–524.

Crosby, N. (1996) Valuation and arbitrage: a comment, *Journal of Property Research*, 13, 211–220.

Crosby, N., Lavers, A. and Murdoch, J. (1998) Property valuation variation and the 'margin of error' in the UK, *Journal of Property Research*, 15, 4, 305–330.

Crosby, N. and Goodchild, R. (1992) Reversionary freeholds: problems with over-renting, *Journal of Property Valuation and Investment*, 11, 67–81.

Crosby, N. and Murdoch, S. (1994) Capital valuation implications of rent-free periods, *Journal of Property Valuation and Investment*, 12, 2, 51–64.

Fraser, W. (1993) *Principles of Property Investment and Pricing*, 2nd edn, Macmillan, Basingstoke, Hampshire, UK.

French, N. (2001) Uncertainty in property valuation: the pricing of flexible leases, *Journal of Corporate Real Estate*, 3, 1, 17–27.

French, N. and Mallinson, M. (2000) Uncertainty in property valuation, *Journal of Property Investment and Finance*, 18, 1, 13–32.

French, N. and Ward, C. (1995) Valuation and arbitrage, *Journal of Property Research*, 12, 1–11.

French, N. and Ward, C. (1996) Applications of the arbitrage method of valuation, *Journal of Property Research*, 13, 47–56.

Gallimore, P. (1994) Aspects of information processing in valuation judgement and choice, *Journal of Property Research*, 11, 2, 97–110.

Gallimore, P. and Wolverton, M. (1997) Price-knowledge-induced bias: A cross-cultural comparison, *Journal of Property Valuation and Investment*, 15, 3, 261–273.

Hagar, D. and Lord, D. (1985) The property market, property valuations and property performance measurement, *Journal of the Institute of Actuaries*, (112, Part, 1), No 450, 19–60.

Havard, T. (2000) *Investment Property Valuation Today*, Estates Gazette, London, UK.

Hutchison, H., MacGregor, B., Nanthakumaran, N., Adair, A. and McGreal, S. (1996) *Variations in the Capital Valuations of UK Commercial Property*, Research Report, Royal Institution of Chartered Surveyors, London, UK.

Kinnard, W., Lenk, M. and Worzala, E. (1997) Client pressure in the commercial appraisal industry: how prevalent is it? *Journal of Property Valuation and Investment*, 15, 3, 233–244.

IPD/Drivers Jonas (1988) *The Variance in Valuations*, Drivers Jonas, London, UK.

IPD/Drivers Jonas (1990) *The Variance in Valuations*: 1990 Update, Drivers Jonas, London, UK.

IPF (2005) *Understanding Commercial Property Investment: A Guide for Financial Advisers*, 2005 Edition, Investment Property Forum, London, UK.

IVSC (2005) *International Valuation Standards*, 7th edn. International Valuation Standards Committee, London, UK.

Lavers, A., Williams, M., Crosby, N. and Foster, H. (1996) *Commercial Property Loan Valuations: Liability, Process and Changes*, Cutting Edge Conference, Royal Institution of Chartered Surveyors, London, UK.

Lizieri, C. and Venmore-Rowland, P. (1991) Valuation accuracy: a contribution to the debate, *Journal of Property Research*, 8, 115–122.

Martin, D. (1991) Valuation: over-rented property, Estates Gazette, December 7, 52

McAllister, P. (2001) Pricing short leases and break clauses using simulation methodology, *Journal of Property Investment and Finance*, 19, 4, 361–374.

Chapter 5

McAllister, P. and O'Roarty, B. (1999) Pricing Break Clauses: a Fundamental Approach, Proceedings of the RICS 'Cutting Edge' Property Research Conference, Royal Institution of Chartered Surveyors, London, UK.

RICS (2002) The Carsberg Report on Property Valuations, Royal Institution of Chartered Surveyors, London, UK.

RICS (2003) *RICS Appraisal and Valuation Standards*, 5th edn. (as amended), Royal Institution of Chartered Surveyors, RICS Business Services Ltd, Coventry, UK.

RICS (2005) Valuation and Sale Price, 2005 report, Royal Institution of Chartered Surveyors, London, UK.

Sayce, S., Smith, J., Cooper, R. and Venmore-Rowland, P. (2006) *Real Estate Appraisal: from Value to Worth,* Blackwell Publishers, Oxford, UK.

Sykes, S. (1981) Property Valuations: a rational model, *The Investment Analyst*, 61, 20–26.

Syms, P. (1996) Contaminated land and other forms of environmental impairment: an approach to valuation, *Journal of Property Valuation and Investment*, 14, 2.

Ward, C. and French, N. (1997) The valuation of upward-only rent reviews: an option pricing model, *Journal of Property Valuation and Investment*, 15, 2, 171–182.

Chapter 5

Chapter 6
Property Development Valuation

6.1 Introduction

The need for development arises in three situations; where new buildings are to be created on previously undeveloped or 'greenfield' land (new development), where existing buildings on vacant/derelict or 'brownfield' sites are to be replaced by new structures (redevelopment) and where existing buildings are to be substantially converted or modernised (refurbishment). The generic term **development** will be used for all of these situations. Redevelopment sites compete with new development sites for potential uses. New or 'greenfield' development sites may have the advantage of being clear of any previous development but redevelopment sites often benefit from existing infrastructure and services. In the UK there is a strong political impetus to redevelop brownfield sites in favour of developing greenfield ones.

Our primary concern in this chapter is with property development from the financial perspective of the **developer**. Development activity is a highly visible, often intrusive process that is responsible for creating a landscape that influences the way that we interact with each other and with the built and natural environment. But we need to remain focused on the financial economics of development here because that is where valuation fits in to the process of development. Development valuations differ markedly from other areas of valuation, principally because the properties being valued do not yet exist. The process, therefore, needs to appraise the financial viability of increasing supply. The main concerns of the developer are how much should be paid for the development site, what will the construction costs be and what profit might be expected? For the development of a particular piece of land or site to be economically viable, the value of the completed development less all expenditure on land, construction and profit, must exceed existing use value. This concept was introduced in Chapter 3 where the residual method of valuation was described. In this chapter, we advance the idea of valuing a development site to appraise the level of profit generated. This will determine whether the proposed scheme will provide the developer with an acceptable return. The chapter will therefore extend the conventional residual method of valuing development sites to consider how it can be adapted to help assess profitability. By doing so, we make our first journey into the world of worth appraisal, a theme that will be the focus of the next and final chapter.

Development, it should be noted, is always a risky business because there are many things that can go wrong or at least work out differently to the initial plan. Management or control of the level of risk taken is, therefore, an important part of the valuation process and ways in which risk can be managed during the various stages of the development are also considered in this chapter. Finally, discounted cash-flow techniques are investigated because, once the initial feasibility has been established, a more detailed financial assessment is usually required not only by the developer but also by the lender (who may be financing the development) and the investor (who may be acquiring the scheme on completion). Being able to identify the cash-flow at any point in time during a development project has obvious advantages over the 'snap-shot' estimate produced by a residual valuation.

6.2   The economics of property development

6.2.1   Property development activity

The development or supply of new commercial property resulting from activity in the development sector adds only a tiny fraction to the existing stock of commercial property each year. We learnt in Chapter 1 that this helps explain why property exchange prices and their associated valuations are largely explained by demand-side factors. Supply-side factors (the supply of new developments) have little impact on overall stock availability. Remember, property is a durable good. Figure 6.1 shows the Government's analysis of the age of rateable hereditaments in England and Wales. The substantial increase in supply that resulted from the property boom in the late 1980s is clear to see, as is the subsequent sharp drop in building activity shortly thereafter, when the market went into deep recession. Throughout the 1990s and the first few years of the new millennium, activity has increased steadily in most sectors, driven principally by office development.

Table 6.1 focuses on commercial development activity in 2004, the latest year for which figures are currently available. Approximately 9500 hereditaments were built that year and the total number of existing hereditaments as on 1 April 2005 was approximately 1.4 million. If development activity was to continue at this rate it would take around 150 years to completely replace the existing stock. In terms of floor-space it would take around 100 years. Clearly then it is price signals from the buying and selling of investments and occupational interests in the *existing* stock that influence the supply of and demand for *new* stock.

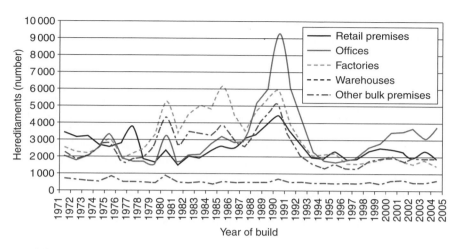

Figure 6.1   Year of build of bulk-class hereditaments in England and Wales, 1971–2004 (Commercial and Industrial Rateable Value and Floor-Space Statistics 2005).

Table 6.1   Bulk class hereditaments and floor-space newly built in 2004.

	Retail	Office	Factory	Warehouse	Other	Total
Number of hereditaments newly built in 2004	1838	3714	1458	1909	570	9489
Total number of hereditaments as at 1 April 2005	548221	324981	262156	200895	59194	1395447
Proportion of new to existing hereditaments	0.34%	1.14%	0.56%	0.95%	0.96%	0.68%
Floorspace newly built in 2004 (000 m²)	1188	1477	911	2199	192	5967
Total floorspace as at 1 April 2005 (000 m²)	103095	97895	220392	149007	20203	590592
Proportion of new to existing floor-space	1.15%	1.51%	0.41%	1.48%	0.95%	1.01%

Source: Commercial and Industrial Rateable Value and Floor-Space Statistics (2005).

6.2.2   Type and density of property development

As demand for urban property increases it becomes worthwhile to pay more for land (land rent increases) to avoid the rising expense of building on the existing site more intensively. This increased demand (and increased land rent) will stimulate supply in the form of new construction in the development sector. Sub-marginal land might become marginal (break-even) or even super-marginal (profit-making) if demand increases sufficiently. This process is subject to the principle of diminishing returns which can be delayed by more efficient use of the land, perhaps by using technology to use the land more intensively by building upwards. If the fixed unit of land is expensive or less marginally productive in comparison with the variable units of capital then a developer will employ more capital on the fixed unit of land, use it more intensively in other words, perhaps by building at a higher plot density – a high-rise building for example. This is why land in the city centre is more intensively developed than land in more peripheral urban locations (Fraser, 1993).

Marshall (1920) was the first economist to consider how the principle of diminishing returns may be applied to the intensity of development on an urban site. If a site has no scarcity value the amount of capital employed per unit area which would yield the maximum return varies with the use to which the site is put. So the use that yields the maximum return for a given amount of capital per unit area will tend to be the use to which the site is put, all other things being equal. But when the site has scarcity value it may be worthwhile to go on applying capital beyond this maximum rather than pay the extra cost of land required for extending the site. In places of high levels of scarcity (and therefore high land value) this intensified use of land will be much greater than on sites used for similar purposes but where land is less scarce (and therefore of lower value). Marshall used the phrase 'margin of building' for that floor-space which it is only just worth adding to a site and which would not be added if the land were less scarce. The example he used was the top floor of a building; by erecting this floor instead of building on extra land a saving equivalent to the cost of that land is effected which just compensates for the expense of constructing the extra floor. In a nutshell, if land is cheap a developer will take much of it and if it is expensive he will take less and build higher. So a combination of things is going on: competition between different land uses ensures that land is used in its most efficient way (maximising return for a given amount of capital per unit area) up to the margin of building at which point it is no longer profitable to apply more capital to the same site. Referring back to Chapter 1, we are considering land use intensity from the point of view of new development activity rather than intensifying an existing use.

Fraser (1993) illustrated Marshall's ideas in a diagram similar to that shown in Figure 6.2. A characteristic that makes property development so exciting – if not risky – is that every scheme is different but, to illustrate the underlying economic principles, consider an 'average' development project as follows. The marginal cost (MC) curve shows the additional cost for each extra unit of floor-space added to a site of fixed size. At low density levels, there are economies of scale to be reaped by adding more floor-space so that the cost per unit of floor-space initially falls; consider the cost saving per unit of floor-space that might be gained by building two storeys instead of one. After a certain point, however, it becomes progressively more expensive to add more floor-space to the fixed amount of land. For example, a high-rise building will need bigger foundations, faster lifts and so on. The time taken to build it will be longer so finance costs will be higher. Moreover, the uncertainty over what the market will be like at the time of completion will be greater and this will mean that the risk and hence profit required by the

Chapter 6

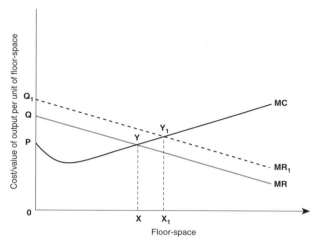

Figure 6.2   Optimum development density (Fraser 1993).

developer will be higher. All of this means that the cost of adding each extra unit of floor-space increases. The marginal revenue (MR) curve is the addition to revenue or development value that is obtained from the completed development for each additional unit of floor-space. It slopes downwards because the principle of diminishing returns means that users of the property will obtain less and less utility for each additional unit of floor-space. The highest value space is usually found on the ground floor – that is why retail users outbid all other commercial users – and the rent per square metre on upper floors may well be less than on the lower floors. Fraser (1993) shows that the optimum amount of floor-space is OX units of accommodation and the area bounded by PQY represents the price the developer would pay for the site, that is the capital value of the site for this particular development.

Harvey and Jowsey (2004) also reiterate Marshall's ideas and note that by building higher the developer is effectively saving on land cost. Consequently a developer will only build more intensively so long as it is cheaper than acquiring extra land. So there is a margin of building in terms of the intensity of use of each piece of land (or density of development) and the extent to which additional land is used. Under free market conditions competition for land between different developers ensures that, in the long run, development everywhere will be pushed to the point where MR is equal to MC of capital.

Fraser (1993) extends his analysis of development density by demonstrating that site values and development density are affected by changes in costs and revenue. For example, an increase in property values will cause the marginal revenue to increase to MR_1, raising the optimum density to OX_1 and increasing site value to Q_1Y_1P. Fraser also argues that the diagram can be used to explain differences in site value and building density that are observed in different locations. Quite simply, if more revenue can be obtained from a particular site, perhaps because of its accessibility advantages in a city centre for example, then its marginal revenue will be higher at say MR_1. The value and development density of such a site will be high. A less accessible site on the edge of town would yield less marginal revenue at say MR and its value and density of development will be lower.

The type of development that is allowed to take place on a site and the intensity to which that site is developed is not determined solely by free market economics; they are regulated by planning policy and development control. Evans (1985) demonstrated how Government controls intervene to determine land use independently of the market. Landowners may also dictate the type, density and timing of development.

6.2.3　The timing of redevelopment

According to Fraser (1993) there are two conditions necessary for property development to be economically viable, assuming developers and landowners seek to maximise profit. First, expected development value must exceed development costs, including the price of the land and the developer's profit, and second, development site value must be at least the same as existing use value. Achievement of the first condition is measured using the residual method of valuation (see Chapter 3) which is advanced in subsequent sections of this chapter. If the second condition is not met then the developer would be unable to purchase the site at a price that would allow sufficient profit to be made. Equally the owner would be unlikely to sell to a developer at a price below existing use value.

We have seen from Chapter 1 that land use is determined by the highest bidder. The amount paid is the present capital value of the future income stream for that use. It follows that the use of an existing property will change if another user can bid a higher price than the existing occupant, subject to planning constraints, inertia of ownership and occupation and so on. But we know that buildings last for a very long time and a change of use might require redevelopment of the site. In this case, rather than comparing the present value of the existing use with the present value of the best alternative use, we need to compare the present value of the existing use with the present value of the site cleared and ready for development to its optimum use. Calculation of the latter is the role of the residual method of valuation introduced in Chapter 3. Assuming competition among developers to acquire a site, the residual site value for development purposes will be the highest price which the most efficient developer would be willing to pay (Fraser, 1993). This value can then be compared with the value of the site in its existing use and, if higher, means that development is viable.

By now you may have realised that the relationship between existing use value and development value of a specific site will vary over time. The value of a site that has just been developed for a particular use will be the highest value that could be obtained for that site; otherwise it would have been developed for another (more profitable) use. To investigate the relationship between existing use value and development value[1] of a site in more detail we need to consider the economic life of a building. Lean and Goodall (1966)

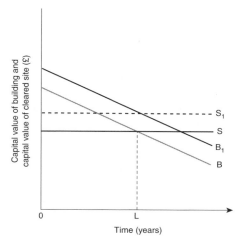

Figure 6.3   The economic life of a building (after lean and Goodall, 1966).

stated that the economic life of a building will be the period for which the present (capital) value of the existing use is greater than the present value of the site cleared and ready for development. It is possible to illustrate the relationship over time between the capital value of a cleared site and the capital value of the buildings on it (improvements made to it). Figure 6.3 shows the capital value of a site and buildings which are currently used as offices.

Lean and Goodall argue that, if we assume that office space was the most profitable use at time 0, the line B shows how the capital value of the office building falls over time as depreciation takes hold, maintenance costs increase relative to rental value and a better standard of accommodation is expected. S shows the capital value of the cleared site assuming no change in supply and demand over time and that land and construction costs remain constant over time. The diagram shows that it is not economically viable (profitable) to redevelop the site until L. In reality, redevelopment is likely to occur some time after L, perhaps when the lease ends, and the decision is subject to planning constraints and sunk investment in the existing use. The economic life of the building depends primarily on its earning power and only secondarily on its structural durability. S may increase to S_1 due to infrastructure improvements and this will reduce the economic life of the building. Similarly B may increase to B_1 due to refurbishment or conversion to a more valuable use and this will increase the economic life of the building. The model can also be used to explain urban structure. In the central area buildings fall into disrepair as owners anticipate redevelopment (B_1 to B) while, at the same time site values may increase (S to S_1). Further out from the centre the built environment is characterised by lots of conversions and refurbishments, increasing building values (B to B_1) but the infrastructure usually worsens (S_1 to S). In the suburbs buildings tend to be well maintained (B to B_1) but development forces are strong (S to S_1).

In the long-term and within the regulatory framework, land in private ownership tends to move to its most profitable use but many factors can slow the development process down (Lean and Goodall, 1966). In reality, according to Fraser, development site value will have to exceed existing or alternative use value sufficiently to overcome landowner's inertia. Evans (1985) expands on this theme: expectations of landowners as to what might be the 'right' price for land may lead to a refusal of a bid that is different from expectations either now or in the future. This is known as speculation if the price expectation is higher or inertia if it is lower. Also, an owner-occupier may be unwilling to relocate without compensation sufficient to overcome the costs and possible loss of revenue, even though it may be more profitable to operate from a different location (Lean and Goodall, 1966). This means that the price paid for development land must be significantly in excess of the pure existing use value. Finally, Evans (1985) notes two landownership issues that may affect development activity. The first issue is tenure. Landlords may be more willing to sell and displace their tenants whereas owner-occupiers would have to displace themselves. Allied to this are possible statutory rights that a business tenant might have that legally secure occupation beyond the end of the current lease – the security of tenure provisions that were discussed in Chapter 4. The second issue is fragmentation of ownership. The larger the development proposal the greater this issue becomes. Trying to assemble a large development site from several smaller sites that are separately owned can be time-consuming, arduous and expensive. Sometimes developers will work with local authorities – which have powers of compulsory purchase – to ensure that these types of development can proceed.

Often, especially in the case of previously developed land (brownfield sites), it is the decline in existing use value through obsolescence that brings about the redevelopment of a site well before the buildings are incapable of economic use, so the impact of depreciation on property is considered in the next section.

6.2.4   Depreciation in the value of existing buildings

Throughout a building's life both its investment value to the owner and utility value to the occupier will tend to depreciate. There are two causes of **depreciation**: deterioration and obsolescence.

In terms of deterioration (sometimes referred to as physical obsolescence) the physical fabric of a property will deteriorate simply through use and by wearing out over time. It is not easy to generalise about the life of various building types but prime shop units are much less prone to deterioration than modern industrial units due to the nature of the use of the building and the proportion of total value attributable to land. The aim of every occupier and owner is to delay the onset of deterioration as much as possible and this is achieved by good design and construction and active property management. Sound maintenance and management policies help to identify, plan and budget for the onset of deterioration. But inevitably as the building gets older the maintenance cost increases and the rental value falls because the building is no longer modern and attractive. Consequently, the value of the building declines relative to site value until it becomes economically viable to redevelop the site.

Obsolescence refers to a decline in investment and/or utility value resulting from changes which are extraneous to the property. In other words, the physical condition of the building may be sound but external influences have rendered it obsolete. It is a decline in utility not directly related to physical usage or the passage of time. A good quality, flexible design can combat obsolescence but to a certain extent matters are beyond the control of the property owner or occupier and management and maintenance will have little impact. A building may become obsolete for any number of reasons that rarely work in isolation. Common causes are

- *Functional*: the property can no longer be used for its intended purpose, perhaps as a result of technological changes rendering layout, configuration or internal specification of the property obsolete and adaptation is not economically viable.
- *Social*: due to changes in the social fabric of the locality or change in consumer demand, working environment, and so on.
- *Technical*: the property may no longer be physically capable of meeting its intended use, for example, automated production line.
- *Geographic*: the property may be perfectly adequate in terms of its physical characteristics but it is in the wrong location.
- *Economic*: changes in the optimum use for a site due to market movements may render the existing use obsolete; the building may not fall but site value appreciates due to developmental potential.
- *Aesthetic*: image and design requirements are constantly changing and a property that no longer projects the right image may become obsolete.
- *Planning policy, environmental regulations and legislation*: new legislation or regulations, changes in wording of leases (rent review period), for example.

So deterioration may be a continual but gradual process whereas obsolescence may strike at irregular intervals regardless of age. The responsibility for maintaining the physical condition of a property is usually passed on to the tenant when a commercial property is let on full repairing and insuring (FRI) lease terms, but the risk of obsolescence cannot be managed in this way and is ultimately borne by the owner. The onset of deterioration or obsolescence can be measured by looking at depreciation in the value of the building in relation to modern replacements and by looking at the development value of the land in comparison to its value in its existing state. A sudden switch in the relative magnitudes of development land value and existing use value may occur as a result of a 'trigger event' that presents an opportunity for a more valuable use. A trigger event may be the granting of planning permission. For example, suppose a small industrial estate located on the edge of a town is around 15 years old and the units are looking a little tired. The owner is able to fill the units with small businesses paying low rents. A by-pass has been constructed around the town and accessibility to the industrial estate is greatly improved. At the same time 'factory outlet shopping' has become popular and planning permission to allow an element of retail trade from the industrial units is forthcoming. The owner of the industrial estate now finds that he can charge higher rents to the factory outlet traders and therefore decides to redevelop the site.

Baum (1991), building on the work of Salway (1986 and 1987), Miles (1987) and Harker (1987) found, for offices in the City of London, a straight-line relationship between age and market rent over first 20 years of a building's life, and also found that only 39% of the depreciation in value can be explained by age. Instead, a classification of building quality (measured in terms of internal specification, physical deterioration, configuration and external appearance) was a stronger determinant (73%) of depreciation. Indeed Baum found that building obsolescence factors (internal specification, external appearance and configuration) were more important causes of building depreciation than physical deterioration and went on to argue that internal specification (e.g. partitioning, layout) was a form of depreciation that was curable and that configuration (building design, walls and doors, etc.) was not, thus underlying the need for flexible buildings to combat obsolescence. Depreciation in rental value strikes hardest after the third and fourth rent review and internal specification and configuration deficiencies are the two predominant causes of depreciation in office buildings in the City of London. For industrials, deterioration was the most important factor. For a more detailed examination of depreciation in the property market, see Salway (1986), Baum (1988 and 1991) and Barras and Clark (1996).

Key points

- The supply of new property each year represents only a tiny fraction of existing stock. This is why the property supply is regarded as inelastic in every time frame except the very long-run.
- The use to which a piece of land is put depends on competitive bidding between developers who are, in turn, interpreting the requirements of occupiers and investors. The amount of land used for a particular development and the intensity with which it is used depends on the cost of capital and revenue that can be obtained. Because these factors vary over space they also help explain why different land uses are located where they are and why they are developed to densities varying.
- Development of a site is economically viable when the present value of the site cleared and ready for development is greater than the value of the existing use.
- Deterioration and obsolescence are the causes; depreciation in value is the effect. Property, although rightly regarded as a long-term investment and factor of production, does depreciate over time. Physical deterioration can be mitigated through an active property management programme. Obsolescence is harder to predict and control but good design helps.

6.3   Residual land valuation

The residual method of land valuation was introduced in Chapter 3 and the reader should read that chapter before going any further. As a reminder of what was covered Section 6.3.1 provides a detailed example of a residual land valuation.

6.3.1 Case study – valuation of a development site in Bristol

Bristol is located in the south west of England and serves as the region's capital. The Bristol conurbation has a population in excess of 500 000. The city is well served by infrastructure links and lies approximately 120 miles west of London and 90 miles south of Birmingham. Intercity trains run frequently from the nearby Bristol Parkway station and take 95 min to London Paddington and 70 min to Birmingham New Street. An international airport serves Bristol and is located to the south of the city. The greenfield site is located on Bristol Business Park on the northern fringe of the Bristol conurbation. The Park comprises large office buildings of two storeys and is adjacent to the ring-road (A4147), which is well linked to the motorway network being one mile from the M32 and M4 motorways. The city centre is approximately 20 minutes by car or bus. Bristol Parkway and Filton Abbeywood train stations are within walking distance of the site.

The site is approximately 0.33 ha in size and has the capacity to incorporate 2000 m² of office space including landscaping and car parking to the standards laid down by the Local Planning Authority and the freeholders of the Park.

South Gloucestershire Council has informally advised that the subject property falls under their local plan. Discussions prior to the submission of a planning application have indicated that an office development, which includes car parking and landscaping, would be appropriate. It is suggested that a planning condition may constitute a financial contribution to a nearby park-and-ride site. It is anticipated that there will be no contamination at a level that would affect the value of the completed office development.

Over the last 12 months there has been a 40% increase in space under construction on the business parks of south west England. Of this, over 80% has been pre-let. This is an increase of nearly 40% compared with the previous year. Significant shocks to the economy appear temporary and demand in the region remains high. Office requirements in the larger size bands are encouraged to pursue the pre-let and forward-sale route.

The Bristol office market is characterised by shortages of supply in the city centre and along the northern fringe, despite considerable development over recent years, and particularly in the city. Most new office space in the city centre is occupied and there are two large mixed-use schemes firmly in the pipeline that will provide over 4600 m² of office space. Both are in prime city centre locations. The North Bristol area has less substantial supply in the pipeline and pre-lets here are dominating the market. Locations outside and with access to Bristol are now experiencing speculative activity. There are also signs that some investors and occupiers are looking further west, to Newport and Cardiff, to serve their accommodation needs. Rents remain high and evidence of lengthening lease terms indicates a positive outlook for landlords and developers. Prime office space on the north fringe of Bristol is currently let at £210 per square metre. This represents a continuing growth in rental levels, which is attributed to the scarcity of modern, prime space in the Bristol area.

As in Chapter 3, the residual valuation presented below includes numbered items that refer to subsequent explanations.

Chapter 6

Development value

[1] Gross Internal Area (m²)	2000		
Net Internal Area (m²)	1700		
[2] Estimated rent/m²	£200		
Estimated rental value (ERV)		£340000	
Capitalised into perpetuity @ 7%		14.2857	
Gross development value (GDV)		£4857143	
[3] less disposal costs (@ 2% NDV)		£95238	
Net development value (NDV)			£4761905

Construction costs

Building Costs @ £969/m² × gross internal area	£1938000		
External Works	£120000		
		£2058000	
Professional fees @ 13% of above costs		£267540	
Ancillary/Miscellaneous Costs		£80000	
Contingency @ 3% above costs		£72166	
[4] Other costs and fees			
(a) Site investigations, say		£25000	
(b) Planning fees, say		£5066	
(c) Building regulations, say		£20000	
(d) Bank's legal/professional fees @ 0.5% NDV		£23810	
(e) Bank's arrangement fee @ 1% NDV		£47619	
(f) Developer's legal fees @ 0.5% NDV		£23810	
Total construction costs		£2623010	

Interest: [5]

On <u>half</u> total construction costs for <u>whole</u> building period @ 10% pa		£201565	
On total construction costs & finance for void period @ 10% pa		£0	
Total interest payable		£201565	

Letting and sale costs

Letting agent's fee @ 15% ERV	£51000		
Marketing	£10000		
Total letting and sales fees		£61000	
Total development costs		£2885575	
[6] plus **Developer's profit on total development costs @ 15%**		£432836	
			£3318411
Future residual balance (inc. profit on land)			£1443493
less **Developer's profit on land costs @ 15%**			£188282
Future balance (inc. interest on land & acquisition costs)			£1255212
less interest on land and acquisition costs for total development and void period (2 years @ 10%)		0.8264	£217847
Present residual balance for land and acquisition costs:			£1037365
[7] *less* Acquisition Costs @ 5.5% site acquisition price			£54081
[8] **Residual site valuation**			**£983284**

[1] *Gross internal area, efficiency ratio, building costs, external works, contingencies and professional fees.* The gross internal area (GIA) is 2 000 m². The proposed development is ideally suited to an open plan design and so an efficiency ratio of 85% was used. Spons Architects and Builders Price Book 2005 (Davis et al., 2004) indicates low-rise offices cost between £850–1000 per square metre to build. £120 000 was estimated to cover highways, landscaping and car parking. A figure of 3% has been used for contingencies. Professional fees have been extracted from Spons and include; Project Manager (2%), Quantity Surveyor (3%), M & E Engineer (1%), Structural Engineer (1%) and Architect (6%). In using these figures it is assumed that the development will be of a conventional design and construction method.

[2] *Estimated rent and yield.* Comparable evidence was drawn from recent transactions relating to office space located on the North fringe of Bristol and is shown in Table 6.2.

Though agents suggested rents in the region of £210 per square metre, evidence of recent transactions in the Bristol North Fringe indicate rents levels slightly lower than this. On this basis an estimated rent of £200 per square metre was used for the proposed development. Comparable evidence suggested an investment yield of 7% and since the current market is characterised by low supply and pre-letting, a yield of 7% is deemed appropriate.

[3] *Disposal costs.* These are payable to an agent when the completed scheme is sold by the developer, often to an investor. The fee is for marketing the scheme and negotiating sale terms. In this case the developer will not be disposing off the investment, hence disposal costs will not be incurred. However, as this is a market valuation, such costs should be included in the valuation and so a 2% reduction in net development value has been made.

[4] *Fees.* For a full site investigation these are estimated to be £25 000. Fees for a full planning application are currently £250 per square metre payable to South Gloucestershire Council. However, under current government proposals, these may increase quite considerably in the next couple of years. A typical bank legal fee is 0.5%, letting agent's fee is 10% of the first year's rent and the marketing fee is estimated to be £10 000.

[5] *Interest.* The level of risk is considered to be comparatively low and a premium of 4% above the base rate has been added to reflect this. A typical range for the risk premium would be 2–6%. A lead-in period of six months is considered appropriate. Comparable evidence from developments schemes at Bristol Business Park indicates a building period of between 12 and 18 months for total completion including external works.

Table 6.2 Comparable evidence.

Scheme	Size (m²)	Rent (£/m²)	Capital value (£)	Yield (%)	Tenant/agent
550 Bristol Business Park	1 550	206.45	4 571 389	7.00	Thales
Building 650, Aztec West	3 817	202.50	11 042 250	7.00	Thales
530 Bristol Business Park	425	186.22	1 128 207	7.00	King Sturge
310 Bristol Business Park	282	188.37	760 750	7.00	Hartnell Taylor Cook

A downside assumption of 18 months has been used to allow for any delays. In light of the market analysis, it is assumed that the property will be pre-let. On this basis no letting void has been assumed. Given that the development will be purpose-built offices and the buoyant market demand for this type of property in Bristol, no rent-free period has been assumed.

[6] *Developer's profit.* It is expected that the scheme will be pre-let and so developer's profit has been calculated at the lower end of the typical range of developer's profit margin of 15–25% of development and land acquisition costs.

[7] *Acquisition costs.* Acquisition costs comprise Stamp Duty at 4%, agent's fee at 1% and solicitor's at 0.5%.

[8] *Valuation.* The residual valuation of the site is £983 284. This has been rounded to £980 000 and should be the maximum price paid for the site. The valuation has not taken account of taxation (Capital Gains Tax or VAT).

6.3.2   Problems with the residual method

Now that our memories are suitably refreshed, let's take a closer look at what the residual method of valuation is actually telling us. The method is a simple but effective means of estimating development site value and profitability. However, its simplicity comes at a price and the method is often criticised for being inflexible and overly sensitive to small changes in the key input variables.

6.3.2.1   Inflexibility

By calculating interest on half of the building costs over the construction period it is assumed that these costs are incurred evenly throughout this period. But, more often than not, building costs are not incurred in regular, equal instalments. In general, the initial build up of costs tends to be gradual, peaks at 60% and then tails off. Typically only 40% building costs are incurred half way through the construction period whereas the residual method assumes 50%. Consequently accrued interest is actually less than the amount estimated using the residual method. In addition, interest on money borrowed usually accumulates monthly rather than annually as assumed in the residual method.

Another drawback of the residual method is that it cannot accurately deal with revenue that may be received and expenditure that may be due at various times during the development period. For example, a development may be undertaken in stages; an industrial estate may be constructed a few units at a time rather than developing the whole site in one go. Consequently development costs will be phased and revenue from lettings and sales will probably be received incrementally. Another example is the redevelopment of a town centre; shops and other key sites such as car-parks and service access areas may well be purchased incrementally, sometimes over a long period of time. The shops might be let on short-term leases until the whole site has been assembled and income from these lettings should be reflected in the development valuation.

6.3.2.2   Sensitivity

It is evident from the above example valuation that there are many inputs into a residual valuation and the final residual amount can be small compared to the size of some of the input variables such as development value and construction costs. Indeed, the final answer is very sensitive to changes in the key variables. This is illustrated in the following example:

Two development sites are to be evaluated: Site A is a prime city centre location with high land cost relative to other costs; Site B is out-of-town, in a greenfield location with low land cost relative to other costs. Residual valuations have produced the following estimates of development value, development cost and site value:

Site A: Development on a prime site:	
Development value (£)	10 000 000
Development cost, inc. finance (£)	7 000 000
Site value (£)	3 000 000
Site B: Development on a cheap site:	
Development value (£)	10 000 000
Development cost, inc. finance (£)	9 000 000
Site value (£)	1 000 000

Three scenarios may be constructed based on changes to development cost and value over the period of the development:

1. Development value and cost increase by the same percentage:
   If this happens, site value at both locations will increase by the same percentage amount.
2. Development value increases by 25% and cost by 5%:
Site A: Development value (£)	12 500 000	
Development cost, inc. finance (£)	7 350 000	
Site value (£)	5 150 000	(+72%)
Site B: Development value (£)	12 500 000	
Development cost, inc. finance (£)	9 450 000	
Site value (£)	3 050 000	(+205%)
3. Development value increases by 5% and cost by 25%:
Site A: Development value (£)	10 050 000	
Development cost, inc. finance (£)	8 750 000	
Site value (£)	1 300 000	(−57%)
Site B: Development value (£)	10 050 000	
Development cost, inc. finance (£)	11 250 000	
Site value (£)	1 200 000	(−220%)

The sensitivity of site value to changes in development cost and value is due to the fact that it is a geared residual. This means that changes in development cost and value are magnified in changes in site value. If the residual (site value) is small relative to other costs, changes in development value and development cost will magnify changes in the residual, so much so that it can easily disappear. Therefore, sensitivity analysis (first encountered in Chapter 5

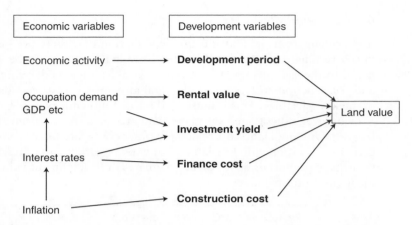

Figure 6.4   Key input variables in a development valuation (Fraser 1993).

and which will be developed further in Section 6.6.2) is undertaken to observe the effect on the residual site valuation when key input variables are altered. The key variables that significantly influence the land valuation are construction cost, rent, investment yield, finance cost (interest rate) and the length of the development period. Regarding the last variable, Fraser (1993) notes that the longer the development period the greater the impact of finance cost, so bigger projects tend to be regarded as more risky. As we shall see later these variables do not move in isolation – they tend to vary concurrently. The developer may attempt to fix one or more of them as a way of reducing risk but this can reduce the land valuation as well. We will look at these risk management techniques in Section 6.6.2. Figure 6.4 shows the key input variables in a development valuation.

6.3.3   Marriage gain valuations on merger of interests

Before we move on to consider how developer's profit might be calculated, it is perhaps a good opportunity to consider a particular way in which development value may arise. **Marriage value** can occur where the combined value of two or more property interests is greater than the simple addition of their separate values. The interests might be adjacent land parcels on a development site or they might be the freehold and leasehold interests in the same property. The marriage value is the difference between the value of the merged interest and the sum of the values of the separate interests. Break-up or 'divorce' value is the opposite of marriage value and refers to the division of property interests, leading to the value of the resultant separate interests being greater than the whole. For explanatory purposes let us consider separately an example of a merger of physically distinct properties and an example of a merger of distinct legal interests in the same property.

6.3.3.1   Physical merger

You have been asked to value two adjacent shop units, both with narrow frontages. You realise that if they were combined they could form a single standard-sized shop unit. The value of each shop in its existing state is £200 000 but if combined the merged value would be £500 000, giving a marriage value of £100 000. All other things equal, you would expect half of this gain to go to each shop owner, assuming they are in the same negotiating position and neither can hold the other to 'ransom'.

6.3.3.2   Legal merger

The freeholder of commercial development land let it to a head-lessee on a 125 year ground lease which has 24 years remaining at a ground rent of £5000 per annum with no provision for rent reviews. The head-lessee developed the site as offices and sub-let on a typical FRI occupational lease with 5-year rent reviews. The current market rent for the offices is £500 000 per annum and a rent review has just taken place. With just 24 years remaining the head-tenant is considering purchasing the freehold interest and wishes to know how much should be offered assuming a freehold all-risks yield of 6%, a leasehold all-risks yield of 8% (single rate) and a ground lease all-risks yield of 10%. The valuation of the freehold interest is

Term rent (£)	5 000	
YP 24 years @ 10%	8.9847	
		44 924
Reversion to market rent (£)	500 000	
YP perpetuity @ 6%	16.6667	
PV £1 24 years @ 6%	0.2470	
		2 058 337
Valuation (£)		2 103 261

The valuation of the head-leasehold interest is

Market rent (£)	500 000	
Less ground rent (£)	−5 000	
Profit rent (£)	495 000	
YP 24 years @ 8%	10.5288	
Valuation (£)		5 211 756

So the aggregate value of the separate freehold and head-leasehold interests is £2 013 261 + £5 211 756 = £7 315 017.

If the two legal interests were combined the valuation of the freehold in possession would be

Market rent (£)	500 000	
YP perpetuity @ 6%	16.6667	
Valuation (£)		8 333 350

And so the marriage value would be
£8 333 350 − £7 315 017 = £1 018 333

In which case, to purchase the freehold interest, the head-tenant could offer an amount equating to the existing value of freehold interest (£2 103 261) plus some proportion of the marriage value. A simple 50:50 split is one solution but it might be more equitable to apportion it according to the value of the exiting separate interests. So the freehold proportion of the marriage value would be

$$\frac{£2\,103\,261}{£7\,315\,017 \times £1\,018\,333} = £292\,798 \quad (29\%)$$

Leaving 71% or £725,535 for the head-tenant.

Key points

- The residual valuation of a site is calculated by first estimating the value of the proposed development and then deducting construction costs, including payments for any money borrowed and expected profit.
- The residual valuation method is usually employed at the evaluation stage and is often regarded as inflexible and sensitive to small but compounded changes in the increasing number of variables that are input as a development progresses.
- An illustration of a residual valuation is shown in Figure 6.5.

6.4   Residual profit valuation

If the development proposal progresses to successful site acquisition, the basic equation for the residual valuation can be transposed to determine the level of profit achieved given construction and site costs. Referring back to the simple example introduced in Section 3.5 of Chapter 3 in which a site

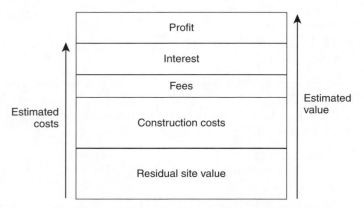

Figure 6.5   Diagrammatic representation of a residual site valuation.

value of £2 847 059 was estimated; let us assume that the two hectare site was successfully acquired for £2 670 000

> Value of completed development – Development costs – Site cost = Developer's profit
> Therefore: £7 647 059 – £4 000 000 – £2 670 000 = £977 059 (say £980 000)

This profit margin clearly compares favourably with the £800 000 that was estimated under the assumption that the site should be purchased at the original estimated price of £2 847 059. The profit sum can be (and usually is) expressed as a percentage of costs, which were estimated to be £4 000 000, giving an expected 'return on costs' of 24.5%. Therefore, the developer's return on construction costs more than matches the pre-determined target rate of 20%. Now look at a more detailed example based on the second valuation undertaken in Section 3.5 of Chapter 3. Explanatory notes relating to key elements of this valuation appear below:

Development value:			
Gross internal area (m²)	5 000		
Net internal area (m²)	3 750		
Estimated rent/sqm	£150		
ERV		£562 500	
YP in perp. @ 8%		12.5000	
Gross Development Value			£7 031 250
Less disposal costs @ 2% NDV			£137 868
Net Development Value (NDV)			£6 893 382
Site Costs:			
[1] Site price		£200 000	
[2] Acquisition costs @ 3.5% site price		£7 000	
			£207 000
Construction Costs:			
Building Costs @ £800/ m² GIA	£4 000 000		
External Works	£80 000		
		£4 080 000	
Professional fees @ 14% building costs		£571 200	
Ancillary / Miscellaneous Costs		£150 000	
Contingency @ 2% above construction costs		£96 024	
Other costs			
(a) Site Investigations, say		£10 000	
(b) Planning fees, say		£5 000	
(c) Building Regs, say		£20 000	
(d) Bank's legal / professional fees (0.5% NDV)		£34 467	
(e) Bank's arrangement fee (1% NDV)		£68 934	
(f) Developer's legal fees (0.5% NDV)		£34 467	
Total Construction Costs (£'s):			£5 070 092

Interest:

on <u>half</u> total construction costs for <u>whole</u> building period @ 7%	£270 785	
on total construction costs and interest for void period @ 7%	£278 011	
[3] on site costs for <u>total development period</u> @ 7%	£42 331	
Total Interest Payable (£'s):		£591 127

Letting & Sale Costs:

Letting agent's fee @ 15% ERV	£84 375	
Marketing	£5 000	
Total development costs		£5 957 594
[4] Developer's profit on completion		**£935 789**
x PV £1 for development period @ 7% discount rate		0.8302
Developer's profit today		**£776 913**

[1] *Site acquisition.* The site acquisition is assumed or is known and can therefore be inserted.

[2] *Site acquisition costs.* Costs associated with site acquisition (typically agent and legal fees) must be added to the costs.

$$\text{Site acquisition costs} = \text{Site price} \times 3.5\%$$
$$= £300 000 \times 0.035$$
$$= £7000$$

[3] *Interest on site costs.* Assuming the site was acquired at the very beginning of the development process, interest will accrue on this cost over the whole development period. Here the site costs will incur interest for 2 years and 9 months at an annual interest rate of 7%.

$$\text{Interest on site costs} = \text{site costs} \times [(1 + 0.07)^{2.75} - 1]$$
$$= £207 000 \times 0.2045$$
$$= £42 331$$

[4] *Developer's profit.* This is the developer's profit realisable at the end of the development period. In order to calculate profit in current prices this figure must be discounted at a suitable discount rate to reflect the time value of money. In this example, the lending rate has been used.

$$\text{Developer's profit today} = \text{developer's profit at end of scheme} \times \text{PV}$$
$$£1 \text{ at } 7\% \text{ per annum for 2 years and}$$
$$9 \text{ months}$$
$$= £935 789 \times [1/(1 + 0.07)^{2.75}]$$
$$= £935 789 \times 0.8302$$
$$= £776 913$$

The estimated developer's profit can be expressed in a number of ways in order to assess the viability of the development and to compare it to other development opportunities. The following are simple methods of expressing development viability:

- *Profit as a percentage of cost*: This measure expresses profit as a percentage of development costs. It is useful for **trader developers**, who need to sell the completed development in order to raise capital for future projects.

    Return on capital = developer's profit at end of scheme/total development costs employed
    = £935 789/£5 957 594
    = 15.71%

- *Development yield*: This equates to rent expressed as a percentage of development costs and the measure is useful for **investor developers** who, in contrast to trader developers, retain the development as an investment. Just as the difference between total costs and total capital value represents capital profit, so the difference between the investment yield and development yield represents the developer's annual profit.

    Development yield = Estimated annual rent/total development costs
    = £562 500/5 957 594
    = 9.44% per annum

Finally there may be non-financial reasons for proceeding with a development. For example, a developer may be keen to design and construct a market-breaking concept or an investor may be looking for a specific type of property asset to balance risk in a portfolio.

So far we have considered developments that involve a single land use but the residual valuation method can be adapted to value **mixed-use developments** too. An example of a profit valuation of a mixed commercial, industrial and residential development is presented below:

Development value:

Estimated rent for office use	£142 500		
YP perpetuity @ 7%	14.2857		
		£2 035 714	
Estimated rent for retail use	£112 000		
YP perpetuity @ 6%	16.6667		
		£1 866 667	
Estimated rent for industrial use	. £133 000		
YP perpetuity @ 9%	11.1111		
		£1 477 778	
Gross value for residential use		£500 000	
Gross development value		£5 880 159	
less developer's disposal costs			
@ 2.5% NDV		£143 419	
Net Development Value			£5 736 740
Site Costs:			
Site price		£1 200 000	
acquisition costs @ 4% site price		£48 000	
			£1 248 000

Construction Costs:

Building costs	
Residential construction cost	£300 000
Office construction cost	£1 200 000
Retail construction cost	£500 000
Industrial construction cost	£600 000
External works	£25 000
Professional fees @ 12% building costs	£315 000
Ancillary/Miscellaneous costs (£)	£0
Contingencies @ 5% above construction costs	£147 000
Other costs:	
(a) site investigation fees @ say	£65 000
(b) planning fees @ say	£11 000
(c) Building Regs	£2 000
(d) bank's legal fee (% NDV)	
(e) bank's arrangement fee (% NDV)	
(f) developer's legal fee (% NDV)	
Total Construction Costs (£)	£3 165 000

Interest:

On site costs for development period of 1.75 yrs @ 12%	£273 760	
On construction costs half bldg period (0.75 yrs) @ 12%	£280 778	
On all costs @ 12% for void period	£0	
Total interest payable (£)		£554 537

Letting & Sale Costs:

Letting agents fee @ 10% ERV	£38 750	
Marketing	£10 000	
Total development costs		£4 967 537
Developer's profit on completion		**£769 203**
x PV £1 for development period @ 12% discount rate		0.8201
Developer's profit today	.	**£630 826**

6.5 Cash-flow land and profit valuations

Whereas a residual valuation is often used at an early stage to provide a snap-shot of development feasibility, a cash-flow development valuation is a more detailed assessment, usually reserved for larger, more complex proposals. Projecting a cash flow is particularly useful for developments where the initial land acquisition or disposal of the completed development is phased, such as residential or industrial estates, where some units may be sold before others are constructed; or complex central area shopping schemes where parts may be let or sold before the remainder is complete. In short, the advantage of the cash-flow technique is its dynamic capability.

The essential difference between a residual development valuation and a cash-flow development valuation is the way that the *timing* of expenditure and revenue is handled. The residual technique assumes that revenue from the development is received at the end of the development and expenditure is handled on the understanding that 50% of all costs are incurred half-way through the development. In contrast the cash-flow technique divides the development project into time periods (usually months or quarters) to allow more accurate judgments to be made regarding the flow of income and expenditure. Payments and receipts which were stated as aggregate figures in the residual valuation may now be estimated as to when they are likely to occur. This permits a more accurate calculation of interest payments to be incorporated and allows the valuer to examine how changes in the timing of costs and revenue might affect value or profitability of the development. Throughout the construction phase adjustments can be made to the cash flow as and when costs and income are realised. This will determine how the project stands at any point in time in terms of potential profit and what began as a valuation becomes an appraisal tool.

As an example, assume that a cash-flow needs to be prepared for the construction of a small commercial building. The cost of construction is estimated to be £250 000, professional fees £25 000 (the majority of which will be incurred early on in the development), marketing £10 000, agent's sale fee £10 000, legal fees of £20 000, a contingency fund of £20 000 and interest on money borrowed is charged at 2% per quarter. This is a very simple set of costs but the principle remains the same regardless of the complexity of the cash-flow. Assuming the project will take 15 months to complete the cash flow grid is shown in Table 6.3.

Table 6.3 Simple cash-flow.

| | Calendar quarter | | | | | |
Costs (£)	1	2	3	4	5	Total
Construction	−40 000	−50 000	−70 000	−50 000	−40 000	−250 000
Professional fees	−20 000	−2 000	−2 000	−1 000		−25 000
Contingency	−5 000			−2 000	−3 000	−10 000
Marketing					−10 000	−10 000
Agent's sale fee					−10 000	−10 000
Legal sale fee					−20 000	−20 000
Net flow	−65 000	−52 000	−72 000	−53 000	−83 000	−325 000
Opening balance	0	−66 300	−120 666	−196 519	−254 510	
Interest on opening balance	0	−1 326	−2 413	−3 930	−5 090	
Interest or quarterly flow	−1 300	−1 040	−1 440	−1 060	−1 660	
Total interest	−1 300	−2 366	−3 853	−4 990	−6 750	−19 260
Quarterly cost/receipt (net flow + total interest)	−66 300	−54 366	−75 853	−57 990	−89 750	
Closing balance (net flow + quarterly cost/receipt)	−66 300	−120 666	−196 519	−254 510	−344 260	

By dividing the project into quarters the expenditure in each period can be examined. It shows peaks in the third and fifth quarters and lower cash needs in the second and fourth quarters. These fluctuations will be reflected in the interest rate charged by the bank. The final column shows the total and appears as it would in a residual valuation. The costs for each period are added to produce a net flow and from this an accurate assessment of interest charges can be calculated.

In residual valuations, it was assumed that income is received (and costs incurred) annually in arrears. The cash flow in Table 6.3 assumes that costs and revenue are incurred and received quarterly in arrears. In reality, there may be a mixture of timings for incurring expenditure and receiving revenue: construction costs are usually paid in arrears whereas income from property in the form of rent is usually receivable quarterly in advance.

6.5.1   Cash-flow land valuation

Continuing the example above and assuming the project has a net development value of £750000 and the developer would like to show a profit of £150000, we can use the cost and interest figures to complete a cash-flow land valuation; an example is shown below. The residual amount of £255740 is reduced by the amount needed to finance the purchase of the land, and one quarter has been added to the cash-flow period to create a reasonable void period.

Net development value (£)		750000
Less costs (£)	−325000	
Less interest payments (£)	−19260	
		−344260
		405740
Less profit (£)		−150000
Residual amount (£)		255740
Less finance: PV£1 @ 2% per quarter for 6 quarters		0.8880
		227090
Reduced by fees @ 3% (£)		1.03
Residual site value (£)		220476

As emphasised above, a key advantage of a cash-flow valuation is that it can deal with non-standard patterns of revenue and expenditure. Whereas a residual valuation assumes sales must come at the end of the development (albeit after a possible void period), the cash-flow method easily deals with phased schemes, allowing rental income to be accounted for when rent commences before the investment is sold. This is simple to include by incorporating two income lines; one for rent and one for sales. In Table 6.4 sales commence in the fifth quarter although construction continues until the eighth quarter. Notice that where phased sales occur the associated costs, such as agent and legal fees, also appear in the calculation at the appropriate time.

Table 6.4 Cash-flow for a phased development.

Costs (£)		Calendar quarter									Total
	1	2	3	4	5	6	7	8	9		
Construction	−40000	−50000	−70000	−140000	−160000	−160000	−100000	−60000	−40000		−820000
Professional fees	−20000	−2000	−2000	−6000	−6000	−4000	−2000	−2000	0		−36000
Contingency	−1800	−1560	−2160	−4380	−4980	−4920	−3060	−1860	−1200		−25920
Sales					200000	300000	400000	500000	600000		2000000
Marketing					−10000	−15000	−20000	−25000	−30000		−100000
Agent's sale fee					−10000	−15000	−20000	−25000	−30000		−100000
Legal sale fee					−20000	−30000	−40000	−50000	−60000		−200000
Net flow	−61800	−53560	−74160	−150380	−10980	71080	214940	336140	438800		718080
Opening balance	0	−63036	−118928	−196950	−354276	−372342	−308709	−99943	234198		
Interest on opening balance	0	−1261	−2379	−3939	−7086	−7447	−6174	−1999			
Interest or quarterly flow	−1236	−1071	−1483	−3008							
Total interest	−1236	−2332	−3862	−6947	−7086	−7447	−6174	−1999			−37082
Quarterly cost/receipt (net flow + total interest)	−63036	−55892	−78022	−157327	−18066	63633	208766	334141	438800		
Closing balance (net flow + quarterly cost/receipt)	−63036	−118928	−196950	−354276	−372342	−308709	−99943	234198	672998		

Chapter 6

Also, when the net flow becomes positive in the sixth quarter, no interest is charged on the quarterly flow and, similarly, when the opening balance becomes positive in the ninth quarter, no interest is charged on the opening balance.

The results from this cash-flow can then be used to value the development site as follows:

Net development value (£)		2 000 000
Less costs of construction, professional fees, contingency, marketing, agents and legal fees (£)	−1 281 920	
Less interest payments (£)	−37 082	
		−1 319 002
		680 998
Less profit (£)		−150 000
		530 998
Less finance: PV£1 @ 2% per quarter for 6 quarters (£)		0.8880
		471 526
Reduced by fees @ 3% (£)		/1 03
Residual site value (£)		457 792

6.5.2   Cash-flow profit valuation

Another possibility offered by the cash-flow technique is an assessment of developer's profit, often referred to as a **viability statement**, provided the land cost is known. To illustrate this Table 6.3 has been adapted by adding two extra rows to the calculation: land cost and acquisition fees. This filters its way through the cash flow presented in Table 6.5 to allow a relatively simple

Table 6.5 Simple cash-flow viability statement.

	Calendar quarter					
Costs (£)	1	2	3	4	5	Total
Land	−250 000					−250 000
Acquisition fees	−7 000					−7 000
Construction	−40 000	−50 000	−70 000	−50 000	−40 000	−250 000
Professional fees	−20 000	−2 000	−2 000	−1 000		−25 000
Contingency	−5 000			−2 000	−3 000	−10 000
Marketing					−10 000	−10 000
Agent's sale fee					−10 000	−10 000
Legal sale fee					−20 000	−20 000
Net flow	−322 000	−52 000	−72 000	−53 000	−83 000	−582 000

Continued

Table 6.5 (Continued)

Costs (£)	Calendar quarter					
	1	2	3	4	5	Total
Opening balance	0	–328 440	–388 049	–469 250	–532 695	
Interest on opening balance	0	–6 569	–7 761	–9 385	–10 654	
Interest or quarterly flow	–6 440	–1 040	–1 440	–1 060	–1 660	
Total interest	–6 440	–7 609	–9 201	–10 445	–12 314	–46 009
Quarterly cost/receipt (net flow + total interest)	–328 440	–59 609	–81 201	–63 445	–95 314	
Closing balance (net flow + quarterly cost/receipt)	–328 440	–388 049	–469 250	–532 695	–628 009	

assessment of profit. As shown in the valuation below the result is a profit of £121 991 on total costs of £628 009 (19.43%); an acceptable return.

Net development value (£)	750 000
Less costs (£)	–582 000
Less interest (£)	–46 009
	–628 009
Profit (£)	121 991

Case study-cash flow profit valuation

A client has been offered a site which is cleared and ready for the development of four shops with offices above. All statutory consents have been obtained and the price is £3 050 000. A fixed tender price of £1 800 000 has been received for the building works and these are expected to be completed in 18 months. Payment is to be in equal amounts for each quarter of the contract. It is estimated that the shops will command a rent of £70 000 per annum each and the offices £200 000 per annum total. Short-term finance will cost 3% per quarter, paid quarterly in arrears, and the project could readily sell, showing an initial yield of 6%. It is assumed that: there is a three month pre-contract (lead-in) and 3 month disposal (void) period; land purchase fees are 3% of the land purchase price; architects' fees are £50 000 at the outset, £50 000 in first quarter, £100 000 in fourth quarter and £25 000 in sixth quarter of the construction period; disposal costs are 3% of the gross development value and the letting fee is 10% of the first year's rent. A cash flow for this scheme is set out in Table 6.6 and the evaluation of profit is shown in the viability statement below.

Profit on costs equates to 18.19%, return on value is 14.33% and the development yield is 7.62%. This viability statement adopts a rather simplistic approach to calculating development value as it assumes that the shops and offices attract the same investment yield.

Finally, expanding the developer's profit calculation shown at the end of Section 6.4, it is possible to illustrate how a residual valuation of a mixed use development can be expanded to incorporate a cash flow, as illustrated in Table 6.7.

Case study-cash flow profit valuation (continued)

Rent on 4 shops (£)	280 000	
Rent on offices (£)	200 000	
Total estimated rental value (ERV) (£)	480 000	
YP perpetuity @ 6%	16.6667	
Gross development value (£)		8 000 000
Less disposal costs @ 3%	−240 000	
Less development costs	−6 302 165	
Less letting fee @ 10% ERV	−48 000	
		−6 590 165
Profit		1 409 835
PV 1 for 7 quarters @ 3% per quarter		0.8131
Profit at today's prices (£)		1 146 325

The cash-flow shows that the total development costs amount to £4 907 22 when analysed using a cash-flow technique. This compares with £4 967 537 that was calculated using the residual technique. Deducting £4 907 922 from the net development value of £5 736 740 (calculated earlier in Section 6.4) this leaves a developer's profit on completion of £828 818. This figure must be discounted to arrive at the developer's profit at today's prices and this is done here by discounting the future profit amount at the lending rate of 12% per annum. This produces a developer's profit today of £679 717, a 16.89% profit on costs. There are two reasons why the profit margin calculated using a cash-flow technique is higher than that calculated using a residual technique. The first is that the quarterly interest rate of 2.75% is slightly more favourable than the annual rate of 12% that was used in the residual valuation (2.75% per quarter compounds to 11.46% per annum). The second reason is that the explicit breakdown of costs over the development period permits a more accurate calculation of interest payments. In this case the interest liability is lessened because the bulk of the construction costs occur in the second half of the construction period rather than assuming that all payments are incurred at the half-way point. Obviously, use of a cash flow will not always reveal a reduction in interest liability but it will at least allow that liability to be considered in more detail over the development period.

It would be possible to build more detail into this sort of cash flow by perhaps phasing the letting and sales of the commercial and residential premises. By adding more detail we move out of the realm of what can be squeezed on to the printed page of a book without the aid of a magnifying glass. Spreadsheet software would be used to construct such a valuation. Alternatively it is possible to purchase proprietary software that automates much of the calculation work. One such software package is called Visual Investor which is produced by Circle Software. Appendix 6A (see Appendix 6A at www.blackwellpublishing.com/wyatt) presents an example of the mixed use developer's profit valuation from Section 6.4 developed using this software package.

Table 6.6 Development cash-flow.

Costs (£)		Calendar quarter						
	0	1	2	3	4	5	6	7
Balance brought forward		−3 287 245	−3 746 362	−4 167 753	−4 601 786	−5 151 839	−5 615 395	−6 118 606
Site cost	−3 050 000							
Site fees	−91 500							
Site clearance	0							
Construction cost	0	−300 000	−300 000	−300 000	−300 000	−300 000	−300 000	
Architect fee	−50 000	−50 000			−100 000		−25 000	
Interest	−95 745	−109 117	−121 391	−134 033	−150 054	−163 555	−178 212	−183 558
Total expenditure	−3 287 245	−3 746 362	−4 167 753	−4 601 786	−5 151 839	−5 615 395	−6 118 606	−6 302 165

Table 6.7 Cash-flow cost estimate for a mixed use development.

Cash-flow (£)		Calendar quarter						
	1	2	3	4	5	6	7	8
Balance brought forward		-1538322	-1817978	-2127981	-2737806	-3526232	-4174508	-4549316
Site price	-1200000							
Acquisition costs @ 4% site price	-48000							
Building costs								
(a) Residential construction cost		-50000	-50000	-50000	-50000	-50000	-50000	
(b) Office construction cost		-100000	-100000	-200000	-300000	-300000	-100000	-100000
(c) Retail construction cost		-50000	-50000	-100000	-150000	-50000	-50000	-50000
industrial construction cost		-20000	-30000	-150000	-150000	-100000	-30000	-20000
External works	-25000							
Professional fees @ % building costs	-138000		-11000	-11000	-11000	-11000	-11000	
Ancillary/miscellaneous costs	0							
Contingencies @ % above construction costs	-8150	-12050	-12050	-25550	-33050	-25550	-12050	-8500
Other costs								
(a) Site investigation fees @ say	-65000							
(b) Planning fees @ say	-11000							
(c) Building regulation fees @ say	-2000							
Funding fees								
(a) Bank's legal fee (% NDV)	0							
(b) Bank's arrangement fee (% NDV)	0							
(c) Developer's legal fee (% NDV)	0							
Letting agents fee (% ERV)								-38750
Marketing								-10000
Interest	-41172	-48656	-56953	-73275	-94376	-111727	-121758	-131356
Cumulative balance	-1538322	-1817978	-2127981	-2737806	-3526232	-4174508	-4549316	-4907922
Total development costs								-4907922
Developer's profit on completion (net development value of £5 736 740 less development costs of £4 907 922)							828818	
× PV £1 for development period @ 12% discount rate							0.8201	
Developer's profit today								679717

> ## Key points
>
> - The cash-flow method enables the valuer to be explicit about the break-down of costs and revenue. It provides a reasonably accurate assessment of monetary flow over a specified time period.
> - A detailed projection of construction and related costs over the development period can provide a more considered estimation of land value. Once the acquisition price of a development site is known the cash-flow projection can be used to keep a close eye on how actual costs compare to the estimates and thus how the developer's profit might be affected by any variation.
> - A development cash flow also provides a useful statement of potential viability – an essential ingredient of any negotiations with possible lenders, and can deal with phased acquisition and disposal costs and revenues.

6.6 Development risk

Property development is a risky business. It has been said that the first rule of successful property development is never to use your own money! The second rule is to think big; if you owe the bank £10 000 then you have a problem, if you owe the bank £10 million then the bank has a problem. Witticisms aside, being able to judge the risk involved in a particular development opportunity goes hand-in-hand with the estimation of likely return. Remember, the higher the risk of an investment the higher the required return. In this section we will consider ways in which various types of risk associated with property development might be managed and we will look at how development risk might be analysed and quantified. Before that, though, clarification of two key terms might be apposite. These are 'uncertainty' and 'risk'. Hargitay and Yu (1992) provide a useful illustration of the relationship between risk and uncertainty and this is reproduced in Figure 6.6.

Byrne (1996) suggests that uncertainty is anything that is not known about the outcome of a venture at the time the decision is made. Fisher and Robson (2006) argue that uncertainty lies at the root of property development – a process which produces a product in anticipation of unknown future demand. On risk Byrne suggests that this is the measurement of loss. Fisher and Robson point out that development is a complex stochastic process, the features of which vary with time and place and developers need to be aware of risks and approaches to risk management in the letting, investment, land, construction and finance markets. Development risk occurs because we are unable to forecast the outcome of future events with certainty.

Both the residual and cash-flow versions of a development valuation are built using a deterministic model that contains numerous point estimates of the input variables. The large number of these variables, their potential for variation and correlation are what lead those who rely on the method to exercise caution. When trying to value a development site or estimate likely profit from a proposed scheme there are many variables that must be

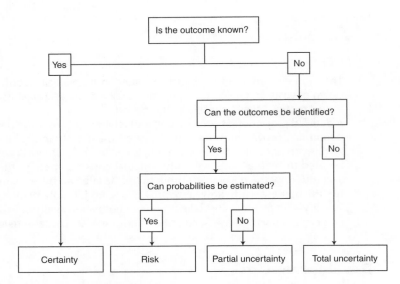

Figure 6.6   The spectrum of uncertainty (after Hargitay and Yu, 1993).

estimated and mistakes can quite easily be compounded in a residual valuation where these variables are brought together in additive, multiplicative and possibly interdependent relationships. For example, there are several downside risks such as: increases in construction costs; delayed completion; reduced investor demand leading to an increase in the investment yield; reduced occupier demand leading to delays in letting or sale of the property, decreased rental and capital value; and increases in the cost of borrowing money. To make matters worse these do not happen in isolation. As explained in Chapter 3 a downturn in the economy will impact on investment and occupier markets. Reduced demand from investors will cause the investment yield to rise and reduced demand from tenants will cause rents to drop. The combined effect may lead to a substantial shift in the view of development viability. It is important therefore to mitigate the influence of the key downside risks as much as possible and potential ways of doing this are discussed in Section 6.6.2. Before that Section 6.6.1 considers various ways that risk might be analysed.

6.6.1   Risk analysis

Fisher and Robson (2006) suggest that the various risks associated with property development may be assessed qualitatively, by detailing and ranking them, perhaps using some sort of 'probability-impact matrix'. Or risks may be analysed quantitatively, by undertaking sensitivity analysis, probability simulations or other techniques that were introduced in Chapter 5.

As mentioned above there may be variation in anticipated construction costs during the development or movements in the level of rent obtained prior to completion. As a consequence the actual return received from a development will probably differ from the estimate made in the residual valuation at the start of the development. Techniques for analysing such risks vary from simple but intuitive relationships such as rent cover, interest cover and break-even rent through to deterministic simulation models such as sensitivity analysis and scenario modelling.

6.6.1.1 Simple ratios and thresholds

Rent cover is the number of years it would take to eliminate the profit assuming letting (and hence sale of the investment) were delayed. The calculation determines the length of the void period before the project would generate a loss. This is relevant in pre-funded arrangements where the developer may guarantee the rent to an investor from the end of any pre-arranged void period until the scheme is fully let. Two schemes with the same return on value will have different rent covers if their investment yields are different; the higher the yield the lower the rent cover. So, using the information from the residual valuation of developer's profit in Section 6.4,

Rent cover = developer's profit at end of scheme/estimated annual rent
= £935 789/£562 500
= 1.66 years

Interest cover is the number of years from the end of the void period before profit is eroded by interest payments to the bank. This is a useful measure for **speculative development** that has been financed through a bank loan and which is converted to a long-term loan (mortgage) at the end of the development period. Assume that in the valuation in Section 6.4 the total costs that need to be paid back to the lender (£5 957 594) is converted to a mortgage secured against the property at a long-term interest rate of 6% per annum over 25 years. The annual mortgage repayments are calculated by adapting the future value £1 per annum formula. So, recalling Equation 2.11 from Chapter 2

$$FV£1\,pa = A\left[\frac{(1+r)^n - 1}{r}\right]$$

where A is the annual instalment and r is the rate of interest charged by the lender. But these instalments must accrue not just to £5 957 594 but to this amount compounded over the mortgage term at r rate of interest. So

$$A\left[\frac{(1+r)^n - 1}{r}\right] = M \cdot (1+r)^n$$

where M is the mortgage amount (£5 957 594) and $(1+r)^n$ is the formula for compound interest (FV £1). Rearranging this formula we can solve for A

$$A = \frac{M(1+r)^n \cdot r}{(1+r)^n - 1} = \frac{5\,957\,594(1+0.06)^{25} \times 0.06}{(1+0.06)^{25} - 1} = £466\,043$$

We can now calculate the interest cover ratio:

Interest cover = developer's profit at end of scheme/annual interest
payable
= £935 789/£466 043
= 2.01 years

Break-even analysis or **profit erosion** is a recalculation of the valuation in which the developer's profit is set to zero. For example, break-even rent indicates the minimum rent required to ensure that no loss is incurred. This sort of analysis is very straightforward if the valuation is set up in a spreadsheet; the interpolation/trial-and-error function (called 'goal-seek' in Excel) can be used to set the cell containing the figure for the developer's profit to zero by altering one of the input variables such as rent, yield, interest rate, development period or building costs to identify break-even values for these variables. Using the residual valuation of developer's profit from Section 6.4, Table 6.8 lists the break-even values of the key input variables.

This simple analysis shows which variables to keep a close eye on. It should be remembered that developers and investors are risk averse and will generally seek to determine the extent to which the most pessimistic case might impact profit.

6.6.1.2   Sensitivity analysis and scenario modelling

A conventional residual valuation does not give any indication of the uncertainty inherent in the development process. Cash-flow methods overcome some of the inaccuracies of the conventional approach but are still only snapshots of viability. **Sensitivity analysis** permits a better understanding of the dynamics of the development by quantifying risk in a very simplistic way. It forces the developer to think more carefully about how assumptions and point estimates of key input variables might vary. Univariate sensitivity analysis seeks to quantify the effect of changes in the values of certain input variables on the output variable one variable at a time. As an example the four key input variables from the now familiar developer's profit valuation in Section 6.4 will be altered by a margin of 10% either side of the best estimate and the effect on developer's profit measured. The results are shown in Table 6.9.

This type of analysis indicates which inputs have the greatest impact on profit. Changes to the investment yield have the largest impact, followed by

Table 6.8   Break-even analysis.

Input variable	Original value	Break-even value	Change (%)
Rent	£150.00	£128.91	A drop of 14.06
Yield	8%	9.29%	A rise of 16.13
Building cost	£800/m²	£945/m²	A rise of 18.13
Interest	7%	17.25%	A rise of 146.43
Void period	0.5 years	2.69 years	A rise of 438

Table 6.9 Sensitivity matrix.

Variable	Original value	+10%	New profit	Change in profit	−10%	New profit	Change in profit	Range
Rent	£150/ m²	£165/ m²	£1 329 527	+71%	£135/ m²	£224 299	−71%	142%
Yield	8%	8.8%	£268 168	−65%	7.2%	£1 398 712	+80%	145%
Building cost	£800/ m²	£880/ m²	£348 962	−55%	£720/ m²	£1 204 864	+55%	110%
Interest rate	7%	7.7%	£713 187	−0.08%	6.3%	£842 485	+0.08%	1.6%

Table 6.10 Univariate sensitivity analysis using Excel.

Rent change	Rent	Profit	Yield change	Yield (%)	Profit
+10%	£165.00	£1 329 527	+10%	8.80	£268 168
+5%	£157.50	£1 053 220	+5%	8.40	£510 428
Original value	£150.00	£776 913	Original value	8.00	£776 913
−5%	£142.50	£500 606	−5%	7.60	£1 071 449
−10%	£135.00	£224 299	−10%	7.20	£1 398 712

Table 6.11 Bivariate sensitivity matrix.

Rent	Yield				
	7.20%	7.60%	8.00%	8.40%	8.80%
£165.00	£2 013 506	£1 653 517	£1 329 527	£1 036 393	£769 908
£157.50	£1 706 109	£1 362 483	£1 053 220	£773 410	£519 038
£150.00	£1 398 712	£1 071 449	£776 913	£510 428	£268 168
£142.50	£1 091 315	£780 415	£500 606	£247 445	£17 298
£135.00	£783 918	£489 382	£224 299	−£15 538	−£233 572

rent, building cost and then the finance rate. A developer may be prepared to pay a high price for a site if a small increase in rent would more than offset the increase in land cost.

It is possible to set up a similar type of table using standard tools on a spreadsheet. Assume that examination of the results reported in Table 6.9 prompt you to focus on the impact on profit resulting from more refined changes in the estimates of rent and yield inputs. Using Excel the 'table' function produced the outputs shown in Table 6.10.

Bivariate sensitivity analysis extends univariate analysis by examining the impact of changes to two variables at the same time. A simple matrix/cross-tabulation/contingency table can be used to report the results. Table 6.11 shows a simple bivariate sensitivity matrix that reports the effect on developer's profit as a result of combined changes in the rent and yield variables.

Despite this being a bivariate analysis it does not take account of any possible correlation between the input variables, instead they are assumed to move independently. But logic tells us that as rents rise, yields should fall and vice versa of course. So the profit estimates highlighted in grey along the bottom left to top right diagonal are more likely to occur than the other combinations. Some of the output is repeated from the univariate sensitivity analysis but you can see that this bivariate analysis provides more information about what happens when changes coincide, such as an increase in yield and a drop in rent. A combination such as this would not be unusual in a market downturn.

By now you should be asking what you can do to model changes in several variables all happening at the same time, after all, that's what happens in the real world. If an increase in the rate of inflation is anticipated, this may cause the developer to reconsider the level of some of the key input variables. The finance cost may increase if the Bank of England Monetary Policy Committee decides to raise the Base Rate as a means of releasing inflationary pressure. Such an action may simultaneously cause businesses to hold off relocating and renting new premises. This may, in turn, increase the void period at the end of a development scheme as the search for tenants takes longer or more substantial rent-free periods are offered. Moreover, developers may have to reduce rents to attract tenants and investors may increase their yields expectations. As Fraser (1993) notes a combination of small changes in several variables could reduce land value or profitability sufficiently to render the development economically unviable.

There are two ways of examining the impact on land value or profit resulting from simultaneous changes in multiple input variables, what may be termed a multivariate sensitivity analysis. The first is called **scenario modelling** and was devised in the days before spreadsheets. Scenario modelling extends sensitivity analysis by examining the residual land value or profit obtained when alterations are made to several input variables at the same time.

It does this by calculating the output value given input values that correspond to best, worst and most likely scenarios. Extending our example to three variables; rent, yield and building costs, we can create different scenarios for different combinations of values of these variables. In theory we can construct many scenarios using many different combinations of values of input variables but it is perhaps better to think carefully about practical combinations of values rather than try and input every permutation. Part of the value of doing this sort of thing is to force careful consideration of the input values. Table 6.12 reports the developer's profit under three scenarios; best, worst and realistic. These scenarios are constructed by inputting suitable values of the three input variables; rent, yield and building cost.

The second way is using pivot tables. These are interactive cross-tabulations of data and utilise a spreadsheet's ability to perform 'what if' modelling to the full.

The main drawback with the simple ratios and thresholds, the sensitivity analyses and scenario modelling that we have looked at so far is that they do not consider the likelihood of various outcomes. As Byrne (1996) points

Table 6.12   Scenario modelling.

| | Scenario | | |
	Realistic	Best	Worst
Input variable			
Rent (£/m²)	150	152	148
Yield (%)	8.00	7.80	8.25
Building Costs (£/m²)	800	790	820
Output variable			
Land value (£)	776 913	1 049 494	428 923

out with regard to scenario modelling, the best and worst scenarios are in fact the two extremes and both may be pretty unlikely. This leads us to the consideration of probability in our analysis.

6.6.1.3   Probability and simulation analysis

Where a deterministic valuation model contains many uncertain inputs, predicting variables with a comfortable degree of confidence can become difficult. The valuation output (site value or developer's profit) might be better expressed as a range of values rather than a single value, but how big is the range and how is it distributed? The valuation of a property development opportunity, unlike the valuation of a standing property investment, typically involves the estimation of a larger number of input variables and the uncertainty that surrounds their estimation is usually greater because the property exists only in the mind of the developer at this stage. Furthermore, the correlations between the variables can be very complicated. Sensitivity analysis and scenario modelling may therefore be of limited use in indicating the extent of the risk. There are ways of reducing the level of uncertainty and these are explored in the next section. Before that though we should look at how the valuation model itself might be adapted to quantify the risk associated with this increased level of uncertainty.

A more robust analysis of risk requires the range and distribution of input variables to be identified and this means that a form of analysis called **probabilistic modelling** may be used. Values for some of the input variables occur more often than other values. In other words, they are more likely to occur. For instance, in any one location, at any one time, there will be a range of possible rents for a particular type of property. However, some will occur more often than others and are therefore said to be more probable. For example, you may calculate the mean and standard deviation of achieved rents from a sample of comparable properties for new office space in the locality of your proposed office development. The same procedure can be undertaken for each input variable and the mean values similarly calculated, assuming the valuer has a sample of sufficient size (rare in practice). If it is assumed that the distribution of the values of each variable is normal, it is a characteristic of normal distributions that approximately 68% of values will occur within one standard deviation either side of the mean and 95% within two standard deviations. Similarly, continuous distributions of values of key variables such as construction costs, development period and finance costs can be modelled to estimate a likely range in which the residual site valuation or profit estimation might lie.

As we know from Chapter 5, a procedure known as simulation can be used to assign probability distributions to input variables in a valuation model as a way of reflecting the uncertainty that surrounds their estimation. The same technique can be applied to development valuation. We consider how this is done below but for a detailed exposition on development appraisal using probabilistic simulation models see Byrne (1996). Values of input variables that cannot be stated with a high degree of certainty can be input as probability distributions of some sort. Specifying these distributions and inputting the key parameters such as the mean and standard deviation or maximum, minimum and mode, is the key to using probabilistic modelling. When the simulation is run, a value for each variable is selected from the range of possible values in accordance with the given probability distribution, so values are more likely to be drawn from areas of the distribution which have higher probabilities of occurrence. These values are then fed into the residual valuation and, through a process of iteration, repeated many times; simulating a range of possible outcomes.

But, if we are not careful, the complexity can increase exponentially as we try to model uncertainty in a large number of input variables. To keep things simple let's model the effect of uncertain *key* input variables on developer's profit. We will do this for the cash-flow profit valuation of the mixed use development shown in Table 6.7. The key variables are land price, rent, yield, building cost, interest rate and development period, and we shall begin by assuming that the land has been purchased so the price is fixed, the rent is fixed via a pre-let agreement and the building costs and construction period have been agreed under a fixed-price contract. The development period can also be predicted with a high degree of confidence because the building contractor has agreed to pay a penalty payment equivalent to the market rent for the duration of any over-run, and the pre-let ensures there is no rent void. That leaves uncertainty over the yield and the interest rate. The parameters for these variables have been input as shown in Table 6.13. Byrne (1996) notes that, generally, uncertainty increases over time (for example, the standard deviation of a normally distributed variable would increase) so it may be necessary to reassess distribution of values of a variable at various intervals. In the following simulation, as with Byrne, it is assumed that all distributions are static throughout the development period.

It is also necessary to examine correlations between variables and these have been set up subjectively as shown in Table 6.14.

Using the @RISK simulation software add-in to Microsoft Excel, the cash-flow profit valuation of the mixed use development is simulated 10,000 times. There are four input variables (office, retail and industrial yields and the bank base rate) and one output variable (developer's profit). Values of the input

Table 6.13 Probability distributions of yield and rent input variables.

Variable (%)	Distribution type	Distribution parameters			
		Mean	SD	Truncated min	Truncated max
Office yield	Normal	7.00	1.00	4.00	10.00
Retail yield	Normal	6.00	0.50	3.00	9.00
Industrial yield	Normal	9.00	2.00	5.00	13.00
Bank Base rate	Normal	4.75	2.00	3.00	6.50

Table 6.14 Input variable correlation matrix.

	Office yield	Retail yield	Industrial yield	Bank base rate
Office yield	1			
Retail yield	0.8	1		
Industrial yield	0.7	0.7	1	
Bank base rate	−0.5	−0.5	−0.5	1

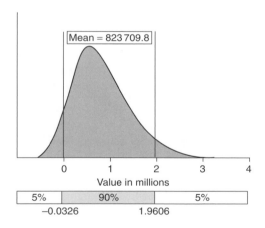

Figure 6.7 Probability distribution for developer's profit.

variables for each iteration of the cash flow were sampled from the probability distributions using the 'Latin Hypercube' sampling method.[2] Figure 6.7 shows the probability distribution for the output variable, developer's profit. It can be seen that there is roughly a 5% probability of making a loss. Table 6.15 reports the main descriptive statistics for developer's profit.

Another useful result produced by the software is a sensitivity matrix. This shows the sensitivity of the output variable to the input variable distributions. Two measures of sensitivity are reported; the first is calculated by regressing each output value with each input variable for each iteration. The overall fit of the regression analysis is measured by the R-squared of the model.

Table 6.15　Descriptive statistics for developer's profit.

Statistic	Result	Percentile (%)	Value
Minimum	−£558157	5	−£32582
Maximum	£3506258	10	£114953
Mean	£823710	15	£219501
Std Dev	£608975	20	£306105
Skewness	0.7088	25	£318119
Kurtosis	3.5165	30	£454995
Median	£739269	35	£525618
Mode	£386876	40	£595763
		45	£669862
		50	£739269
		55	£819985
		60	£899535
		65	£981040
		70	£1082331
		75	£1185950
		80	£1307929
		85	£1453386
		90	£1651971
		95	£1960565

Table 6.16　Sensitivity matrix.

Rank	Input variable	Regression sensitivity	Correlation coefficient
1	Industrial yield	−0.444	−0.897
2	Office yield	−0.428	−0.914
3	Retail yield	−0.227	−0.870
4	Bank base rate	−0.021	−0.529

The lower the R-squared, the less stable the reported sensitivity. The input variables are then ranked according to their influence on the volatility of the output variable. Spearman's rank correlation coefficient is calculated between the output variable and the samples for each of the input distributions; the higher the coefficient, the more significant the input is in determining the output's value. The results for the developer's profit cash-flow simulation are shown in Table 6.16. Developer's profit is most sensitive to the level of industrial yield and the negative signs for all four input variables mean shifts in their standard deviations cause a shift of in the opposite direction for developer's profit, as expected. There is a positive rank correlation coefficient for the bank base rate and this is counter-intuitive; we would not expect a rise in the base rate to reduce developer's profit. This result may be caused by multicollinearity[3] between the input variables and would require further statistical investigation.

If we now add further uncertainty by varying the rents, void period and building costs, as shown in Table 6.17, let us see what happens. Table 6.18

Table 6.17   Probability distributions of input variables.

Variable	Distribution type	Distribution parameters		
		Mode	Min	Max
Office rent	Triangular	95	92.50	97.50
Retail rent	Triangular	140	137.50	142.50
Industrial rent	Triangular	70	67.50	72.50
Office build cost	Triangular	600	580	650
Retail build cost	Triangular	500	480	550
Industrial build cost	Triangular	300	290	330
Void period	Normal	0	0	0.5

shows that the correlation matrix can get really complicated. The subjectively chosen correlations between the 11 input variables have been kept as simple as possible in this example. Again, 10 000 iterations were undertaken using the Latin Hypercube sampling method. Figure 6.8 shows the probability distribution of developer's profit. The mean value has dropped to £808 552 but the probability of making a loss is still around 5%. Summary statistics are reported in Table 6.19 and they show that not much has changed apart from the measures of central tendency (the mean, median and mode), all of which show a reduced level of profit. Basically, the distribution has shifted very slightly to the left. The sensitivity matrix in Table 6.20 shows that yields and rents have the most significant influence on developer's profit.

Simulation techniques can also be used to perform an advanced sensitivity analysis. Using @RISK, a full simulation is run at a range of values (typically the percentile values) of each input variable distribution, tracking the results at each value. The results are summarised in a 'tornado' sensitivity chart (Figure 6.9) which shows the extent of the change in developer's profit as the input value changes and thus shows the sensitivity of the output to the specified input.

French and Gabrielli (2006) note that simulation tests the robustness of single point estimates and produces a range of possible outcomes, the mean of which can be considered as the expected land value or developer's profit and the variance or standard deviation can be considered as measures of uncertainty. The problem with this sort of analysis is the inability to confidently predict distributions and correlations of input variables such as rents, yields, building costs, and so on. Statistical confidence requires sample sizes that are significantly larger than the typical pool of comparable evidence available when valuing a property. A great deal more research is needed to confidently base the choice of probability distributions and selection of co-relationships between variables on empirical evidence.

6.6.2   Risk management

According to Fisher and Robson (2006) developers may respond to risks that they have been able to identify by avoidance, reduction, transfer or retention.

Table 6.18 Input variable correlation matrix.

	Office construction costs	Retail construction costs	Industrial construction costs	Letting void	Office rent	Retail rent	Industrial rent	Office yield	Retail yield	Industrial yield	Bank base rate
Office construction costs	1										
Retail construction costs	0	1									
Industrial construction costs	0	0	1								
Letting void	0	0	0	1							
Office rent	0	0	0	0	1						
Retail rent	0	0	0	0	0	1					
Industrial rent	0	0	0	0	0	0	1				
Office yield	0	0	0	0	-0.5	0	0	1			
Retail yield	0	0	0	0	0	-0.5	0	0.77	1		
Industrial yield	0	0	0	0	0	0	-0.5	0.67	0.67	1	
Bank base rate	0	0	0	0.5	-0.5	-0.5	-0.5	0	0	0	1

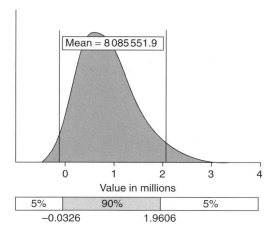

Figure 6.8 Probability distribution for developer's profit.

Table 6.19 Descriptive statistics for developer's profit.

Statistic	Result	Percentile (%)	Value
Minimum	−£576 389	5	−£39 568
Maximum	£3 687 974	10	£99 440
Mean	£808 552	15	£203 913
Std Dev	£608 123	20	£289 696
Skewness	0.7495	25	£366 529
Kurtosis	3.6274	30	£439 362
Median	£729 154	35	£510 404
Mode	£360 389	40	£583 389
		45	£654 858
		50	£729 154
		55	£806 058
		60	£874 454
		65	£960 820
		70	£1 052 842
		75	£1 157 693
		80	£1 284 008
		85	£1 430 191
		90	£1 644 644
		95	£1 947 761

Risk avoidance, reduction and transfer will invariably come at a price and that is usually expressed as a reduced return. Risk may be avoided altogether by, for example, not proceeding with the development. Risk may be reduced in various ways and we shall explore some of these below. Alternatively, risk may be transferred by taking out an insurance policy or agreeing with another party or parties to share some of the risks. This would be done using legal contracts and perhaps by forming joint ventures. Risks that are only partially transferred are shared. Risk may be retained, of course, but

Chapter 6

Table 6.20 Sensitivity matrix.

Rank	Input variable	Regression sensitivity	Correlation coefficient
1	Industrial yield	−0.421	−0.889
2	Retail yield	−0.373	−0.851
3	Office yield	−0.268	−0.903
4	Office rent	0.112	0.251
5	Industrial rent	0.050	0.257
6	Retail rent	−0.044	0.141
7	Letting void	−0.038	−0.055
8	Office construction costs	0.000	−0.005
9	Retail construction costs	0.000	−0.021
10	Industrial construction costs	0.000	−0.008
11	Bank base rate	0.000	−0.095

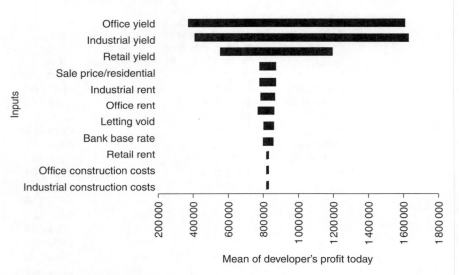

Figure 6.9 Tornado sensitivity chart.

it is wise for the developer to estimate in some way the magnitude of any retained risk and it is also important to remember that 'a risk ignored is a risk retained'. Retained risks must be managed by setting up procedures designed to reduce their probability of occurrence or mitigate their impact. Table 6.21, which is taken from Fisher and Robson, allocates typical risk responses by UK office property developers to these four categories.

There are various ways of managing the risks associated with property development. For example, the developer may decide to set up a contingency fund, agree a pre-let by offering an incentive, or arrange a fixed-rate loan with a lender. Some of these strategies are described below but it is worth bearing in mind that the risk-return trade-off is pertinent here; the greater the perceived risk, the greater the potential return. Therefore, the

Table 6.21 Risk responses in property development.

	Avoidance	Reduction	Transfer	Retention
Planning permission conditions and agreements	Location/site selection Land use/mix Option to purchase	Location/site selection Design		
Site assembly and purchase price	Location/site selection Purchase price Option copurchase	Location/site selection	Joint venture	Purchase price
Site or building condition including contamination	Location/site selection Purchase price Option to purchase Site investigation	Location/site selection Remediation design Site investigation	Col. warranties Insurance Contract terms	Purchase price Insurance Contract terms
Building procurement cost and over-runs	Site investigation Land use/mix	Site investigation Design Phasing	Col. warranties Contract terms Joint venture	Contract terms Joint venture
Debt finance and interest rates	Equity only	Level of gearing Phasing	Rate cup Limited recourse	
Letting market and voids. Rental value and incentives	Location/site selection	Market research Land use/mix Design Phasing	Pre-letting joint venture	Letting Joint venture
Investment market and yields	Location/site selection	Location/site selection Market research Land use/mix Design Phasing	Advanced sale Joint veneure	Sale Joint venture

Source: Fisher and Robson (2006).

Chapter 6

more risk is controlled, the less profit/return should be expected from the development.

6.6.2.1   Site acquisition

Byrne (1996) notes that the period of time for which a site is held prior to development can be significantly reduced if it is purchased with planning permission in place. But a site with planning permission for the development in question means that the developer faces much less site purchase risk so the price will be higher. This risk/return trade-off should be compared against the higher potential return (and higher risk) associated with acquisition of the site without the relevant planning permission.

As a means of reducing risks associated with site purchase and perhaps allowing an opportunity to investigate the condition of the site for the intended development, developers often try to delay acquisition of the site for as long as possible. This can be achieved by entering into a conditional contract with the landowner to purchase the site should permission be forthcoming. It is important to carefully word the terms of such a contract so that conditions relating to planning permission, remediation of possible contamination, density of development, and so on are unambiguous. Alternatively the developer could pay an option fee for a 'right to purchase' the site. This usually lasts for a specified period at a specified price and can also be conditional. There are two types; short-term (fixed price or fixed price with index) and long-term (perhaps 75–80% of market value of the site with relevant planning permission). These purchase arrangements are usually limited by time. The option fee is probably the best choice for the developer and the conditional contract for the landowner. The developer can also agree a right of pre-emption or 'first refusal,' should the landowner decide to sell. The pre-emption may confer a right to make the first offer or match the offer of another. In return the developer would pay a fee or obtain the necessary planning consent. This type of arrangement is not as straightforward as an option and only possible if the owner decides to sell. Using these strategies developers can assemble land banks, or virtual land banks, in which the land itself is not owned but some option, right or contract to purchase is held over the land.

With large sites in multiple ownerships it is particularly important to identify which land parcels are essential to the development. In town centres much development flows from the opening up of 'back land'. Major acquisition programmes can be complicated and conditional contracts and options to purchase are common. The aim of the developer is to purchase each site at or near to existing use value so that, if necessary, it can be sold with minimum loss if the development scheme does not proceed. It is important to note that there are two levels of development value for such sites: the first is the value of the site if developed in isolation and the second includes a share of marriage value that is released when developed with neighbouring sites. The aim of the vendor is to maximise potential development value. Given the potential for conflict, partnerships can arise where risk and profits are shared in some way, often with a minimum guaranteed return to the landowner. This type of arrangement is described in Chapter 7.

6.6.2.2 Construction costs and professional fees

An obvious means of transferring risk associated with the construction phase of the development is to agree a fixed-price contract and, indeed, this was found to be the most common risk management technique among UK office developers (Fisher and Robson, 2006). Alternatively prices of specific materials can be agreed in advance, perhaps with anticipated variation scales. The developer should also seek to control the labour cost. There may be circumstances where it is desirable for the developer to obtain bonds and warranties from contractors to guarantee work and cost. In doing so, the size and reputation of a contractor or consultant is an important consideration when attempting to ensure effective risk transfer (Fisher and Robson, 2006).

Various professionals such as architects, surveyors and engineers are commissioned to give advice throughout a typical commercial development. By doing so the developer is purchasing information about certain aspects of the development and transferring some risk. The fee paid to a professional depends on the extent of the advice given but also contributes to the indemnity insurance premium that professionals must pay to protect themselves against any losses arising from negligent advice and other legal liabilities. Professional fees should be agreed at the outset whenever possible. It may be possible to adopt a method of fee tendering. Diligence and professionalism within the professional team can be encouraged by instituting an agreed system of performance related fee scales and penalties for under-performance. Interest on professional fees can be separately calculated over two thirds of the building period. This is likely to produce a more realistic figure because many professionals are appointed early on in the development period and therefore are likely to need paying before the main contractors and materials suppliers.

6.6.2.3 Finance

Lean and Goodall (1966) suggested that smaller businesses tend to rely on short-term finance and larger ones on long-term finance. The former tend to borrow from banks and liquidate debt by selling the property on completion of the development. A larger developer, although relying partly on bank credit, will make issues of stocks and shares or borrow on a long-term basis from insurance companies and pension funds. These fundamentals of development financing have remained intact for many decades but the details have become increasingly complex. There are many ways in which the financing of a development, particularly a large or complex scheme, can be arranged and some of these financing options are discussed in Chapter 7. Essentially the developer will be seeking to reduce exposure to finance costs as much as possible. This can be done by controlling the rate at which interest is charged on money borrowed by fixing it at an agreed rate or within a specified range. Alternatively it may be possible to reduce the length of time over which the money is borrowed. With large developments such as business parks or industrial estates this can be achieved by purchasing parts or plots on the site in stages; each stage might be developed, let and sold before remaining stages are complete. Finally it may be possible to enter into an arrangement or joint venture with a lender, site owner or investor in order to share risk, funding and profit and this is a particularly useful way of sharing the risk associated with large development schemes.

6.6.2.4   Rent, yield and sale price

Fisher and Robson (2006) found that letting was the greatest perceived risk at the development feasibility stage and, once it is fixed on satisfactory terms, many other risks can be resolved. For most developers, letting the property to a good quality tenant was regarded as more important than the initial level of rent. If the development is to be let to several tenants, some units may let before others and the letting period would therefore be an average (Byrne, 1996). Some of the uncertainty surrounding the letting of a completed development and achieving the estimated level of rent can be removed by using a risk transfer technique known as a **pre-let**. This is where the developer seeks to secure a tenant at an agreed rent before the development is finished. The advantage to the developer is the removal of any possible void period. It also helps when negotiating a **forward sale** to an investor and when negotiating development finance with a lender as the risk of delayed loan repayment is reduced. The risk-reduction benefit of pre-let and forward sale arrangements must be weighed up against the potential increased return that might be achieved if the developer decides to wait until completion before letting and sale negotiations are finalised. The strategy will usually depend upon the strength of the market for the proposed development; if demand is weak then it is sound policy to seek a pre-let arrangement.

Key points

- The developer is a risk-taker: construction costs and interest rates may alter and anticipated rent and investment value may not be forthcoming
- Simple ratios and thresholds, sensitivity analysis, scenario modelling and probability analysis are all recognised methods of analysing risk
- A fall in tenant demand may lead to a fall in rent, increases the likelihood of voids, incentives and rising yields. If this coincides with rising borrowing rates then it can wipe out highly a geared residual value. A sophisticated analysis of risk should recognise the interdependence of these variables
- In terms of risk management, Fisher and Robson (2006) found that the following methods were employed (in decreasing order of popularity): fixed-price contract, pre-let, forward sale, option to purchase site, joint venture, phased disposal, mixed or flexible use and interest rate cap.

Notes

1. The value of a site depends on the use to which it is put and a change to alternative use realises that value. Rather confusingly, development control in the UK regards many changes of use as 'development'. For the purposes of this chapter though, development involves a more tangible replacement of buildings.

Development value is thus regarded as a specific form of alternative use value calculated using the residual method of valuation.

2. Byrne (1996) provides a clear explanation of the difference between the two sampling methods available in the @RISK software program. 'Monte Carlo' sampling is random and, given a probability distribution, the more probable values are likely to be sampled. If the number of iterations is small, events in the tail may not get sampled. 'Latin Hypercube' uses a form of stratified sampling where each input distribution is divided into equal strata. This is done according to the number of iterations to be run; if there are to be 1000 iterations then the distribution is divided into 1000 strata. A stratum is selected randomly and a value sampled from within: this is done 'without replacement' so, over the entire run, every stratum is sampled once. The consequence of stratification is a higher standard deviation because values are sampled from right across the distribution.

3. Multicollinearity refers to linear inter-correlation among two or more variables, that is, they actually measure the same phenomenon to a significant degree.

References

Baum, A. (1988) Depreciation and property investment appraisal, in MacLeary, A. and Nanthakumaran, N. (Eds), *Property Investment Theory*, E. & F. N. Spon, London, UK.

Baum, A. (1991) *Property Investment Depreciation and Obsolescence*, Routledge, London, UK.

Barras, R. and Clark, P. (1996) Obsolescence and performance in the Central London office market, *Journal of Property Valuation and Investment*, 14, 4, 63–78.

Byrne, P. (1996) *Risk, Uncertainty and Decision-making in Property Development*, 2nd edn, E. and F. N. Spon, London, UK.

Davis, Langdon, and Everest (eds) (2004) *Spon's Architects' and Builders' Price Book*, Taylor and Francis, London, UK.

Evans, A. (1985) *Urban Economics: An Introduction*, Blackwell, Oxford, UK.

Fisher, P. and Robson, S. (2006) The perception and management of risk in UK office property development, *Journal of Property Research*, 23, 2, 135–161.

Fraser, W. (1993) *Principles of Property Investment and Pricing*, 2nd edn, Macmillan, Basingstoke, Hampshire, UK.

French, N. and Gabrielli, L. (2006) Uncertainty and feasibility studies: an Italian case study, *JPIF*, 24, 1, 49–67.

Hargitay, S. and Yu, S. (1992) *Property Investment Decisions: A Quantitative Approach*, Spon Press, London, UK.

Harker, N. (1987) The valuation of modern warehouses: inflation and depreciation implications, *Journal of Valuation*, 5, 138.

Harvey, J. and Jowsey, E. (2004) *Urban Land Economics*, 6th edn, Palgrave Macmillan, Basingstoke, UK.

Lean, W. and Goodall, B. (1966) *Aspects of Land Economics*, Estates Gazette Ltd, London, UK.

Marshall, A. (1920) *Principles of Economics*, 8th edn, Macmillan, London, UK.

Miles, J. (1987) Depreciation and valuation accuracy, *Journal of Valuation*, 5, 125.

Salway, F. (1986) *Depreciation of Commercial Property*, CALUS, College of Estate Management, Reading, UK.

Salway, F. (1987) Building depreciation and property appraisal techniques, *Journal of Valuation*, 5, 118.

Chapter 7
Property Appraisal

7.1 Introduction

It is easy to become confused by the terms that are used to describe various concepts surrounding price, value and worth. One important distinction to draw at the beginning of this chapter is between a market valuation and an appraisal of worth. You may remember that, in Chapter 1, we made a distinction between value-in-exchange and value-in-use. In economic terms market value is equivalent to value-in-exchange and worth is equivalent to value-in-use. Furthermore, a market *valuation* is an estimation of exchange price that relies on the interpretation of market information, which is usually available in the form of comparable evidence. An appraisal of worth, or *appraisal* for short, is an estimation of worth to a specific individual at a certain time and usually involves an assessment of personal circumstances, together with wider property and market factors, to consider the risk and return characteristics of some property-related decision that is being made. These personal circumstances might encompass the following:

- The financial resources available for a property acquisition, including the split between debt and equity finance.
- The timescale for holding a property asset, referred to as a holding period by investors (as encountered in Chapter 5) or a write-off period by business occupiers.
- The tax position, personal tastes and specific requirements of the decision-maker.

These specific requirements may relate to the way in which the property is to be managed if it is to be held as an investment (a small-scale niche investor may wish to manage the property much more actively than a large institutional investor) or the way in which the property might be used by an occupying business. Wider considerations relating to the investment portfolio of an investor or the property estate of an occupier will also need to be considered. Moreover, all of these issues must be considered in the light of the macro-economy.

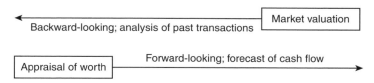

Figure 7.1   Valuation and appraisal.

In a perfect market, where buyers and sellers have instant access to market information, their economic requirements are identical and properties are homogeneous, we could assume that market participants would arrive at similar decisions and thus individual appraisals of worth might converge on a market value. In other words there would be no difference between exchange prices, market valuations and appraisals of worth for each unit of property. However, the property market and its primary sectors (development, occupation and investment) are not perfect; the product is heterogeneous, as are buyers and sellers, and there are many typologically and geographically distinct sub-markets, as we know from Chapter 1.

Methodologically, appraisals of worth have tended to ignore the simple comparison-based techniques that have been used in valuation for many years. These essentially backward-looking techniques focus on the analysis of past transactions in order to support an estimate of current market value, as illustrated in Figure 7.1.

Instead cash-flow techniques and other sophisticated approaches have been adapted from other financial markets. In recent years the economic basis of market value – supply, demand and equilibrium price – has been extended to include a more analytical treatment of the pricing decision and the distinction between valuation and appraisal has blurred. Cash-flow modelling seeks to quantify not only the price at which a property might exchange in a market situation but also the criteria on which such pricing decisions are made; for example, the required rate of return, the holding period for the property and risk factors. These concepts were considered in detail in Chapter 5 and will be revisited here from the perspective of an appraisal rather than a valuation. An appraisal is usually performed by determining the risk and return characteristics associated with holding the property and often includes a valuation, forecasting of key variables and some form of performance analysis. For an investor the future income stream, quality of the tenant and property are important. For a business property appraisal, undertaken on behalf of an occupier, the cost of the property as a factor of production or its contribution to profit, as well as its future sale price or write-off cost will need to be considered. An appraisal of worth can be undertaken for different clients for different reasons. For example, a pension fund may need to know how an asset might contribute to portfolio performance, whereas a property company (usually a more active investor) might be more interested in a building's redevelopment potential. An occupier will evaluate the business requirements and the cost of debt and equity capital amongst other things. The aspirations and therefore the appraisal assumptions (such as discount rate, holding period, and so on) will undoubtedly vary to some degree. Having said this, groups of similar types of investors and occupiers will behave in a similar way (institutional investors for example) and therefore certain assumptions can be made.

It is therefore normal for a range of appraisals of worth to exist for a property but only one exchange price. There is no reason that just because something trades at a given price that it will represent and will deliver good value to a particular buyer, especially in a relatively information-starved market like commercial property and where there are many sub-markets and heterogeneous buyers. Differences between price or value of a property and its worth to an individual emerge because of different perceptions about either the utility to a business or potential return to an investor that the property may offer. Perceptions may vary in terms of how utility or return will vary over time (its volatility) and how long that utility or return will last. So worth and value can be different and provide evidence of mispricing from the perspective of certain decision-makers. This leads to the debate concerning market efficiency and the fact that the property market offers opportunities for buyers to exploit pricing inefficiencies, mainly due to informational gaps and inaccuracies. Also, market correction is likely to be slower than is the case for other more liquid investment markets such as equities and bonds.

Ball *et al.* (1998) boldly claim that 'the influence of valuations on price and the focus on price estimation, rather than worth, can lead to systematic mispricing'. What is being suggested is that because property is a thinly traded and heterogeneous investment asset or factor of production, valuers are not only *interpreting* market prices when attempting to estimate the market value of a property, but they are also *influencing* them. Not only that, what is being suggested is that valuers' methods have erroneously focused on price estimation rather than worth appraisal – looking too much at market price data rather than the fundamental requirements of clients. These criticisms are harsh but not unfounded: conventional valuation techniques are increasingly being supplemented and in some cases replaced by contemporary approaches that place more reliance on client fundamentals than market signals. But it should be remembered that valuation must always have interpretation of market activity at its heart and market-generated price signals will always provide a very reliable source of intelligence. It is important to distinguish, then, between market value and worth; the latter is worth to a particular buyer, which may coincide with market value if the buyer's decision criteria are typical of other buyers in the market. Apart from the latter half of Chapter 6, this book has been about property valuation. In Chapter 6 we did move into the world of appraisal by attempting to estimate and evaluate developer's profit as well as market exchange price. This chapter extends the consideration of appraisal to cover not only development but also investment and business appraisal.

> ### Key points
>
> - Valuation is a market-based concept; an appraisal of worth is an individual-based concept and represents a means of assessing whether a price/valuation represents 'good value' to a particular individual.
> - A different information set is used to conduct appraisals of worth, using more information specific to the individual. An appraisal of worth may vary more than a market valuation – as the financial estimation moves away from being based on an analysis of market information to greater consideration of personal investor or occupier requirements, using more sophisticated techniques.
> - In this chapter appraisal is considered from the point of view of the investor and the occupier. The developer, who was the focus of attention in Chapter 6, is considered to be a particular type of property investor for the purposes of this chapter.

7.2   Property investment appraisal

In the investment sector an appraisal of worth typically refers to an estimation of an individual's perception of worth. Much of the research effort and practical development of worth appraisals to date has concentrated on appraisals of investment worth. In simple terms, an investor considering the purchase of a property investment needs to compare its asking price with his or her own assessment of worth. Similarly, a holder of a property investment would periodically compare its worth with its market value. This helps the investor decide whether to acquire a new property or whether to hold, refurbish, redevelop or dispose of an existing property. Property investment appraisals are also required to help choose between different investment opportunities, to assess the viability of redevelopment or refurbishment projects and as a decision tool for financing arrangements. The latter is also relevant to business appraisals.

7.2.1   Appraisal information and assumptions

Investment appraisal involves making explicit judgments (based on evidence) about depreciation, risk, expenditure, exit value, any rental growth, taxation, financing and all costs.

Information needs range from the property-specific to the macro-economic. Table 7.1 is an attempt to classify the information typically sought prior to conducting an appraisal of worth.

This is a lot of information to assimilate in an appraisal of worth, and many of these factors can be grouped together and handled by adjusting either the cash-flow or the target rate of return. Nevertheless, it is important to concentrate on those factors considered to affect the assessment of worth to the greatest extent, in other words, the most important or value significant factors. This concept of focusing analysis on key variables was

Table 7.1　Typical appraisal information.

Information	Example
Economic indicators	Economic output (GDP, GNP)
	Employment and unemployment statistics
	Movements in corporate profits (by sector), money supply, public sector borrowing, inflation and interest rates
Market indicators	Current market rents
	Rental growth and depreciation rates
	Future redevelopment or refurbishment costs
	Current yields and forecasts of exit yields
	Purchase and sale costs
	Movements in market indices
Portfolio information	Asset returns and correlations (to aid diversification)
	Sales and purchases
	Risk indicators
Property information	Physical attributes (areas, ancillary space, quality, improvements)
	Financial details (yield, rent passing, rental growth, market rent and capital value)
	Legal terms (tenancies and lease details, number of tenants, expiry dates, review dates, voids, future leases)
	Outgoings and capital expenditure (vacancies, voids, unrecoverable service and management costs, letting, re-letting and rent review costs, purchase and sale costs)
	Depreciation, costs and timing of redevelopment and refurbishment, cost inflation
	Planning
	Taxation (Business rates, VAT)
	Occupancy/holding costs (management, review, purchase and sale costs)
	Dilapidations, service charge and other payments for repairs and insurance if leasehold
Client-specific information	Target or discount rate
	Individual tax position (capital allowances, IHT, loan/finance tax on income and on capital gain in the form of Income Tax/CGT and Corporation Tax)
	Holding period
	Loan facilities
	Risk profile

introduced in Chapters 5 and 6 when we looked at sensitivity analysis and simulation. In fact, an investment appraisal may be less volatile than a development appraisal (which we looked at in Chapter 6) because there are fewer key variables, and changes in these variables are often less pronounced. This results in a more stable cash-flow. In an investment appraisal, the key factors are rent, target rate of return, holding period and exit yield. These have been discussed in Chapter 5, and we will expand on that discussion here in the context of appraisal.

7.2.1.1   Rent and rental growth

The rental value and rental growth must be identified. Associated variables include timing of rent reviews (which usually occur every 5 years in the UK), the length of the lease, the existence of any break options and the level of management costs, taxation and inflation. Rent can be volatile over short term but rental growth tends to be fairly stable over the medium to long term. Forecasts of market rents and rental growth are available and typically relate to prime business space in the locality concerned because the thorny issue of how rents may depreciate as premises age can be avoided. These forecasts are produced at a national, regional or local level and are usually based on econometric models of the economy and the property market. Forecasting requires future levels of revenue and expenditure to be predicted and this can be problematic because the market is cyclical and it can be difficult to predict turning points. Another difficulty is a lack of good quality data, especially at the local level. Forecasts of rent and rental growth at the town level may be misleading if they are applied at individual property level. Little is known about the way rents depreciate over time, either owing to physical deterioration of the property itself or owing to some form of obsolescence. There is a clear demand for appraisal to allow for such items as obsolescence and deterioration, but particular care is needed when considering how these phenomena affect value and it is important to ensure that double-counting does not occur. This is a frequent problem when trying to be explicit about all value influences in an appraisal. For example, if refurbishment expenditure is included in the cash-flow then any enhanced value should be reflected either in the estimated rental value, the rental growth rate or in the exit yield.

It is important to consider the potential impact of gaps or voids in the receipt of rent, particularly as lease lengths shorten and break clauses become more prevalent. Of key concern is the likelihood that a tenant operates a break clause or vacates the premises at the end of a lease. Other matters then follow, including the costs of holding a vacant property, the length of time to re-let and any works that need to be done to enable a new letting.

7.2.1.2   Target rate of return

The target rate of return from an investment must adequately compensate an investor for the risk taken. It is typically derived by adding a risk premium to a 'benchmark' risk-free rate of return. The risk-free rate is a baseline rate defined by reference to the return from a low-risk or risk-free asset and was conventionally derived from an examination of the income yields on medium/long-dated (15–25 year) gilts. The rationale for basing the risk-free rate on this benchmark was because the term coincided with typical lease lengths. As lease lengths shorten it may be more appropriate to base this risk-free rate on short-dated gilts or 5–10-year swap rates. A risk premium is added to the risk-free rate to compensate for holding a property asset. This risk premium is difficult to estimate for property, as each asset is unique. Investment characteristics that are best handled by adjusting the target rate are generally market-related and include liquidity, rental growth prospects, possible yield movements and depreciation. Property-related risks include the quality of tenant, potential for letting voids, cost of ownership and management and lease structure. The financial impact of these factors can be built into the cash-flow. But determining a risk premium for each factor is difficult given paucity of data, complexity of the market and confidentiality of client data. Also, the significant overlapping influence of these risk factors complicates this sort of analysis. Consequently, attempting to derive risk premiums for individual property assets is not easy and not recommended. It may be more helpful to group similar types of property in order to determine a property risk premium for each group. A market risk premium can then be adjusted up or down to reflect the risk associated with the sub-sector being analysed. Market and property risk premiums are added to the risk-free rate. So, for example, consider the high street shops sub-sector;

risk-free rate

+

market risks (sub-sector risk of market failure, such as illiquidity, poor rent or yield performance, allowance for sub-sector depreciation)

+

property risks (including property-specific risks such as adjustments for tenant quality, and grouped property risks such as adjustments for sub-sector lease structures)

= risk-adjusted discount rate

Remaining costs (fees, management, dilapidation, etc.) are incorporated in the cash-flow.

This 'risk-adjusted discount rate' approach to deriving a target rate of return is frequently used by property analysts and investors but, according to Sayce *et al.* (2006), there are two main limitations. First, only one discount rate is applied to all cash-flows and it therefore fails to distinguish those parts of the cash-flow that are risky and those that are not. For example, rental income return might be regarded as fairly secure, whereas capital return might be considered to be more volatile over the holding period. It is possible to discount different parts of cash-flow at different rates using a 'sliced income approach' (Baum and Crosby, 1995) or an arbitrage approach (French and Ward, 1995), but such methods are not frequently used in property investment appraisal. In property valuations a core and top-slice approach is used when the risk profile of a rent changes significantly at some future date. The second limitation is that the target rate heavily discounts distant cash-flows regardless of whether they are actually more risky. It is unlikely that the growth in risk is going to be at exactly the same exponential rate as the growth inherent in the risk premium. Furthermore, cash-flow after a refurbishment or redevelopment programme is likely to be more uncertain.

7.2.1.3   Holding period

The holding period is normally specified by the client and is usually between 3 and 5 or 10 and 15 years depending on the type of investor. As a rule of thumb, large institutional investors might be considered to have longer holding periods than niche investors and investor-developers who may be more interested in the capital growth opportunities afforded by redevelopment potential than long-term income growth. The duration of the holding period can also be influenced by lease terms, particularly the dates of any break clauses and lease expiry, or by the physical nature of property itself; particularly depreciation factors and redevelopment potential. A longer holding period will mean that it is more difficult to predict the values of key variables in the medium to long term (a problem that is usually hidden by using an exit yield or exit value at the end of a shorter holding period). So a long holding period is associated with greater risk of fluctuation from predictions of long-term trends and a greater chance of error in selecting exit variables. An additional consideration is whether the market is assumed to be stable over the holding period.

7.2.1.4   Exit value

Exit value refers to the value of the property at the end of the holding period. The usual method of calculating exit value is to capitalise the rent forecast at the end of the holding period. In selecting an appropriate exit yield at which to capitalise the rent, we are asking what yield a purchaser would require for the property at the point of (notional) sale. The exit yield is usually based on fairly stable prime yields and is normally derived by comparison with similar investments. It is important to consider the impact of depreciation, but care should be taken so as not to double-count its effect on value by, say, reducing the forecast rent and raising the exit yield. The choice of exit yield is central to the appraisal when the holding period is less than 20 years, as the resulting exit value forms a substantial element of the overall worth of the investment. The exit value may reflect land values if demolition is anticipated.

7.2.2   Appraisal methodology

Investment appraisal requires a rational basis for comparing different investment propositions and some of the methods for doing so are considered below.

7.2.2.1   Payback method

Payback measures the time taken to recoup expenditure and is a widely used investment appraisal method, mainly because it is simple to perform and interpret. The method favours investments where the greater cash-flow is received in the early years. It does this because any income received after payback has been attained is simply ignored. The method therefore tends to view investments in the short term, only focusing on cash-flows within the payback period; the shorter the payback the more attractive the investment. The method fails to measure long-term profitability beyond the payback

Table 7.2   Payback.

Year	Property A	Property B
0	−100 000	−100 000
1	60 000	20 000
2	40 000	60 000
3	20 000	60 000
4	20 000	70 000
Total net cash-flow	40 000	110 000

period. Some types of investment may yield low returns in the short term but benefit from substantial increases in income and capital value in the medium to long term: a reversionary freehold property investment or a shopping centre, where units are let on periodic tenancies while redevelopment is planned are examples of this type of cash-flow. The payback method would not be able to adequately reflect the potential worth of these types of investment opportunity. The method also ignores the time value of money, the total return that can be expected from the investment and volatility of that return. For example, consider the cash-flows of the two investment opportunities in Table 7.2.

Property A would be chosen because the payback is in 2 years despite the total net cash-flow for B being much greater. The only justification for this method can be that as one projects further into the future the more volatile returns are expected to be, so it is better to have returns sooner.

Discounted payback is a variation of the payback method that considers the time value of money by calculating how quickly a project recoups initial expenditure in discounted (present value) terms. It is really a version of the net present value method (see below) truncated to the payback year so cash-flows beyond this point are, once again, ignored. The payback method should be used as an initial screening device prior to more sophisticated methods.

7.2.2.2   Yield

A key measure of investment quality is the ratio of net annual income to capital outlay.

In property investment this ratio is known as the yield (see Chapter 2). For example, assume that a small pension fund wishes to invest £5 000 000 but insists on a 9% return. A shop comes on to the market for £5 000 000, which has been let at £400 000 per annum. Should the pension fund purchase this investment?

Yield = income/capital value
      = £400 000/£5 000 000
      = 0.08 or 8%

On the face of it, the shop investment does not produce a sufficient return. The yield is simple to calculate and can be compared to a 'hurdle' or target rate of return set by the investor, as illustrated in the example above or it can be compared to the investor's overall return on capital or weighted average cost of capital. Of course, the shop investment has only been analysed in terms of its initial return and the simple relationship between initial income and price paid reveals nothing about future income and capital growth prospects. To do this a slightly more sophisticated measure is required. Assume that an analysis of recently achieved yields in the local prime office property market has revealed that they average 6.40%. Typically, properties are let on 15-year leases incorporating 5-yearly rent reviews. Your client requires an annual rate of return of 11% from this type of asset. The IPD office property index indicates that, recently, rents have been growing at an average rate of 4% per annum. Does office property currently look attractive? Initial yields average 6.40%, and this, together with the target rate of 11%, implies rental growth of 5.17% per annum. This is the growth rate that would need to be achieved if your client's target rate of return is to be realised. If past performance of rental growth reported by the IPD index is indicative of future performance, then this level of growth appears to be unsustainable. In other words, offices look unattractive, unless your client is willing to accept a return of less than 11% or rental growth prospects look set to improve.

Like the payback method, the yield is simple to calculate and easy to understand. But the method cannot account for financial magnitude of the investments under consideration because it is a percentage measure. The fact that a yield, like payback, ignores the time value of money and ignores the concept of cash-flows, means that it should only be used to screen investments prior to a more detailed appraisal.

7.2.2.3   Discounted cash-flow (DCF) methods of investment appraisal

The way in which the appraisal methods described so far have handled the relationship between money invested, future cash-flows and time ignores the time value of money. This crucial investment concept must be reflected in any serious appraisal method and the most popular way of doing so is to construct a discounted cash-flow or DCF. DCF was developed by financial appraisers as a tool to assess overall profitability. A DCF is a summation of the present values of all revenue, including rent, premiums and sale price, and expenditure, such as the purchase price and any periodic expenditure. The present value of a future sum, whether it is revenue or expenditure, is dependent on the discount rate and the length of time over which it is discounted: the higher the discount rate and/or the longer the discount period, the lower the present value. The main advantage of a DCF approach over payback and yield methods is that it can adjust the cash-flow in each period to account for changes in inflation, rental growth, tax, and so on. DCF also allows direct comparison of investments because the cash-flows are converted to a common denominator – present value. We have already looked at the application of DCF to property valuation. Because DCF can be expanded to incorporate explicit assumptions about rental growth, holding period, depreciation, refurbishment, redevelopment, management and transfer costs, tax and financing costs, it is used as a worth appraisal technique as well as a market valuation technique. In fact, DCF techniques are often used to test the estimate of market value rather than derive it; in other words, they are more frequently used in appraisal than valuation.

There are two commonly used approaches to investment appraisal using a DCF: net present value and the internal rate of return.

Net present value (NPV). NPV calculates a money amount by summing known or projected cash-flows over a holding period discounted at an appropriate discount rate, usually the target rate of the investor but it could equally reflect the cost of borrowing, the return required from alternative investments or the rate on government stock. Earlier income is deemed more valuable as the effect of discounting diminishes the value of more distant cash-flows. Any investment with a positive NPV is viable at the specified discount rate. If we ignore periodic expenditure for the moment and assume that the purchase price is the only cost, mathematically, NPV is simply the total present value (TPV) less the purchase price *P*. The TPV of an income stream of £1 per annum was derived in Chapter 2 (Equation 2.15) and takes the form of a geometric progression, repeated below for convenience:

$$TPV = \frac{1}{(1+r)} + \frac{1}{(1+r)^2} + \frac{1}{(1+r)^3} + \cdots + \frac{1}{(1+r)^n} = \sum_{i=1}^{n} \frac{1}{(1+r)^i} \qquad [7.1]$$

And, for any other income *A*:

$$TPV = \sum_{i=1}^{n} \frac{1}{(1+r)^i} \cdot A = \sum_{i=1}^{n} \frac{A}{(1+r)^i} \qquad [7.2]$$

Net present value is TPV less purchase price *P*:

$$NPV = \sum_{i=1}^{n} \frac{A}{(1+r)^i} - P \qquad [7.3]$$

For example, calculate the NPV of a property investment on the market for £880 000 and which generates the cash-flow shown in Table 7.3.

Assuming a target rate of return or discount rate of 10%, the NPV is positive, which means that the target rate of return required by the investor has been exceeded by this investment opportunity.

If the NPV approach is used to compare a number of investment opportunities then the one with the highest NPV will be the best, provided the capi-

Table 7.3   Net present value.

Year	Cash-flow (£)	PV £1 @ 10%	DCF (£)
0	−880 000	1.0000	−880 000
1	200 000	0.9091	181 820
2	400 000	0.8264	330 560
3	440 000	0.7513	330 572
4	220 000	0.6830	150 260
NPV			113 212

tal outlay on each opportunity is the same. For example, a restaurateur can install a new bar for £140 000 (Project A) or have alterations done to increase the seating capacity for the same cost (Project B). The returns in Table 7.4 are anticipated.

Assuming that the target rate of return for both projects is 10% and they are mutually exclusive, advise the restaurateur as to which should be undertaken.

Table 7.5 shows that Project B has the greater NPV.

Now compare two property investments where each involves the same initial outlay and produces identical net total cash-flows. However, the timing of payments is different; Property A yields a higher income in the early years and then requires refurbishment in year 7, whereas Property B is in need of refurbishment in year 1. The NPV will be higher if the majority of the cash-flows are received early on, as illustrated in Table 7.6.

If the capital outlays are different, the *benefit-to-cost ratio* can be calculated as follows and the project with the highest ratio should be chosen:

$$\text{Benefit-to-cost ratio} = \frac{\text{NPV}}{\text{PV of total costs}} \qquad [7.4]$$

For example, which of the two mutually exclusive investments in Table 7.7 would you recommend, assuming a target rate of return of 10%?

Table 7.4 Two investment opportunities.

Year	Cash-flow from Project A (£)	Cash-flow from Project B (£)
1	60 000	20 000
2	40 000	40 000
3	20 000	40 000
4	40 000	60 000
5	40 000	60 000

Table 7.5 Comparing investment using NPV.

Year	Cash-flow from Project A (£)	PV £1 @ 10%	DCF (£)	Cash-flow from Project B (£)	PV £1 @ 10%	DCF (£)
1	60 000	0.9091	54 546	20 000	0.9091	18 182
2	40 000	0.8264	33 056	40 000	0.8264	33.056
3	20 000	0.7513	15 026	40 000	0.7513	30 052
4	40 000	0.6830	27 320	60 000	0.6830	40 980
5	40 000	0.6209	24 836	60 000	0.6209	37 254
		TPV	154 784		TPV	159 524
		Less outlay	−140 000		Less outlay	−140 000
		NPV	14 784		NPV	19 524

Table 7.6   The effect of timing of investment return on NPV.

Year	Property A (£)	Property B (£)
0	−750 000	−750 000
1	90 000	−500 000
2	90 000	70 000
3	90 000	70 000
4	90 000	90 000
5	70 000	90 000
6	70 000	90 000
7	−500 000	90 000
8	2 000 000	2 000 000
Net total	1 250 000	1 250 000
NPV	563 303	323 484

Table 7.7   Comparing two investment with different capital outlays using NPV.

Year	Cash-flow from Project A (£)	PV £1 @ 10%	DCF (£)	Cash-flow from Investment B (£)	PV £1 @ 10%	DCF (£)
1	30 000	0.9091	27 273	40 000	0.9091	36 364
2	20 000	0.8264	16 528	30 000	0.8264	24 792
3	15 000	0.7513	11 270	20 000	0.7513	15.026
		Total	55 071		Total	76 182
		Less outlay	50 000		Less outlay	−70 000
		NPV	5 071		NPV	6 182
		PV total costs	50 000		PV total costs	70 000
		Benefit: Cost ratio	10.14%		Benefit: Cost ratio	8.83%

Table 7.8   The effec of inflation on a cash-flow.

Year	Cash-flow	Discount/inflation rate (4%)	DCF
0	−200 000	1.0000	−200 000
1	15 000	0.9615	14 423
2	20 000	0.9246	18 492
3	200 000	0.8890	177 800
Net	35 000	NPV	10 715

Despite a lower NPV, because of its magnitude in relation to the outlay, Project A would be chosen.

If the rate of inflation is used as the discount rate then it is possible to determine whether an investment meets the minimum requirement of transferring purchasing power through time. The effect of an inflation rate of 4% per annum on a cash-flow is shown in Table 7.8.

The NPV is a lot less than the net cash-flow in nominal terms because the bulk of the value of the cash-flow is received at the end of the holding period in year 3. The nominal increase in value is £35 000 and the real increase is £10 713 after a loss of purchasing power to inflation at a rate of 4% per annum. This shows the relationship between nominal and real present value. A loss to inflation is the first barrier to investing and is a financial cost just like operating expenses and taxes. But inflation is only one component of the discount rate; others include a return for risk taken and possibly adjustments to reflect depreciation.

The calculations for these cash-flows can be undertaken on a spreadsheet. In fact, there is an NPV function on Excel that simplifies the process even more. Consider a conventional rack-rented freehold property investment opportunity which is on the market for £100 000. An appraisal is required to determine whether this opportunity is one that your client, who has a target rate of 16%, should pursue. The rent is £12 000 per annum, rent reviews are for every 5 years, the assumed holding period is 20 years, over which time you expect rent to grow at an average rate of 5% per annum. At the end of the holding period you assume a sale at an exit yield of 11%.

In Table 7.9, the cash-flows from this particular investment have been concatenated into 5-yearly income blocks because the annual rental income between each rent review is identical. The exit yield may well be higher than current initial yields because the property will be 20 years older, so it is important to use comparable evidence of similar but 20-year-older properties than the subject property. Also, the rate of rental growth will probably decline, become static or even negative, so a spreadsheet can be used to model various outcomes.

Consider another example but this time where a year-by-year cash-flow is constructed. One of your investment clients is thinking of purchasing the freehold interest in an office refurbishment opportunity in the centre of Cardiff. The property was constructed in the 1960s and is ripe for refurbishment upon expiry of the existing lease in 7 years' time. The current lease is on full repairing and insuring (FRI) terms, the present rent is £100 000 per annum

Table 7.9 Appraisal of a rack-rented freehold property investment.

Period	Net cash-flow (£)	Growth rate	Real cash-flow (£)	YP 5 years @ target rate	PV £1 @ target rate	Discounted income (£)
Initial outlay						−£100 000
0–4	12 000	1.0000	12 000	3.2743	1.0000	39 292
5–9	12 000	1.2763	15 315	3.2743	0.4761	23 876
10–14	12 000	1.6289	19 547	3.2743	0.2267	14 508
15–19	12 000	2.0789	24 947	3.2743	0.1079	8.816
20–perp.	12 000	2.6533	31 840	9.0909[a]	0.0514	14 874
Net present value						£1 365

[a]YP perpetuity at exit yield of 11%.

and the final review is in 2 years' time. The asking price is £1 200 000. Your client plans to hold the property until lease expiry, refurbish and then sell the freehold interest. The current cost of refurbishment is £1 000 000 and will take 1 year to complete. The current market rent of the property in its existing state is £120 000 per annum and £200 000 per annum when refurbished. The freehold all-risks yield after refurbishment is 7%. Rental growth for the existing property is estimated to be 4% per annum and for the refurbished property 7% per annum. Building cost inflation is running at an average of 6% per annum. Assuming your client's target rate of return is 15% advise your client as to whether this is a good investment opportunity at the asking price stated. With a year-by-year cash-flow, shown in Table 7.10, the YP column is dispensed with. If the investment is purchased for £1 200 000 then, as the NPV is positive, a target rate of 15% will be achieved.

This final example assume the rental growth rate changes during the holding period. Your client, who has a target rate of return of 11%, is considering the purchase of a freehold office building in the centre of Bristol. It is let on an FRI lease, having 1 year left to run. The current rent is £140 000 per annum. The open market rental value is £160 000 per annum. The present occupier intends to vacate the premises at the end of the current lease. Refurbishment works, estimated to be £480 000, would increase the market rental value to £240 000 per annum (at today's levels). Rental values are predicted to rise by 4% by the end of the current lease. They will rise to 7% per annum for the following 5 years, and then to 9% per annum thereafter. Your client wishes to sell the freehold interest after 10 years and investment yields at that time can be assumed to be the same as those reflected by the current asking price. You are required to provide an investment appraisal to help determine whether it would be worth your client paying the asking

Table 7.10 Appraisal of a reversionary freehold property investment with refurbishment potential.

Period	Description	Cash-flow (£)	PV @ 15%	DCF (£)
0	Purchase price	−1 200 000	1.0000	−1 200 000
1	Rental income	100 000	0.8696	86 957
2	Rental income	100 000	0.7561	75 614
3	Rental income	129 792[a]	0 6575	85 341
4	Rental income	129 792	0.5718	74 209
5	Rental income	129 792	0.4972	64 530
6	Rental income	129 792	0.4323	56 113
7	Rental income	129 792	0.3759	48 794
8	Sale proceeds	4 909 138[b]	0.3269	1 604 797
	Refurb costs	−1 593 800[c]	0.3269	−521 013
NPV				375 343

[a]MR of £120 000 compounded over 2 years at 4% pa rental growth rate.
[b]£200 000 compounded over 8 years at 7% pa rental growth rate and capitalised at 7% ARY.
[c]£1 000 000 build cost compounded over 8 years at 6% pa build cost inflation rate.

price of £2 000 000. A period of 1 year for refurbishment is assumed and, given a buoyant rental market for refurbished office premises in the subject location, a swift letting on FRI terms at a rent subject to 5-yearly reviews is also assumed. The rental income profile is shown in Table 7.11.

To determine the capital value or exit value of the property at the end of year 10, we are told to 'assume that investment yields at that time will be the same as reflected by the current asking price' and, therefore, we need to analyse the investment whilst disregarding the refurbishment proposals. The analysis is as follows:

Purchase price (£)	2 000 000
Rent passing (contract rent) (£pa)	140 000
Initial yield	7%
Market rental (£pa)	160 000
Reversionary yield	8%
Years to reversion	1
Equivalent yield, say	8%

Table 7.11 Cash-flow of a reversionary property investment with varying rental growth.

Year	Activity	Current rental values (£)	Rental growth rate (%)	Compounded rental growth	Projected rental values (£)
0	Purchase				
1		140 000			140 000
2	Refurbishment		4		267 072
3	New MR	240 000	7	$1.04 \times 1.07 = 1.1128$	267 072
4		240 000	7		267 072
5		240 000	7		267 072
6		240 000	7		267 072
7		240 000	7		381 576
8	Rent review	240 000	9	$1.04 \times 1.07^5 \times 1.09 = 1.5899$	381 576
9		240 000	9		381 576
10	Sale	240 000	9		381 576
11		240 000	9		381 576
12		240 000	9		381 576
13	Rent review	240 000	9	$1.04 \times 1.07^5 \times 1.09^5 = 2.2443$	538 637

[a]Note that the compounded increase in any year is the compounded increase from the previous year multiplied by the increase over the last year. For example, there is to be a 4% increase in rental values over the first year followed by a 7% increase over the second year. The compounded increase to the start of Year 3 is therefore $1.04 \times 1.07 = 1.1128$, and so on.

We can now value the property at the end of year 10, when it will be a reversionary investment, as the rent passing will be below the then market rental value. The capital value at the end of year 10 will therefore be

Term rent (£pa)	381 500
YP for 2 years @ 8%	17 833
	680 329

Reversion to market rent at next rent review (£pa)	538 637
YP perpetuity @ 8%	12.5000
PV of £1 in 2 yrs @ 8%	0.8573
	5 772 168
Capital value (£)	6 452 495

The appraisal is shown in Table 7.12

Internal rate of return (IRR). NPV is a means of assessing whether an investment reaches a target rate but it does not tell you exactly what the rate of return (the IRR) of the investment is. The IRR is the rate at which the discounted cash-flow of income equates to the discounted cash-flow of all expenditure, in other words where NPV equals zero. But the relationship between NPV and the discount rate is non-linear. This means that if a cash-flow is discounted at various rates and the resultant NPVs are plotted on a graph a curved line results. This can be illustrated with an example. A rack-rented freehold property investment is currently let at a rent of £17 500 per annum on a lease with 5-year upward-only rent reviews. Rent is forecast to grow at 3% per annum compounded at each review. The holding period is 20 years and the exit yield is 8%. Using a range of discount rates between 1% and 20% the NPVs presented in Table 7.13 are calculated, and these are plotted in Figure 7.2.

The IRR is found where the curve cuts the *y* axis, where the NPV is 0. Using the IRR to appraise an investment avoids having to select an appropriate discount rate for a particular investment. Instead the IRR of an investment can be compared with the investor's generic target rate of return or the cost of borrowing capital. Also, the IRR of a property investment can be compared with IRRs of non-property investments. The IRR can also be monitored throughout the life of an investment; if it drops below market rates it may be time to sell.

Table 7.12 Apprisal of a reversionary property investment with varying rental growth.

Period	Activity	Net cash-flow (£)	PV @ 11%	DCF (£)
0	Purchase price	−2 000 000	1.0000	−2 000 000
1	Rental income	140 000	0.9009	126 126
2	Refurbishment	−480 000	0.8116	−389 568
3	Rental income	267 000	0.7312	195 230
4	Rental income	267 000	0.6587	175 872
5	Rental income	267 000	0.5935	158 465
6	Rental income	267 000	0.5346	142 738
7	Rental income	267 000	0.4817	128 613
8	Rental income	381 500	0.4339	165 533
9	Rental income	381 500	0.3909	149 128
10	Rental income	381 500	0.3522	134 515
	Sale price	6 452 495	0.3533	1 951 188
NPV				937 689

Table 7.13 NPVs, resulting from different discount rates.

Discount rate (%)	NPV (£)
1	519 724
2	421 400
3	339 330
4	270 580
5	212 780
6	164 006
7	122 697
8	87 578
9	57 607
10	31 932
11	9 852
12	−9 210
13	−25 732
14	−40 108
15	−52 667
16	−63 681
17	−73 377
18	−81 948
19	−89 552
20	−96 325

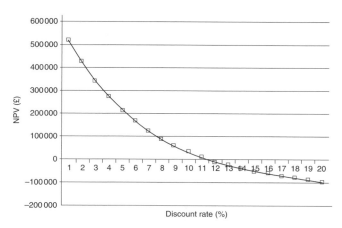

Figure 7.2 Relationship between NPV and disscount rate.

Because investment cash-flows vary there is no single formula for calculating the IRR. Instead the IRR can be estimated by linear interpolation on paper or, more usually, derived by iteration (trial and error) on a computer. Looking at linear interpolation first, consider the cash-flow from Table 7.3 once again. When we discounted this cash-flow at 10% the NPV was positive so we know that the IRR (which produces an NPV of zero) must be higher than 10%. So let us take two trial IRRs of 15% (TR_1) and 16% (TR_2) and discount the cash-flow as shown in Table 7.14.

Because we get a positive NPV when the discount rate is 15% and a negative one when it is 16% we know the IRR lies somewhere between 15% and 16%. We also know that the true relationship between discount rate and NPV is curvilinear, but because our two trial rates are pretty close to the IRR we could assume that, between them, the relationship is linear. Figure 7.3 shows how this might look.

Using similar triangles, we can interpolate a linear estimate of the IRR between the two trial rates as follows:

$$x = \left(TR_2 - TR_1\right) \times \frac{NPV_1}{NPV_1 + NPV_2} \text{ (ignoring + and – signs)}$$

$$x = (1\%) \times \frac{11546}{18432} = 0.63\%$$

[7.5]

Table 7.14

Year	Cash-flow (£)	PV £1 @ 15% (TR₁)	Present value (£)	PV £1 @ 16% (TR₂)	Present value (£)
0	−880 000	1.0000	−880 000	1.0000	−880 000
1	200 000	0.8696	173 920	0.8621	172 420
2	400 000	0.7561	302 440	0.7432	297 280
3	440 000	0.6575	289 300	0.6407	281 908
4	220 000	0.5718	125 796	0.5523	121 506
		NPV₁	+11 456	NPV₂	−6 866

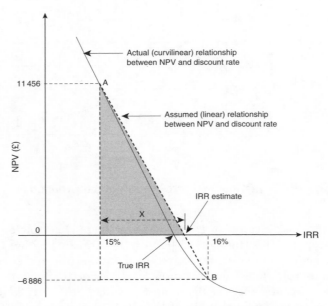

Figure 7.3   Linear interpolation of the IRR using similar triangles.

Therefore, the estimate of the IRR is 15% + 0.63% = 15.63%.

This method can be applied to a property investment. For example, a freehold office investment totalling 400 m² NIA is advertised for sale at an asking price of £800 000. The rent is currently under review and 20 years remain on the lease, which is on FRI terms with rent reviews every 5 years. A comparable property measuring 500 m² NIA was recently let at a market rent of £75 000 and subsequently sold for £937 500, revealing an initial yield of 8%. Advise your client whether the investment opportunity offers an acceptable return when compared to the client's target rate of return of 12%.

Analysis of the comparable property reveals a market rent of £150 per square metre and when this is applied to the subject property a market rent of £60 000 per annum is estimated. The growth rate implied by a target rate of 12% and an initial yield of 8% is 4.63%. Assuming trial IRRs of 10% and 14% the NPVs are calculated as shown in Table 7.15.

$$\text{IRR} = 10\% + \left[(14\% - 10\%) \times \frac{125752}{125752 + 180599} \right]$$

$$= 10\% + \left[4\% \times \frac{125752}{306351} \right] = 11.64\%$$

This does not meet the target rate of the client.

The other way of deriving the IRR of an investment is by iteration on a computer, usually using a spreadsheet. Consider the following cash-flow of a rack-rented freehold property investment. The rent is £17 500 per annum and rent reviews are 5 yearly. The all risks yield is 8% and rental growth is estimated to be 3% per annum. The asking price for the property is £200 000. The cash-flow is set up in Excel, as shown in Table 7.16 and, using the IRR function, the IRR of this investment is found to be 11.25%.

NPV or IRR? By using a discount rate based on the investor's target rate of return, the NPV method makes a relative comparison with the opportunity cost of capital or the capital market. IRR, on the other hand, cannot be reliably used to judge between alternative investments because it assumes that cash-flows from an investment are reinvested at a rate equal to the IRR of the investment generating those cash-flows. So, rather than compare each investment against the capital market as the NPV method does, the IRR method compares investments relative to one another under a scenario of unequal reinvestment rates. A workaround is to calculate the IRR of the differential cash-flow between the two investments being compared, and if this is greater than the target rate, accept the investment with the smallest IRR. If this 'incremental' IRR is less than the target rate, accept the project with the highest IRR. Clearly, if more than two investments are being compared this process of calculating incremental IRRs will become lengthy, whilst all that is needed to make the investment decision using the NPV method is the calculation of each investment's NPV. It is argued that IRR is an inferior method for two further reasons: first, when appraising investments with cash-flows that fluctuate between positive and negative (a large,

Chapter 7

Table 7.15 Estimating an IRR from two rial discount rates.

Years	FV £1 @ 4.63%	Projected rent (£)	PV £1 @ 10%	YP 5 years @ 10%	PV (£)	PV £1 @ 14%	YP 5 years @ 14%	PV (£)
0–4	1.0000	60 000	1.0000	3.7908	227 880	1.0000	3.4331	205 986
5–9	1.2540	75 237	0.6209	3.7908	177 085	0.5194	3.4331	134 163
10–14	1.5724	94 344	0.3855	3.7908	137 874	0.2697	3.4331	87 353
15–19	1.9717	118 303	0.2394	3.7908	107 360	0.1401	3.4331	56 904
20–perp.	2.4724	148 346	0.1486	12.5000	275.553	0.0728	12.5000	134.995
			Total PV		925 752			619 401
			less outlay		−800 000			−800 000
			NPV		125 752			−180 599

Table 7.16 Finally the IRR by iteration using a spreadsheet.

Year	Income (£)	Growth rate (3% pa)	Projected cash-flow (£)
0			−200 000
1	17 500	1.0000	17 500
2	17 500	1.0000	17 500
3	17 500	1.0000	17 500
4	17 500	1.0000	17 500
5	17 500	1.0000	17 500
6	17 500	1.1593	20 287
7	17 500	1.1593	20 287
8	17 500	1.1593	20 287
9	17 500	1.1593	20 287
10	17 500	1.1593	20 287
11	17 500	1.3439	23 519
12	17 500	1.3439	23 519
13	17 500	1.3439	23 519
14	17 500	1.3439	23 519
15	17 500	1.3439	23 519
16	17 500	1.5580	27 264
17	17 500	1.5580	27 264
18	17 500	1.5580	27 264
19	17 500	1.5580	27 264
20	17 500	1.5580	27 264
20–perp.	17 500	1.8061	395 087[a]
IRR			11.25%

[a]This is the projected rent (£17 500 × 1.8061) capitalised in perpetuity at a yield of 8%.

phased property development project for example), more than one IRR may result or there may be none at all in the time frame being considered. IRR is therefore more likely to be used by investors who wish to retain the scheme after completion and measure its IRR against other investments in the portfolio or against a target rate of return. Second, the IRR cannot be calculated directly, only by interpolation or by iteration on a spreadsheet.

So NPV is mathematically superior but still leaves the problem of selecting the appropriate discount rate. Using the IRR it is simpler to appraise a stand-alone opportunity against its own benchmark. But an IRR overlooks the rate at which finance is available and assumes income is reinvested at the same rate as the model. And this may be an unrealistic assumption. Peculiar cash-flow patterns frustrate the IRR as a measure of investment worth: an investment project could break even at high IRR but give no profit. Furthermore, the highest IRR does not necessarily mean the highest NPV and therefore the highest profit. However, IRR is by far the most commonly used appraisal method in commercial property investment, particularly amongst institutional investors because they like a common benchmark that allows discussion, comparison through time and benchmarking. It also allows one-off appraisal of a single project against a pre-determined hurdle rate. Basically though, NPV and IRR are the same; variables are examined and then cash-flows are estimated and discounted.

7.2.3   Risk analysis in property investment appraisal

An appraisal of worth must consider both return and risk. In the investment appraisal methods discussed so far risk is quantified by making adjustments to the required rate of return or by making adjustments to the investment cash-flow. In this section we are going to look at how risk can be examined in a little more detail. According to Hutchison *et al.* (2005) risk analysis is now a chief concern of property lenders. This is because of proposed revisions to international standards for measuring the adequacy of a bank's capital.[1] The proposed regulatory requirements mean that banks must be more explicit about the risks of lending. As property is a major destination for debt finance, the identification, analysis and communication of the risks involved are becoming more central to the lending decision. But how is risk handled in the appraisal process?

Because most investors are risk averse they are concerned with the probability of making a loss, estimating the most likely return and the variability or volatility of that return. In the case of the property investor, a property asset is likely to form part of a portfolio of assets. As such, it will either exacerbate or help to reduce the year-on-year volatility of income (or 'risk') within that portfolio. An investor for whom a property reduces portfolio risk should, in theory, be willing to pay more for an asset than an investor for whom the same property increases risk. An appraisal needs to reflect both the intrinsic value of the asset and the contribution to risk within the portfolio. Clearly, the former is likely to dominate but fund managers need to keep an eye on the latter.

In investment terms there are two types of risk: systematic risk arises from market conditions and affects all investments. It is caused by inflation, economic cycles, interest rate movements, tax and cannot be diversified away in a portfolio of investments. Non-systematic risk affects particular investments and is caused by business, financial or liquidity risks. It can, theoretically at least, be diversified away by constructing a portfolio of property investments and actively managing that portfolio. Choosing good-quality tenants, delaying the onset of depreciation by implementing a regular maintenance and refurbishment programme, and arranging staggered lease renewals to avoid simultaneous voids are all recognised methods of reducing the impact of non-systematic property investment risk. Sources of risk can be categorised as follows:

- Tenant risk, including non-payment of rent or non-performance of other contractual obligations.
- Sector and geographical risk, the IPD index of total return illustrates the different return characteristics of various property sectors and regions. The 'lumpiness' of property investment accentuates this type of risk and international diversification can ameliorate some of this type of risk.

- Physical risk, this is quantified by estimating the magnitude of likely future expenditure. Prime city centre retail property investments are much less prone to this type of risk.
- Legal risk; including the effect of landlord and tenant legislation, fiscal policy, planning, ownership and other legislation such as the Disability Discrimination Act, 1995.

Unlike portfolio-level risk analysis, empirical tests of property-specific risk have not been developed to a point that enables risk-return analysis to be widely practised in the property industry. There is a lack of reported data on the risk associated with investing in property assets. Traditionally, in valuation, the all-risks yield takes account of the risks at the individual property level. As we have seen, in DCF-based valuation and appraisal, the discount rate used to calculate an NPV can be derived by building risk premiums on top of a risk-free rate to reflect different elements of systematic and non-systematic risk (RICS, 1997). In this way, a 'risk adjusted discount rate' is constructed. Similarly, when using the IRR investment appraisal technique, the setting of a high hurdle rate will allow potentially more risky investments to be excluded from further consideration. Issues of inflation, interest rate and tax changes can be handled within the cash-flow itself regardless of whether NPV or IRR method is used to appraise the investment. But these are rather simple approaches to risk analysis. Hutchison *et al.* (2005) point out that

> Whereas in the equities market, pricing models have been developed to identify the required rate of return from risky investments; a risk premium of around 2% is usually suggested for property. While this figure may apply to the market as a whole, at the individual property level the premium will vary. In the absence of a robust pricing model and data limitations, it is likely that target rates for property will continue to be estimated subjectively. Consequently, errors in the estimation of discount rates tend to exacerbate the error in the worth calculation especially when longer holding periods are used.

Increasingly investors are seeking to quantify risk and allow for it separately through the use of more sophisticated techniques that have long been used in the analysis of non-property investments. These include sensitivity analysis, scenario modelling, probability analysis and simulation, and they were described in Chapters 5 and 6 in the context of property investment valuation and property development appraisal. These techniques may be applied with some variation. For example, as a means of reflecting downside risk, 'Domesday analysis' looks at the continuity of guaranteed income-flow, and the risk of loss is exaggerated by assuming that rent will fall to zero at every opportunity such as lease expiry and breaks and will not grow at rent reviews. Nevertheless, the underlying risk analysis techniques used in the appraisal are the same.

Baum (2003) discusses how some of these modelling techniques are being extended in relation to the analysis of risk relating to rent in particular. An investor investing in a property let on a flexi-lease (see Chapter 4) may regard the rental income as more uncertain or volatile and would wish to

Chapter 7

analyse possible risk. A cash-flow model might therefore incorporate adjustments to the rent to reflect the probability of costs associated with tenant vacation as well as the more typical cash-flow variables of expected rental growth and rent review times. Simulations may be carried out that look at the effect of moving from a standard lease (with a 15-year term and 5-year upward-only rent reviews) to a flexi-lease (with a 10-year term and a break option in year 5). Assumptions can be made about the probability of the tenant renewing the lease, exercising a break option, how long a rent void might be expected to last for and the probability of it varying from this expected void period. Anticipated empty property costs and re-letting costs can also be incorporated and modelled if necessary, alongside the more conventional key variables of rent and rental growth. Using this sort of analysis the investor can look at the impact of agreeing flexi-lease terms as opposed to more conventional terms. The investor could focus on how much the initial rent should alter to put him in a similar risk/return situation.

A more qualitative approach to risk analysis is suggested by Hutchison *et al.* (2005): investment quality risk may be scored in a way similar to that employed by credit-rating agencies. The technique uses an analytic hierarchy process (AHP), a multi-criteria decision-making tool, to rank and quantify the various sources of risk described above. The risk score would be reported to the client, enabling a more detailed understanding of the property investment.

Key points

- There is widespread use of DCF for property investment appraisal. Discounting is the popular method of investment comparison because cash-flows are converted to a common denominator, present value.
- Any mismatch between the market value or price of a property investment and its worth to a particular investor should be investigated. A rational investor will buy an asset if its price is equal to or below his assessment of worth and vice versa. The range of worth estimates is typically wider in property market than in equities market where a great deal more trading takes place on the more marginal differences between price and worth.
- Investment appraisal should include a detailed analysis of risk and return culminating in a judgement as to the worth of the investment. Investors are primarily concerned with return performance, typically measured against a portfolio benchmark. This is because investors are remunerated on the basis of total return performance rather than risk. In the property investment market, when risk measurement is undertaken, risk is pragmatically regarded rather simplistically as the chance of not achieving a benchmark return. The main measure of risk is standard deviation and the focus is always on downside potential. More sophisticated measures of risk in terms of volatility are not in general use in the property investment market yet.

> ### Key points (continued)
>
> - Having said this there are competition, globalisation and securitisition pressures on property, an essentially deal-driven business, to align with other investment classes. There is, therefore, demand for greater market transparency and more research at the market and asset level that will lead to explicit pricing of risk. Perhaps too much attention has been paid to sector and region portfolio weightings rather than examining the income, tenant quality and lease terms of individual assets. Consideration of specific risk at this level is warranted because it might impact on the property portfolio more than would be the case with other asset classes.

7.3   Property occupation appraisal

7.3.1   Business property appraisals

So far, the appraisal of worth of property has been considered almost entirely from the perspective of the property investor. The application of investment analysis techniques from other investment markets, such as DCF techniques, have driven this, as has demand from investors for the development of more sophisticated tools to appraise property investment opportunities. The results of these pressures for innovation have been described in Section 7.2. We now turn our attention to appraisals of property worth from the perspective of business occupiers. This aspect of property appraisal has received much less attention than the investment sector but its importance is growing as businesses seek to make much more effective use of their property assets. A glance at national and property-specific press demonstrates this, as high street retailers such as Marks and Spencer, financial institutions such as Abbey and even manufacturers and extractive industries such as British Coal regularly revalue their property estate with a view to maximising its return. To achieve this, businesses have sold properties they own to investors who, in turn, lease them back. This generates sales proceeds that can be reinvested in the core business. Other financial arrangements are also made but all with the aim of maximising return from property assets. Before these sorts of financial arrangements can be made, it is essential that the business occupier has a full understanding of the worth of each property asset to its business. Otherwise how will it know which assets are surplus to requirements, which should be rented, owned outright or sold and leased back?

In the occupier sector, as far as businesses are concerned, the key consideration is worth as a business asset rather than as an investment asset, and so in this section we will look at value-in-use from the perspective of the occupier rather than the investor. As French and Byrne (1996) state, an investor will view worth as a discounted value of the rental income stream produced by the asset, whereas the owner-occupier will see the asset as a factor of production and assign to it a worth derived from the property's contribution to the profits of the business. The appraisal methodology may be the same but the assumptions are now based on business factors rather than investment market factors. So, rather than consider the opportunity cost of capital on the investment market, a business occupier may consider the opportunity cost of investment in the core business.

A distinction should be made between valuing the property assets that make up a business and valuing the business itself. Whereas the latter would include the value of any goodwill, work-in-progress, order book and so on, the latter might ignore these aspects and the value of the property assets would simply be the addition of individual property valuations assuming vacant possession. Alternatively, if the property assets are to be valued assuming continuing occupation of the business, value attributable to the business might be allocated in some way to each property (or group of properties). For the purposes of financial accounting, the value of an operational business entity that is expected to continue in operation (its going concern or business value) includes the value of all tangible and intangible assets, including goodwill. In the UK, business valuations are the remit of accountants, and valuers are not perceived as professionals in this field. This is in contrast to practice in the US and Europe where, according to Champness (1997), property valuers in a number of European countries carry out business valuations for mergers, acquisitions and disposals. Property advice in these cases is usually required to be at a more strategic level than a valuation of an individual property asset, but the valuation is an important part of that advice, so much so that in some countries the distinction between a property valuer and a business valuer is an artificial one.

Wyatt (2001a) has considered ways in which property valuations and business valuations might be applied to business property appraisal. A useful form of business property appraisal would be for businesses to compare the market value and business value of individual property assets (Miles *et al.*, 1989). But Guidance Note 7 in the Appraisal and Valuation Manual (RICS, 2003) states that 'The going-concern value of a company in the open market will reflect its overall potential earning capacity' and 'cannot normally be apportioned to any individual property asset which is part of the whole; individual properties cannot have a going concern value by themselves' Sayce and Connellan (1998) agree that the apportionment of business value amongst individual properties is unrealistic in practice. In terms of appraisal this is a problem; how can the market value, existing use value or depreciated replacement cost (DRC) of business property assets be compared with their value to the business or going concern value if the latter cannot be apportioned between individual property assets?

A possible solution might be to look at the value-in-use of each asset. As well as an economic concept value-in-use is also an accounting term that refers to the maximum amount recoverable from continuing ownership and ultimate disposal of an asset (not necessarily a property asset). International Accounting Standard (IAS) 36 (UK's Financial Reporting Standard (FRS) 11 is analogous to IAS 36) requires that where the balance sheet value (the historic cost or fair value plus additional investment and less depreciation) exceeds its recoverable amount, the asset should be valued at the higher of market value or value-in-use. If the higher figure is the market value, there is clearly no logic in the asset being retained by the company or for production to continue. In this way calculation of the recoverable amount is a form of appraisal with a decision rule that asks whether the business can financially justify the performance of an asset in the context of the current business operation. If not then the rational decision is to sell (Dunckley, 2000) and realise the net selling price. So value-in-use can be regarded as an appraisal of the business worth of an asset, often calculated as the present value of the estimated future cash-flow discounted at a pre-tax rate that reflects current market assessments of the time value of money and the risks specific to the asset.

A business property appraisal is thus taken to refer to an appraisal of the worth of a business property asset (rather than an investment property asset) on behalf of an occupier (rather than an investor). It is a worth concept for property that contributes to the profitability of a business. A business property appraisal is specific to the business occupier because it utilises occupier-specific information. A generalised approach to the appraisal of worth of business property might be as follows (Wyatt, 2001b):

1. Identify the nature and extent of the business and its property assets. Key information will include details of the legal interests (freeholds, long leaseholds, short leaseholds, serviced accommodation, accommodation regularly taken in hotels), classification as operational or surplus property and specialised or non-specialised property, physical and locational characteristics such as age, depreciation, obsolescence, use and intensity of use (floor area, number of staff).

2. Determine the information requirements regarding the property assets to be valued and appraised. Valuations will require market information and appraisals will require market and occupier-specific business information. Information in published accounts will not be adequate; more detailed financial information will be required. Business property appraisals require close liaison with the occupier and a detailed understanding of the client's business.

3. Value surplus property assets on a market value basis and operational property assets on either an existing use value or depreciated replacement cost basis. It should be noted that a business property appraisal can only be performed if the current value of property assets is known; it is, therefore, a pre-requisite. Conventionally, many businesses did not regularly revalue their property assets but the introduction of revised International Financial Reporting Standards and a heightened awareness of the value of many property holdings means that this situation is changing.

4. Estimate the going concern value of the business. There is an established methodology for estimating the going concern value of a business. See, for example, the International Valuation Standards published by the IVSC (2005) and the RICS Red Book (RICS, 2003).

5. Appraise the worth of property assets to the business. A cash-flow approach could incorporate profit and cash-flows, taxation and corporate finance alternatives (Colborne, 1995) and could be used to examine alternative property holding strategies, cost charging structures, tax and finance arrangements, for example. Business cash-flows need to be assigned to individual properties. Cash-flow analysis at the individual property level means that expenditure (occupancy costs) must be assigned, which is relatively straightforward, but it can be difficult to apportion business revenue to a single property, particularly when financing and taxation issues are taken into account. The definition of value-in-use in IAS 36 offers some guidance here. It states that some assets form part of a wider business process and so the asset may be absorbed into an entity referred to as a cash-generating unit. This is the smallest identifiable group of assets that generates a cash-flow that is distinct from cash-flows from other assets or groups of assets. IAS 36 adds that businesses should use cash-flow projections based on reasonable and supportable assumptions that reflect the asset in its current condition and represent management's best estimate of the economic conditions that will exist over the remaining useful life of the asset.

6. Apply decision rules
   (a) compare aggregate market value of property assets with the going concern value of the business to determine efficient use of property in the business at the aggregate level;
   (b) compare the market value, existing use value or depreciated replacement cost of each property asset with its appraisal of worth to the business. If the worth appraisal exceeds the market value then acquisition or continued holding would be financially viable. If not then this may signal disposal of the property asset but the appraisal must consider implications for the business as a whole when disposing of a property asset. An appraisal of worth of a property to a business depends on its purpose but fundamentally companies need to be able to identify the property with its earning capacity.

7.3.2 Business property performance measurement

A worth appraisal of a business property asset provides, at a strategic level, information about return on property assets. At an operational level, performance measurement provides similar information. Property performance measures need to consider property as a cost and as an asset and integrate these considerations with strategic decision-making criteria. Most performance measures that are currently employed focus on the cost of providing a working environment for each member of staff and include measurements of property cost as a percentage of revenue and total costs, annual occupancy cost per unit area or per capita. However, property is a significant asset as well as a cost and, as businesses examine return on property assets, valuers must adapt their service to meet demands for property performance measures that are based on value rather than cost. Return-on-asset-based performance measures are driving the reduction in owned property, and funds are being redirected to core activities that yield a higher return than property, but what is the benchmark against which these measures are considered? Varcoe (1993) suggests that to enable comparison between businesses and business sectors, performance measures need to relate to benchmark properties whilst reflecting objectives of the specific occupier but further research is needed. Varcoe also argues that property and facilities have a unique influence on the performance of a business' most important asset – staff – so cost and performance measures for property assets must have regard for the overall performance of the business. In other words, do not pursue cost savings without regard for the wider business impact.

The initial financial measurement of property assets will always be cost, but this cost should be considered in the light of a worth appraisal undertaken by the business prior to purchase of the property asset. Subsequent treatment of property assets in accounts permits the recording of depreciated cost or up-to-date fair value. The majority of businesses adopt the former approach but recording historic cost does not allow an accurate appraisal of the worth of that asset to be undertaken. At the moment, UK and international accounting standards state that when businesses are acquired, the assets and liabilities of the acquired company must be included at fair value; in other words, the acquirer's purchase price. As acquisition activity increases, the need to know the current value of property assets also rises. This presents an opportunity to use this information to inform appraisals and property asset decision-making in the way outlined above.

Key point

- Property advice to business occupiers needs to be linked to the core functions of the relevant business and valuers need to appreciate the implications that property has for business processes. This requires a good knowledge of the occupier's business.

7.4   Financing property investment

It is not the intention in this book to cover the financing of property investment and occupation in detail; the reader is referred to Adair *et al.* (1996) and also Brett (1998) and Isaac (1996). This section outlines the typical ways in which funding is arranged, how risk is managed and concludes by considering indirect property investment.

7.4.1   *Property funding*

According to DTZ (2006), the UK commercial property market recorded a net capital inflow of £69.5 billion in 2005, an increase from £22.6 billion in 2004; see Figure 7.4.

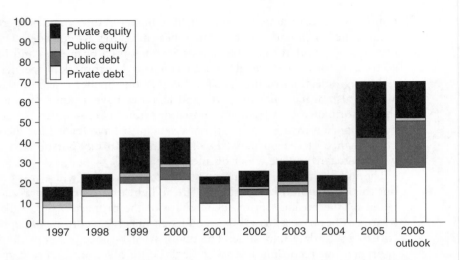

Figure 7.4   Net capital flows to UK commercial real estate (DTZ Research).

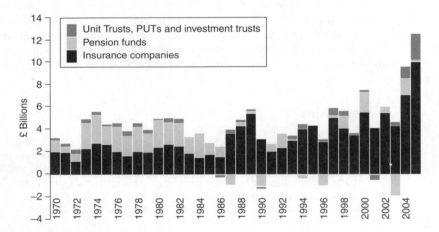

Figure 7.5   Institutional direct net investment in UK commercial real estate (Office for National Statistics, DTZ Research).

An influx of private debt and equity capital has driven the UK market in recent years. That said, the UK All-Property yield was 4.88% at the end of May 2006 and this is a drop of 0.75% from 1 year earlier. Consequently, it is mainland Europe rather than the UK that is likely to offer a more significant yield premium over debt financing costs. The substantial increase in money flowing into the UK property investment market is fuelled by a much greater use of debt than was the case in previous years and this represents increased gearing in commercial property market, leading to greater risk.

Institutional investment in direct and indirect commercial property increased in 2005, as can be seen in Figures 7.5 and 7.6. Sayce *et al.* (2006)

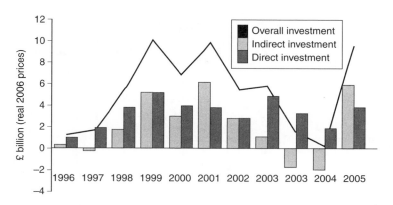

Figure 7.6   Indirect Institutional net investment in UK commercial real estate (Office for National Statistics, DTZ Research).

comment that there is now substantial internationalisation of property investment activity in the UK with investors from the US, Ireland, the Middle East, India, Russia and Canada.

Institutional investors tend to fund property investment (including development) activity using their own money, known as equity finance, and the measure of return is return on equity. But other investors often use a combination of debt and equity finance. Debt finance refers to the amount that is borrowed to fund the acquisition of a property investment and can remain fixed throughout the loan period (an interest-only loan) or it can be gradually paid off over the term alongside the interest payments (a repayment loan). Capital and interest repayment can be deferred for a period of time (this is known as a 'balloon payment' loan), and it is the preferred method of financing a property development where there will be no return until the scheme is let and/or sold. The interest payable on a loan may be fixed or variable. For short- and medium-term fixed rate loans the interest rate will relate to the prevailing swap[2] rate plus a risk premium. Swap rates as on 13 October 2006 are shown in Table 7.17. For long-term fixed rate loans of 10 or more years the rate may relate to the gross redemption yield on long-dated gilts that have a comparable life but with the addition of a suitable risk premium. If it is a variable rate loan the rate may be linked to the Bank of England Base Rate[3] or, more usually, the 3–6 month LIBOR.[4] The Base Rate and LIBOR rates as on 13 October 2006 are shown in Table 7.18.

Funding the acquisition of a property investment through the use of debt and equity finance allows the investor to increase returns through gearing (at the expense of higher risk) and also allows the investor to invest in a greater number of properties, thus reducing risk through portfolio diversification. Gearing enhances return on equity when the IRR of the investment is greater than the rate of interest payable on the debt (loan). Conversely, gearing erodes return when the loan interest rate is higher than the investment IRR. There may be occasions, perhaps because the interest rate on a variable loan has gone up, when an investment switches from equity enhancing to equity

Table 7.17   Swap rates (13 October 2006).

Year	UK (£) current (%)
1	5.36
2	5.28
3	5.25
5	5.18
7	5.11
10	5.00
12	4.94
15	4.85
20	4.72
25	4.59
30	4.49

Notes: The rates shown are based upon a loan of circa £5 million and interest only throughout the term.
Most loans are, either in whole or in part, likely to be on an amortising basis which may mean that the actual rate will differ from those indicated above.

Table 7.18   Base rate and LIBORs (13 October 2006).

Market rate	UK (£) current (%)
Base rate	4.7500
Overnight LIBOR	4.8375
1 month LIBOR	4.8938
3 month LIBOR	5.0963
6 month LIBOR	5.2056
12 month LIBOR	5.3225

eroding owing to the impact of gearing. A an investor accepts a higher level of gearing to finance an investment acquisition so too does the potential volatility of the return from that investment. In other words, the return on equity becomes more sensitive to underlying return (the IRR) of the investment itself. The extra volatility of equity return that occurs as the gearing level increases is proportionate to the **income gearing ratio**.

Property, particularly the landmark buildings in prime locations, are expensive. Property investment is, therefore, capital intensive and many investors usually look to raise debt finance (borrow money) to help fund acquisition. Property development, which may be considered as a sub-set of property investment, is also capital intensive and many developers are typically not holders of vast equity resources and invariably need to raise finance to fund all aspects of their development projects, including site acquisition, planning, site clearance, preparation, construction, fitting out, marketing and disposal. Lenders therefore play a critical role in the development process and a residual valuation is often used to convince them that a project is viable and that they will receive an adequate return (given the risk profile) on their loan finance. In financial terms developers seek short-term loan finance for the development itself and the interest on the loan is usually 'rolled up' until the scheme is complete, let and sold. Consequently, the loan finance rate is relatively high in order to reflect the risks associated with this type of lending; there is limited loan security during construction phase and void period. The ability to borrow money and the lending rate depend on the financial status, track record and experience of the developer and the quality of and risks associated with a particular scheme. Once the development is complete the developer may be looking to sell it to an investor or retain it as an investment. With the latter, long-term finance will need to be arranged.

7.4.1.1 Sources and types of property funding

There are many ways to raise finance for the purchase of a property. In practice, each purchase could be financed in a unique way depending on the status of the borrower and the type of property being acquired. As a means of simplifying matters property funding (finance) can be categorised as corporate or project specific and each are considered below.

Corporate property funding. Property investors and developers (property companies) that are listed on a Stock Exchange will be able to raise corporate finance. This typically takes two forms: equity finance (new shares, rights issues and retained earnings to name but a few examples), and debt finance secured against the borrower rather than the property (such as bonds, debentures, loan stock, unit trusts and securitisation). An advantage of raising corporate finance is that there is no direct link between the investment itself and the debt finance. Consequently, the acquisition of a specific property investment will not attract the attention of or intervention by a lender, and interest payments (dividends) are covered by overall company performance rather than the performance of an individual scheme. The disadvantages are that a sale of new shares in a company may dilute its control over a long term or even on a permanent basis – a period far in excess of the needs of a single investment acquisition. Also one unsuccessful investment may collapse an otherwise healthy company.

Project-specific property funding. Project-specific loans are made by a lender to fund a specific property acquisition or development project. Project loans are often secured against the value of the scheme rather than the borrower and therefore provide an independent assessment of the viability of the investment or development opportunity. Consequently, this method of funding is less reliant on credibility of borrower and more reliant on the quality of the project.

Sources of project-specific property funding include; financial institutions such as insurance companies and pension funds, banks and building societies, and equity investors from UK and overseas. Financial institutions such as banks and buildings societies typically lend between 70% and 80% of the total acquisition or development cost and do not usually require equity participation but an arrangement fee is usually payable. Borrowers who have a good track record or a particularly attractive investment opportunity (a very good tenant in occupation for example) may attract a higher loan-to-value ratio, thus allowing more to be borrowed, but the interest rate may be higher. Overseas investors may be prepared to take more risk than UK-based financial institutions and may become involved in long-term, more complex, schemes. For some acquisitions and developments a single financier is not enough and some form of joint venture, where parties share risk and profit, is common for large, complex developments. Also, as far as development is concerned, certain sites may attract tax incentives or other financial help from the UK Government or from the European Union in the form of tax incentives, grants and simplified planning procedures.

There are many arrangements by which project loans may be made; some of the more common include mortgages, syndicated loans, bridging or interim finance in the case of development projects, and partnership and equity-sharing arrangements. A **mortgage** is a long-term loan secured against the property asset (or completed development) and interest is paid in instalments throughout the period. This is a traditional form of long-term lending to property investors, including developers who wish to retain a development as an investment. Syndicated project loans spread the risk among several lenders and allow smaller lenders to participate in larger investment and development projects. In the case of bridging or interim finance, upon completion the development is sold to pay capital and interest (a forward sale can attract short-term finance at a more favourable rate as the risk to the lender is reduced). Partnership and equity-sharing arrangements are popular methods of funding property development and it is worth looking at one or two examples of how these arrangements work so that the impact of gearing can be demonstrated.

In order to help finance a development, spread risk and/or retain some degree of equity, a developer may enter into a partnership arrangement with another party. This may be the landowner, say a local authority, who does not wish to dispose of the freehold interest in the site. The landowner may grant a long lease to the developer in return for a ground rent which is, itself, often geared to enable growth. There may also be an arrangement whereby the landowner shares in the profit from the development. The risk to the developer is that the development will not succeed in generating sufficient profit to cover the ground rent and equity-sharing arrangement. Detailed explanations and examples of various arrangements for funding developments can be found in Darlow (1990). The aim here is to present examples from a range of funding arrangements.

The way in which any profit from the development is split usually depends on the level of risk that each party takes, the amount of equity put in and the relative bargaining position of the parties. In these types of equity-sharing arrangements the first claim on the development profit would normally be by the landowner and equal to the existing use value of the land, followed by a fixed return to the developer related to his financial investment and risk, with the surplus, if any, being shared on an agreed basis. Consider a developer who wishes to retain ownership of a completed development as an investment and receive an annual return on this investment. The cost of the development is estimated to be £5 000 000, the expected rent is £500 000 per annum and the long-term fixed rate of interest at which money can be borrowed to enable the property to be retained as an investment is 7% per annum. Once let the return from the completed scheme is calculated as follows:

Development yield = annual return (rent)/development cost
= 500 000/5 000 000
= 10%

If money can be borrowed at 7% per annum then the return to the investor-developer is 3% per annum. If we now assume that, instead of selling the site outright to the developer, the landowner wished to retain the freehold interest and let the land on a long lease at a ground rent to the landowner. Obviously, the ways that this arrangement could be made is at the discretion of the parties involved, but assume that a ground rent of £50 000 per annum is required by the landowner. The developer now receives a profit rent of £450 000 per annum (£500 000 per annum rent received less £50 000 per annum ground rent) and the return to the developer is calculated as follows:

Development yield = 450 000/5 000 000
= 9%

So the developer receives a 2% annual return over the debt finance rate, with the landowner receiving the other 1% (£50 000/£5 000 000). The developer receives 90% (£450 000/£500 000) of the rental income and the landowner receives 10% (£50 000/£500 000) and any future growth in rent received may be split in the same proportions. In this case the ground rent would be geared to the rack rent at a 10% proportion and the investor-developer's return would be geared at a 90% proportion. For example, assume that, by the time the development is complete, the rent achieved on letting is actually £600 000 per annum rather than the initial estimate of £500 000 per annum, an increase of 20%. Moreover, the actual cost of the development increases by 10% from £5 000 000 to £5 500 000. It was agreed that the ground rent would be £50 000 per annum and any return in excess of initial estimates would be split 90% to the developer and 10% to the landowner. Therefore

Actual income	£600 000
Actual cost	£5 500 000
× development yield	0.09
	£495 000
Residue	£105 000
Less agreed ground rent	−£50 000
Therefore, excess	£55 000

Ten per cent of this excess goes to the landowner who therefore receives £50 000 ground rent plus £5 500, totalling £55 500 per annum. Any further growth in rent (equity) may be apportioned at the same ratio as that calculated on completion, that is, £55 500/600 000 = 9.25% to landowner and 91.75% to the developer. Alternatively, the equity can be geared (recalculated at each review). The former is known as a proportional arrangement where future growth is apportioned proportionately at each review. The latter is known as an equity arrangement, for example assume a rent increase of 50% at the first rent review and a 50:50 split in excess rent between the investor-developer and the landowner:

Actual income	£900 000
Development yield payment (from above)	£495 000
Residue	£405 000
Less ground rent	−£50 000
Excess	£355 000
50% excess to landowner	£177 500
Plus original ground rent	£50 000
Total income for landowner	£227 500

So the landowner's income is now 227 500/900 000 = 25.3%, resulting in a geared effect.

If the developer borrowed money to finance the long-term investment at 7% and this is paid out of the 90% share of rack rent then there is a gearing effect here too. Clearly there is a great deal of opportunity for the parties to negotiate subtle differences to each arrangement depending on their bargaining strength, risk profile, tax position, and so on. For example, assume a premium of £500 000 is paid to the landowner in lieu of £45 000 of ground rent. This would leave an annual ground rent payable to the landowner of £5 000 per annum. The developer's return would be

$$\text{Development yield} = 495\,000/5\,000\,000$$
$$= 9.9\%$$

And this leaves a ground rent yield of just 0.1% (£5 000/£5 000 000) to the landowner. Now the developer receives 99% of the rack rent and the landowner receives 1%. The landowner has traded off an equity share in the form of future rental growth potential for immediate capital payment in the form of a premium.

The sale and lease back arrangement, although more risky than a pre-let, is the most popular vehicle for equity sharing. Types of arrangement vary but a typical example might be that the developer buys a site, completes the scheme and sells the freehold interest to an investor below market value on condition that the investor then grants a long lease back to the developer below market rent. At rent reviews in the head lease any increase in rent (equity) can be apportioned at the same ratio as that calculated on completion, or the equity can be geared so that the investor takes a share of the initial rent plus a small proportion of subsequent rent increases). The developer (now the head tenant) sublets to occupying subtenants at a rent above that paid to the investor, thus retaining an equity share in the completed development. Advantages to the investor are a share of equity and security of income and capital. Management obligations are the responsibility of the developer under the leaseback arrangement. A disadvantage to developer is that it has disposed of the valuable freehold and retains only a profit rent which, if sold, is likely to be capitalised at a higher yield.

For example, a developer sells the freehold of a recently completed retail development to an investor for £750000, who then agrees to lease back the completed development to the developer. The development has an estimated rental income of £100000 per annum. The investor requires a 7.5% yield plus 50% of all rental income over £100000 per annum.

If, on letting, the rent achieved is £120000 per annum the ground rent will be

Initial lease-back rent @ 7.5% of £750000	£56250
Plus 50% of excess rent of £20000	£10000
Initial ground rent	£66250

Future rent reviews in the ground lease may be geared to the same percentage or a participation clause may be incorporated whereby the split between investor (freeholder) and developer (head-leaseholder) varies at an agreed percentage. In the above example the investor receives a ground rent of £66250 per annum (55.2% of the actual rent received from occupying tenants) and the developer receives a profit rent of £53750 per annum (44.8%). If these proportions are maintained at future rent reviews the developer would not increase his share of the income from the development. Such an arrangement would be ungeared. If the arrangement is left on the original (geared) basis and, at the first rent review, the rent increases to £150000 per annum;

Leaseback initial rent 7.5% of £75000	£56250
Plus excess rent 50% of £50000	£25000
	£81250

The developer now has a profit rent of £68750 (57.3%) and so is slightly favoured by the geared arrangement.

It is worth spending a few moments looking more closely at the effect of gearing on the return that a developer might receive. Gearing refers to the use of borrowed funds to exaggerate capital and income growth. Consider three financing arrangements for a development:

1. No loan is taken out and the development is financed entirely by the developer (100% equity input) and, for the purposes of this example, assume no opportunity cost of capital.
2. A loan is secured to cover 70% of the development costs, the remaining 30% is equity input from the developer.
3. As (2) but a ground rent equating to 10% of the annual rental income is paid to the landowner.

Table 7.19 and Figure 7.7 illustrate how the return on equity increases at a faster rate on geared funding arrangements compared to 100% equity funding as progressively higher amounts of rental income are projected.

Chapter 7

Table 7.19 Gearing

Rent (£)	(a) No loan			(b) Loan			(c) Ground rent		
	Cost (£)	% equity input	% return on equity	% equity input	% return on equity	Rent net of 10% ground rent	Cost (£)	% equity input	% return on equity
500 000	5 000 000	100	10.00	30	33.33	450 000	5 000 000	30	30.00
550 000	5 000 000	100	11.00	30	36.67	495 000	5 000 000	30	33.00
605 000	5 000 000	100	12.10	30	40.33	544 500	5 000 000	30	36.30
665 500	5 000 000	100	13.31	30	44.37	598 950	5 000 000	30	39.93
732 050	5 000 000	100	14.64	30	48.80	658 845	5 000 000	30	43.92
805 255	5 000 000	100	16.11	30	53.68	724 730	5 000 000	30	48.32
885 781	5 000 000	100	17.72	30	59.05	797 202	5 000 000	30	53.15
974 359	5 000 000	100	19.49	30	64.96	876 923	5 000 000	30	58.46
1 071 794	5 000 000	100	21.44	30	71.45	964 615	5 000 000	30	64.31
1 178 974	5 000 000	100	23.58	30	78.60	1 061 076	5 000 000	30	70.74
1 296 871	5 000 000	100	25.94	30	86.46	1 167 184	5 000 000	30	77.81
1 426 558	5 000 000	100	28.53	30	95.10	1 283 903	5 000 000	30	85.59
1 569 214	5 000 000	100	31.38	30	104.61	1 412 293	5 000 000	30	94.15
1 726 136	5 000 000	100	34.52	30	115.08	1 553 522	5 000 000	30	103.57
1 898 749	5 000 000	100	37.97	30	126.58	1 708 874	5 000 000	30	113.92
2 088 624	5 000 000	100	41.77	30	139.24	1 879 762	5 000 000	30	125.32
2 297 486	5 000 000	100	45.95	30	153.17	2 067 738	5 000 000	30	137.85

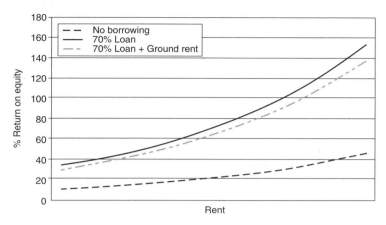

Figure 7.7   Gearing.

7.4.2   Risk management in property financing

As well as sharing risk and return through the use of various equity-sharing, partnership arrangements and joint ventures there are other ways to try to manage risk exposure when borrowing money to fund property investment and development activity. Risk management instruments offer risk protection, flexibility of funding arrangements, potentially lower borrowing costs over time and the ability to avoid unforeseen changes in interest costs.

Among the most popular risk management instruments are techniques designed to control the rate of interest on debt finance. There are many ways in which interest rates might be managed and a few of the more common ones are outlined below.

- Fixed rate: the interest rate on a loan is fixed for all or part of the term. This removes the risk of interest rate movements but the rate is invariably higher than a variable rate loan and can involve early redemption penalties and loss of profit if the interest rate falls.
- Interest rate cap: a variable interest rate is prevented from rising above a pre-determined ceiling rate. The instrument is essentially an insurance policy purchased by the borrower which puts a 'cap' or upper limit on the variable rate of interest on the loan and therefore is a hedging instrument. The cap rate is the price a borrower pays (in basis points) as a percentage of the capped loan amount in order to place an upper limit on a floating rate of interest. This cost is incurred up-front and the cost of the cap will vary according to the degree of protection required. If the interest rate expected to increase a capped rate is more expensive than when the interest rate is expected to remain stable or fall.
- Interest rate floor: a variable interest rate is prevented from falling below a pre-determined 'floor' rate. This type of product provides the lender with a minimum interest rate for the loan. The cost of a cap can be reduced by selling a floor.

- Interest rate collar: this is a combined cap and floor product and is useful to reduce the cost of a cap. A floor (which is clearly more attractive to the lender) might be used to lower the cost of a cap (which is more attractive to the borrower). It is possible to structure a 'no-cost collar' where the cost of the cap is fully offset by the price received for selling a floor.

Nothing remains static in the world of investment finance, and each of these products may be traded, offset, insured against, and so on. In fact, a vast market in SWAP instruments now exists and these allow, amongst other things, one party to exchange variable interest rate obligations with fixed interest ones. There are also property-specific risk management techniques such as letting to a good quality tenant, requiring a long lease term, arranging non-recourse debt where, on default, the lender is given access only to the property asset and not the assets of the company. For development finance to be forthcoming substantial pre-lets and in some cases forward sales are generally required by lenders. Ultimately, when lending money to finance the purchase of a standing property or the development of a property, the lender will wish to confirm that it provides adequate security for the amount lent. A valuation will therefore be a key piece of information on which the lending decision is based.

7.4.3   Indirect property investment

Commercial property performs well in terms of rental and capital growth and is a good portfolio diversifier. The main means by which investors can gain exposure to property is by purchasing standing investment properties or becoming involved in property development, either as a developer or as a lender. But because of the illiquidity, lumpiness and high transaction costs that characterise **direct property investment** many investors cannot take full advantage of this investment type. Valuable, high yielding investments such as city centre office buildings and shopping centres are often not on the shopping list of small to medium-sized investors looking for exposure to property. For example, at the moment commercial property represents less than 10% of pension funds' total investment holdings and this is perhaps underweight given its return performance. Good-quality property investments are very expensive and building a diversified portfolio of property investments is very, very expensive. Some of the larger UK properties can be accommodated only in the portfolios of major institutions. Consequently, smaller or medium-sized funds may decide not to invest in property. Each asset takes a long time to transact and convert into cash with no guarantee that the transactions will actually complete, thus possibly incurring abortive costs. Transaction costs (stamp duty, lawyer and surveyor fees) and property management costs can be high; trading information is much thinner than in other investment markets and market participants must rely on valuations and related advice supplied by surveyors, much of which is usually historically based. The difficulty investors face when trying to move funds around speedily to control risk, reflect market movements, vary the weightings in particular sectors, reflect the relative attraction of other forms of investment or to take advantage of special (sometimes speculative) trading opportunities means that they have a restricted ability to diversify risk and return.

Joint ventures, syndicated loans, equity sharing and other partnership arrangements that were discussed in Section 7.4.1 are ways of reducing the lumpiness of direct property investment by spreading the investment amongst two or more investors, but these instruments are not tradable. Investors can invest in property indirectly. Perhaps the most obvious form of **indirect property investment** is the purchase of shares in property development and investment companies. But share prices and thus investment returns tend to correlate more closely with the equity markets than the property market. Where returns are heavily influenced by equity market factors, indirect property investment may not offer the same diversification benefits as direct property. It may be possible to purchase a property, or a portfolio of properties, via a takeover bid for a quoted property company. Takeover bids, or rumours of them, often cause substantial share price movements, especially if the share price of the property company is at a discount to its capital value. Alternatively, it is possible to invest in property unit trusts or property investment trusts, or trade in synthetics (such as investments based on property indices).

Securitisation, where a property is financed or owned by tradable investment instruments or securities, makes it a more 'liquid' investment. Securitisation is considered suitable for properties worth more than £25m and can be equity based or debt based. The equity securitisation of property would see investors own shares in a property that yields income through dividend payments and produces capital gains (or losses) through share price movements. The securitisation of property by debt is achieved by issuing bond-type securities, which can also be traded. Equity markets are more volatile and higher profile than bond markets and require high-quality management to enhance performance and value. In the UK securitisation has been used mainly by property companies that have issued debt backed by a single building or a portfolio. Securitised property appeals to smaller institutions, overseas investors and private individuals. Securitisation of property ownership provides greater opportunity to access market information and therefore affords greater efficiency than direct markets. The market value of a property, in terms of the price it would achieve if exposed to the market as a single direct property investment, will not necessarily be the same as its price as a securitised investment vehicle. In the latter case, the securitised price may be assessed by reference to its 'discount' or 'premium' to the market value of the property. If, in the longer term, securitisation predominates in certain markets, the diminished trading in non-securitised properties will reduce the quantity of direct property transactions and, accordingly, the quality of overall market evidence. This may result in a weaker link between share prices and capital values, giving further scope for price variability.

Chapter 7

Until 2007 income and capital gains on indirect property investments were taxed twice; on income and capital gains at the corporate level (via corporation tax) and again when the investor pays tax on dividends and on capital gains on the sale of shares. With direct ownership, income tax and capital gains tax is paid only once. From 2007 the UK government has allowed indirect property investment vehicles to have a special status that exempts them from corporate taxes, thus avoiding the problem of double taxation. This has been achieved by introducing Real Estate Investment Trusts or REITs in the UK. A REIT is a tax-efficient collective property investment vehicle where the investor owns shares in a quoted company that invests in and manages a range of commercial and residential property. The company, which must be fully listed and resident in the UK for tax purposes, pays no corporation tax but must distribute at least 90% of its taxable earnings to its investors each year by way of a dividend. This makes them particularly attractive to income-seeking investors. Tax is then paid by these investors at their normal rates. The REIT must obtain at least 75% of its income from rent, its interest charges must be covered at least 1.25 times by net income and it must own and retain three or more properties for at least 3 years. REITs provide smaller investors with indirect access to, possibly very large, professionally managed and diversified portfolios of property investments. They also offer liquidity because the purchase of shares is rapid and low cost; stamp duty on direct property investment can be as high as 4% of the purchase price, but for shares it is 0.5%. They are also easily tradable; the search for finance to help purchase high-value direct property investment, along with the gearing risk that this involves, is no longer necessary.

REITs are not new; currently they exist in 23 countries. In fact, Germany and the UK are the last two G8 countries to introduce REITs. As at 2006, worldwide they account for 48% of listed property investments and are capitalised at £285bn with 63.5% in the US, 14.6% in Europe, 11.8% in Australia, 5.7% in Asia and 4.4% in Canada. At the time of writing this book (late 2006) it is too early to tell what effect the introduction of REITs will have on the UK property development, occupation and investment markets. According to the REITs and Quoted Property Group (www.reita.org) most existing quoted property companies are expected to convert to REITs and that other major landlords, including pension funds, major retailers and pub and hotel chains, might also be tempted to convert their property assets into REITs. Whereas the impact on existing direct and indirect property investment might be inferred from experiences in other countries the effect on the occupation sector might be harder to predict. It may lead to a decrease in the amount of commercial property owned by occupiers as they sell assets that are not regarded as essential to their core business activity and decide to rent rather than own an increasing proportion of their own assets. Who knows what effect the growth of indirect property investment vehicles in general and REITs in particular will have on property occupation, investment and development activity in the UK. As a valuer, I have a built-in capacity not to make forecasts so let us just wait and see!

Key points

- Whereas investors look at upside and downside potential risk, lenders focus on downside.
- Sources and methods of property investment and development funding are numerous and some, particularly for large, complex schemes, may be very sophisticated arrangements indeed.
- Finance may be in the form of debt or equity and may be project/property asset specific or corporate. Debt-based project-specific finance would be an asset-based mortgage whereas corporate debt would be secured against company, for example, a debenture (mortgage debenture or other bond-style debt). Equity-based project-specific finance might take the form of a special purpose vehicle (SPV), joint venture or an equity-sharing arrangement such as a partnership arrangement. Corporate equity would be raised by the issue of shares, and so forth.
- Investing in commercial property has long been an effective tool to diversify larger investment portfolios. Indirect property investment vehicles in general and REITs in particular enable smaller investors to acquire shares in diverse property portfolios.

Notes

1. International Convergence of Capital Measurement and Capital Standards – A Revised Framework, also known as Basel II or The New Accord.
2. A swap is a method whereby borrowers can swap a London Inter Bank Offer Rate (LIBOR) (floating) rate of interest for a fixed rate over a given period. Swap rates are the borrowing rates between financial institutions, usually with high credit ratings. Interest rate swaps are normally 'fixed against floating', but can also be 'fixed against fixed' or 'floating against floating' rate swaps. Interest rate swaps are often used by companies to alter their exposure to interest-rate fluctuations, by swapping fixed-rate obligations for floating rate obligations, or swapping floating rate obligations to fixed-rate obligations. By swapping interest rates, a company is able to synthetically alter its interest rate exposure.
3. The Base Rate is the rate at which prime banks can borrow from the Bank of England. They use this as a base rate for general loans. The Bank of England Base Rate is reviewed by the Monetary Policy Committee, which announces its decision at midday on the first Thursday of each month.
4. LIBOR is the rate at which banks are prepared to lend to each other for different periods of time. Loans for property are normally linked to this rate and expressed as a margin over LIBOR, for example, 50 basis points over LIBOR (1 basis point equals one hundredth of a percentage point).

References

Adair, A., Downie, M., McGreal, S. and Vos, G. (eds) (1996) *European Valuation Practice*, Spon, Oxford.

Baum, A. (2003) Pricing the Options Inherent in Leased Commercial Property: A UK Case Study, ERES Conference, Helsinki, June 2003.

Baum, A. and Crosby, N. (1995) *Property Investment Appraisal*, 2nd edn, Routledge, London.

Brett. M. (1998) *Property into Money* , 2nd edn, Estates Gazette, London.

Champness, P. (1997) *Approved European Property Valuation Standards*, Estates Gazette, London.

Colborne, A. (1995) Valuation of Business Properties, Cutting Edge Conference, RICS, University of Aberdeen, Aberdeen, September 1995.

Darlow, C. (1990) *Valuation and Development Appraisal*, Estates Gazette, London.

DTZ (2006) *Money into Property*, DTZ Research, Summer, 2006.

Dunckley, J. (2000) Financial Reporting Standards: is market value for existing use now obsolete? *Journal of Property Investment and Finance*, 18, 2, 212–224.

French, N. and Byrne, P. (1996) Concepts and models of value, in Adair, A., Downie, M. L., McGreal, S. and Vos, G. (Eds) *European Valuation Practice: Theory and Techniques*, E. and F. N. Spon, London, pp.15–29.

French, N. and Ward, C. (1995) Valuation and arbitrage, *Journal of Property Research*, 2, 1–11.

Hutchison, N., Adair, A. and Leheny, I. (2005) Communicating investment risk to clients: property risk scoring, *Journal of Property Research*, June–September 2005, 22, 2–3, 137–161.

Isaac, D. (1996) *Property Development*: *Appraisal and Finance*, Macmillan, London.

Isaac, D. (1998) *Property Investment*, Macmillan, Basingstoke, pp. 256–270.

IVSC (2005) *International Valuation Standards*, 7th edn, International Valuation Standards Committee, London.

Miles, M., Pringle, J. and Webb, B. (1989) Modeling the corporate real estate decision, *The Journal of Real Estate Research*, 4, 3, 47–66.

RICS (1997) *Calculation of Worth: An Information Paper*, Royal Institution of Chartered Surveyors, London.

RICS (2003) *The RICS Appraisal and Valuation Standards,* 5th edn (as amended), Royal Institution of Chartered Surveyors, RICS Business Services Ltd, Coventry, UK.

Sayce, S. and Connellan, O. (1998) Implications of valuation methods for the management of property assets, *Property Management*, 16, 4, 198–207.

Sayce, S., Smith, J., Cooper, R. and Venmore-Rowland, P. (2006) *Real Estate Appraisal: from Value to Worth*, Blackwell Publishers, Oxford.

Varcoe, B. (1993) Facilities performance: achieving value-for-money through performance measurement and benchmarking, *Property Management*, 11, 4, 301–307.

Wyatt, P. (2001a) Property Advice for Business Occupiers: From Asset Valuation to Business Property Appraisal, RICS Research Paper, 6, 2, Royal Institution of Chartered Surveyors, p. 33, electronic ref: PSO404.

Wyatt, P. (2001b) An investigation of the nature of the valuation service offered to business occupiers, *Journal of Property Investment and Finance*, 19, 2, 100–126.

Glossary

Acquisition costs The costs associated with purchasing a property, such as solicitor's and estate agent's fees.

Alienation Sale of freehold or leasehold interest (see also **Assignment**).

All-risks yield (ARY or *y*) Conventional metric used to capitalise rental income to determine the capital value of a property. The yield is usually derived from comparable evidence and encapsulates future expectations of the investor regarding income and capital growth, the qualities of the property and the tenant. But these factors are not explicitly quantified in this unit of comparison. Instead they are implicitly handled by adjusting the yield. Initial, term and reversion yields are all examples of all risks yields.

Ancillary costs Development costs over and above direct building costs such as site clearance, landscaping and so on.

Appraisal (of worth) Estimation of the financial value of a property to a particular investor.

Arbitrage A method of dealing in (typically large quantities of) financial assets in order to secure a profit from a (usually small) variation in the price quoted in different markets.

Arm's length A description of a market transaction that takes place between parties that are believed to have no connection or special relationship.

Assignment Transfer of ownership of a leasehold interest in a property between an **assignor** (the transferor) and an **assignee** (the transferee).

Asset valuation Undertaken on behalf of a company for the purpose of reporting the financial value of a property held as a tangible fixed asset.

Base rate Underlying interest rate set by the Bank of England.

Break option Some leases include an option for the landlord and/or the tenant to terminate the lease before it expires. The option usually defines the period of notice to be given and may be subject to financial penalties if exercised.

Break-even rent The rent that would need to be achieved when letting a new development to ensure the profit margin is maintained.

Business Rates Property tax paid by occupiers of business premises in England and Wales.

Commonhold A form of property ownership introduced in England and Wales in 2004 which involves the freehold tenure of part of a multi-occupancy building with shared ownership of and responsibility for common parts.

Contingency allowance Money put aside in the development costs to help pay for any unforeseen expenditure.

Contract rent The rent specified in the lease contract at the valuation date (see also **rent passing** and **term rent**)

Cost The financial expenditure used to produce something.

Covenant A binding one-way agreement whereby the covenantor is the only party bound by the promise.

Deed A legal instrument used to grant a right, typically a transfer of title in property.

Depreciation The diminution in value caused by the physical deterioration and obsolescence that a building undergoes during its life.

Depreciated replacement cost The current cost of reproduction or replacement of a property less deductions for all relevant forms of obsolescence.

Derived demand Demand created in a market to help meet other demands. For example, the demand for factories is derived from the demand for manufactured goods.

Developer An entrepreneur who is responsible for the creation and renewal of properties. Two types can be distinguished: the 'investor-developer' who retains completed schemes as part of an investment portfolio and the 'trader-developer' who disposes of completed schemes in order to raise collateral for the next development.

Development The process by which buildings are constructed for occupation or for sale / investment. Property development for occupation and investment is like any other economic activity – satisfying needs through the allocation of scarce resources.

Development yield Rent achieved upon letting a new development divided by the cost of the development. This is often calculated for the benefit of investor developers (see **developer**).

Diminishing returns (The law of) **diminishing returns** or **diminishing marginal returns** refers to the principle that, in a production system, having fixed and variable inputs, keeping the fixed inputs constant, as more of a variable input is applied, each additional unit of input yields less and less additional output.

Direct property investment Investment in physical properties as opposed to **indirect property investment**.

Discount rate Rate at which a cash-flow is discounted to present value.

Discounted cash-flow Cash-flow expressed in present values by discounting.

Dual capitalisation Using the profits method of valuation the net adjusted profit can be split into two components and capitalised separately. This is normally done so that the element of profit to be (notionally) paid as rent can be capitalised at a lower rate than the remaining profit return to the operator.

Dual rate Traditional approach to capitalising a profit rent from a leasehold interest where the return *of* capital is calculated at a lower rate than the return *on* capital.

Easement The right over a property to do or prevent something. A right of way or a right to fish are typical examples of easements.

Economics A social science studying the way in which individuals and societies choose among the alternative uses of scarce resources to satisfy wants.

Economic rent Sometimes referred to as scarcity rent. The surplus earned by any factor of production over and above the minimum earnings necessary to induce it to do its work.

Effective rent Rent net of financial concessions, such as discounted rent-free periods

Efficiency ratio The ratio between net and gross internal area which provides a measure of how efficiently the space in a building can be used.

Elements of comparison Specific characteristics of properties and transactions that cause prices to vary, for example, the nature of the legal rights conveyed, location, physical and economic characteristics and use.

Equated yield The **internal rate of return** of a growth explicit cash-flow, see **target rate of return**.

Equivalent yield Single yield that can be used to capitalise both the term and reversionary incomes. It is the **internal rate of return** of a growth implicit cash-flow, meaning that any future growth in the income stream is allowed for in the choice of the yield. Most reversions occur within a 5 year period due to frequency of rent reviews so, unless the reversion is many years away or the term income is very low compared to the reversionary income, the equivalent yield will be very close to the yield used to value the reversionary income stream.

Exchange price See **price**

Existing use value (EUV) This is a basis of value published by the RICS for valuing business premises under the assumption that alternative uses are disregarded.

Exit value The market value of a property at the end of an assumed **holding period**.

Exit yield The yield used to capitalise the projected rent at the end of a **holding period** to calculate the **exit value**.

External works Development costs not directly attributable to the main building construction such as car-parking, access roads and so on.

Factors of production Often grouped under four headings – land, capital, labour and entrepreneurial ability – these are the resources, or inputs, of any economic activity.

Fair value The price at which a property could be exchanged between knowledgeable, willing parties in an arm's length transaction, regarded as synonymous with the IVSC definition of market value.

Fixtures, fittings & equipment (FF&E) Items associated with a particular trade operating from a property and which are usually transferred with the property when the business is sold as a going concern (see also **plant and machinery**)

Flexi-lease A generic term used to describe modern business leases that are short and include incentives such as rent-free periods and options such as break clauses.

Freehold The legal term used to describe ownership of property held in fee simple.

Freehold ground rent The (usually very low) rent paid to the owner of a freehold interest in property by the owner of a long leasehold interest in the same property.

Forward sale The sale of a property development to an investor or owner-occupier before completion.

Full repairing and Insuring (FRI) lease terms The most common lease arrangement in England and Wales whereby the tenant is responsible for internal and external repairs and insuring the property.

Future value The market value of a property at some future date.

Gearing How borrowed funds increase or decrease the equity return.

Going concern (and going concern value) An operating business (and the value of an operating business).

Goodwill Future economic benefits arising from intangible business assets. Transferable or inherent goodwill may be generated from a property-specific name and reputation, customer patronage or location and would be included in a property valuation. Personal goodwill, which is excluded from the valuation, refers to profit generated over and above market expectations, perhaps due to the particular skills of the business operator and which

would not be transferred when the business is sold.

Gross development value (GDV) The value of the project before any costs associated with its sale have been deducted.

Gross internal area (GIA) The area of a building measured from the inside of each external wall.

Gross rent (as opposed to **net rent**) The rental income before any deductions have been made for management, repairs and so on.

Growth rate Rate at which rents or capital values have increased in the past or are expected to in the future. The actual growth rate may differ from the expected rate or a growth rate implied by the relationship between initial yield and target rate of return.

Headline rent The rent paid before the annual equivalent of any incentives has been deducted.

Hereditament A hereditable property.

Holding period The period for which an investor intends to hold a property investment.

Hope value That part of market value over and above existing use value that could be attributed to a change of use or development potential.

Imputed rent An estimated rent to account for property costs when a firm uses its own capital to purchase the asset – it is usually based on the opportunity cost of the capital.

Income yield Annual income as a proportion of capital value.

Indirect property investment Investment in financial shares in a company or units in a trust that owns properties as opposed to **direct property investment.**

Initial yield A particular type of **income yield**, being the *initial* income divided by purchase price. It is a common market measure of investment performance. The initial yield is lower than target rate because investors expect income and capital growth in the future.

Internal rate of return The rate at which a cash-flow (including the purchase price) must be discounted to give an NPV of 0.

Internal repairing and insuring (IRI) lease terms An alternative to an FRI lease where the landlord takes responsibility for external repairs.

Investment The act of spending money or time on something with the expectation of profit in terms of an acceptable flow of income and/or appreciation in capital value.

Investment value Discounted value of expected net revenue.

Key money Money paid to an existing tenant who assigns a lease to a new tenant where the contract rent is below market rent (see also **premium**).

Landlord Owner of the freehold interest in a property. The term 'landlord' was coined to reflect the aristocratic nature of land-ownership in the UK.

Lead-in period An initial phase, before construction activity starts; allows for preliminary matters such as planning and the assembly of the project team to take place.

Leasehold A form of tenure where one party buys the right (usually in the form of regular rental payments) to occupy a property for an agreed length of time.

Legal interest The entitlement in law to the ownership of an interest in property.

Lessee See **tenant**

Lessor See **landlord**

Letting fee A payment to an agent instructed to find tenants for a vacant property, normally calculated as a percentage of the first year's rent.

Liquidity refers to the time taken to transfer ownership of a property interest, from initial marketing to sale completion. Transaction costs are high for property when compared to other investments. They typically comprise agent and legal fees (approximately 1.75% of the sale price) plus Stamp Duty Land Tax (4% of the sale price if it is over £500000, 3% if less than £250000 and 1% if less than £120000) but the holding period for a property investment is usually longer than for other types of investment so annualised costs are lower.

Macroeconomics The study of economy-wide phenomena, such as total consumer expenditure.

Market An abstract concept concerning all the arrangements that individuals have for exchanging goods and services with one another. Economists often study the market for particular goods and services, such as the labour market, the car market, the commercial property market, the housing market, the building materials market, the credit market, and so on.

Market rent The rent that a property would probably command in the open market as indicated by current rents on comparable properties as at the valuation date.

Market valuation See **valuation**

Market value An estimate of the most likely selling price for a property at a particular point in time.

Marriage value The value in excess of the sum of the values of individual interests that might be produced when they are merged.

Microeconomics The study of economic behaviour of individual households and firms and how prices of goods and services are determined.

Mortgage A legal instrument for guaranteeing a specified property interest as security for the repayment of a loan under certain terms and conditions.

Net development value (NDV) The value of the development after costs associated with its sale have been deducted.

Net internal area (NIA) The area of a building measured from the inside of each external wall and deducting non-useable space such as corridors, lift lobbies, toilets, etc.

Net present value Discounted (present) value of a cash-flow (including purchase price).

Net realisable value The amount at which an asset could be disposed of, less any direct selling costs. In valuation terms it is a market value less costs of sale; it is an exit value.

Net rent (as opposed to **gross rent**) The rental income after any deductions have been made for management, repairs and so on.

Normal profit Profit sufficient to keep a firm it in its current line of business.

Opportunity cost The highest valued alternative that has to be sacrificed for the option that was chosen.

Over-rented property A property where the contract rent is higher than the market rent.

Overage Difference between the contract rent and market rent on an over-rented property.

Option fee A financial payment by a developer to a landowner for the right to purchase land at some future date for development.

Phased development A development that is completed a few units at a time.

Pre-let An arrangement reached before construction is complete for a tenant to lease the premises.

Premium Financial consideration paid by a tenant to a landlord (or by an assignee to an assignor) as a capital sum in lieu of rent. A **reverse premium** is paid by a landlord to a tenant (or by an assignor to an assignee).

Present value Discounted (present) value of a cash-flow.

Price Recorded consideration for a property.

Professional fees Payments to professionals involved in the development process, such as architects, project managers and engineers.

Profit rent The difference between the rent received from the owner of an inferior interest and the rent paid to the owner of a superior interest. It is the rental income return to the owner of a leasehold property investment.

Property Legal right(s) and interest(s) in land and buildings.

Rack-rented A property investment that is let at the current market rent

Rateable value "The rateable value of a non-domestic hereditament … shall be taken to be the amount equal to the rent at which it is estimated the hereditament might reasonably be expected to let from year to year if the tenant undertook to pay all the tenant's rates and taxes and to bear the cost of the repairs and insurance and other expenses (if any) necessary to maintain the hereditament in a state to command the rent" (Paragraph 2(1), 6th Schedule, LGFA 1988).

Real estate A term used to describe immovable property which includes land and improvements to the land such as buildings.

Real property A legal term used to describe ownership rights over real estate.

Recoverable amount The amount which the enterprise expects to recover from the future use of an asset including its residual value on disposal.

Rent A regular payment made by a tenant to a landlord for the right to occupy a property, usually as a condition of a lease.

Rent cover The number of years it would take to eliminate profit assuming letting (and hence sale of the investment) was delayed.

Rent-free period A fixed length of time within the term of a lease during which no rent is paid.

Rent passing See **contract rent**

Rent review The mechanism by which the rent is periodically reviewed. If the rent review is upward-only (and most are) and if market rents have fallen, the rent will stay the same. If the landlord and tenant cannot agree the new rent then the matter can be referred to an independent expert or arbitrator (as specified in the lease).

Residual method of valuation The mathematical technique used to value a development site.

Residual value The estimate of site value resulting from a residual valuation.

Reverse yield gap Because bond-type investments are less risky than equity-based investments (including property) logic would dictate that yields on the former are lower than the latter. But in an inflationary economy the fixed income from bonds is eroded whereas the dividends and capital values from equities inflates. Consequently yields on equities may be lower than yields on bonds to reflect their real growth potential. This phenomenon is known as the reverse yield gap.

Reversionary property investment A property investment where the current rental income is below market level and is expected to revert to a market rent at some point in the future.

Reversionary yield When valuing a reversionary property using the term and reversion technique, it is necessary to capitalise the initial term income at a term yield and capitalise the reversionary income and a reversionary yield.

Risk premium An additional element of return over and above the risk-free rate of return

Royal Institution of Chartered Surveyors (RICS) The professional body that regulates the UK valuation profession.

Running yield The current income expressed as a proportion of capital value.

Sale and leaseback The simultaneous sale and leasing back of a property by the same party. The purchaser of the freehold interest becomes the new landlord-investor while the seller becomes the occupying tenant.

Scarcity A reference to the fact that at any point in time there is a finite amount of resources, in relation to the infinite amount of 'wants' for goods and services.

Scenario modelling A means of evaluating the impact of uncertainty on a valuation by modelling pre-determined combinations of input variables, usually a range of scenarios is tested.

Sensitivity analysis A means of evaluating the impact of uncertainty on a valuation by changing the value of an input variable by a pre-determined amount, say plus or minus 10%.

Service charge A payment by a tenant in addition to rent for items such as maintenance of common parts, building insurance and so on.

Specialised trading property A property which is usually bought and sold as part of a going concern.

Stepped rents Rent which increases in stages at predetermined points.

Target rate of return (or equated yield) Discount rate selected by an investor, often based on a risk-free base rate plus risk premium but may be derived from comparison with other investments. It is to be distinguished from the **internal rate of return** which is ultimately achieved from the investment.

Tenant The leaseholder or owner of a lease.

Tenure Although the concept of feudal tenure has little relevance today, tenure now generally refers to the way in which a tenant holds an interest in property from a landlord or other holder of a superior interest.

Transfer earnings The opportunity cost of the land in its current use.

Upward-only rent reviews A clause inserted into most UK commercial leases which prevents the rent agreed at rent review from falling below the existing contract rent.

Utility In economics this is a measure of relative satisfaction gained by consuming different combinations of goods and services.

Valuation An estimate of the exchange price achievable in the market for a property. The estimate is supported by experience and knowledge of the valuer together with

an interpretation of market transactions, drawing out units of comparison from comparable properties, adjusting evidence and applying it to the subject property.

Value Estimation of price that would be achieved if the property were to be sold in the market.

Value-in-use Defined in FRS11 as "the present value of the future cash-flows obtainable as a result of an asset's continued use, including those resulting from its ultimate disposal". Unlike replacement cost, which represents the cost to a typical occupier conducting the same class of business as the actual occupier, value-in-use is a measure of the value of the asset to the specific occupying business.

Value to the business The worth of a property to a business occupier.

Viability statement Usually a cash-flow based assessment or valuation of developer's profit.

Void period A time allowance after construction is finished to allow for tenants or investors to be found.

Worth In investment terms, a specific investor's perception of the capital sum he or she would be prepared to pay (or accept) for the stream of benefits expected to be produced by the investment. There is likely to be a range of prices at which purchasers would be willing to transact an investment. Each investor will estimate the worth of the investment taking into account tax, borrowing, risk and other criteria specific to that investor. The concept is similar to **value-in-use** in the context of occupiers.

Years' purchase Multiplier used to convert income to capital value.

Yield Capitalisation rate, divisor or ratio (usually expressed as a percentage) between the income received from an investment and its capital value. Its level depends on several factors, such as expectations of future growth and perceived risk. The yield is therefore used to describe the quality of an investment.

Index